RELIGIOUS EDUCATION in GERMAN SCHOOLS:

An Historical Approach

Ernst Christian Helmreich

RELIGIOUS EDUCATION

in GERMAN SCHOOLS

An Historical Approach

1959

HARVARD UNIVERSITY PRESS

Cambridge, Massachusetts

Publication of this book has been aided
by a grant from the Ford Foundation

Library of Congress Catalog Card Number : 59-11509
Printed in Great Britain

To my wife
Louise Roberts Helmreich

PREFACE

There have been many books written on the relation of church and state in Germany, but historical presentations of one aspect of that problem, the place of religious education in the schools, are notably lacking. Numerous volumes and articles cover phases of the subject, but none survey the whole field. This volume is meant to contribute not only to an understanding of the present status of religious instruction but also to a better appreciation of the German educational system in general. The German experience affords interesting comparisons and contrasts to conditions in other countries as well.

The place of religious education in the German school curriculum, not only as a concern of the churches but also as a political and pedagogical problem, can scarcely be understood outside of its historical setting. It is important at the outset to stress the fact that there is no attempt here to deal with the whole history of religious education as such in Germany, but rather to give an account of religious instruction as it developed in the curriculum of German elementary and secondary schools. Emphasis is laid on how religious education worked out in practice, how it affected school administration, and how the problem of religious education in the school has been and in certain places still is one of the most disturbing political questions of the day. While there is considerable complexity arising from the number of petty states and principalities in Germany, to which school affairs have traditionally been relegated, there is also a certain continuity of problems and issues which runs through the whole story. Along with the basic problem of the relationship of church, state, and school appear such questions as: a confessional or interdenominational basis for public schools, the place of private schools in the educational system, religious prayers and services in schools, teacher training and qualification for teaching of religion, supervision of instruction, the content of the curriculum, and not least of all, the method of instruction.

Fundamental to an understanding of the German school tradition are the early origins of the schools. Hence an introductory section deals with the beginnings of an educational system, the development of a religious curriculum and the influence of certain religious and educational movements. The major portion of the book lies within the modern period, following the establishment of the German Empire in 1871. Here the educational theories of the churches, the Socialist position, and attitudes of the teaching profession are discussed. Particular emphasis is given to the Hitler regime and the postwar period. The complicated problems arising from the reconstruction of the whole school system after the war and the partition of Germany, and also the unique position of Berlin call for more detailed analysis.

To name the many individuals who have helped me in various libraries and archives, or who have taken time to grant interviews would be impractical. In the early years of the study, I was privileged to use the facilities of the libraries of Harvard University, Columbia Teachers' College, University of Chicago, Union Theological Seminary, Concordia Seminary in St. Louis, and Wartburg Seminary in Dubuque, Iowa. Dr. J. M. Reu of the latter institution put his excellent private library on German school questions at my disposal. Sabbatical leave enabled me to study in Germany in 1950 and again in 1957. Education officials at the office of the U.S. High Commissioner for Germany were very helpful in 1950, and on this occasion I was also generously permitted by Frankfurt school authorities to use their archives. Professor Erich Hylla, former director of the Hochschule für Internationale Pädagogische Forschung in Frankfurt am Main read the manuscript with great care, and I am deeply grateful to him for this and many other kindnesses. Not only did he make the facilities of this research center with its excellent library on recent German educational problems available to me, but through his introductions my work was greatly facilitated. Authorities at the Catholic Diocesan Headquarters in Fulda, Munich, Berlin, as well as at the Bischöfliche Arbeitstelle für Schule und Erziehung in Cologne, at the Evangelische Landeskirchenamt in Munich, and the Lutherische Kirchenamt in Berlin were all most helpful. I should also like to mention individually Dr. Gerd Buchwald and Dr. Martha Engelbert of the Hauptstelle für Erziehungs- und Schulwesens in Berlin, and Pastor Hans Lokies, Dr. Gerhardt Giese, Karl Bunke, and O. Schikora of the Kirchliche Erziehungskammer in Berlin. To all these people I am deeply indebted; to many others who must remain nameless, I am grateful for opportunities to visit schools, to talk with teachers and pupils, to observe and to ask endless questions.

I wish I could do more than express my heartfelt gratitude to my wife whose share in the volume is a very real one indeed. Mr.

Leroy Cross helped with the typing of the manuscript, and I stand in awe of his skill. It should be added that the editors of the *Lutheran School Journal, Lutheran Education, Current History,* and the *Journal of Central European Affairs* have kindly permitted me to include goodly portions of articles which first appeared in their respective journals.

Bowdoin College   E. C. HELMREICH
Brunswick, Maine
   June, 1958

CONTENTS

Part Two

The Empire, 1871–1918

Part Three

The Weimar Republic, 1918–1933

Part Four

The Third Reich, 1933–1945

Part Five

The Post-World War II Era

TABLES

Part One

Introduction:
Before the Establishment
of the Empire, 1871

Chapter I

The MIDDLE AGES and
The REFORMATION

The history of the German school system, like that of western Europe in general, is rooted in the history of the Christian church. The early Christian missionaries, especially Boniface (d. 755), the apostle to the Germans, established monasteries in which the Benedictine rule was prescribed. This rule permitted taking small boys into the community so that from their early years they might be schooled for their career as monks. These so-called *pueri oblati* (boys offered to God) formed the core of the pupils of the early monastery schools.[1] The Benedictines in their humane and liberal fashion taught not only religion but also, in their upper classes, the famous encyclopedia of medieval knowledge, the Trivium—grammar, dialectic, rhetoric—and the Quadrivium—arithmetic, geometry, music, and astronomy. Although the schools were designed primarily for the education of future monks (regular clergy) they soon were attended by a number of students who after their education did not take vows but returned to the world. The monastery schools developed apace and constituted the most important educational institutions of the Middle Ages. In similar fashion the nunneries provided the few educational facilities which were available for girls.

It was Chrodegang, Bishop of Metz (742-766), who did much to inaugurate another important type of school. Seeing how successful the monasteries were, he established a system of communal life for the numerous secular clergy attached to his cathedral. Faced with the task of taking care of the young men (*scholares canonici*) who attached themselves to the cathedral chapter in anticipation of an appointment, and with the necessity of educating a young priesthood, he ordained that a school should be established under the direction of a member of the cathedral chapter, the *Scholasticus*. The cathedral schools had much the same curriculum as the monastery schools and also were attended by lay scholars. Since they were usually located in the larger cities they came to play an important part in the education of the rising burgher class. As chief educational officer of the diocese the Scholasticus asserted the monopoly of the church over education.

These two school types were encouraged and extended when the great Emperor Charlemagne issued a capitulary in 789 decreeing that every monastery and every cathedral chapter within his realm should erect a school. He further expressly ordained that lay students should be permitted at these schools, although the great majority of the students continued to be clergy, both regular and secular. Charlemagne encouraged learning in many ways, and the group of scholars he gathered at his court—the palace school of the Carolingian Renaissance—is rightly famed.

Eventually at some foundation an "inner" school developed for the future clergy and an "outer" school for the other students, an early manifestation of a secular school system. Theology and religion dominated the curriculum; the more worldly subjects received official sanction when Pope Eugene II in 826 ordered his bishops "to name masters and doctors diligently to teach letters and liberal arts as well as sacred dogma."[2] The study of grammar, that is, the Latin language and literature, actually occupied the center of attention for all students since it was the language of the medieval Bible, of the church, of administration, and of learning in general.

Schools also came to be established about churches and parishes that were not seats of bishoprics and had no monastic connections. This was particularly true of those churches which were administered by a group of clergy (*Stifts- oder Kollegialkirchen*). These actually were often only an extension of the old *Pfarr- oder Parochialschulen*, which was a name given to the ancient practice of simple oral instruction in the fundamentals of Christian belief. Even in the Pfarrschulen the instruction was sometimes extended to the rudiments of reading.

Gradually as cities increased in size and wealth the citizenry demanded that more schools be established. The few schools associated with the churches and monasteries were often far distant, and very often inadequate. Besides, there was a demand for more instruction on a lower level in secular subjects. Often the city fathers had to obtain the special consent of the neighboring bishop or abbot before opening a school. Heated controversies arose over this issue, and it had an economic aspect, for lay schools meant a drop in fees going to church authorities. Usually the conflict would be settled when the church granted to the city the right to open a school. The city fathers in turn would recognize the school monopoly of the church and would promise to endeavour to prevent a decline in the receipts of the Scholasticus. The Latin schools, as the lay schools were known, were actually parallel to the church schools and there was no intention of establishing a new program of instruction. As in the monastery and cathedral schools the emphasis was on Latin, religion, and music. The main purpose, however, came to be the training of the lay citizenry, business men and administrators, rather than the clergy.

The other type of city school, which reached prominence somewhat later, was the reading-and-writing school (*Lese- und Schreibschule*). These taught the reading and writing of German, arithmetic, and usually a few fundamentals of religion. In a sense the lack of Latin instruction was their most distinguishing characteristic, for instruction in German was not entirely lacking in the other schools. This development bears witness to the increased importance of the vernacular which was an essential feature of the Renaissance. Using the common language of the people these schools constitute one of the important foundations of the modern public-school system of Germany.

The later Middle Ages also saw numerous private schools established. Many pious ladies and often not-so-pious vagabond clerics, students, artisans, in fact any one who could make a pretense of knowing how to read or write, established schools as a means of earning a living. They aroused the opposition of the clerical authorities, for as one of the contemporary accounts put it, they "took up school fees and put them in their own pocketbooks."[3] A regulation soon decreed that one-third of such fees was to go to the local clerical Scholasticus while the master might retain two-thirds. These private schools, often called *Winkelschulen* (hole-in-the-corner schools) in contrast to the city and church schools, gave elementary instruction in "reading, writing, and arithmetic." Religion was not regularly taught. The entrepreneurs who ran them eventually organized themselves into guilds. Schoolmasters were now distinct from clergymen. The historical process repeated itself, however, and soon men outside the guilds set up their own establishments. Their schools (particularly in the sixteenth century) took over the opprobrium of being classed as Winkelschulen and were denounced by the guildsmen quite as much as by the clerics.

German Schools at the Close of the Middle Ages

Medieval education was climaxed by the rise of universities during the twelfth-century Renaissance. German universities were founded relatively late; Emperor Charles IV, who founded the University of

Prague in 1348, is usually credited with their initiation. Soon after came the University of Vienna in 1365, Heidelberg in 1385 and many others in the succeeding years. The rise of universities affected the lower schools, and certain ones distinguished themselves by their better preparatory courses.

There also came to be in the late fourteenth century, certain religious centers very different from the older orders. The members of these communities, known as "The Brethren of the Common Life," or sometimes as the Hieronymians, lived ascetically, devoted most of their energies to the study of the Bible, and directed their efforts toward making the teaching of the Bible available to all. Although the first of these communities was formed in the Netherlands, the movement spread throughout northern Germany in the fifteenth century. Numerous houses were set up where the brethren did much copying and translating, and also taught the young. Since their aim was neither to develop clergy nor men of secular learning, but primarily to teach Christianity stripped of theology and scholasticism, the Hieronymians have some claim to be called the founders of Christian popular education. Their efforts to make the Bible accessible to everyone were the essential background of some of the reforms of Luther. They had a part, too, in exploiting the printing press to spread knowledge of the Bible.

The early products of these schools seem to have been mystics, devoted to the study of holiness (Thomas à Kempis was a notable instance), but the order later became famous for learning and exercised considerable influence over the men of the northern Renaissance. The Hieronymians were the first in the north to introduce into their schools the study of classical literature, and the Christian character of humanism in the north can be traced in large part to their influence. No less a person than Erasmus was a student in one of their schools as a boy, and the power of their great philosopher, Wessel, was felt by Reuchlin and recognized by Luther himself.

The Renaissance even in the north, was, however, primarily concerned with higher learning based on classical antiquity, and it brought a more worldly intellectual climate to the universities especially. The new learning also touched some of the schools, where Greek and in a few instances even Hebrew, became a part of the curriculum. Yet despite the secular trend of the Renaissance, it was among humanist scholars that certain men appeared whose work contributed greatly to the tremendous changes of the Reformation period; indeed one of the ablest of these, Melanchthon, became Luther's staunchest ally. The study of Greek and Hebrew and the return to original sources resulted in a new study of the Bible itself, an important stepping-stone on the road to the Reformation.

The close of the Middle Ages found in Germany a rebirth of learning in the ranks of scholars, but only a very inadequate and variegated school system, beset by many rivalries. The clerical authorities were constantly forced into conflicts to maintain their monopoly rights as well as their fees; German instruction challenged that of Latin; and the privileged masters, mostly qualified as guildsmen by the city authorities, were in rivalry with those early advocates of the doctrine that "anyone can teach." City, not state, schools were in the vanguard of the gradual but growing movement to separate the schools from the church. The number of people who could read had risen steadily, as the demand after 1450 for products of the new printing presses shows. Yet when all is considered, education was still designed primarily for a small group of clerical and lay intelligentsia. There was actually no attempt to provide education for the common man, and the concept of the *Volksschule*, a school serving all the people, did not exist. However, in spite of the diverse forms and the uneven development among the multitude of petty German states, there was a uniformity which colored the whole educational system. This was the control and teaching of the church. The schools were either church-run or under close clerical supervision. It was the Protestant Reformation which was to break the educational monopoly and control of the Catholic church and to bring about fundamental changes in the German school system.

The ideas and beliefs of the leaders of the Reformation led to a new emphasis on education. Cardinal among the teachings of the reformers was that of the universal priesthood of all believers.[4] It broke the power of the church hierarchy and made every man responsible for his own salvation. To this end each individual was to search the scripture and study the foundations of his faith. Clearly such a doctrine necessitated an extensive program of education and one that would reach the masses of the people.

The reformers early became aware of the need not only to provide a religious program for instruction, but also to establish new types of schools, if the people as a whole were to be taught to read. The main purpose of instruction in the schools was to educate Christians and to prepare the children for participation in the life of the church. The reformers retained the pre-Reformation practice of having school prayers, and as attendance of the children at daily Mass ended, the importance of these opening and closing school services as integral parts of the schoolday increased. They became a regular feature of all German schools in the following centuries.[5]

Development of a Religious Curriculum during the Reformation

As far as material for instruction, in other words, a religious curriculum, is concerned, three things may be singled out: (1) the popularization of the scriptures through Luther's translation of the Bible; (2) the publication of Luther's Small and Larger Catechisms; (3) the increased use of hymns in worship and as a means of instruction.

During the Middle Ages the Bible was known practically only in the Latin translation of the original Hebrew and Greek texts made by Saint Jerome in the fourth century. This translation, known as the Vulgate, was an exceedingly able production, but in the course of time inaccuracies had crept in as one manuscript was copied from another. It has been estimated that in the early fifteenth century twenty-thousand Bible manuscripts were in circulation. With the coming of the printing press the number of Bibles, Bible histories, and prayer books increased tremendously. A conservative estimate would place the number of Latin Bibles printed in Germany alone before 1520 at twenty to twenty-seven thousand. In addition there were fourteen different High German and several Low German editions of the Bible and many German Psalters and service books before Luther began his work. These figures make it clear that the Bible was not an "unknown book" and was already in the hands of the people before the Reformation. It is true that Archbishop Bertold of Mainz in 1486 did forbid the laity of his diocese to read the Bible, but this was exceptional and contrary to the general practice of the clergy.

While Luther was not the first translator of the Bible into German, he was the first translator who went back to the original Greek text of the New Testament and the Hebrew text of the Old Testament. Not as accomplished a Greek scholar as Erasmus or Melanchthon, nor as good a Hebrew scholar as Reuchlin, he nevertheless knew these languages. Of course he was well acquainted with the Vulgate, and in preparation for his lectures at the university, he had studied the New Testament thoroughly. While confined at the Wartburg after his meeting with the Emperor at the Diet of Worms he translated the New Testament, this translation being published in 1522. Luther and his friends took great pains with their work and struggled to get the proper German word for a Greek or Hebrew phrase. For example in a letter in 1528 he strikes a note with which many will sympathize:

We are now sweating over the translation of the prophets into German. O God, what great and hard toil it requires to compel the writers against their will to speak German. They do not want to give up their Hebrew and imitate the barbaric German. Just as though a nightingale should be compelled to imitate a cuckoo and give up her glorious melody, even though she hates a song in monotone.[6]

As Luther became engaged in a multitude of other tasks, the translation of the Old Testament went even more slowly. The task was also more difficult. In 1530, he wrote a friend: "In Job we had such hard labor, M. Philipp, Aurogallus and I, that sometimes we could hardly finish three lines in four days. Beloved, now that it is translated into German and is completed, everyone can read it and master it."[7] The sacrifice rituals of the Mosaic law were also very difficult to translate, and Luther was forced to call on the local butcher to furnish correct German terminology. The crown jewels of Saxony were borrowed for study in order to name accurately the precious stones mentioned in the Bible. Finally in 1534 the first complete translation of the Bible by Luther was published. But he was never satisfied with his work. He called in a commission of fellow scholars with whom he discussed the translation, and between 1534 and 1541 two thorough revisions of the entire Bible and three of the Psalter were made. Minor corrections were made in three later editions, two of which appeared before his death in 1546.

The Bible in Luther's translation at once won great popularity. Between 1534 and 1584 the printing presses at Wittenberg alone produced 100,000 copies, and presses throughout Germany were doing the same. Not only was this new availability of the Bible important in the education of the people, but the language in which it was written provided a new instrument of education. Heinrich Heine's tribute is no exaggeration, that "Luther created the German language and he did so by translating the Bible."[8] Luther actually gave literary form to the common German language which was slowly developing in this period. As Luther himself stated:

I do not write in a language peculiar to myself alone but in the common German so that everybody, both in north and south Germany, can understand it. I use the language of the Saxon chancellery, which is today spoken by nearly all the German princes, from the Emperor Maximilian to the Elector and the Duke of Saxony, after having blended into one tongue the various dialects of the empire.[9]

Luther's German Bible was not only a translation but in a sense was a new Bible, for he rearranged the order of the books. He esteemed scripture in accordance with the degree it taught Christ. Since he held that the Epistle to the Hebrews, the Epistles of James and Jude, and the Revelation of St. John were the most backward in this respect, he put them at the end of the New Testament. To this day German Bibles follow this arrangement which at first was also followed by the English translators. Of more importance was Luther's influence on the Apocrypha. These books were in the Vulgate and with one exception in the Septuagint, but were not in the Hebrew canon. Luther did not consider them part of the true canon, although he held that they were valuable and good for the people to read. He therefore translated them but gathered them together as a separate unit, putting them between the Old and New Testaments. All the early English Bibles followed this practice and the King James Bible as first printed was no exception. Puritan repugnance to many things in the Apocrypha, however, led to its omission. This happened as early as 1599 in the Geneva Bible, and as early as 1629 there is an edition of the King James version where this was done. If Luther had not separated out the Apocrypha, it would not have been so easy for the Puritans to have omitted it altogether.[10]

While Luther was working on his translation of the Bible he continued to teach at the university and performed many other tasks. He had long been urging the Prince of Saxony to do something for education and in 1527 drew up a detailed set of instructions for a commission which was to inspect the churches and schools. Luther and Melanchthon themselves shared in this work. The commission disclosed a sad state of affairs. Out of 718 parishes in Saxony only 71 were provided with schools. The people were ignorant of the mere essentials of Christianity. Luther, always a man of action, decided to write a concise summary of the main points of Christian teaching to be used as a manual of instruction at home and in the schools.

There had been catechisms before this; the system of questions and answers was a favorite method of instruction in the Middle Ages. Luther, too, had been wont to give practically every year a series of expository sermons dealing with the Ten Commandments, the Lord's Prayer, and the Apostles' Creed. As early as 1520 he had published, as a treatise for the common people, a confessional mirror entitled "A Short Form of the Ten Commandments, A Short Form of the Creed, A Short Form of the Lord's Prayer." In October 1528 Luther began the writing of his catechism, using as a basis his sermons delivered earlier that year. He soon realized that the book was getting too long (it eventually appeared as the Larger Catechism), and so he interrupted his composition to draw up in the shortest possible compass a statement explaining the Ten Commandments, the Apostles' Creed, and the Lord's Prayer. These were then printed as charts to be posted on the walls of the home. He soon added a similar chart dealing with the sacraments of the Lord's Supper and baptism. In the spring of 1529 these charts were published in book form with the addition of prayers for the table, for morning and evening.

Known as the Small Catechism, this book had tremendous influence. Others paid him the compliment of imitation. Among similar treatises the Heidelberg Catechism of 1563 is important because it was drawn up for the Reformed Churches of Germany and came to have a place alongside Luther's catechism in the Protestant schools. It differed in organization, being divided after some introductory questions into only three parts: "Of Man's Misery," "Of Man's Redemption," and "Of Thankfulness." It also grouped the Commandments differently, reverting to the numbering that was common before the days of St. Augustine, while Luther was content to follow the usage which had been established in the Roman church. This difference in the numbering of the Commandments was to create some difficulties for German teachers in future years.

The catechism was central to Luther's plan of elementary education, since faith was the first principle of a moral life. For all his emphasis on learning and languages, on understanding of the Bible and individual responsibility to God, faith in "the redemption of the world by our Lord Jesus Christ" was the rock on which he built. This faith, then, must be presented to the child at the earliest possible moment, and made an integral part of his educational experience. It is only in the light of this cardinal Lutheran principle that the continued stress in German schools on memorization of the catechism, even into modern times, can be understood.

Luther himself thought highly of his catechism, and he once stated that he would be willing to have all his books perish except for it and his essay on "Unfree Will." Ranke maintained in his *Deutsche Geschichte im Zeitalter der Reformation*: "Luther's catechism is at once childlike and profound, lucid and unfathomable, simple and sublime. Happy is the man who constantly returns to it to nourish his soul. To him it will ever remain a living fountain of comfort, a frail shell that contains the heart of truth which satisfies the wisest of the wise."[11] The catechism immediately achieved wide distribution and by the end of the century had been translated into seventeen languages.

In 1528, the same year in which he wrote his catechism, Luther stated:

I condemn no ceremonies but those opposed by the gospel. . . . For the font stands, and baptism is administered with the same rites as heretofore, though the language used is the vernacular. I even leave the images undisturbed, except those destroyed by the rioters before my return. We also celebrate mass in the customary vestments and forms, only adding certain German songs, and substituting the vernacular in the words of consecration.[12]

In this brief quotation there are two references to the use of the vernacular, and this is a key to Luther's influence on hymnology as well as on education in general. The chants sung during divine service were translated into German and were sung in unison by the whole congregation seated in the nave of the church rather than only by the small group in the choir. Soon original German hymns were added to the order of service. The first German evangelical hymnbook, the so-called *Achtliederbuch* appeared in 1524, containing four hymns by Luther, three by Speratus, and one by an unknown writer. Later in the same year two other hymnbooks appeared, one containing twenty-five hymns, eighteen of which were by Luther, the other thirty-two hymns, twenty-four of which were his. The number of German hymnals multiplied rapidly in the next years; Luther himself edited one in 1529. In all, Luther composed thirty-seven hymns. Some of them are new or improved translations of Latin hymns, others are paraphrases of holy scriptures such as "Dies sind die heil'gen zehn Gebot'" or "Vater unser im Himmelreich." He drew on Psalm 46 for his famous "Ein' feste Burg ist unser Gott" and on the 130th Psalm for his great passion choral, "Aus tiefer Not schrei ich zu Dir." Some of his most original hymns were written for special occasions. "Vom Himmel hoch da komm ich her" was written for Christmas 1535, and his "Erhalt uns Herr bei deinem Wort" was a summons against the Pope as well as the Turkish danger in 1541.[13]

Luther not only wrote the words but he also composed the music for some of his hymns. At times the music was original—more often it was a modification of established tunes. He enjoyed singing and was an accomplished musician, playing both the lute and the flute. Genuinely fond of music, he considered it one of the best antidotes for the work of the devil. Luther's hymns did much to develop the great choral school of music. Funck-Brentano writes: "One learned historian of music assured me that Germany owes her Bachs, her Handels, and her Beethovens entirely to Luther's action."[14] Whether this statement is too enthusiastic or not, a moment's reflection will

give an idea of what a difference it would have made, had Luther
not elevated music and congregational singing to such a high position
in his church service. Calvin and Zwingli were not nearly so interested
or able as Luther in the field of music. They held that only the word
of God should have the supreme place in worship and that productions
of man should not be permitted to take its place. They raised the
Psalter to a new dignity, and versified versions of the Psalms became
the first hymnbooks of the Reformed Church.

Luther's contribution did not end with the composition of hymns.
He also did much to make music and the singing of songs a regular
part of the educational curriculum. He was of the opinion that "a
school master must know how to sing; otherwise I do not look at
him."[15] Or as he stated on another occasion: "Music is of great assistance in discipline and education; it makes men gentler, better, more
sociable, and reasonable."[16] He ordained that in Protestant schools
and parishes religious instruction should include not only the Ten
Commandments, the Creed, the Lord's Prayer, but also hymns. From
that day to this the learning and studying of hymns has been an
integral part of the teaching plan of most German schools. How many
hymns German school children have had to learn has varied from
district to district and from period to period as the years passed, but
they have always remained a part of the education of a German child.

The Relation of the State to Education

The Reformation brought the existing school system into disorder. Many of the old monastery and cathedral schools ceased to
function; the municipal Latin schools were disrupted. There was of
course a tremendous shortage of properly educated Protestant teachers
and also of necessary funds. Confiscated lands and endowments were
all too often diverted to other than religious or educational purposes.
Parents were loath to pay the necessary school fees, although formerly
they might well have paid far larger sums under the guise of charity
or church exactions, sums which had made possible the maintenance
of the church schools. Moreover some of the more extreme sectarians
also began to question the need for education if everything came from
the spirit.

Under these circumstances, as in so many other instances, Luther
turned to the princes—to the state—for aid. In one of his earliest
writings, his famous address "To the Christian Nobility of the German
Nation on Improvement of the Christian Estate," he wrote: "Each
city should have schools for boys and girls, where the gospel should be
read to them either in Latin or German." Four years later (1524) he

wrote a "Letter to the Aldermen and Cities of Germany on the Erection and Maintenance of Christian Schools." This was his most important educational summons, of which it has been said: "The book had a great success and, followed up as it was by unremitting efforts in the same direction, it undoubtedly had an incalculable effect in popularizing and raising the standard of education in Germany."[17]

The schools as Luther envisaged them were lineal descendants of the city Latin schools of an earlier period. He insisted on the necessity of studying Latin, Greek, and Hebrew, for without a knowledge of them true religion would perish. He wrote:

The languages are the scabbard in which the Word of God is sheathed. They are the casket in which this jewel is enshrined; the cask in which this wine is kept; the chamber in which this food is stored. . . . If through neglect we lose the languages (which may God forbid), we will not only lose the Gospel, but it will finally come to pass that we will lose also the ability to speak and write either Latin or German.[18]

Clearly Luther believed it was necessary for the followers of the new religion to know languages as it had been in the past. The humanistic influence continued, for Melanchthon, with his broader classical interests, valued the ancient languages and literature for their own worth, not only as religious tools.

Although Luther was primarily interested in schools because he considered them essential for religion, he also insisted that education must serve both church and state. On more than one occasion he pointed out the need for properly trained officials, "for ignorant governors are as bad as wolves." A city might pride itself on its wealth, its fine houses, its strong walls, but its "greatest glory, blessing and power are many fine, educated, intelligent, honorable, and well-brought-up citizens."[19] The following quotation demonstrates his insight into the need for popular education.

Even if we had no souls, and schools and languages were not needed for God's sake and the Bible's, there would still be ground enough for establishing the best possible schools both for boys and girls, for the world needs fine and capable men and women to conduct its affairs, that the men may rule land and people wisely and the women keep house and train their children and servants as they should. Such men are made of boys and such women of girls, and hence it is necessary to educate the boys and girls properly.[20]

Luther always hoped that education could rest on a broad foundation. Early he wrote: "For my part, if I had children they would have to learn not only the languages and history but also singing, music, and the whole mathematics. . . . It is a sorrow to me that I was not taught to read more poetry and history."[21]

At this time Luther was chiefly concerned with maintaining the higher schools. For the great group of children he thought it might suffice if the boys attended school two hours and the girls one, spending the rest of the time at home learning a trade or household duties. The ablest pupils were to be selected for education as teachers, ministers, and officials.

Luther always recognized the primary obligation of the family to train and educate their children. In 1530 he published his famous "Sermon on the Duty of Sending Children to School." This was directed not only to parents but to the public authorities as well.

I am of the opinion that the government is obligated to compel its citizenry to send their children to school. If a government can compel its citizens to bear spear and gun, to run about on the city wall and assume other duties when it desires to carry on war, how much more can and should the government compel its citizens to keep their children at school.[22]

Thus Luther was an early advocate, not only of the principle of schools supported and organized by the state, but also of compulsory attendance laws.

The Sacristan Schools

In the Great Visitation of Churches and Schools of 1528-1529 in Saxony the visitors had admonished the sacristans (Küster) of the parishes to gather the children at least once a week and teach them the Ten Commandments, the Creed, the Lord's Prayer, and some German hymns. It was to furnish a guide for this instruction that Luther had written his Small Catechism. At first this instruction consisted largely of reciting the catechism and getting the children to repeat it until it was learned, a heritage of memorization which has plagued German school children ever since. As Luther put it: "vorsprechen, nachsprechen, auswendiglernen." This instruction was gradually expanded, and in the regulations drawn up by Bugenhagen for Brunswick in 1541 the sacristans, in addition to teaching the catechism, are called upon to teach school, that is to teach reading. Thus there developed a new type of school connected with the parish churches, not only in cities but in the host of scattered villages.

Such schools were often expressly provided for by the state in the many church and school regulations which were issued in this period. In this the state of Württemberg took the lead.[23] In 1559 the prince ordered the establishment of schools in connection with the parish church in which reading, writing, arithmetic, religion, and church singing were to be taught. Supervision of the schools was given to the local pastor and to the church authorities. Catechism instruction was made compulsory, and parents were to be punished if their children failed to meet this obligation. This ordinance thus embodies in early form later educational developments: state schools, compulsory attendance, and clerical supervision.

It should be remembered that in these early days the man who was in charge of these sacristan schools (*Küsterschulen*) was by no means a trained teacher. He regularly practiced a trade. He might be a tailor, cabinetmaker, or shoemaker, who had undertaken various duties as custodian or janitor of the church. To these he now added that of teaching.[24] All accounts testify that he was grossly underpaid, and the possibility of getting an additional fee of a few pennies often made him willing to undertake a new service. At times he was given perquisites, as for example in some sections of Germany in the early period the sacristan schoolteacher had the privilege of dispensing spirits and even beer. This practice of combining church and school duties was to continue until very modern times, many years after teaching had become a full-time job and the incumbent of the office had been dignified by the title of schoolmaster. The sacristan schools were antecedents of many of the elementary schools of Germany.

At first, in these joint positions, in some cases even until the nineteenth century, church duties (*Kirchenamt*) held dominance over school duties (*Schulamt*), but in general the situation was gradually reversed. The church duties became secondary, the *Nebenamt*, and the occupant came to think of himself as a schoolteacher rather than as a sacristan. This shift was naturally carried through more rapidly in some sections of Germany than in others. Then, too, educational institutions and procedure in Germany as elsewhere are inlaid with local usages and customs, and there has always been a vast difference between one-teacher and multiple-teacher schools. It was the elementary schoolteacher in rural congregations who usually held the dual church-school position.

The multiple church duties undertaken by the sacristan-teacher in various periods of history permit of several classifications. There were his duties first of all as custodian of the church. Here might be enumerated such tasks as the cleaning of the church building, opening and locking the church, changing the altar and pulpit cloths, preparation of the altar for communion service, polishing the candlesticks, snuffing the candles during the service, pouring water into the baptismal font and holding the cloth at baptisms, entering names in the baptismal records, supervising the church cemetery—at times even digging the graves—shoveling the church walks in winter, and in general caring for the church property. He also assisted the minister in his pastoral duties, especially in the attached preaching stations, usually reading sermons (although sometimes he gave his own) when the pastor was absent. In some localities it was customary in the case of house communion for the teacher to carry the cup, bread, wine, and also the robe of the pastor.[25]

Secondly, there were a whole series of duties connected with the church bell and the tower clock (*Glöcknerdienst*). The bells had to be greased and kept in repair. Then, too, they had to be rung for all church services, burials, weddings, etc., and in the early morning, usually four a.m. in the summer, at noon, and in the evening. In sections of Bavaria, at least ever since the time when the Turks stood before the gates of Vienna, there was also an eleven o'clock morning bell, when the people paused and united in a prayer which is appropriate even today:

Da pacem, Domine

Verleih uns Frieden gnädiglich,
Herr Gott, zu unsern Zeiten!
Es ist ja doch kein andrer nicht,
Der für uns könnte streiten,
Denn du, unser Gott, alleine.
Gib unserm Land und aller
Obrigkeit
Fried' und gut Regiment,
Dass wir unter ihnen ein christlich,
ehrbar, geruhig Leben führen
mögen
In aller Gottseligkeit und
Wahrheit.

Amen.[26]

The teacher often called upon his older pupils to help with the bell ringing, a task which they no doubt enjoyed if it took them from their classes. After all, one man alone could not always ring the two or three church bells which some of the towers contained. The daily task of climbing the creaky ladder of the church tower to wind the clock was all too often a regular pedagogical chore. If the clock was fast or slow, it was obvious to all who was to blame.

More important than the above tasks were those connected with the posts of cantor and organist. The teacher played the organ, not always a pleasant task in the unheated churches, and pulled the congregation along with a good strong voice through verse on verse of the great chorals. He had to post the numbers of the hymns, which,

when you consider the usual place of the hymn boards, was not a
simple task. Training the children's choir, the men's choir, and the
mixed choir, if these were at hand, was expected. No doubt the teacher's
most disagreeable task was to lead the singing at burials, notably at
the cemetery. The necessity for discipline among the school children
in a funeral procession, to keep them from tripping each other, and
to see that they maintain a demeanor proper to the occasion, is
often mentioned in the regulations. Singing at weddings and baptisms,
and the teacher's deportment at the accompanying festivals also
occasioned many an ordinance. On the whole, however, the duties
of cantor and organist, since they required special skills, tended to
increase the standing of the teacher and were looked on with favor
by the profession.

In addition a variety of miscellaneous duties sometimes fell to
the lot of the teacher. He often had to keep the church books, act as
clerk of the congregation, and at times act as clerk of the local court.
Unfortunately in some sections he also became involved in petty
squabbles as a makeshift lawyer.

In many congregations the teacher performed his tasks willingly
and in perfect harmony with the pastor. In many cases, however,
friction arose, especially when difficulties were added because of the
supervisory rights which the ministers had over the schools. Konrad
Fischer in his monumental history of the German elementary teacher
states: "The sacristan is—ideally—the helper of the pastor, but
according to the usual conception he is his servant."[27] Tucked away
in the files of the *Evangelisch-Lutherisches Schulblatt* is a touching
account of the services to the Lord of an old schoolteacher, how he
thought of an appropriate verse of Scripture or a hymn as he performed
his many and varied duties. But even he concludes his reminiscences
with the statement: "I know well indeed that in recent times the
special church duties have aroused opposition among many teachers,
and I cannot deny that many of the obligations of *Glöckner* and *Küster*
at times interrupt school hours and in addition are often very burdensome."[28]

Other Types of Schools

In the village school many of Luther's ideas bore fruit, but
Melanchthon's interest was in higher learning and his plan of study,
issued in 1528, was intended for the Latin schools. Here boys were
to learn to read, write, and even speak Latin, to become familiar
with classical authors, and to receive a graduated program of religious
instruction. Underlying this plan was the idea common to all the

reformers that only through learning and particularly through the study of grammar (by which they meant Latin) was it possible to arrive at an understanding of the Holy Scriptures and hence of true religion. That all instruction was to be bound together with prayers, church services, and church attendance was an accepted principle. The Protestant city Latin schools were not sufficient in number and often were unable to maintain the standards desired by the reformers.

In 1543, Moritz, Duke of Saxony, founded state as distinct from municipal schools at Pforta, Meissen, and later (1550) at Grimma. Soon other states followed his example. These *Landes-* or *Fürstenschulen* were open to promising children from any part of the state and were supported by public funds, much of this money coming from the secularization of ancient church property. In some states these were known as Cloister schools for this reason, and did, indeed, have the task of preparing students of theology for the university, as well as future state administrators and teachers. Such schools did not give elementary instruction, and some knowledge of Latin was necessary for admission. At these schools the influence of Melanchthon's educational theories was even more pronounced. The Fürstenschulen at their highest levels even approached the university course and provided an example to the more ambitious of the city Latin schools. At Strassburg the renowned Johannes Sturm founded the most famous of the sixteenth-century Protestant schools. To it came students from all over Europe to undergo its ten-year course in which Latin and Greek classics were stressed to the exclusion of all other subjects except religion—and this too was largely reduced to a linguistic exercise. Translation of the catechism into Latin and memorization, with some explanation, of some of the Epistles of Paul in Greek constituted most of the religious part of the curriculum, and was confined to a few hours a week. Sturm also introduced the presentation of dramas at his school. Although many religious themes were dramatized in this period, he stressed classical Greek and Latin plays, which provided a magnificent opportunity for linguistic practice in the ancient languages, moral-ethical motives being for him a secondary consideration.[29] He exemplified the blending of religious and secular elements common in German higher education at this time. Yet Sturm himself believed that he was serving the cause of religion, indeed subscribing to the motto that "a wise and eloquent piety is the aim of education." About the middle of the sixteenth century a school which taught at least two ancient languages came to be called a *Gymnasium*, and for such schools Sturm's became the model. Here is the beginning of the long tradition, reaching to the present day, of the German Gymnasium, with its emphasis on ancient languages. Humanistic as this tradition was in essence, its breadth and impact derived from the Reformation, and from this fact came the continued acceptance of religion as a necessary part of the educational program, even after this instruction had lost much of its vitality.

In Catholic schools the most important change which the period of the Reformation introduced was the domination of the Jesuit order in the higher schools and at the universities. The Society of Jesus, founded in 1539–40, also held fast to the humanistic subjects, and there was little difference as to the formal curriculum between Catholic and Protestant higher education. The Reformation led to Catholic efforts to give parish priests a sounder education including the ability to understand more than the simplest Latin. The Jesuits did not concern themselves primarily with elementary education, this field being usually left to the Piarist Order which was founded in the seventeenth century. Whatever advances were made in Catholic elementary education were chiefly the result of Protestant example.

Although Erasmus had published a Catholic catechism in 1534 and G. Wicelius had followed with a more polemical one in the following year, it was the first Provincial of the Jesuit Order in Germany, Peter Canisius, who laid the foundation for later Catholic catechetical instruction. He published a Large Catechism in 1554 at the request of Ferdinand I and followed it with a Small Catechism in 1564. Both are divided into five chief parts: (1) of Faith, (2) of Hope, which contains the Lord's Prayer and the Ave Maria, (3) of Love and the Decalogue, which also contains the precepts of the church (*praecepta ecclesiae*), (4) of the Sacraments, and (5) of Righteousness and Good Works. "The text of Canisius is a masterpiece of brevity, precision and learnability which from beginning to end bears the mark of the intention to excel the great and influential Protestant example in skill of presentation,"[30] This catechism won great popularity and influenced all later Catholic catechisms. The so-called "Roman Catechism" issued by the Council of Trent in 1566 was meant more as a directive to the clergy as to what should be taught than for use in instruction of the laity. In Catholic parishes a system of regular instruction in the catechism was gradually introduced, designed primarily to instruct the children in what was needed in order to participate in the life of the church: confession, prayers, and the forms of worship. Catholic princes also interested themselves in the problem of education. For example, in 1564 Albert V, Duke of Bavaria, issued a school ordinance which established certain regulations for school teachers, demanded instruction in reading, writing, and Christian doctrine, and admonished the clergy of his lands to erect German schools. In Catholic lands in Germany the foundations were thus also being laid for a common Volksschule system.

The expansion of municipal and state activity in education did not eliminate the private schools; if anything their number increased. In Munich, for example, in 1560, alongside the three Latin schools, sixteen German schoolmasters ran their own schools. They operated on a fee basis, usually charging double if instruction was to include arithmetic. Church and civil authorities as a rule did not take kindly to the private schools, but they continued to meet a real need. Private schools were now either Protestant or Catholic, and in contrast to the private schools of pre-Reformation times, religion was a regular subject of instruction. This raised special problems of supervision for the church authorities.

The most important result of the Reformation for the German school system is the obvious one; it brought about a basic division of German schools into Catholic and Protestant. This in fact paralleled the political division of the time, for a state or territory was Catholic or Protestant according to the religion of the ruler. In the Protestant sections the princes took a very direct part in organizing both the churches and the schools. There was still no thought of separating church and school, and even the Peace of Westphalia (1648) considered the schools as annexes of the churches. The beginning of the secularization of the schools, however, had been made. The state henceforth undertook to serve the cause of education not only financially but through its inherent coercive power over its citizens. The concept appeared at this time that an educated citizenry was necessary to serve the cause both of religion and of the state. There is no question but that the Protestant teaching of the universal priesthood of all believers and its insistence upon the reading and studying of the scriptures did much to further the cause of universal education. In addition the education of women received a tremendous impetus at this time.

While religion had always been studied in the medieval schools, under the influence of the Protestant movement it became much more a subject of instruction. A regular religious curriculum came into being which centred in the study of the Ten Commandments, Creed, Lord's Prayer, and the sacraments as explained in the various catechisms of the period. The singing of hymns, and regular participation in church and school religious services was a part of the program.

In fact the sermons of the period took on an instructional note and became the primary instruments of "adult education." The Protestant leaven in the field of education did not leave the Catholic schools untouched, and in general it can be said that the two school systems proceeded along parallel paths.

Chapter II

The IMPACT of PIETISM and RATIONALISM

The seventeenth and eighteenth centuries which brought pietism, a movement close to the church, also witnessed the growth of rationalism, mainly outside of the church. It is not strange, therefore, that the schools, which were controlled in part by the church, in part by the state, and were held to have the dual task of training citizens and making Christians, were torn by the basic differences between pietism and rationalism. Whereas pietism stressed inward feeling, faith, meditation and prayer, rationalism stressed reason, knowledge, and understanding. Pietism was bent on strengthening religion and re-awakening the church; rationalism on breaking the control of the church and strengthening and revitalizing the state. One point the two movements had in common. This was their emphasis on the practical in education, although their concepts as to what was practical were at variance. Both welcomed with somewhat different emphasis more instruction in the vernacular, and in such subjects as arithmetic, history, geography, and nature study—but when it came to religion they differed sharply. While one stressed inner piety and prayer, the other stressed rational inquiry and training in ethics and morality. One wanted a Christian education tied to the catechism and the historic confessional creeds; the other wanted a general religious instruction based on nature and reason.

Precursors of the Great Leaders of Pietism

The beginning of the seventeenth century brought a reaction to the still dominant humanistic education of the upper schools. Schools were to be made more practical, and above all there was to be more teaching of German. Latin was not objected to so much as Greek and retained its dominant place in the curriculum. In this movement Wolfgang Ratke (1571–1635) took a leading part, as did Johann Amos

Comenius (1592–1670). Born in Moravia, educated in great part in Germany but spending most of his active life in eastern Europe, Comenius nevertheless had great influence on German education. He devised an educational plan which called for education by the parents in the home until the sixth year of age, to be followed by attendance until the twelfth year at a parish school. Here instruction was to be in the vernacular. After finishing the common school, pupils were to pass on to the Gymnasiums or Latin schools and later to the universities. His highest goal was education for piety and morality. As he put it: "He who advances in learning and backslides in morality, steps more backwards than forwards."[1] Another of his sayings was: "If we in truth want to have Christians we must make practical Christians, not theoretical ones, and this from the earliest educational period on, for religion is a living not a formalized matter."[2] Although his personal interest lay in nature study and in the general curriculum, he always stressed the place of religion in education. In this field he advocated extending the work of memorizing beyond the catechism to selected verses from the Bible and some of the Bible stories.

Comenius' work was handicapped by the disorder and destruction of the Thirty Years' War. In many places schools disappeared in the general barbarization of the period. Yet the very disorder in some ways proved a blessing, for it created a need for building anew. Even before the end of the conflict, Ernst the Pious, Duke of Gotha, issued his famous educational ordinance (1642), which incorporated many of Comenius' ideas. Pupils were not to study Latin until they were adept at reading and writing German. Of even more importance, the ordinance established compulsory education for children between the ages of five and fourteen, with a system of fines for noncompliance. These fines were to be used for the benefit of poor people. Provision was also made for school inspections, new text-books, and new school buildings. In the curriculum religious instruction was emphasized, for the Duke considered it part of his Christian duty as a ruler to provide for the moral education of his subjects. The system he devised did much to further the state-supported church school in conformity with the ideas of the Protestant reformers.

Other states also undertook to encourage schools, but advances were slow. Württemberg, which had a rather well-developed system of primary schools before the war, had in 1672 only reached a stage where the state could provide summer instruction once or twice a week in a few villages. In Brandenburg, Frederick William, the Great Elector, issued a church ordinance in 1662 which ordered that churches and local authorities should take care to organize good schools. This

ordinance is the key to the future development of the Prussian educational system. The state orders and makes the laws, but they are to be
implemented and administered by the churches and the local communities.

Some attempts were made to improve the quality of religious
instruction in this period. In the schools of Gotha under Ernst the
Pious, there was not to be so much memory work. Students were to
be encouraged to present the catechism material in their own words
instead of learning it by heart. A Bible history with pictures—a sort
of school Bible—came into use. Justus Gesenius, who published in
1638 a collection of Bible histories of the Old and New Testament, is
often called the father of Bible-history instruction. Although there
had been some Bible history taught before, it was usually incorporated
into the instruction of the catechism. Luther, for example, included
it in a discussion of the Apostles' Creed. Luther, however, did publish
in the same year as his Small Catechism (1529) a collection of fifty
Bible stories, his so-called *Passionale*. On one side of the page was a
woodcut and on the back a text of varied length explaining the picture.
It was a booklet of fifty-two pages and between 1529 and 1604 went
through at least twenty-seven editions.[3] Melanchthon also published
a collection of Bible stories, but it was not until the seventeenth and
eighteenth centuries under the influence of pietism that Bible history
became a separate part of the curriculum in Protestant schools. It
began to infiltrate into Catholic schools in the last quarter of the
eighteenth century; but it was only in the second decade of the nineteenth century that it became a regular subject of instruction apart
from the catechism.[4]

The Influence of Spener and Francke

Although the Pietists laid emphasis on personal piety and an
inward direct relationship with God, it was in the field of method
that they made their greatest contribution. Philip J. Spener (1635–
1705) and August Hermann Francke (1663–1727) were Pietism's
greatest representatives. Spener was especially interested in giving
new life to the instruction in the catechism. In 1677 he published his
"Einfältige Erklärung der christlichen Lehre nach der Ordnung des
kleinen Katechismus Luthers." He developed and furthered a more
systematic type of catechization through which the truths of Christian
doctrine were to be taught. He always stressed meaning and understanding rather than memorization. Spener not only influenced the
schools but also started a movement for more instruction in the
churches. He held a special series of catechism sermons, instituted

study groups, and soon was applying his technique of catechization to adults.

At this time, no doubt due to pietistic influences, it became general practice to have confirmation preceded by a special period of instruction by the pastor. These confirmation classes, which lasted from one to three years according to local custom, were started as a supplement to what was considered inadequate instruction in religion on the part of the schools. They did not simplify church–school relations, although confirmation itself came to be closely integrated into the school program. Actually it often came to serve more or less as the graduation ceremony from elementary school, since it usually coincided with the school-leaving age. There was always the problem as to what should be learned in school, what in the confirmation classes. Pastors, often with good reason, were likely to complain that the teachers did a poor job of preparing the children. Teachers, with an eye to pleasing the pastor, who was also the school supervisor, were likely to hound the pupils into memorizing the material so that they had a ready answer when facing the pastor. Through the rite of confirmation, which both church and populace considered very important, the church maintained an important entree into the schools.

Francke, the greatest of the Pietists, was, like Spener, interested in the development of religious attitudes by skillful use of the discussion technique. His greatest contribution was the establishment of the School and Home for Orphans at Halle, which did much to spread the idea that education should be available to even the very poorest children. He was the founder of the system of Protestant orphanages in Germany.[5] In his school Francke attempted to teach the children a trade, for he desired to make them self-supporting citizens. He wrote: "It is highly necessary to inculcate in tender youth industry and love for work."[6] The introduction of work education added a new feature to elementary schools which was copied by various private as well as state institutions. The idea of educating the poorer classes so that they would not become out-and-out paupers, but could contribute to the economic prosperity of the state, naturally appealed to the mercantilist-minded rulers of the day. But Francke, motivated by real love for his pupils, also insisted on new standards of instruction. By the emphasis he laid on teacher training he gave an impetus to the establishment of special teacher-training academies. Interested as he was in a trade education, he always considered that the main purpose of schools was the glorification of God, and "the heart of his piety" consisted in placing the individual will under the will of God. "A dram of living faith is to be valued higher than a hundred weight of historical wisdom, a drop of real love higher than a whole sea of learned mysteries."[7]

With such emphasis on personal piety it is not surprising that Francke expanded religious instruction until it occupied close to four out of seven classroom hours. More and more Bible reading was inserted in the teaching plan. The number of Bible verses the children had to memorize was increased. Neander had published (1580) one of the first collections of Bible verses (*Spruchbuch*) and several others had followed it. In the "Age of Pietism" one collection contained close to 9000 "selected" verses, not all of which were, of course, learned. This marked the high tide, and the later Spruchbücher again became slimmer; in 1839 Württemberg's included 689 verses, Bavaria's, 485.[8] Francke also increased the number of prayer and meditation services. Added to this was a strict renunciation of many so-called worldly pleasures. The theater was denounced, and pupils in his schools were even forbidden to skate or swim. That there was a reaction to such a regime under the influence of rationalism is not surprising.

It was a pupil of Francke's who made a most significant contribution to the religious curriculum. In 1714, Johannes Hübner, rector of Hamburg, published his *Zweimal zweiundfünfzig auserlesenen biblischen Historien aus dem Alten und Neuen Testament*. This "Two times fifty-two selected Biblical Histories from the Old and New Testament" broke a new path in religious instruction. The stories were told as much as possible in the language of the Bible, and Hübner added a series of questions which required definite answers. To these he appended useful lessons to be drawn from the story and a verse of six lines dealing with what he labeled a "godly thought." Pictures illustrated the accounts. With this volume German schools had a good textbook, which meant a great deal considering the lack of training of most of the teachers. So successful was the volume that it was soon translated into Latin, French, Italian, Swedish, and Polish. From now on Bible history became a regular and separate subject of instruction on a level with the study of the catechism and the hymns of the church. With the later addition of instruction in church history and the explanation of the regular Sunday Gospel and Epistle lessons, the religious curriculum of the Protestant German schools was complete.

School Legislation

Francke and his pedagogical ideas had a particularly strong influence on Frederick William I (1713–40) of Prussia. In an ordinance of 1717[9] the latter made education compulsory in those places which had schools, and public money was made available for children whose parents could not afford the fees. He did much for education in all his various lands and in 1739 gave to East Prussia 50,000 thaler for schools "to build the Kingdom of God." As the King put it: "If I build up and improve the province, and make no Christians, then all will be of no aid to me."[10] Soon over a thousand village schools were established in this province alone. He also tried to raise the educational standards of the teacher and did take steps to establish teacher-training schools. Yet in most places slightly schooled artisans continued to serve as sacristans and as such were also the local schoolmasters. Frederick William undertook to better the lot of these sacristans, giving them free firewood and ordering that they should have the use of an acre of land next to their houses.

Frederick the Great (1740–1786), although himself a disciple of the Enlightenment, in general followed the policy of his father in the educational ordinances which he issued. This is largely accounted for by the fact that the educational philosophy of the Enlightenment, as expounded by a group known as the Philanthropists, did not strike Germany in force until the last quarter of the eighteenth century. It was Julius Hecker, a disciple of Francke and minister at the Church of the Trinity in Berlin, who was the dominant influence in the many educational reforms of the mid-eighteenth century.

Hecker was aware of the gradual separation of a Latin and German school system. Francke had himself divided his school at Halle into these two divisions, the Latin school being for those students who intended to go on to advanced work. Gradually the need arose for more advanced education in German for the growing middle class. Business men, military officers, landed squires, all sought more education. Hecker decided that something must be done to meet this need. He organized a school in three divisions; a German, a Latin, and a *Realschule*—the latter devoted to the more practical subjects, taught in German. He conceived of these three forms as serving in general three dominant groups in society: the peasants and day laborers; the intelligentsia; and the businessmen, artists, military officers, and landed aristocracy. The Realschule was destined for great expansion and development in the next century. Hecker was also instrumental in starting a Sacristan and Teacher-Training School (1748) which in a few years became a royal institution.

Hecker's greatest contribution by far can be found in Frederick the Great's general state school regulation, the *Generallandschulreglement* of 1763.[11] This was the first school law which applied to all lands of the Prussian crown and, as its name implies, dealt with the rural and village schools. It expressly provided for a Christian school system, for, as Frederick himself stated, "teachers should take care that people retain their attachment to religion." Again compulsory attendance was required, and religious instruction was given a dominant place in the curriculum. Children were to attend Sunday services and were to be questioned on the sermon in school the following Monday. For administrative purposes schools were considered a part of the church organization. Local ministers were to visit the school two times a week and to have a monthly conference with the schoolteacher. Failure to do this was cause for suspension or even dismissal of the minister. Further, each superintendent of the churches was to visit the schools in his district once a year. Incompetent schoolteachers were to be reported to the higher church authorities by the local pastor. Schools had long been under the supervision of the church, but these general regulations wrote into law clerical inspection of schools. Disputes over the continuation of this practice became one of the great issues between clergy and schoolmen in the later nineteenth century.

In 1765 Frederick II supplemented his general state school regulation by issuing a special ordinance for the schools of Silesia.[12] This province had only recently been won from Austria, and its schools had suffered from the series of wars which had been fought over this territory. The population, too, was predominantly Catholic, and so special regulations, worked out with the aid of Catholic advisors, seemed necessary.

Frederick II's youthful remark, on refusing to dissolve a Catholic garrison school in Küstrin, has often been quoted: "All religions have to be tolerated, . . . for here every one must go to heaven after his own fashion" ("hier muss jeder nach seiner Fasson selich werden"). The comments which he made as an aged ruler on the problem of Catholic schools indicate that he remained steadfast in his views.

It is criminal coercion, when one takes from fathers the right according to their desire to educate their children . . . ; it is a criminal coercion if you send the children to a school run according to the precepts of natural religion, when the fathers want the children to become Catholics like themselves. There are few lands in which all citizens have the same religion, and the question arises: is such unity to be forced, or can one permit every one to think according to his own views? To this the answer must be, that it is impossible to establish such unity. . . . General tolerance alone guarantees the happiness of the state.[13]

These views of an enlightened and skeptical despot would not be a bad prescript for a democratic state of the twentieth century.

Issuing the school laws was one thing, carrying them out another. Nobility and peasantry did not give their full support. So great was the lack of teachers that Frederick found himself forced to decree that retired soldiers who could read and write and were adapted to teaching should be appointed as school teachers in the rural areas. This edict has been often criticized and described as a militarization of the Prussian schools. This it certainly was not. Frederick the Great rightly deserved praise for his educational activity; Prussia now began to take a leading role in the development of German education. It is also about this time that the term "Volksschule," with its implication of universal education, was generally applied to the elementary schools. Officially, however, the Prussian legislation of 1794 did not use the term, still speaking of the *Gemeine Schulen* or common schools.

The pietistic influence extended to the schools in most of the German states. Thus in Württemberg the revised ordinance for German schools (1729) proclaimed: "Schools are not to be viewed only as a place of preparation for civil life, but as workshops of the Holy Spirit, because the Lord is served best by people who are not only well trained but are also pious."[14] Under the influence of pietism, there was an increased emphasis on religious instruction, with Bible history playing a regular and important part in the education of the child. The Pietists also emphasized the obligation of the church, apart from the schools, to further religious instruction. The development of confirmation instruction, which received great stimulus from them, was in fact a recognition that the religious training received in the schools needed supplementation.

Christianity to the Pietists was not merely a matter of knowledge and faith, but above all a matter of deeds.[15] Francke's orphan schools began an important social service of the Protestant church in Germany. His introduction of what might be termed useful trade schooling with more emphasis on the German language has given him credit for giving a practical turn to German education, a movement which was brought to flower later by men of more rationalistic persuasion. Pietistic influences also did much to strengthen the growing concept that there should be universal education.

Rationalism and the Philanthropists

The practical in education also found support in a very different philosophy of life from that of the Pietists. The Rationalists, basing their educational ideas on reason rather than piety, stressed the importance of an education suited to a man's role in society. For many of their ideas they turned to France, which during the age of Louis XIV (1643–1715) set the cultural standards of Europe.

French influence extended everywhere, but it had its greatest effect upon the aristocracy and the upper classes of society. French became the fashionable language and in Germany it was added to the curriculum of the Gymnasiums. Special *Ritterakademien*, catering to the sons of the nobility, had been established as early as 1589 in Tübingen, but they only came into flower during the late seventeenth and early eighteenth centuries.[16] In organization these academies resembled Gymnasiums, but instruction in modern languages—French, Italian, Spanish, English—replaced Greek and Hebrew. Physics, chemistry, botany, mathematics, all on a rather rudimentary plane, and other "useful" subjects were stressed. Among the latter were fencing, horsemanship, dancing, and the art of conducting a genteel conversation. Instruction in religion often degenerated into sterile religious disputations. Despite its aristocratic coloration, the curriculum of the Ritterakademien was a manifestation of the general movement towards making education more practical, in the sense of bringing it closer to the immediate needs of the students. Knowledge of the French language was considered essential for the man of birth or culture, and French ideas had already made a place for themselves in Germany before the French *Philosophes* began to write. The latter, however, had a profound influence on German thought.

Jean Jacques Rousseau (1712–1778) was the most original of the French thinkers in pedagogical matters, and his theories were propagated and reworked in Germany by a group known as the Philanthropists (*Philanthropen, Philanthropisten*). They were given this name because as "friends of the people" they advocated doing away with the harsh discipline of the schools and replacing it with a spirit which would attempt to make learning a pleasure. Great stress on the use of educational aids, insistence on physical training including dancing, fencing, and other similar activities, forecast many of the practices of our modern schools. The new movement sought to change the whole tone of the schools and thus inevitably came to question the place of religious instruction in the curriculum.

Johann Bernhard Basedow (1723–1790) was the founder of the Philanthropist movement. Without completing his ministerial training he became a teacher and taught in several schools attended mainly by scions of the aristocracy. At this time the nobility were among the strongest supporters of liberal ideas, particularly in regard to religion. Basedow began to write a series of pamphlets and books attempting a rational appraisal of the Holy Ghost, the inspiration of the Bible, baptism, the Lord's Supper, eternal damnation in hell, and other Christian doctrines.[17] He was soon denounced for his theological views, but he continued his efforts to reform the schools. Finally in 1774 he was able to organize his own school through the aid of Prince Leopold of Anhalt. The school at Dessau was known as the *Philanthropinum* and catered to the sons of the aristocracy. A seminar for the training of teachers was opened in connection with this school, and in this way the ideas of the Philanthropists were spread. Joachim Heinrich Campe (1746–1818), Christian Gotthilf Salzmann (1744–1811), and, most influential, Friedrich Eberhard von Rochow (1734–1805) were among Basedow's foremost followers. Whereas the movement as a whole was oriented chiefly to the needs of the upper classes, Rochow achieved renown for improvement of the rural schools. He is often praised as the reformer of the Evangelical village and rural schools of North Germany. The constant emphasis of the Philanthropists on better instructional methods brought beneficial results to the lower schools.

The Philanthropists, in their insistence that the schools were to be made pleasant, objected vigorously to the memorizing which still constituted the main method of instruction in religion classes. First understand, then memorize, was their motto. They always insisted on a rational approach to religion and advocated introducing children first to the truths of natural religion and proceeding from there to revealed religion, which they belittled. Ethics and morality were the things to be stressed. One of their greatest contributions was to popularize the Socratic method of teaching, starting with commonplace things and thence proceeding to great truths. They sought to discover meaning through skillful questioning. A good field for this procedure was the traditional instruction in the catechism, a book they did not like. One of the more moderate rationalist Christians, Friedrich Dinter (1760–1830) wrote thirteen small volumes describing a new method of instruction in the catechism and also dealing with the teaching of Bible history. His motto was: "What a pupil can find himself, should not be given to him."[18] This renewed emphasis on the technique of teaching by questioning, however, also had its less attractive side, for it often degenerated into mere cleverness with little progress in understanding. Instead of promoting faith and piety, Socratic questioning was all too likely to encourage skepticism and a general doubt of religious values.

In regard to Bible history the Philanthropists insisted that the various episodes be recounted as stories. This method of presentation had, on the whole, a good influence. although it tended to place the Biblical accounts on a par with fairy tales. This tendency was enhanced through the use of allegories, parables, and aphorisms, in an attempt to make the instruction interesting. Moreover they objected strenuously to teaching some of the traditional episodes in Biblical history. Especially critical of the Old Testament which they regarded as a "Jewish Chronicle," they would have liked to eliminate it from the schools. As Heinrich S. Stephani (1761–1850) wrote: "How wrong has been our previous practice, by teaching the Old Testament to our children, first to make them into Jews in their religious views and only after this preparatory instruction, to lead them to Christianity."[19]

The most constructive contribution of the rationalists to religious education was perhaps the distinction which they drew between theology and religion. In their efforts to make this distinction, it is true that their religion took on the characteristics of natural rather than revealed or evangelistic religion. It would not be correct to say that the philanthropists wanted to abolish religion from the schools, but they were opposed to narrow confessional instruction. They constantly sought to uncover what they considered superstition and ignorance masking under the guise of religion. They advocated that schools should have only a loose connection with the church, and their movement constituted the first concerted assault on the traditional religion-dominated school curriculum which had been established by the Reformation.

The New Humanism

The man who stands as the finest expression of the eighteenth century Enlightenment in Germany is Lessing (1729–1781). His was a position too lofty for the average man, for he believed it possible to hold firmly to conceptions and accepted symbols of one's own faith, while expecting those of other beliefs to do the same. Out of his tolerance he argued that the ultimate aim of all religions is one, and that moral character is the final objective. Thus there is room for confessional instruction, so long as tolerance and understanding of others remain our guiding principles. In his play *Nathan der Weise* and in his essay *Die Erziehung des Menschengeschlechts*, he expressed ideas which greatly influenced German education in the following century.

In literature Klopstock (1724–1803) and Lessing broke the bonds of a purely French classicism. German culture was at this time too poor to act as a wellspring, and German intellectuals turned again to the classics much as the leaders of the Renaissance had done three centuries earlier.[20] The study of Greek was revived and the ideas of

classical philosophy were acclaimed. The whole tone of instruction at
the Gymnasium became more and more colored by classical paganism;
it ceased to be religiously centered. At the universities the faculties
of philosophy took on equal status with those of theology and became
seedbeds of a new but yet very old orientation towards man, rather
than towards God.

The New Humanism as manifested in higher education also
helped to bring about a change in the teaching profession. Formerly
many school positions were filled by men who considered teaching
a stepping-stone to a career as a minister. Others were held by men
who had not quite made the grade as theologians. Now men began to
be educated as teachers directly, and their status was recognized by
the establishment of separate qualifying examinations. This was
regularized in detail in Prussia by the examination ordinance of 1810.
In line with this gradual separation of the teaching profession from
the ministry in higher education, the Prussian state in 1787 established
a separate school authority—the *Oberschulkollegium*. Both higher and
lower schools were now under the direction of their own bureaus and
were no longer treated as annexes of the church. In 1808 a special
cultural section was established in the ministry of the interior.

New School Legislation

The administrative separation of schools from the church, although
by no means complete, was of course fully in keeping with the spirit
of the time. The influence of rationalism was also manifested in
the Prussian legislation in regard to schools that formed part of the
Allgemeine Landrecht of 1794. This codification laid the basis for the
Prussian schools of the nineteenth century and established a system
which was imitated in many other German states.

The law of 1794 declares flatly that schools and universities are
state institutions for the purpose of instructing the youth in useful
information and scientific knowledge and are under the supervision
of the state. They must at all times submit to visitation and examination by state authorities. For this supervision, however, the state in
practice regularly relied in large part on clergy and other church
authorities. Schools were to be supported by public funds and attendance was compulsory. Children were to attend from the age of five
until they had reached a state of learning which the supervisor
(regularly the pastor) considered proper for their particular status in
society. Although the law did not expressly require it and the way
was left open for interdenominational schools, public schools continued
to be organized along confessional lines. This meant that Protestant

schools were staffed by Protestant teachers and attended by Protestant pupils, and that Catholic schools had Catholic teachers and pupils. Since the population of any one district usually belonged to the same religion, this system worked no hardship. In cities or localities where there were sufficient numbers of each persuasion, both Protestant and Catholic schools were to be maintained. No person was, however, to be denied the right to attend a public school because of differences in religious belief. A child belonging to a different confession from that of the school he was attending could not be forced to participate in the religious instruction. Religion was, nevertheless, a regularly required subject of instruction, and if a pupil was excused from these classes, parents were to see that the child received equivalent instruction. The law did not abolish private schools, although they were obliged to receive a permit from state authorities. Here too religion was continued as a subject of instruction.

While the law of 1794 placed the state in a commanding position, there was no thought of taking religion out of the school. In fact, Minister Woellner, who had charge of schools, wished to combat the religious rationalism of the Enlightenment and as early as July 9, 1788, issued a famous edict on religion intended to bring about a return to more orthodoxy.[21] In the same year in which the schools were definitely placed under state control (1794), he issued a directive to the teachers reminding them that indifference and skepticism had raised havoc in the schools, and that they should remember it was their duty to educate the children to be Christians. Appointment as a teacher was made dependent on passing an examination in regard to orthodoxy. By an ordinance of 1794 all new teachers at Gymnasiums and city schools had to take an oath containing the following promises:

I, ————, promise and swear solemnly before God the omnipresent that after I have been made teacher at the school of ———— by His Majesty, my most gracious Lord, and by my superior, I will take it on my conscience as my holy and constant duty at all times to avoid carefully everything through which I might strengthen the youth in disdain [*Verachtung*] for the Christian religion, Holy Writ and public church service, and, needless to say, to avoid leading them to this; but even more to contribute with all my power to the end that love for religion, submission to its precepts and true godliness shall ever more rule among youth.   I promise especially; that I, neither in nor outside of my teaching hours, in writing or orally, either directly or indirectly, will introduce anything against Holy Writ, against the Christian religion, or against the provincial ruling and ordinances in religion and church matters, even more I will conduct myself exactly in accordance with the prescriptions of the Religion Edict of July 9, 1788, in every detail.[22]

The hand of the past still lay heavy on the German schools in spite of all the efforts of the rationalists to introduce a better new world. Yet there can be no question that German schools had become more secular and that the state was replacing the church as the controlling force. The general extension of the principle of compulsory education, first advocated by the Protestant reformers as a means of bringing about education in Christian doctrines, actually became a most important milestone in the gradual secularization of the schools. The Catholic authorities recognized this and adopted a hostile attitude to compulsory attendance laws, for they maintained that these struck at the freedom of the family and church, in whose province lay the education of children. In Bavaria, where the Jesuits were long dominant, the first compulsory education law was not enacted until 1802.[23]

Under the influence of the Enlightenment religious instruction in the schools was broadened, and rationalist-minded schoolmen would have liked to do away with the confessional aspects entirely. Less orthodox views made particular headway in the higher schools where the New Humanism, with its distinctly worldly orientation, was strongly entrenched. Nevertheless, the Pietist idea that schools were meant to educate Christians did not disappear, as the later history of religious education in German schools amply demonstrates.

Chapter III

The NINETEENTH CENTURY to 1871

While the main trends in the development of the German educational system were not broken by the events of the French Revolution —the New Humanism continued to dominate higher education and also indirectly to influence the lower schools—the revolutionary period was not without effect upon German education. Even before 1789, books had appeared in Germany which showed the influence of Caradeuc de la Chalotais' *Essai d'éducation nationale* (1763). Thus Friedrich Eberhard von Rochow in 1779 published his *Vom National-charakter durch Volksschulen*. Interest in things German and the development of national feeling received tremendous stimulus from the movement to free Germany from Napoleonic domination. That a national state required nationally-oriented schools was a doctrine popularized by French revolutionary legislation.

The decline of the number of German states in 1815 from over 300 to 39 also brought the surviving state governments more control over education. As a result of the *Reichsdeputationshauptschluss* of 1803 the remaining church states were secularized and those of petty princelings also disappeared. State boundaries were shifted hither and yon, and very often the new states no longer were predominantly of one faith. Political boundaries had ceased to be confessional boundaries. Württemberg, for example, up to this time had been almost completely Protestant, but now received important Catholic lands. Bavaria emerged with such significant Protestant additions that henceforth its population was to be approximately one-third Protestant. The postrevolutionary states found their old legislation no longer sufficient. There was need for the prince to unify his state and his administration. Everywhere new educational regulations and laws were issued, which invariably clarified and strengthened the hold of the state over the schools.[1] The abolition of feudalism in Germany was a manifestation of the revolutionary epoch which also benefited the state. The patron rights over education that traditionally were

37

exercised by large estate holders were now diminished, if not always completely abolished. Public schools increased in number rapidly during this period, and more and more the state came to supervise all schools.

If the French Revolution brought an extension of the activity of the state and its increased secularization, it also brought a movement, particularly on the part of the Catholic church, for emancipation of religious organizations from state control. The Civil Constitution of the Clergy in France had brought home to the hierarchy what it meant to be under the complete domination of the state. The secularization of ecclesiastical states and the seizure of other church lands also broke ties with the state and enhanced the spiritual character of the church. The clergy felt less secure and sought support through closer ties with the Pope. Ultramontane tendencies were strengthened. The re-establishment of Catholic hierarchies in England (1850) and the Netherlands (1853) are striking illustrations of the organizational strengthening of the Catholic church which was going on all over Europe. This movement of Catholic consolidation, in a measure the result of a general religious revival, was also partly a reaction against the weakening of confessional dogmatism through the Enlightenment, with its doctrines of natural religion and tolerance. In Germany the Catholic resistance to state control was manifested in the conflict over mixed marriages, the so-called *Kölner Kirchenstreit* of the 1830's. A state that tolerated all religious beliefs—or at least recognised religious equality—was not considered to be a state that ought to have much say in the internal affairs of a church. The Catholic church also strove constantly to protect its interests in regard to education. It sought to have its claims recognized in constitutions and laws and also endeavored to negotiate concordats. During the Revolution of 1848 Catholic leaders in Germany demanded the separation of church and state, not realizing fully what this actually implied. They were under the illusion that the schools would remain with the church, certainly something no state in nineteenth-century Germany would have been willing to grant.

In the early nineteenth century the Volksschule came into its own as the democratic basis of all education. The practical training that had infiltrated the lower schools from the time of Francke was now replaced by the idea of a common basic education of mankind. This idea had stemmed originally from Rousseau, but was deepened and enriched by the idealism of the national awakening. A spirit of brotherhood was manifested in what is sometimes referred to as the New Protestantism of which Friedrich Schleiermacher (1768–1834) was the guiding spirit. He was a liberal theologian, who, as preacher at Trinity Church in Berlin and professor at the university there, achieved great prominence. Through his lectures on pedagogy and his study *On the Position of the State in Regard to Education* he came to exercise a wide influence on German education. The schools were to develop a child for active participation in the community, state, and church. Schleiermacher turned from the extreme and oftentimes shallow rationalistic approach of the previous period, which saw catechism instruction at times degenerate into sheer mental gymnastics from the abuse of the Socratic method. Schleiermacher did not entirely throw out this method of instruction, but held that it should be supplemented by explanatory and illustrative lectures so that the pupils would not only have a knowledge of religious truths, but would become true Christians with a living faith. Schleiermacher was a strong supporter of the union of the Lutheran and Reformed churches in Prussia in 1817 under the direction of the government. Thus the trials and tribulations of the period of French domination under Napoleon and the enthusiasm of the liberation movement in Germany encouraged a spirit of brotherhood unmarred by petty denominationalism.

Establishment of Simultanschulen

Another manifestation of the spirit of brotherhood was the establishment of a new type of elementary school. Up to this time public schools had as a rule been organized on confessional lines, that is, either Catholic or Protestant, the latter being either Lutheran or Reformed depending on the religion of the community. Now a new type of interdenominational school came into prominence, particularly in the small Duchy of Nassau. In 1806 the two duchies of Nassau-Usingen and Nassau-Weilburg were united and joined the Confederation of the Rhine.[2] The new state was made up of bits of territory from all sorts of lands, the result of the Napoleonic zeal for consolidation. The ruler was now faced with the problem of bringing some uniformity into his administration. Religiously he ruled over a mixture of peoples, there being, in 1816, 133 Catholic, 124 Lutheran, and 67 Reformed parishes. The Nassau school edict of 1817 recognized this situation and decreed that schools should not be separated according to confessions. The *Simultanschulen,* as these interdenominational schools came to be called, were staffed by both Protestant and Catholic teachers according to the ratio of Protestant to Catholic pupils. The law provided that there should be general instruction in religion, and in addition the pupils should be separated into special classes for instruction along confessional lines. Only the general religious instruction was obligatory for Gymnasiums and teachers' seminaries. This general instruction did not work out too well and was abolished in Gymnasiums in 1838 and at elementary schools in 1846 in favor of purely denominational instruction. This has since been the general practice for Simultanschulen: all instruction is in common except for classes in religion, where the pupils are separated along denominational lines. In general both teachers and the local clergy share in this religious instruction. In Nassau if there was no teacher or clergyman in a village to give such denominational instruction, a person from a neighboring village was called upon. If there were less than twelve pupils, the church bore the cost, if more than twelve, the state.

The Simultanschule offered advantages and in general was advocated by progressive schoolmen. It created an opportunity to improve school standards, for it cut down the number of single-teacher schools and made it possible to erect units that were better equipped and staffed. It also was more convenient for parents and pupils. Where schools were organized on confessional lines a Catholic child, living next to a Protestant school, might have to walk blocks or even miles to get to the school in which he was legally enrolled. In Nassau the princes thought that interdenominational schools would unite the people and educate them to tolerance and the unified support of the state. This has ever since been one of the important arguments for this type of school.

Defenders of the old confessional schools were quick to point out what they believed to be disadvantages in the new schools. Teachers would have to curb their free expression in teaching certain worldly subjects, notably history. A Protestant or Catholic portrayal of the Reformation, it was held, would bring objection from respective church authorities if not from laymen. Then, too, such interdenominationalism would raise havoc with traditional school prayers, school communion services, group attendance at church services, and instruction in singing, which consisted in large part of hymns. Instead of diminishing denominational differences Simultanschulen would increase them, notably through separating pupils into special religion classes. Even if a nondenominational opening or closing school prayer were used, the Lutheran child would fold his hands while the Catholic would cross himself, and was likely to add a "Hail Mary" under his breath. If a child belonged to a minority, this set him apart from his fellows, which was psychologically bad. The Simultanschulen above all disrupted the common spirit which ought to pervade all instruction. Religion was not something to be separated out, but was an integral part of a whole school. Without unified Catholic or Protestant instruction the complete education of a child would suffer.

It is to be noted that the Simultanschule did not remove religion from the schools, nor did it do away with the confessional nature of the religious instruction. There were pedagogical reformers who wanted to do this, and it became one of the issues of the later nineteenth century. The establishment of Simultanschulen instead of solving the problem of the relationship of church, state, and school only increased its complexity. Church authorities as a rule supported the confessional school system and fought the establishment of Simultanschulen. The debate has always been heated and at times bitter. As a result, their development was long and slow. Although permitted in Baden since 1834, the Simultanschule did not become the legally established school there until 1876. It was also largely adopted in Hesse, in parts of Prussia (West Prussia, Posen) where it was supposed to unite Poles and Germans, and rather exceptionally in Bavaria and in Alsace-Lorraine after 1871. In the end Simultanschulen, where established, often won the support not only of parents but even of the clergy.

Pestalozzi and Other Educationists

The decrease in emphasis on denominationalism which was characteristic of Germany in the post-Napoleonic period was also evidence of the spirit of rationalism which continued to influence educational development. Here the name of Johann Heinrich Pestalozzi (1746–1827) must be mentioned. This impractical and yet practical Swiss schoolman had a profound effect on German schools. His emphasis on the natural development of the child's personality, the importance of the home, the need for general education of the masses, his insistence on trained teachers, and his new technique of instruction all left their mark on German schools. Pestalozzi was not anti-religious like Rousseau, and never made attacks on a positive belief in religious truths. His was a generalized natural religion without dogmatic foundation. He was no friend of the catechism and the prevailing practice of memorizing, nor was he fond of Bible history as it was generally taught. He felt that the religious development of a child started with a feeling of love, trust, and thanks, which he must first learn in respect to people and then in relation to God. The general effect of his philosophy was to maintain classes in religion in the schools, but to use them for ethical and moral, not doctrinal purposes. Teachers trained in his theories and practices came to have a different view of how to teach religion from that of the clergy, who still supervised religious instruction and determined the teaching plan.

These ideas are found again in the writings of Friedrich Froebel (1782–1852), the father of the kindergarten, and a believer in the unity of spirit and nature. He stated that "all education not founded on religion is unproductive," yet "the naturally trained child requires no definite church forms." He feared that as the child becomes a man he "runs the danger of casting away his whole higher life along with the dogmatic religious forms which he has been unable to assimilate."[3]

Johann Friedrich Herbart (1776–1841), Tuiskon Ziller (1817–1882), and Adolf Diesterweg (1790–1866), to name but a few men, were also influenced by these ideas. Diesterweg, from 1832 to 1847 director of a newly founded teachers' seminary in Berlin, was one of the most important so far as religious education was concerned. Imbued with a rationalistic concept of Christianity, he was opposed to religious instruction on a confessional basis and would have liked to dispense with the catechism in the schools. He became the champion of the movement to do away with clerical supervision and inspection. His views were not acceptable to the authorities and he eventually lost his position as director of the seminary at Berlin.

If Diesterweg was a good representative of rationalist Pestalozzianism, Christian Wilhelm Harnisch (1787–1864) may be considered an exponent of orthodox Pestalozzianism. His viewpoint was always that of orthodox Christianity. "In the true meaning of the word," he declared, "there is no other education (*Erziehung*) than a Christian one, an education in sanctified love to the glory of God in the name of his Son."[4] He published a volume on Luther's catechism which did much to revitalize this instruction, although he believed that the catechism should be taught only in the upper grades. There were others of Harnisch's persuasion. Christian von Palmer's (1811–1875) *Evangelische Pädagogik* is one of the chief studies of orthodox Protestant educational theory. Franz Ludwig Zahn (1798-1890) made an important contribution to the teaching of Bible history by publishing his *Biblische Historien nach dem Kirchenjahr geordnet mit Lehren und Kinderversen versehen* (1832). This volume, where Bible stories were arranged according to the church year, superseded Hübner's eighteenth-century volume. In place of the moral teachings and pious thoughts of Hübner, Zahn substituted Bible verses and hymns. This book tended to bring about more unity in religious instruction.

Conservative Reaction

A more conservative religious group soon gained the support of the state authorities, who felt called upon to counter the prevailing rationalism of the schools. In 1808 a special bureau (*Sektion*) for education and instruction had been created in the Prussian ministry of the interior, which tended to separate the administration of school and church affairs. In 1817 however the two were again brought closer together when the bureau of education was transformed into a ministry for spiritual, instructional, and medicinal affairs. For the next twenty-one years this ministry was headed by Karl Altenstein, (1770–1840), a man of moderate views. Under his able, if not exactly vigorous direction, great progress was made, on the whole, along liberal lines. He was fortunate in being able to prevent reactionary political measures from penetrating to the teachers' seminaries and to the Volksschulen. Disillusionment with pure rationalism, however, was gaining momentum, and in 1826 Altenstein issued a decree that had lasting influence. He pointed out that the Prussian state wanted to bring up true Christians in schools and that religious instruction must have real content, permeated with belief in Jesus Christ and the doctrine of Christian salvation. Under him more orthodox and positive texts were favored.

With Altenstein's death another kind of reaction set in, hastened by the ardor displayed by various schoolmen in the Revolution of 1848. King Frederick Wilhelm IV, in a speech at a conference of seminary teachers in 1849, gave vent to his spleen:

You and you alone are to blame for all the misery which the last year has brought upon Prussia. The irreligious pseudo-education of the masses is to be blamed for it, which you have been spreading under the name of true wisdom, and by which you have eradicated religious belief and loyalty from the hearts of my subjects and alienated their affections from my person. This sham education strutting about like a peacock has always been odious to me. I already hated it from the bottom of my soul before I came to the throne [1840], and since my accession I have done everything I could to suppress it. I mean to proceed on this path, without taking heed of any one, and, indeed, no power on earth shall divert me from it.[5]

With a ruler of these views it is not surprising that the dictated Prussian constitution of 1850 made no fundamental changes in the education system. It specifically stated in Article 24: "In the organization of public elementary schools (Volksschulen) all possible consideration is to be accorded the confessional situation. Religious instruction in the elementary schools is under the direction of the respective religious bodies. Physical matters pertaining to the school are under the direction of the local authorities. ... " Parents and guardians were to see that their children received the instruction prescribed by the state. This clearly obligated them to have a child attend the classes in religion in the public schools or provide alternative instruction.

Schools were to be publicly supported, and teachers were to have all the duties and privileges of public employees. Until the passage of a special law regulating school affairs (which did not come until 1906 and then was not complete) existing laws and practices were to prevail. As heretofore, matters relating to schools were thus subject to ministerial ordinances.

The Prussian regulations of 1854, drawn up by Ministerial Councillor Stiehl, mark the high point of this conservative reaction. Religion was again made the center of the teaching plan, with some reading, writing, and a little arithmetic, much as in the schools of the Reformation. Four hours a week were to be devoted to Bible history and Bible reading and two hours to the catechism. Memorization of much of the material was required. Pupils in the Volksschulen were to be able to recount the Bible stories and to repeat the catechism by heart. In addition they were to learn the common church prayers, parts of the liturgy, some of the gospel lessons, at least 30 hymns and 180 Bible verses. Clearly this was an overdose of memory work, stemming from a zeal to eradicate revolutionary thoughts by administering a larger dose of religion. Up to 1854 provinces and individual schools had been given great leeway in establishing the details of their curriculum. Stiehl's ordinance, however, now established a uniform teaching plan for teachers' seminaries and for all Prussian Volksschulen. Within the next few years many of the Simultanschulen, even in West Prussia and Posen, were converted into confessional schools.[6]

The movement for a return to orthodoxy was also concerned with the teachers' seminaries, for after all they had considerable influence on what was being taught at the schools. But at the same time teachers were gaining in selfconsciousness and developing a pride in their profession. They chafed under clerical supervision, and their demands for supervision by pedagogically trained schoolmen became more insistent. While not advocating the abolition of religious education, they campaigned more boldly for the separation of the schools from the church. To forestall such radical ideas the government ordered an increased emphasis on the religious training of the elementary-school teachers. Stiehl himself declared that the purpose of his regulation was to put an end to the movement which aimed "at the emancipation of the schools from the church, the emancipation of the teaching profession from authority, the organization of an independent teaching profession, which is based on its own members. Such agitation must come to an end and must never be permitted to start again. The school is the daughter of the church and the helper of the family."[7] In Prussia a candidate for admission to a teachers' seminary was required to know fifty hymns, eighteen Psalms, the Bible histories of the Old and New Testament and of course the catechism. Moreover the teachers at the seminaries were specifically ordered to stay close to the prescribed textbook in religion and not to insert their own ideas.

The reaction, however, had gone too far, and by the end of the eighteen-fifties the trend was reversed. Again the more secular subjects came to the fore, and the amount of material to be memorized in religious instruction was lessened. What was true in Prussia held true in general for the rest of Germany, although there were always more conservative states—the Mecklenburgs, for example—and more liberal ones—Bremen, Baden, and some of the Thuringian states. Neither extreme rationalism nor extreme orthodoxy was dominant in elementary education as the German states united in an empire in 1871.

Jewish Education

There was another development in elementary education in the first half of the nineteenth century which should be noted. This was the recognition of Jewish schools on the part of the state. Up to the nineteenth century as a rule Jewish children were educated by their parents or house teachers. Gradually the practice developed that several families got together and hired a teacher, and a private school came into being. In Württemberg Jewish schools were organized in the 1820's and were recognized by law as Volksschulen. In 1825 the Evangelical Consistory in Württemberg decreed that where Jewish children had no special schools, they were to attend the elementary schools of their villages, but were to be exempt from the religion classes.[8]

The establishment of compulsory education by the state obviously applied to the Jewish as well as the Christian population, and the state could no longer neglect these children. The Prussian Allgemeine Landrecht of 1794 specifically stated that no one could be denied entrance into a school because of differences of religious belief and, secondly, that no one should be compelled to attend the religion classes of a school if he belonged to a different confession. It was not until the law of June 23, 1847, that Jewish schools were recognised in Prussia and entitled to some public support. This was, however, done under the proviso—which was clearly in contradiction to the Allgemeine Landrecht—that attendance at these schools should be limited to Jewish children.[9] Special Jewish school societies or synagogue congregations were recognized as the equivalent of the regular school authorities (*Schulverbände*). Jews supporting such a school were freed from payment of other school fees as well as from all immediate personal obligations for the support of regular public schools.

Where Jewish children attended a state school, the problem arose as to who should provide religious instruction. The laws stated that the Prussian school system was to have a Christian basis and the authorities were under no obligation to include Jewish religious instruction as a part of the regular curriculum. Since Jewish religious instruction meant also instruction in Hebrew, this was not a simple thing to annex to an elementary-school program. The courts at various times declared that compulsory attendance did not apply to Jewish religious instruction as it did to Christian. The Prussian law of 1847, however, stated that every synagogue congregation was obligated to make arrangements that no Jewish child lacked the necessary religious education during the age of compulsory school attendance.[10]

It was not until the end of the eighteenth century that the Jewish communities took notice of a "special subject called 'religious instruction,' since instruction in the Bible and Talmud as well as Jewish family life and community life were performing this function."[11] Under the influence of the Enlightenment, C. G. Salzmann first drew up a syllabus of Jewish religious instruction which combined ethics and religion. The Prussian law of 1847 now made it incumbent upon the Jewish communities to establish religious schools for Jewish children that were attending the regular non-Jewish public schools. After some abortive attempts, a successful religious school in Berlin got under way in 1854, attended at first by 87 children. "Biblical history, Hebrew, translation of Bible and prayer book, Bible reading and religious doctrine" constituted the curriculum.

The provisions in regard to Jewish religious instruction paralleled the position taken in the case of some minority Christian groups, such as Baptists, Methodists, and Mennonites, whose churches had to bear the cost of instruction. Children from these groups, however, usually attended the regular Protestant religion classes. If there were permanently twelve or more Jewish children in a school, the Jewish congregation had a right to a subsidy from the local authorities toward their religious instruction. By a ministerial decree of March 21, 1867, school buildings were put at the disposal of the Jewish congregations, and school authorities were to cooperate in supervising regular attendance. In other parts of Germany the laws were much like those in Prussia. Where the Jewish community had not erected its own schools, Jewish children attended the regular Christian public schools. Nowhere were they obligated to attend religion classes, but on the other hand they were supposed to receive equivalent religious instruction, either at home or through the Jewish congregation.

Two laws of 1867 and 1869 of the North German Confederation removed all legal disabilities resulting from difference in religious confession, and these laws became a part of the imperial legislation. Yet education always remained a state matter, and old practices and laws long held sway. In general it can be said that as far as Jewish religious instruction is concerned separate rules and regulations always applied. This stemmed no doubt to a great extent from the close historic ties between the schools, the Christian churches, and the state.

The Humanistic Gymnasium

In higher education the beginning of the nineteenth century brought about a new emphasis on the humanistic Gymnasiums. They became the embodiment of the idea that an intensive study of Greek and Latin literature, with a thorough familiarization with the spirit of classical antiquity, was the best preparation for higher professional training. This was the great era of German Idealism when the influence of Kant, Fichte, Schelling, and Hegel was dominant. Although these men differed, and their idealism was far removed from that of Plato, the whole intellectual climate of the period aroused a renewed interest in the classics. The emphasis on ideas, the concept that all reality was to be derived from the mind—that is, from reason which was akin to God's will—tended to less orthodoxy in religion and a greater secularization of learning. This idealism dominated higher education. The Gymnasiums now received a new status and were set apart from the Latin and other secondary schools by the inauguration of a special school-leaving examination (*Abitur*), which entitled the successful candidate to admission to a university. In 1788 Prussia had established these final examinations, but it was not until the ordinance of 1812 that they were completely worked out.[12] High standards were set, especially in Latin, Greek, German, and mathematics. Universities, it is true, continued to give their own admission examinations until 1834, but after that no one could study for the professions without having first passed the final Abitur (also called *Reifeprüfung*) from a Gymnasium.

Religion had always been taught at the German secondary schools, but under the national and humanistic influences of the eighteenth and early nineteenth centuries it had lost much of its orthodoxy. In some places the number of hours of instruction approached the vanishing point; in others there were as many as four a week. Some schools gave relatively traditional instruction, others spent much of their time studying the early heretics—Monophysites, Nestorians, Donatists, and other abstruse subjects. In Prussia religious instruction had a rather hard time at the Gymnasium in the first decade of the century. Wilhelm von Humboldt (1767–1835) and Friedrich August Wolf (1759–1824), who had much to do with directing higher education, were Hellenists who had little real interest in religion.[13] Wolf believed that a harmonious development of mind and spirit was best fostered by a study of classical times. In ancient Greece the men of the New Humanism found their ideal man, that is, the individual personality developed to the highest degree, yet dedicated freely to the welfare of all. Since this was considered to be the aim of education, Christianity was relegated to a minor role, not only at the universities, but in the higher schools as well.

Humboldt, who for a time headed the bureau on education and instruction, in 1810 had issued an edict that no one should be appointed as teacher in a Gymnasium in Prussia who had not passed a special qualifying teachers' examination. This was a landmark in separating the teaching from the clerical profession and did much to create an independent professional group of teachers. Three educational commissions (*Wissenschaftliche Deputationen*) were set up at Berlin, Breslau, and Königsberg to administer these examinations.

Schleiermacher was an influential member of the Berlin commission. He believed that religious education was primarily the duty of home and church and raised the question whether religious instruction should be made a part of the teaching plan at a Gymnasium at all. With one exception all the members of the commission, including Schleiermacher himself, voted in favor of its inclusion. The main arguments advanced were that it was necessary to have a tie between more advanced scientific learning and religious education. Religion classes would also provide a good opportunity to awaken higher speculative faculties. Besides it was necessary for all state servants and members of the upper classes to have a full knowledge of Christianity. Schleiermacher drew up the regulations for this religious instruction. He wanted a distinctly Christian education, not one dealing with all religions. He did not want it on a confessional basis, and particularly deprecated distinction between Lutheran and Reformed instruction. The full Bible, not a book of selections as recommended by the rationalists, was to be the basis of instruction. The teachers were to have the greatest possible liberty in choosing portions of the Bible which they wanted to use. Schleiermacher felt that it was impossible to examine in religion, and it was probably due to his influence that the examination regulations of 1812 omitted the examination in religion for the Abitur. Later this was changed, and after 1834 there was also an examination in religion for Gymnasium graduates.

In the reorganization of the Gymnasium, which occurred in other states as well as in Prussia, religion was everywhere maintained as a regular subject of instruction, usually taking two or three hours a week. It was far from being the center of instruction, as the following summary of scheduled hours for the ten-year course in Prussia indicates: Latin 76, Greek 50, German 44, Mathematics 60, History and Geography 30, Nature Study 20, Religion 20.[14] This allotment of two hours a week to religion by Prussian authorities also became the rule in many other states, although there was no uniformity. Under conservative influence in 1856 the number of hours was increased in Prussia to three in the sixth and fifth forms, only to be cut back to two in the fifth form in 1882. The Gymnasiums as a rule were not organized on confessional lines, although they might be designated as Protestant or Catholic according to the confession of the majority of the students. If there were students of more than one confession present, they were separated into special classes for religious instruction. Religion classes in the Gymnasium, unlike those in the elementary school, were and still are in most cases regularly taught by a qualified theologian.

Higher education, however, did not entirely escape the conservative reaction which was so marked in elementary education after 1840. Ludwig Wiese, who was placed in charge of higher education in Prussia in 1852, wrote in his autobiography: "I would have preferred to return to the old simple teaching plan with its emphasis on religious instruction, the ancient languages, and mathematics."[15] This he was not able to do, but the Gymnasium was ready for reorientation in the new united Germany of 1870. The overweight of ancient languages had to make way for modern languages, while religion retained on the whole its established, if modest, place.

It is said, quite rightly, that Germany was culturally one, long before it had any real political unity. In literature, music, and the arts generally, there were no dividing lines. Even in the field of education some common factors had developed—the idea of a Volksschule, forming the basis for all education, the appearance of the Gymnasium and the Abitur examination for entrance to all universities, even the development of the Simultanschule tended to dull political and religious differences.

3+ R.E.I.G.S.

Political particularism, however, played a much larger part in school systems than it did on the higher cultural level. At the time of the formation of the Empire, the educational systems of Germany, while they had many features in common, sharply reflected local differences, traditions, and pride. A mass of local provisions cluttered the educational scene. It is not unusual that there should be local resistance in educational matters to outside ideas. In the United States, the states and even municipalities are still loath to delegate such responsibilities to higher authorities. Local pride and local interest both tend to a particularism in this field above all others.

Ideological differences enhanced this tendency. The long tradition connecting church and school meant that religious divisions were among the most difficult problems of the schools. Between those rationalists, who approved only of ethical instruction, and conservatives, who thought of religion as a necessary weapon against radical forces, there existed all shades of opinion. These centred about various leaders who championed a number of teaching methods and materials. The atmosphere of the age was scientific, and specialization became a magic watchword. The "higher criticism" of the Bible had its part in undermining confidence in the familiar curriculum. Teachers came to feel that they were professionals, who could brook no interference or supervision by the clergy. The weight of tradition, the load of state regulations, the sharp conflict between conservatives and scientific criticism, the mounting professional jealousy between teachers and clergy, presented problems to which the creation of the Empire offered no simple solutions.

Part Two

The Empire, 1871–1918

Chapter IV

RELIGION and the
ORGANIZATION of EDUCATION
in the EMPIRE

The Germanic Confederation of 1815 was made up of thirty-nine states; the German Empire of 1871 numbered twenty-five states plus the Imperial Territory of Alsace-Lorraine. It was a federation of states unequal in size and population. Prussia was by far the largest, including approximately two-thirds of the area and population of the Empire and extending from the eastern frontier with Russia to the borders of Belgium on the west, from the frontier with Denmark on the north to within a short distance of Switzerland on the south. Bavaria was the next largest state, with an area and population about one-sixth that of Prussia. Next came Württemberg in size, but Saxony in population, followed by Baden and the other states, with Bremen being the smallest in area (106 sq. miles), while Schaumburg-Lippe had a population of only 32,059. There was also no uniformity in state governments, as the Empire was a federation of four kingdoms, six grand duchies, twelve duchies and principalities, three free cities and one imperial territory. Some of these states had a more liberal government than others, some were more united in area, population, and legislation than others, but every state had its own administration as well as its own school system. Not all the states had universities of which there were twenty-one in the Empire. The entrance requirements for the universities and the training they offered did, to be sure, exert a unifying influence on the whole educational system.

The Educational Pattern

The new imperial constitution, unlike the proposed Frankfurt Constitution of 1849, contained no important provisions in regard to education. In 1871, it is true, a *Reichsschulkommission* was established,

53

but its only function was to decide under what conditions the secondary schools could award the coveted certificate that permitted a young man to serve only one year instead of the customary two years in the army. Reich authorities also took steps to bring about agreements between the states for the recognition of each other's examinations, and the medical examination that came into being was for all intents and purposes a Reich examination. The Reich also supported some scientific research institutions such as the Kaiser Wilhelm Institute. In spite of demands from teachers for a national educational law, no such law was ever seriously contemplated. Education as heretofore was left to the province of the state governments.[1]

This, however, does not mean that there were only twenty-five educational systems in Germany. The situation was far more complicated than that, for when territorial additions were made to any state the existing school systems were usually retained. This was an old practice; thus when Prussia in 1864–66 annexed Schleswig-Holstein, Hanover, Electoral Hesse, Nassau, and Frankfurt am Main, there was no thought of establishing a unitary school system. Even within most of these territories there was no uniformity, for their school systems, too, were overlaid with the accumulated enactments of centuries. Even if a state had recently passed a so-called comprehensive education law, it usually contained exceptions for certain localities, or more often a general proviso that "until this matter is dealt with by further legislation or regulations, existing laws will prevail." To this day, for example, some of the schools of Frankfurt are in part governed by legislation going back to the days when it was a free city; other schools, in territory administratively annexed to the city since 1870, are under regulations made by the old Duchy of Nassau to which this territory had once belonged. In addition there is Prussian legislation since 1867, Reich legislation since 1919, and various post-World War II constitutional and legislative provisions. As a result of this complexity, in some Frankfurt schools clerics are supposed to give the religious instruction, while in others only lay teachers are permitted to give such instruction.

While there was great diversity—and it would be practically impossible to make any statement in regard to educational matters which would hold for all Germany—there was a general pattern which can be discerned. The spirit which brought about the unification of Germany also created a desire for more uniformity of practice in various fields still controlled by state legislation. Bavaria in 1874 extended its Gymnasium program from eight to nine years in order to bring these schools into line with those of the north German states.

Most states after 1871 issued new teaching plans for their Gymnasiums and these all showed a decline in emphasis on the classics.

The Empire provided a national forum such as there had never been in Germany before. School issues came to be less local and more national. Discussion of problems arising in one state now spread more readily to other states. This did not always mean a progressive solution, for vested interests, frightened by what took place elsewhere, fought strenuously to maintain the *status quo*. Nevertheless the same educational theories and practices were discussed throughout the length and breadth of Germany. Teachers, who had formerly grouped themselves primarily into regional or state organizations of various kinds, began to strike up ties with teachers in other states. There came to be national societies, and the *Deutscher Lehrerverein*, formed in 1871 in Berlin, was later joined by various provincial and state organizations.[2] It replaced the moribund *Allgemeiner Deutscher Lehrerverein*, founded in 1848 at a time when hopes of achieving national unity filled men's hearts. Germany now began to think more on a national level, and as the years passed more consistency in educational practices appeared. How much progress was made is indicated by the complete omission of any reference to education in the Imperial Constitution of 1871, while the educational clauses were among the most important of the Weimar Constitution of 1919. This is, of course, also an expression of the modern trend toward centralization of government.

The Empire brought about political parties on a national scale, and these parties helped to determine how each state should exercise its powers over the schools. Universal manhood suffrage prevailed for national elections, and this was both a means and an incentive for building up a party organization. The Social Democratic party, for example, could hardly have acquired significant status under the restrictive suffrage regulations that still held for many state and local elections. The Social Democratic party came to support everywhere the abolition of church influence over the schools, the erection of schools on a Simultan rather than a confessional basis, and, if not always the complete abolishment of religious education in the schools, at least its drastic revision and curtailment. Actually these policies had for some time been supported in varying degrees by many of the progressive schoolmen in Germany, and the liaison between school reforms and social democracy aroused the suspicion of government and church authorities. There is no doubt that many considered the strengthening of religious instruction in the schools as one of the best antidotes to the growth of socialism. Conservative parties allied themselves with church authorities and became ardent supporters in state legislatures of maintaining church influence over the schools. It is to be noted that the great Catholic Center party, organized in 1870 to protect Catholic interests, became an important factor in German political life only after the formation of the Empire. The existence of a national political arena did much to strengthen political Catholicism in the states, as witness the denouement of the *Kulturkampf*. This struggle had been waged first on a minor scale in Baden and Bavaria, but, as the conflict developed between Bismarck and the Roman Catholic church, it was fought largely over issues arising out of Prussian state affairs. Yet because Bismarck needed the support of the Center party in the national Reichstag, he compromised with the party on state issues.

The Pattern of Religious Affiliation

The formation of the Empire facilitated interchange and mobility in the population with a consequent increase in the intermixture of religious denominations. The census of 1871 showed that the Empire as a whole contained 25,579,709 Protestants, 14,867,463 Catholics, 512,158 Jews and 82,155 members of various Christian sects.[3] The generalization that North Germany was predominantly Protestant and South Germany was Catholic still held true, but this could not be carried over to the individual states. Prussia is usually classed as a North German state, but in 1871 one-third of its population was Catholic. On the other hand, the South German states of Bavaria and Baden were approximately one-third Protestant; Baden even had a Protestant ruling house. These two states, along with Alsace-Lorraine, where the Protestants numbered about a fifth, were the only territories where Catholics had a majority. Württemberg, the other important South German state, was sixty-eight percent Protestant. While there were in general not many Catholics in the north, there were only a few states where they constituted such a small number that they played no role when it came to legislation. In Mecklenburg-Schwerin and Mecklenburg-Strelitz only the Lutheran church had a legal standing, and the organization of a few Catholic and Reformed parishes was permitted by special ordinances.[4] Saxony was overwhelmingly Protestant (2,493,422 Lutherans, 53,642 Catholics), but the ruling house was Catholic.

A close relationship had developed between state and church over the years; indeed it was difficult at times to distinguish what pertained to civil or church law. Historically the state had reserved a means of supervision known as the *Plazet*. This meant that all church laws, ordinances, and decrees had to receive the approval of the state before they could be proclaimed or put into effect. The Plazet gradually lost its importance after 1848, but only Prussia rescinded it. Bavaria, Brunswick, and Saxe-Coburg-Gotha specifically retained it, while it was modified in other states.[5] The state also exercised certain rights of supervision over the erection of new church offices and monastic orders and shared in various ways in the appointment of higher clergy. Thus in the Concordat of 1817 the papacy had granted to the King of Bavaria the special privilege of nominating the two archbishops and six bishops in Bavaria.[6] In some places the clergy had to take a special oath of loyalty. There was, also, state regulation and state review of the administration of discipline and punishment on the part of church authorities.

Thus there was a close relationship between the government and the dominant church bodies and one could speak of established churches (*Landeskirchen*). In some states the ruler was even titular head (*summus episcopus*) of the Protestant church. The usual practice was to have a ministry in each state which supervised church and school affairs, with separate Catholic and Protestant bureaus. The abolition of the separate Catholic bureau in Prussia in 1871 was the opening gun in the Prussian Kulturkampf and aroused great opposition in Catholic circles. Both Protestant and Catholic churches, and as a rule Jewish synagogues as well, received state funds and were entitled to levy taxes on their membership. Some states maintained separate Lutheran and Reformed church organizations.

In Prussia eight Protestant churches were recognized as being on a par with each other, e.g. as Landeskirchen.[7] This was due to the fact that the churches in the provinces annexed in 1866 (*Neue Provinzen*) retained their own independent organization. In the old provinces as a result of the church union of 1817, engineered by Frederick William III, the distinction between Lutheran and Reformed churches was done away with, and the Evangelical church was recognized as the state church. These eight Protestant bodies and the Catholic church were classed in Prussia as privileged corporations under public law. (*Privilegierte Korporationen des öffentlichen Rechts*). The buildings of only these corporations were legally called churches and recognized as privileged buildings by the state. They were not taxable. The clergymen of these bodies had special privileges enjoyed by no other clergy, such as exemption from communal, district, and provincial taxes, exemption from the quartering of troops in time of peace, and exemption from church but not school taxes. They were not exempted from military service although they did not have to serve with arms on the battle field and were entitled to other considerations.

3*

Every religious body in Prussia which held itself separate from the established churches (Old Catholics were considered as Catholics) was classed as "tolerated" (*geduldet*) and had to undergo a special legal process in order to obtain the privileges of a corporate body. This by no means placed them on the same plane with the privileged corporations. They were, however, free from police restrictions applying to organizations (*Vereinspolizeiliche Aufsicht*), were entitled to somewhat greater protection from the state, and were regarded as having a legal identity. In this group were those congregations which had separated from the Evangelical church in old Prussia (Old Lutherans and adherents of the Reformed Netherland Confession), Herrenhuter, Jews, Mennonites, and Baptists. The Mennonites received a special concession in that they were not required to take an oath, or forced to carry arms on a battlefield, but they might be used in hospitals.

There was a third group of religious sects which were not corporate bodies at all but were classed as private organizations (*Privatgesellschaften*) under Prussian law. In this category we find such small sects as the "Nazarener, Irwingianer, Deutsch-Katholiken, Phillipponen" and other free organizations such as the Adventists.[8] These churches were free to carry on their work, and could rely on the article of the constitution guaranteeing religious liberty. The one big restriction was that it was practically impossible for any of these churches to acquire property as an organization.

It was customary in all of Germany that by a judicial act any person could leave an established church and join another church, or, if he wished, remain entirely without religious affiliation. He was then exempted from church taxes, but on the other hand lost all the privileges of church membership, for example, the services of the ministers at baptisms, marriages, and funerals. The church taxes were by no means burdensome and very few availed themselves of the privilege, in spite of the mass exodus advocated by the socialists. In the years immediately preceding the first World War the number who left the church for all reasons was on the increase, but for the Protestants came to only about 30,000 a year (about one-sixth of one percent).[9] Many of these had no interest in religion at all, and the church was certainly not weakened by the dropping of this dead timber. Nevertheless many merely nominal Christians remained within the churches, which is inevitable if there is an attempt to have a *Volkskirche* with universal membership.

Universal membership in an established church has advantages but also disadvantages. It meant that all classes, poor and rich, educated and uneducated, liberal and orthodox, attended the same church, which was very democratic in this respect. Obviously, however, a sermon adapted to one class was not suited to another, and it was hard to satisfy radicals, liberals, conservatives, fundamentalists, even on religious issues, apart from broader ethical, moral, social, or political problems. The result was that many lost interest, particularly in medium-sized cities where the congregations lacked the homogeneity of rural areas or even that of big cities where residential zones often bring a certain unity. All too often young pastors imbibed liberal theology at the state universities, which they had been forced to attend, and then were called upon to preach to congregations whose members had been instructed along orthodox lines in the public schools, which they too had been obliged to attend.

One big advantage of universal church membership, it is often said, is that it brings about a measure of unity among the people; it creates a certain common fund of knowledge and at least in part a common ideology. This thesis should not be unduly stressed, and there are many things to be said pro and con in regard to it. Under this system, however, religious instruction in the public schools was made possible, for it was not plagued by petty denominationalism as would certainly be the case in the United States.

Laws in regard to religious instruction, which was given in the schools in every German state, usually spoke only of Protestants or Catholics, with special provisions for Jews. In practice Protestant instruction bore a Reformed or Lutheran character, depending on the district and particular parish where the school was located. This was largely a matter of using a Lutheran or Reformed catechism, for they differed in the arrangement of material. Members of the dissident sects usually permitted their children to attend the religion classes, and in Prussia they were almost forced to do so. If parents withdrew their children, they had to provide equivalent religious instruction, for religion was a compulsory subject of instruction. In Prussia authorities decided whether this equivalent instruction was adequate, while in Saxony no attempt was made to test it, although it had to be Christian. In Bavaria children of atheistic parents did not have to attend religion classes. There was no compulsion in Württemberg and Baden, and no alternative instruction was required in these states.[10]

The Organization of Schools

Along with the religious pattern in the Empire, there was a pattern to the organization of the schools which must be reviewed. By 1871 everywhere in Germany education had been made compulsory, and the common tuition-free Volksschule, or elementary school, was well established. This normally was an eight-year school and was typed as one-class, two-class, and so on, depending on the number of teachers employed. This was the school for the mass of the people and with slight variations existed in both rural and urban areas. There were also various kinds of so-called middle schools deriving their name from the fact that they were designed to cater to what the Germans called the middle class (*Mittelstand*), a more limited and sharply defined group than is covered by this term in the United States. These schools, at which a tuition charge was paid, were geared to give a more extended and advanced common-school education and usually had a nine or ten-year course. The curriculum provided one foreign language and a measure of trade education, usually of a secretarial nature. There were also vocational schools (*Berufsschulen*).[11]

In addition there were the higher schools—Gymnasium, *Realgymnasium, Oberrealschule* (for boys), *Lyzeum* and *Oberlyzeum* (for girls)—which received pupils after either a three-year course in a so-called *Vorschule* (preparatory school), or four years of Volksschule. These higher schools had a nine-year program, and most of them were public, supported in great part by public funds, and subject to state supervision. There were also numerous private schools, most of them carrying on much the same program as the public schools, but often also providing specialized programs. Private schools played an especially important role in higher education for girls. Many of these private schools were church-run and controlled, particularly by teaching orders of the Catholic church.[12] Although classed as private, these schools very often received a measure of public financial support, usually from the states rather than from the local authorities, which had to bear the brunt of the cost of public elementary-school education.

At all elementary, middle, and higher schools religion was a regular subject of instruction. So far as religious education is concerned, middle schools need not be dealt with separately from elementary (Volk) schools, but higher schools must be placed in a separate category. Sometimes religion was taught at vocational (Beruf) schools, but whether it should be a regular subject of instruction there was a much debated point. The Prussian vocational-school curriculum of 1897 made no provision for religious instruction. These schools took care of students who only wanted a specialized trade education. They were often attended on a part-time or after-work basis, and no attempt was made to present a rounded curriculum.

In 1871 the overwhelming number of elementary schools in Germany were organized as either Protestant or Catholic confessional schools. Some were organized, however, as Simultanschulen, which, as we have seen, were schools staffed by both Protestant and Catholic teachers and attended by children of both confessions. The Simultan-schule, already well established, became the only legal type in Baden in 1876, and was dominant in Hesse and in certain sections of Prussia, chiefly Nassau, West Prussia, and Posen. In Bavaria, on the other hand, a decree of 1873, which was intended to facilitate the erection of Simultanschulen, aroused such opposition that a further ordinance of 1883 restricted the establishment of Simultanschulen to "exceptional cases made necessary by compelling circumstances."[13] Simultan-schulen were represented in a few other states. Many of these legal Simultanschulen were, however, actually confessional schools, for they were located in either purely Protestant or Catholic parishes, and both teachers and pupils belonged to the same denomination. To have a Simultanschule by no means meant that teachers of both faiths cooperated in giving instruction. Teachers were always appointed with reference to the faith of the students, and in single-teacher schools the majority faith won the teaching position. In multiple-teacher schools, a teacher of another confession was often appointed only because of the need to have a religious teacher for the children of the minority. At times this custom led even to the appointment of Jewish teachers, who were likely to have their teaching load rounded out by assignments in technical or manual subjects like drawing. The appointment of a Jewish teacher was always regarded as an exception to the rule.

In spite of the support given to Simultanschulen by most peda-gogical reformers, this type did not show a marked increase in numbers. In Prussia, under Minister Falk (1872–1878) the government per-mitted rather freely the opening of such schools in places where the people wanted them, and there it led to an improvement of the school system. With Falk's dismissal this policy was reversed. Minister Puttkamer, his successor, stated: "I must make clear that these defenders on the tribune and in the press of the principle of the Simultanschule are fighting for a lost cause."[14] The opening of new Simultanschulen was henceforth permitted only in exceptional cases and many Simultanschulen, notably in the Rhine Province, were again converted into confessional schools. A summary of their status in Prussia as of 1906, when the first general education law was finally passed, shows that the Prussian schools were largely on a confessional basis. Of the 37,761 public elementary schools attended by 6,161,378 children, there were only 900 Simultanschulen with 370,079 children. Of the latter there were 449 schools in West Prussia, 184 in Posen,

119 in the District of Wiesbaden (Nassau), which left only 148 for all the other territories of the monarchy.[15]

In 1872 an important educational measure was enacted in Prussia, the so-called general ordinances (*Allgemeine Verfügungen*) which dealt mostly with the regulation of the curriculum. There were of course many other minor regulations issued in the next years, but it was not until July 28, 1906, that the basic school budgetary law (*Volkschulunterhaltungsgesetz*) was passed.[16] This was far more than budgetary legislation, and was the result of many commission reports, long committee and legislative debate, and numerous compromises. Even then it left many things still to be regulated, and the law did not apply to the provinces of West Prussia and Posen. One of the most bitterly contested issues was the question of confessional or Simultanschulen. The whole fourth section of the law was given over to the regulation of this issue.

A few details will bring home the fact that organizing a school system along confessional lines is not a simple matter. Article 24 of the Prussian constitution stated: "In the establishment of public Volksschulen attention is to be paid as much as possible to the confessional situation." The law of 1906 endeavoured to carry out this prescription and boldly declared (Article 33): "Public Volksschulen are as a rule to be organized so that instruction of Evangelical children will be given by Evangelical teachers, Catholic children by Catholic teachers." Although the law carefully avoided the terms "confessional" or "Simultan," the confessional school was now legally the normal school, and the confession of the teachers determined whether it was to be classed as a Protestant or Catholic school. This all seems simple enough, but actually many other details had to be worked out, for it was expressly stated that no child could be denied admission to the public elementary school of his place of domicile because of his religion. This meant that often there were religious minorities among the pupils of a confessional school. With changes in population the religious complexion of a school could easily be altered.

The law made rather complex provisions to deal with such a situation. It provided that under such circumstances an Evangelical teacher should regularly succeed an Evangelical one, and the same held for the succession of Catholic teachers. If, however, in a Protestant school for five successive years two-thirds of the pupils—exclusive of guest pupils from other districts—were Catholic, and during this time the number of Evangelical children had fallen below twenty, then upon a new appointment coming up, a Catholic should receive the position. No change in confessional status, however, was to be made without the approval of the state educational minister. The same rule of course applied if it was a question of changing from a Catholic to a Protestant teacher. If a school had more than one teacher, then the second position was to be filled by a teacher of the other confession, if for five years two-thirds of the pupils had belonged to the other confession, and the number of pupils belonging to the former majority had declined to below forty.

The same law, despite its basic confessional emphasis did permit Simultanschulen to continue in those districts where they already existed. It even stated specifically that "in the territory of the former Duchy of Nassau the existing regulations prevail," and under paragraph 70, the whole law did not apply in the other predominantly Simultan provinces of West Prussia and Posen. Under special circumstances and with express permission of authorities, Simultanschulen could also be established anywhere in Prussia. However, should there be within such a school 60 (120 in cities and larger rural districts) Catholic or Evangelical children for five successive years, and if the parents of these demanded the establishment of a school on confessional lines, this had to be done, unless there already was a confessional school in the district to which they could be sent.

The law confirmed existing practice by providing that if there were permanently at least twelve children in a confessional school belonging to either an Evangelical or Catholic minority (no provision was made for denominational dissidents) then special religious classes had to be provided.[17] This was often done by bringing in teachers from neighboring villages, or by grouping children from different schools for religious classes. If such instruction could be provided only at great cost and inconvenience, then a teacher of the minority confession could be appointed and given other teaching assignments as well. This, however, did not change the confessional status of the school. As a rule only Evangelical or Catholic teachers were to be appointed, although in some special cases Jews could be named. In addition the law stated specifically that in the appointment of teachers for technical subjects (drawing, gymnastics, needlecraft, domestic science) religious affiliation did not have to be considered. The number of these exceptions to the rule indicates the difficulty of establishing a completely confessional system.

The Education of Children of Mixed Marriages

In the ministerial ordinance of March 14, 1908, implementing the educational law, it was decreed that children of mixed marriages would be considered members of that confession in which, according to existing practice in that district, children were being educated. This brings to the fore one of the most complicated problems in regard to confessional religious education, which had long plagued school administrations. As far back as 1650 in implementing the Treaty of Westphalia, the question cropped up as to what should be the religion of orphans. Three solutions were suggested: (1) male children were to take the religion of the father, female that of the mother; (2) both male and female children were to follow the religion of the father; (3) children were to have religious training according to directions agreed upon by the parents before their death.

These three solutions all reappear in legislation which was enacted in various German states in later years. In general the laws held that the will of the father decided the matter. Should he remarry after the death of the mother or should he die himself then new problems arose. Some states decreed that the will of the father prevailed even after his death, while others held the mother then had full rights of determination. (The latter was true in Holstein.) In the case of illegitimate children the mother, of course, decided. In the Palatinate all children of mixed marriages had to be raised as Catholics until as late as 1705. This was in line with the later papal bull of 1741 which permitted mixed marriages only if children were brought up as Catholics. As the state came to tolerate all faiths it had to take a neutral position and could not uphold a type of regulation which benefited one religion. But old provisions continued. Thus different rules applied to male and female children in Bavaria until August 1919, and in Mecklenburg-Schwerin until 1921.

In Prussia a decree of 1803, applying to the eastern province, stated that in order to preserve the harmony of the family all children were to be raised in the religion of the father. This policy was applied to the Rhine provinces in 1825, whereupon a Rhineland bishop turned to the Pope for a directive. The Pope replied that the Catholic church could bless mixed marriages only if children were to be brought up as Catholics. The Prussian government refused to recognise this position, but was able to work out a secret agreement with the Archbishop of Cologne: the Archbishop would not insist on the education rule, while the state promised to do away with civil marriages in the Rhineland. When a new Archbishop of Cologne was named, controversy broke out in what is usually termed the Cologne church dispute (*Kölner Kirchenstreit*). It was a minor church–state conflict which heralded the far more important Kulturkampf of the seventies. In the end Prussia recognized the right of the clergy to inquire into the upbringing of children, but refused to alter its law.

During the nineteenth century there was, in general, a tendency in the enactment of legislation "to order the religious education of children on the basis of the family, and thus give expression to the idea that the natural intermediators between God and children are those to whom a child owes its life."[18] Nevertheless laws still varied greatly among the states as to whether in a disputed case a child should be schooled as a Catholic or Protestant. As population changes brought more confessional diversity, as mixed marriages as well as divorces and remarriages increased, the need for more uniform regulations became apparent. This was not achieved until 1921 when under the Weimar Republic a national law was passed.

Jewish Schools

Since the various state educational systems were definitely organized on a Christian basis, it was customary to have special laws or sections of laws to regulate Jewish schools. The Prussian law of 1906 was no exception. This law extended the provisions of the law of 1847 to the whole monarchy. Previously the Jewish societies could ask for help from public funds only in those places where the obligation to support the schools rested on the civil commune. Now they had the right to ask for aid for their public schools everywhere within the monarchy. Under these provisions there were Jewish confessional schools just as there were Protestant and Catholic confessional schools. Civil communes were not obligated to erect Jewish schools, this being left to special Jewish societies which were recognized as public school authorities in their districts. Prussia, Bavaria, and Württemberg were almost the only states which made provision for public Jewish schools. In regions where Simultanschulen prevailed there were no separate Jewish schools.[19]

Christian children were prohibited in Prussia from attending a Jewish confessional school, as there were always Christian schools at hand. On the other hand, Jewish children were permitted to attend the public Christian schools of their place of residence, but did not have to participate in the Christian religion classes. The ministerial ordinance of 1908 states:

The provision of Jewish religious instruction is a matter for the care of the synagogue congregation. In some instances, civil communes can take on the Jewish religious instruction and for this purpose can appoint a Jewish teacher at the Christian schools. These teachers will also be entrusted with other subjects, the teaching of which by Jewish teachers would not arouse the sensibilities of Christian children. They can under some circumstances act as class masters. The subject matter which is dealt with by ordinance shall not be changed. Such arrangements can, however, be made only when there is real need.[20]

The appointment of Jewish teachers at Simultanschulen was easier than at purely confessional schools. In Baden this was very frequently the practice. Although orthodox Jewish communities liked having their own schools, most Jews favored Simultanschulen so long as the close ties between the Christian churches and the public schools were retained. Although the Social Democrats wanted the complete secularization of the schools, they always directed their sharpest attacks against the confessional schools. This sometimes led opposition groups to combine anti-Semitism with antisocialism. Thus the Conservative party in its program of December 8, 1892, proclaimed:

We consider the confessional Christian Volksschule the foundation of the education of the people and the most important guarantee against the increasing degeneration of the masses and the progressive dissolution of all the bonds of society. We oppose the often forward-pushing and divisive Jewish influence on our Volksschulen. We demand for a Christian people a Christian government and Christian teachers for Christian pupils.[21]

Jews numbered only 512,158 out of a total population of 41,058,641 in 1871. About two-thirds of these lived in Prussia which left only small minorities scattered among the other states. In no place could they exercise a dominant influence on school policy, but they were always well represented at the higher schools. About 1871 it was estimated that one out of every 370 Catholic, 200 Evangelical and 33 Jewish children in Prussia received a higher (Gymnasium) education.[22] This penchant of the Jews for advanced education aroused periodic concern among certain groups, but no official restrictive measures, such as prevailed in Russia at this time, were introduced. On the whole the educational opportunities for Jews steadily improved in the years after 1871. That there was some discrimination against them, notably in the appointment of teachers, was inevitable in school systems which legally and historically were organized on a confessional Christian basis. For that matter the small dissident Protestant and Catholic groups also did not enjoy absolute equality with the major confessions.

The Higher Schools

Secondary education in the Germany of 1871 was provided mainly in (1) the nine-year Gymnasium, where Greek and Latin played a dominant role in the curriculum; (2) in the Realgymnasium, where Latin, but no Greek, was taught and there was more emphasis on

modern languages and technical subjects; and (3) in the Oberrealschule, where modern languages, but no Latin or Greek, were taught
and the emphasis was definitely on mathematics, science, and more
practical subjects. There were, in addition, variations of these basic
types, for example the Progymnasium and the Realschule which were
basically only six-year schools, students having to transfer to other
schools to complete their courses. The Oberrealschulen really came
into their own under the Empire and achieved a status equal to the
other two in as much as they could certify students to the universities.
States had varying requirements in regard to certain faculties, but
all agreed that only a Gymnasium could certify students for the study
of theology at the university. This was a reasonable restriction since
theologians needed to know Greek and Latin. Then, too, Hebrew as
an elective course was available only at a Gymnasium. The availability of instruction in Hebrew also aided Jewish religious instruction
at these institutions.

The secondary schools were generally not organized on a confessional basis, for, as at the universities, close control by the church
had disappeared. The modern trend was more and more towards
Simultan higher schools. In Prussia after 1869 all new state-sponsored
higher schools were Simultan.[23] City higher schools often changed
over also when the population of a city became more mixed. Yet in
actual practice many of the Gymnasiums could still be classed as either
Protestant or Catholic. Here often the origin of the school and its
connection with established foundations was an important consideration. This is brought out by some figures which are at hand for the
Prussian Gymnasiums in 1873-4. At that time there were 110 Gymnasiums at which all teachers were Protestant, 6 where they were all
Catholic; 31 where they were all Protestant with the exception of
the Catholic teacher of religion, 40 where they were all Catholic with
the exception of the Protestant teacher of religion; 30 where the
teachers were predominantly Protestant, 9 where they were predominantly Catholic; only 2 where the number of Catholics and
Protestants were about equally divided. This gives a total of 171
predominantly Protestant Gymnasiums, 55 predominantly Catholic,
and 2 where actual parity existed. The figures for teachers of religion
are slightly different. Of the 228 gymnasiums there were 116 that had
no Catholic religious teacher while only 6 had no Protestant religious
teacher.[24]

The higher schools were all naturally considered to be Christian
schools, and religion was taught everywhere. The instruction usually
consisted of two hours a week, although the time allotted varied

slightly according to grades, types of schools, and regions of Germany. The following summary of total week hours covering a nine-year program at the Gymnasium (figures in parentheses at Realgymnasium) show that the differences between the sections of Germany were not great: Prussia 19 (19); Bavaria 18 (18); Saxony 20 (21); Württemberg 18 (14); Hamburg 18 (18); Weimar 19 (18). Allotted times at the Realschulen were about the same.[25]

As in the elementary schools, Jewish students attending higher schools were excused from the regular religion classes, but were supposed to receive their own religious instruction. In the higher schools, perhaps more often than in elementary schools, Jewish teachers who could provide such instruction were appointed to the faculty. Often they were entrusted with the classes in Hebrew, but technical subjects were also assigned. Just as there were some Jewish confessional elementary schools there were also a few Jewish higher schools.

Agitation for Change

While the period of the Empire thus brought no fundamental changes in the relation of religion to the German schools, there was much agitation for change. This came from two chief sources, the teachers, and the Social Democratic and other liberal parties.

The years of the Empire witnessed the immense strengthening and growth of pedagogy as a separate educational discipline and profession. Professional educators, jealous of their new prestige, strove to break the influence of the theologians on the schools. The church to the theologues, the school to the pedagogues was their watchword. Their attack centered on the right of supervision exercised by the clergy, and in this they had practically the unanimous support of the rank and file of teachers. In their opposition to church influence and out of a sincere desire to improve the schools, most educational leaders opposed the organization of schools on a confessional basis. The national meeting of the German Teachers' Association held at Munich in the spring of 1906 devoted its session to the topic "Simultan or confessional schools," and the Simultanschulen received the greatest support.[26]

Although very few teachers wanted to abolish religion classes entirely, there was, however, a small group that desired generalized religious instruction. A Simultanschule does not, of course, mean nonconfessional classes in religion, in fact the experience of Baden with Simultanschulen showed that generalized instruction did not work well in them. The Saxon Teachers' Organization, which voted overwhelmingly in 1908 for less confessional instruction, did not couple their demands with a request to convert the confessional schools of Saxony into Simultanschulen. Nevertheless, the issues became confused in the public mind. Many held that the adoption of Simultanschulen would also lead to generalized religious instruction. They believed that this would have little content, that it would not prepare children for participation in their churches, and that the one sure way to assure proper instruction was not to change school forms. That confessional schools were necessary for confessional instruction was not a valid argument, but it was an appealing one which carried weight with many people.

From its very beginning the Social Democratic party advocated the establishment of a public-school system independent from church control. This was clearly stated in the Eisenach Program of 1869, which repeated many of the demands made by the Workers' Congress in 1848. The church was to be separated from the state, the school from the church, and the demand was made for universal compulsory education in public schools. The Gotha Program of 1875 was something of a compromise on church matters, and the party line became, "Religion is a private matter." Consistently the party demanded the establishment of a public secular-school system. Liebknecht, the great Social Democratic leader, stated at the party congress in 1890: "We can get at religion only by permitting the religion of the individual to be quietly his religion, and see to it that he gets some enlightenment. The school must be mobilised against the church, the schoolmaster against the parsons—true education puts aside religion."[27] The great Erfurt Program of 1891 which remained the official party program for so many years, boldly proclaimed that religion was a private matter. It demanded the abolition of the use of public funds for church and religious purposes. Education was to be compulsory and free in public secular schools. In an explanatory statement Liebknecht maintained that no religion was to be taught in the schools, but that parents and the churches if they wished could see that children obtained religious instruction.

The demand for compulsory attendance at state-controlled secular schools of course brought the Socialists in direct opposition to some Protestant parties, but above all to the Catholic Center party. The law of the Catholic church (Canon 1375) states: "The church has the right to erect schools of every category, specifically, not only elementary schools, but also middle and higher schools." It is not surprising that the Center party in its first *Soester Program* of October 28, 1870, made a demand for confessional schools.[28] On this point, therefore, there existed a fundamental antagonism between the Social

Democrats and the Centrists. As Dr. Offenstein points out in his excellent study, the Socialists were, however, not always entirely united.[29] Their bitterest attacks were always levied against the confessional schools, where all education was to be carried out in the spirit of the confession, where textbooks had to be picked with a view toward confessional soundness, and where there were confessional school prayers, hymns, and church services. On the other hand the Simultanschulen did not have their full approval, since they too had a religious basis. While Socialists always objected to dogmatic religious instruction and maintained this was a province of the home and church, many were willing to permit general historical religious instruction in the schools.

Thus some Socialists and some professional educationists joined arms in the battle to free the schools from interference by the churches. By 1914 the Social Democrats were definitely moving in a direction which foreshadowed a less intransigent attitude toward a measure of religious instruction in the schools. On this issue, as on many others, the party gradually became less doctrinaire, and its position was to be much more moderate under the Weimar Republic and in Western Germany after World War II.

If the Socialists felt it necessary to attack the school system, it must always be remembered that the government authorities in Germany, as in some other countries, thought it a function of the schools to uphold the government and the existing state system. They were supposed to fulfill the slogan: "Mit Gott für König und Vaterland." Particularly it was held to be the function of the schools to combat socialism. It has already been pointed out that after the Revolution of 1848 there was a general increase in the amount of religious instruction in the schools. Pupils were required to memorize more hymns and Bible verses, and instruction was channeled into more dogmatic lines. When the growing strength of the Socialists caused alarm and the Prussian government took active steps to meet their challenge, the King issued an order on May 1, 1889, which shows clearly that the Socialists were justified in considering religious instruction in the schools a political issue.

I have for a long time been occupied with the thought of making use of the schools in their separate grades for combating the spread of socialistic and communistic ideas. The prime object of the schools will ever be to lay the foundations for a sound comprehension of both civic and social relations by cherishing reverence for God and love for the fatherland. But I cannot fail to recognize that in a time when the errors and misrepresentations of social democracy are spread abroad with increased zeal, the school is called upon to make increased efforts to advance the recognition of the true, the real and the possible in the world. The school must endeavour to create in the young the conviction that the teachings of social democracy contradict not only the Divine commands and Christian morals, but are, moreover, impractical and, in their consequences, destructive alike to the individual and to the community.[30]

The Socialists, of course, did not quarrel with the King about the schools being state schools. What they wanted was that the schools should spread propaganda for a socialist rather than a monarchical capitalist state. The claim that "Divine commands and Christian morals" are opposed to socialism inevitably led to Socialist opposition to religious instruction in the schools.

Chapter V

The SUPERVISION of SCHOOLS

If state schools were to be organized on a Christian basis, and even more narrowly on confessional lines, it was inevitable that many problems would arise in their supervision. As long as state and church were one, the problems were not too acute, for it mattered not if the right or left hand did the administering of the schools. The denominationally neutral state, however, had to maintain its independence from any narrow church control, and equally important, the churches sought with renewed emphasis to assure their independence from the expanding power of the state. Although both movements brought greater secularization, there was actually no desire on the part of either party to sever relations completely.

The teaching profession, nurtured by both church and state, meanwhile became even more insistent on asserting its independent position. In the Peace of Westphalia of 1648, the schools were considered an annex of the church, but no one would have thought of making such a statement in a general international treaty in 1871. The churches now sought the aid of the state in maintaining their influence on education, while the schools looked to the same state to emancipate them from the control of the churches. Since the state needed the support of both churches and schools for its own ends, it had to weigh carefully how to grant its favors.

Problems of Aufsicht and Leitung

In the same year that brought the Franco-Prussian War and laid the foundation of the Empire, a book was published in Leipzig with the title *Die Emanzipation der Schule von der Kirche und die Reform des Religionsunterrichts in der Schule* (The Emancipation of the School from the Church and the Reform of Religious Instruction in the Schools). This book was a prize-crowned volume of the Diesterweg Foundation, which had been established to commemorate the work of Adolf Diesterweg (1790–1866), one of the most influential of nine-

72

teenth-century liberal educators. The author pointed out that there are various views of what constitutes "emancipation," but that in using the term Diesterweg always meant: "Freeing the school from the supervision (*Aufsicht*) of the clergy and the conduct (*Leitung*) of the same by trained experts; the freeing of teachers from sacristan and janitorial duties also of course being included."[1] Related to these two points is a third which bears more directly on religious instruction in the schools. This is the problem of who shall determine the qualifications of the teachers of religion and regulate their appointment.

As we have already noted, the Prussian Allgemeine Landrecht of 1794 stated specifically that, "all public school and educational establishments are under the supervision (*Aufsicht*) of the state and must at all times submit to its examination and visitation." Just what the word "Aufsicht" covered was a matter which even the Germans had difficulty making clear to themselves.[2] A few English definitions given in a dictionary are: inspection, supervision, surveillance, guardianship, care, charge. It seems clear that the lawgivers wanted to put the schools, which were declared to be state institutions, under state officials. At that time the state, however, continued the customary practice of authorizing church officials to carry out this supervision. This was not in a way unreasonable, since the schools were organized on confessional lines, and the minister was often about the only qualified man who could undertake this task in the rural communities. Although some lay officials were appointed on higher levels, the rule was also that district church officials acted as district school supervisors. Very often they did a poor job, for they were more interested in their church offices. If the churchmen really did attend to their job, this aroused the ire of the teachers, who felt they knew more about school problems than men who had been educated as clergymen, not as teachers. This basic problem became more acute as the nineteenth century progressed, bringing an ever expanding and broadening school system with a better trained teaching profession.

As the state took over more active control of the school system the narrower problem of the supervision of the religion classes presented itself. Could the religiously neutral state determine their content and supervise both Catholic and Protestant instruction, which admittedly was to be in accord with confessional principles and spirit? An attempt was made in the Prussian Constitution of 1850 to solve this problem by reiterating the *Aufsicht* rights of the state, while stating that:

The respective religious bodies direct (*leiten*) the religious instruction in the elementary schools. The direction (*Leitung*) of the physical upkeep (*äussere*

Angelegenheiten) is the duty of the commune. The state, with the legally regulated cooperation of the commune, appoints from the number of qualified people the teachers at the public elementary schools.[3]

Here were other words: "leiten, Leitung," which led to various interpretations. The attempt to give them an English equivalent will perhaps demonstrate the difficulties. Without exhausting the possibilities a small dictionary states that the verb "leiten" means to lead, conduct, to guide, direct, to oversee, to manage; while the noun "Leitung" covers direction, guidance, control, management, and conducting. It should also be noted that while the churches oversee, manage, and conduct the instruction in religion, the state appoints the teachers, among them the instructors in religion. Other states used other words, but all meant about the same thing. In Baden the churches had perhaps the greatest influence, for they were granted "care and supervision" (*Besorgung und Überwachung*) of religious instruction. In Bavaria the churches had the right to direct and supervise (*Leitung und Überwachung*); in Württemberg they had just the right of direction (*Leitung*). In Saxony and Hesse the churches were restricted more and only had the right to cooperate (*Mitaufsicht*) in the supervision of religious instruction.[4] The provisions of the Constitution of 1850 did little to change the situation in Prussia, and churchmen still supervised the schools there. Whether their activity was to be considered as *Aufsicht*, a state function, or as *Leitung* of religious instruction, a church function, was not always clear.

In 1872 Prussia passed a short law expressly stating that all schools were under the *Aufsicht* of the state, and that all bureaus and officials charged with this supervision did it at the commission of the state. "This Commission granted to the inspectors by the state is, in so far as they conduct their office as a part-time or honorary duty (*Neben- oder Ehrenamt*), at all times subject to recall."[5] While this law respected the civil-service status of the full-time lay inspectors, under it the state was free to revoke the school inspection privileges of clergymen. School inspection was now officially separated from the ministerial office and established as a separate post. Yet the state continued to commission Catholic and Protestant clergymen as inspectors, and even Jewish rabbis for Jewish schools. This was done partly out of budgetary considerations, for a clergyman received only a small additional fee for his extra duties as school inspector, whereas a full-time lay appointee had to be paid a full salary. Gradually, however, the number of full-time lay school inspectors, particularly on the district level, increased.

The Prussian law was mainly motivated by the desire to replace uncooperative Catholic priests with more conforming inspectors.[6] This was done by Minister Falk during the years of the Kulturkampf. On January 23, 1878, a Catholic petition bearing 100,000 signatures requested that religious instruction in schools should be given only by those who had been authorized by bishops, and that supervisors of Catholic schools be Catholics. While all Catholic clergy were certainly not excluded from supervision of schools in Prussia under Falk's administration, nevertheless in this period (1872–79) 2,148 Catholic clergy were relieved of the conduct of religious instruction in the elementary schools or of the supervision of teachers.[7] On the other hand the privilege of inspection was withdrawn from few Protestant clergymen, and clearly the removal of Catholic supervisors was the by-product of the Kulturkampf rather than a deliberate change from clerical supervision in principle. In fact, when a Protestant clergyman wanted to refuse the commission of the state to act as school inspector, the higher church authorities usually brought pressure to force him to accept the office.[8]

That teachers were almost to a man opposed to the use of clergymen as school inspectors for the whole school did not necessarily mean that they always opposed their supervision of religious instruction. While this was related to the whole problem of clerical inspection it was usually considered to be different in essence and recognized as such by the teachers. It was a matter of *Leitung*, not *Aufsicht*. This difference was not always accepted by the church authorities and was definitely rejected by the Catholic hierarchy, who sought to retain their general inspection rights, for it gave them a measure of control over the whole school and not only over what had become a minor segment of the teaching plan. A school organized on a confessional basis must have a common spiritual unity, so the argument ran, and no one is better qualified to see that this prevails than the clergy. This view is well illustrated, for example, by the statement drawn up by a conference of bishops in Bavaria. Clerical inspection had been regulated in Bavaria by an edict of September 15, 1808, and an attempt was made in 1866–68 to pass a law altering this (*Gressersche Gesetzentwurf*). At that time the bishops stated:

According to the opinion of all positive Christian pedagogues, the entire school—as an educational (*Erziehungs-*) as well as an instructional (*Unterrichts-*) institution—must rest on a religious foundation, and the religious education and instruction dare not be separated from the rest of the school work. Otherwise the essential unity of education and instruction and the natural relationship of religious teachings with the other subjects of instruction would be disturbed, which would be in conflict with the innermost function of the school."[9]

When the Catholic Teachers' Organization in Bavaria asked for more expert lay inspection, the bishops in 1909 took their stand on the 1867 statement and added. "We see no other goal of this desired so-called expert supervision except in the end to make the schools completely into state and secular institutions."

Yet the use of clergymen as inspectors of the schools was doomed, and the practice ended after the first World War. It disappeared earliest in Baden, Coburg, and some of the smaller states. In 1914 local school inspection by clergymen (*Geistliche Ortschulaufsicht*) existed only in Bavaria, Lippe-Detmold, Reuss ä.L., Schwarzburg-Rudolstadt; was partly used in Anhalt, the two Mecklenburgs, Oldenburg, Prussia, Saxony, Waldeck, and Württemberg, but had been abolished in Baden, Brunswick, Hessen, Reuss, j. L., Saxe-Coburg-Gotha, Saxe-Altenburg, Saxe-Meiningen, Schwarzburg-Sonderhausen, Bremen, Hamburg, Lübeck, and Alsace-Lorraine. Inspection by clergymen on a district (*Bezirk oder Kreis*) level existed in Bavaria and partially in Brunswick, Waldeck, Prussia, and Württemberg.[10] With the exception of those states, Bremen for example, where only general non-confessional religious instruction was given, the religious bodies retained the *Leitung* and an influence on the religious instruction.

As things developed *Leitung* came to include the right to visit the religion classes, to ask necessary questions and at times participate in the instruction, and to determine if instruction was what it was supposed to be and whether progress could be seen. The teacher could be set right as to material, but this only in the absence of pupils.[11] Perhaps of more importance was the right of the church authorities to be consulted in regard to the teaching plan drawn up by the state for the religion classes. This teaching plan was an elaborate affair and set forth the norms of instruction—what material was to be taken up in each class, what Bible verses and hymns were to be memorized, and numerous other details. Church authorities had the right to be consulted on textbooks, but the minister of education gave the final approval. In places the clergy had the right to be present at final examinations in religion at the higher schools. Then, too, as will be pointed out in more detail below, they often shared in matters relating to the appointment and dismissal of teachers of religion.

State inspectors—whether Protestant or Catholic—had the right to attend religion classes in all schools. They could not influence the content of the doctrinal religious instruction, except to see that such instruction did not contain things which were contrary to the duties and responsibilities of citizenship. They had a right, of course, to see that the classes were being held in a proper fashion and that the teaching plan was being followed. As a matter of practice the lay state inspectors did not often inspect the religion classes. Naturally no objections were raised to this on the part of the lay teacher—nor on the part of the clergy who in many places cooperated in teaching the religion classes. As a rule state and church administrative officials got along very well, and it is remarkable that there was so little controversy over the actual conduct of religious instruction in the schools under the Empire.

While not exactly a question of school supervision, the churches were often given another opportunity to share in directing school affairs. In Prussia and in other sections of Germany as well, the senior Catholic and Evangelical pastors, and the Jewish rabbi, if there were at least twenty Jewish pupils present, were regularly members of the local school authority.[12] Thus the churches had official representation, along with elected laymen on the school authority. The school boards were mostly concerned with the administration of school property, but they did have certain supervisory rights in regard to the proper functioning of the school. The pastor, because of his position in the community, was always one of the most influential members of these local school boards and could always represent the interests of the church.

Joint School and Church Positions

The relation of state and church in supervision of the schools was complicated by the fact that in many places there was an organic union of the parish and school, between the *Kirchengemeinde* and the *Schulgemeinde*. Property and endowments were held in common, and teachers held both church and school positions. These joint school and church positions had come about naturally because so many of the public schools had originated as sacristan schools (*Küsterschulen*).[13] To appreciate the difficulties of the growing movement after 1871 among schoolmen for the separation of school and church positions, one must understand the conditions as they had developed over the years. Very often the proper desire of pedagogical reformers for teachers to have an independent position was considered an attack against the church and its position in relation to the schools. It is true it did disturb the established church practices and made difficulties for the pastor. Also many rank-and-file teachers themselves were inclined to retain at least some of the church positions because of the additional revenue they brought.

There were many reasons, of course, for the maintenance of the tie between school and church positions. The connection had a natural historic origin and was hallowed by usage. It was also one of the things which helped maintain the control of the churches over education, and powerful conservative forces fought for the *status quo*. Then, too, the teacher was often the only person qualified to carry on the various church duties, especially the duties of cantor and organist. One need not be a Marxist, however, to discern that economic factors were important in maintaining the relationship. The salaries of elementary teachers in Germany have on the whole been pitiful.[14] A pamphlet of the sixteenth century describing their position was entitled "Der arme Teufel," and, after all, there is the German saying: "Wen die Götter hassen, den machen sie zum Pädagogen." (Whom the Gods hate they make into a Pedagogue.) The teachers were glad to have additional funds from the churches, and in many places the two offices were so organically united that it was almost impossible to separate them. The teacher often lived in a house that belonged to the church and not to the school district when these became separate governing bodies. The teacher had certain perquisites, ecclesiastical and feudal in origin, such as the following: his garden was to be plowed, he was to be furnished with firewood, he was entitled to collect a certain number of eggs from the members of the parish, he was to receive gifts at Easter and Christmas, and above all he was to receive incidental fees at baptisms, marriages, and funerals. The separation of these historic church and school properties and privileges has been a difficult task, and although measures have long been taken in Germany towards this end, the situation has not yet been fully straightened out.

If there were many forces working to maintain the tie between the two positions, stronger forces were working the other way. The increased control of the state over education and the general secularization of society that has been the universal aspect of the modern era has tended to a separation. The great pedagogical advances of the nineteenth century above all pushed to this end. Teaching became more and more a full-time profession with a standing and training that simply did not harmonize with what were after all janitorial services. Added to this, teachers began to join in strong associations and so made their demands felt. It was not only the manual laboring classes who in the last century realized that in union there is strength. Extreme and yet indicative of a growing general feeling was the statement made by a teacher at the *Allgemeine Lehrerversammlung* in Hamburg in 1872: "We schoolteachers no longer recruit ourselves from the lackeys and servants of these worthy gentlemen [ministers] but are trained from our youth for our profession."[15]

Gradually, beginning in the cities and extending only by degrees to the country, where the clergy were reluctant to let go any of the "good old customs," more and more the teacher came to be relieved of some, at least, of his church duties.[16] The school regulations of Anhalt of 1850 freed the teachers from the sacristan services, such as ringing the bell, cleaning, heating and lighting the church, regulating the tower clock, and clearing the cemetery paths. In Baden the Protestant teachers were first freed from the lower church duties and in 1874 the Catholic teachers as well were exempted from their services as sextons (*Messnerei*). In Württemberg a law of 1905 provided that, where sacristan duties were still joined with teaching positions, they should be done away with as soon as possible. In Prussia the attempt to separate the joint church and school positions was begun in earnest about 1887. Progress was slow, and the school law of 1906 made no radical changes. For the first time, however, legal provision was made for carrying through this separation. It has been estimated that from 1887 to about 1930, 5,000 joint positions had been separated but that 7,000 still remained at that time, largely on a voluntary basis. And this in spite of the far more aggressive attack made on this problem under the Weimar Republic. To anticipate a bit, however, it can be noted here that there was still need under Hitler's regime for a Prussian law, decreed on September 7, 1938, to the effect that all joint positions were to be considered separated as of October 1st of that year. The actual separation, however, dragged on, because the property and pensions settlements which had to be arranged were extremely complicated.[17]

The Appointment of Teachers of Religion

There were many clergymen who continued to give religious instruction in the schools, particularly in South Germany, and in this connection it should not be forgotten that the clergy also always gave confirmation instruction and this was usually coordinated with the religion classes of the school. Nevertheless, it came to be the case in all Germany, although more in the north than in the south, that regular teachers bore most of the weight of the religious instruction in the schools. This meant that lay teachers had to be prepared to teach these classes, and religion was always one of the subjects of instruction at teachers' academies. Since the schools were mostly on a confessional basis, and religious instruction always on confessional lines (except in Bremen and a few other places), it naturally followed that the teachers' academies should be organized according to confession. This was the position taken as a rule by the churches, and elementary-school teachers were regularly trained in confessional academies. Universities and Gymnasiums were, however, nonconfessional, and they set the example for the professional educators, who, seeking to raise the standing of the normal schools, advocated a Simultan basis for the teaching academies. A few Simultan academies existed, but at both Simultan and confessional institutions the prospective teachers were exposed to a great dose of religious training. Whether or not a candidate wanted to teach religion was not the guiding factor, since religion was a regular subject of instruction, and if a person was not qualified to teach it, chances of an appointment were diminished. Teachers in the great mass of one-teacher schools almost always had to teach religion, for the local ministers, already often burdened with two or three small rural parishes, could not teach all religion classes in as many schools.

This obviously raised great problems. Teachers without religious conviction, skeptics, were supposed to teach religion on a confessional basis. The heterodoxy of teachers in Germany has been a perennial concern to church authorities and at times also to the state. To deal with this situation church officials tried to insist that teachers giving religious instruction have the specific authorization or at least the approval of the church. This raised problems for the state because it meant that its appointees, particularly in one-teacher schools, would be subject to church review. Logically this perhaps should be the case, if schools are to be confessionally organized and instruction carried on in a confessional spirit. A state-controlled educational system, however, can in practice hardly permit the churches to have such a veto power over its appointees. This problem has always been more acute in relation to the Catholic than to the Evangelical churches, for here fundamentally different concepts of doctrine come to the fore.

The Catholic church always has maintained that the family and church have the primary right in regard to education. This is especially true in respect of religious instruction, where the church embodies the commission given in Matthew 28: 19-20 (Douay): "Go therefore, teach ye all nations; baptizing them in the name of the Father, and of the Son, and of the Holy Ghost; Teaching them to observe all things whatsoever I have commanded you; and, behold, I am with you all days, even to the consummation of the world." The Catholic church maintains that this right to teach rests in the Pope for the whole church, and in the bishop for the diocese (Canons 1327, 1328). The Pope and the bishops, therefore, announce publicly the teachings of the church. They can authorize others to give religious instruction and such authorization is regularly given by the bishop. This authorization is known as the *missio canonica* (Canon 109) and is given as a matter of course to holders of certain offices. Thus a priest can give instruction without further qualification; in fact the Council of Trent prescribed that it was the duty of priests to give religious instruction. In Germany, however, a priest was supposed to obtain permission from his superiors before undertaking to teach in the schools. The *missio canonica* can also be expressly granted to other individuals. A teacher who has received it is not required to teach, but if he does, then he must do so in a manner prescribed by the church. This is manifest from the formula of the *missio* as used in the diocese of Osnabrück. It was granted to the teacher only after he had formally made and signed a declaration of Catholic faith in the presence of two witnesses.

Since you have been appointed as teacher at the ———— and have made a declaration of Catholic faith, we hereby grant to you until recall in accordance with Canon 1328, Canon 1381, Paragraph 3 of the *Church Law-book*, the necessary church commission to give religious instruction, the *missio canonica.*

You are to give this religious instruction with special zeal and with the conscientiousness proper to this subject according to the suggestions and under the direction of your priest (Canon 1333, Paragraph 1; Canon 1381, paragraphs 1, 2; Canon 1382 of the *Church Lawbook*) following the teachings, regulations and institutions of our holy church. We are confident that you will always endeavor to bring to the children entrusted to your care the knowledge of religious truths, to introduce them to a churchly life, and to warm their hearts for the holy faith. We also expect that you will set an example for the children by a God-fearing Christian life, and that you will lead them by word and example to be virtuous Catholic Christians.[18]

Canon law makes no definite rules regarding the withdrawing of the *missio*, but it is clear that such action would have to be based on weighty reasons. There is no recourse against such withdrawal except an appeal to the Pope. In Bavaria, Baden, and Württemberg, state law required that Catholic religious teachers have the *missio canonica* and that Evangelical teachers have the approval of the Evangelical church authorities. In Prussia the *missio* was not required. Appointments were made, and then, so far as the state was concerned, Catholic teachers if they wished could apply to church officials for authorization. This was regularly done, for the statement of the Prussian minister of education in the *Landtag* in 1925 was as true for the Empire as for the Republic: "I would like to see the teacher, who would dare to undertake religious instruction at a confessional school, if the hierarchy did not grant the *missio canonica*. That simply does not happen." (Das gibt es nicht.)[19] In the years of the Kulturkampf when the Catholic church pressed for the removal of certain Old Catholic instructors, the fact that the Prussian state did not require the *missio* became significant. In later years, although the state was always careful to maintain its position, in actual practice authorities did take cognizance of teachers' having the *missio*.

While only Protestants might teach Protestant religion classes, they received no special permission from the Protestant churches, such as the *missio* for Catholics. In line with the basic doctrine of the universal priesthood of all believers, any member of the church was entitled, if qualified, to teach religion. The church authorities regularly recognized the qualification for instruction as established by the state examining committees. In some states church authorities could attend these examinations, and they alone or with other members of the examining commission would determine whether the teacher passed his examination in religion.[20] Ministers were regularly given the right to teach religion without examination. In Baden and Hesse they were required to teach. Some states asked teachers to pledge loyalty to a confession much as ministers were required to do. Evangelical church authorities in their capacity as inspectors or observers of religious instruction did not demand adherence to any set symbols or forms, but did expect an adherence to the historic confessions of the church. Teachers were supposed to conform to local church practices, that is, Reformed or Lutheran, no special attention being paid to the small dissentient groups. In Prussia a ministerial decree of August 6, 1910, decreed that Mennonite teachers could teach Bible history and the first three parts of the catechism (Commandments, Creed, Lord's Prayer) at Evangelical schools.[21] This was done in agreement with the highest Evangelical church authorities. Since the last two parts of the catechism (baptism, Lord's Supper) were usually reserved for confirmation instruction, the Mennonite teachers in practice were under no severe restrictions.

As has already been suggested, the state played a dominant role in determining who was qualified to give religious instruction. This was regularly done through regulating the curriculum at the teachers' academies, establishing standards of qualification, administering the examinations, and making the final appointments. Qualifications varied in different states, and, of course, for different grades. Prussia and sixteen other German states had a reciprocal agreement, recognizing their respective elementary, middle, and girls' higher school teacher examinations. The standard as established in 1874 in the Prussian examination ordinance for school mistresses at Volksschulen will, therefore, give a good idea of the minimum requirements.

Religion: General acquaintance with the teachings of the Bible and of the relationship of the holy history of the Old and New Testaments, as well as with the chief events of church history, and of the geography connected therewith. The candidate must be able to recount freely one Bible story as expressed in the Bible—yet without being tied to the exact Bible words— and to explain its religious and ethical content. She must know the catechism of her church, be able to give information in regard to its word and material content, be able to draw on Bible verses, Bible stories, verses and songs to help explain the catechism, and be able to explain with true insight and repeat from memory a number of sacred hymns.[22]

Not only did the state make the final appointment of lay religious teachers, but also it gave its sanction to the clergy who were to give this instruction. Such sanction could of course be withdrawn although this was likely to cause trouble with church authorities. This was true notably in Baden and Prussia during the period of the Kultur-kampf. In 1872 the Imperial Government banned the Jesuit order from all Germany. Individual Jesuits were not even to read Mass or to teach in schools. Needless to say the Catholic school system suffered a severe blow from this law, which, although modified somewhat in 1904, was not repealed until April 1917. Most states had some restrictions on teaching by monastic orders, if no more than that they had to obtain permission from the state. The same year that Jesuits were banned in the Reich, teaching by all Catholic orders or similar congregations was forbidden in Baden.[23] Measures against teaching orders were also taken in Hesse and Saxony. In 1875 all monastic orders in Prussia except those engaged in nursing were dissolved. This law against teaching orders was not repealed until 1887, and even then boys' schools administered by monastic orders were forbidden in Prussia.

Members of monastic orders teaching in the public schools were paid salaries by the state, but these went to the order and not to the individual teacher. People who objected to this practice maintained that the state was thus subsidizing the monastic orders. Since the church itself, and many private (religious) schools as well, received state aid directly, this indirect subsidy was not exceptional. However, it did bring more aid to the Catholic church as an institution than to the Evangelical church, for the latter had no parallel monastic system.

At the Gymnasium and other higher schools, religion was usually taught by full-time instructors (*Oberlehrer*) who had passed the state examinations either in theology or religion and certain other subjects, usually the ancient languages. In addition to religion these men might also be required to teach other subjects. In North Germany the teachers were often not ordained. In Prussia, teachers in the higher forms were theologues, as a rule, while others could teach in the lower grades. All teachers in Saxony and most of those in Württemberg were qualified theologues, while in Bavaria only fully ordained ministers taught religion at the higher schools and teachers' training institutions.

Many of the clerics held their teaching posts as a side position, and they as a rule did not have to take the difficult state examination as teachers. On the other hand clerics who did not hold teaching certificates usually were not appointed to full-time posts, nor were they granted the coveted title of professor. It was hard for a young man studying to be a minister to prepare himself also to pass the regular state teachers' examination. The difficulty of obtaining sufficient clerical personnel in some places led to easing the rigor of the state requirements, particularly in regard to the choice of secondary subjects. In Baden, for example, after 1911, if there was need for a full-time religious instructor, any clergyman who could qualify as a teacher of Hebrew might be appointed as a regular member of the faculty at a higher school. He was, however, restricted to teaching religion and Hebrew. If he wanted to teach any other subjects, he had to pass the regular examinations.[24]

The employment of trained theologians might lead to the assumption that the religious instruction at higher schools was more orthodox than at the Volksschulen. Just the opposite was the case, for the theologues, especially the Protestant ones who elected to teach, had often received a very liberal theological training and were full of the theories of higher Biblical criticism. When they presented their ideas in class, parents often charged that the pupils were being taught skepticism, free thinking, and a concept of religion which was not in keeping with the confessional tenets of their faith. The general spirit of humanism which prevailed at the higher schools also permeated the religious instruction and gave it a liberal slant. This liberal development in the higher schools was at crosspurposes with conservative opinion, and the period of the Empire saw growing differences in the more important field of the content and purpose of religious education in the schools.

Chapter VI

The CONTENT and METHOD of RELIGIOUS INSTRUCTION

Considering the disputes after 1871 over Simultan and confessional schools, over clerical or lay supervision, it would have been surprising indeed if there had been no controversy over the subject matter of religious instruction. Differences of opinion in this field had already occurred, notably in the conflict between pietism and rationalism. The modern scientific educators on the whole were opposed to instruction on a confessional basis, advocating instead general religious instruction. Then, too, just as instruction in mathematics and languages had changed, they believed that techniques of religious instruction also needed reform. Church leaders were willing to grant the latter, for they were under no illusion as to how effective the religion classes were, but were inclined to go slowly lest the child be thrown out with the bath water. With their powers of *Aufsicht* or *Leitung* the churchmen had the controlling voice, and tended to be more conservative than the educators.

There were others who feared that change might bring a diminution of religious fervor. Those who saw in religion the best antidote for revolution, forgetting the revolutionary character of early Christianity itself, accused the schools of falling down on their job. They failed to see that really great doses of religious instruction had not spared Germany the Revolution of 1848, and that the growing number of Social Democrats had all attended schools where there was no dearth of religious teaching. These political conservatives tended also to be religiously conservative, with little inclination to support changes in teaching plans and methods.

In discussing the general religious program of the German schools it should be remembered that this program was far more than merely a matter of classes in religion, for the whole school was supposed to have a Christian character. The school year was regularly begun and closed with religious services. Each day the school opened and ended with a prayer; often there were hymns and a short service. In Protestant schools these were likely to be centered about a "Verse of the Week" (*Wochenspruch*) which the pupils were supposed to learn. There were often more extended religious services (*Schulgottesdienst*), either held regularly or on special occasions. These were more likely to occur at the higher schools, since they had a greater corporative unity and frequently had what we might term boarding students. These special school services were perhaps stressed most by Catholic schools. An ordinance of 1840 regulated this matter for many years in Baden and will give an idea of the system:

Pupils at a higher school which has its own religious services are to attend Mass on week-days two times, or if customary once a week, and, on Sundays and festivals, afternoon vespers in addition to the morning service. Special religious services are to be held on Ash Wednesday, Holy Week, Corpus Christi Octave, All Souls Day, the Grand Duke's birthday, as well as at the opening and closing of the school year. If there is no special religious service, pupils will go to the parish church. . . . All pupils are to go to confession and Holy Communion three times a year or, where it is customary four times. First confession and Communion is to be preceded by a period of special instruction. Before going to church the pupils will all assemble in a classroom where attendance will be taken and then march two-by-two to church, where they will occupy special seats. . . . Teachers are expected to be present; at the chief festivals they must put in their appearance.[1]

In 1916 the Baden ministry stated: "The Ordinance of 1840 has lost its legal validity; the participation of pupils as such at religious services continues in fact to be the same." As so often is the case custom was more important than the letter of the law in continuing old practices. Protestants also had their special school services and school Communion.

School children, particularly those in the upper classes, were expected to attend church services on Sunday and might even be expected to give a report on the sermon the next day. One of the most arduous tasks of teachers was to maintain discipline at church, for this had to be done under the eyes of the whole congregation. The practice of compulsory group attendance gradually disappeared, and teachers found welcome relief from their supervisory duties. The custom of group attendance by the confirmation classes, however, was usually maintained. Choirs trained in the schools regularly took part in the church services and, in rural congregations, generally led the funeral procession to the cemetery.

State authorities always took cognizance of the church festivals.

Christmas, Easter, Pentecost, the great festivals common to Catholics and Protestants alike, always called for longer school holidays. In addition Catholics, Protestants, and Jews all had their special festival days which rated a school holiday, or at least an excuse if the school was maintained in session. Catholics had the largest number of holy days and if Catholic students attended a Protestant school they were usually excused only for the time of the church services. Particularly in schools where confessions were mixed the recognition of church festivals led to difficulties of administration long before Hitler tried to bring about a uniform practice in this matter.

These generalizations—and they must be only that, for practices varied in the many localities of Germany—will emphasize the fact that there was always a conscious effort to put religion into the schools and not to cut the schools off from religion. The goal was to have the schools, particularly the confessional ones, permeated by a common spiritual unity. To this end all instruction was to be in one spirit and to serve a common purpose. All too often this did not occur. Religious teachers had good cause to feel that their pupils were being taught one set of values and ideas in religion classes, another in their language, history, or science classes. Along with the other disciplines, religion had become a departmentalized subject of instruction, especially in the higher schools, with little aid being given by one department to another.

The subjects taught within the department were the historic ones which had been developed over the years: the catechism, Bible and church history, hymns, Bible verses, Bible reading, and various matters connected with the church service such as the festivals of the church year and the pericopes (epistle and gospel lessons). In regard to the latter the Prussian regulations of 1872 for elementary schools specifically stated: "On every Saturday the pericopes of the following Sunday are to be read to the children and briefly explained to them. There shall be no memorization of the pericopes." Such a regulation was certainly beyond the capabilities of many of the elementary school teachers, to say nothing about the receptibility of the students. There can be little wonder that schoolmen began to agitate for changes in the teaching plans as drawn up by the authorities. In this matter it was largely a question of rearranging the material so as to make it more suited to the students.

Purpose of Religious Instruction

One great difficulty about the religious curriculum was always the question as to what exactly was to be accomplished by it. The Prussian regulations of 1872 attempted to be very definite on this point and stated:

The task of the Evangelical religious instruction is to lead children to an understanding of Holy Writ and the confession of the local parish, in order that children will have the ability to read the Bible by themselves and to take an active part in the life of the congregation as well as to participate in the religious services.[2]

This is a good general statement and with proper interpretation could be made to cover various schools of thought in regard to the teaching of religion. There were those who felt that religious instruction should be primarily concerned with imparting knowledge about religion. Like philosophy, literature, or history, it was an important part of our cultural past and an educated person should know something about it. Another group, while interested in knowing about religion, always felt that the chief purpose of religious instruction in the schools was to awaken a religious feeling or attitude. The purpose of the instruction was to make Christians or, as it was usually phrased, to lead children to Jesus. Since this was largely a matter of belief or feeling some believed that religion could not be taught. Schleiermacher and even Pestalozzi had raised this question early in the nineteenth century, and another group of thinkers brought the problem to the fore again about the turn of the twentieth century. It received much publicity when it was debated at a meeting of the *Freunde der Christlichen Welt* in 1900.[3] In general, however, the conclusion was that religion is teachable. Most people obtain their religion, like other things, from hearing about it, and St. Paul's remark could always be cited: "So then faith cometh by hearing, ..." (Romans 10: 17). Likewise most writers held that while there might well be difference of emphasis there must be both teaching *about* and *in* religion, for the two could hardly be separated. This was well put in the teaching plan for Evangelical instruction at the higher schools in Prussia which stated: "Indeed, imparting of information also belongs to the purpose of religious instruction. But this has only the value of being a means to the orientation of the heart and will towards the divine."[4] A decision of the Bavarian Oberkonsistorium of October 31, 1888, for higher schools similarly held that "not the really scholarly but the religious aspects of faith, the personal relation of the pupil to Christ, his Savior, must remain in the forefront."[5]

There were still others who supported religious education in the schools primarily because they felt religion to be "the most valuable character building subject of instruction in the Volksschule."[6] They wanted ethical and moral principles stressed, and thus gave a some-what different emphasis to instruction. The significance of religious training as a means of character building was a broad common ground which did much to unite liberal and orthodox, state and church, in support of religion as a part of the school curriculum. Here one might say lay the essential interests of the government. It was concerned with training good citizens, not with the saving of souls, although this too was usually considered to be a combination package. The funda-mental reason why the teaching of religion in the schools is so difficult is that religion is not just another subject akin to the others among which it has become departmentalized. It is at the same time a body of knowledge, a way of life, and a way of salvation. To try to separate this trinity would be to commit a modern Arian heresy, productive, as of yore, only of sterile discussion and dissension.

Light will perhaps also be thrown on the problem if, for a moment, a negative approach is taken. All agreed that religious instruction should not create an antireligious feeling, or opposition to the church. This was one reason why the churches were given a part in directing the instruction, for a purely state-controlled religious program might easily lose true religious values and even be directed against the churches. That religious instruction in the schools turned some people against religion and the churches caused great concern to many who truly had this matter "on their hearts."

The fact that the religious instruction was virtually compulsory and that this instruction tended to support the existing regimes alienated some liberal leaders. Thrändorf, one of the more liberal but not antireligious education men, highlights this problem well. Writing of the period after 1815, he states:

Throne and altar was now the watchword, and the subjugation of the people to those in authority in state and church was the goal which was sought. . . . This alliance with the political reaction came to cost the church dearly; for the educated middle class saw in it only the tool of the police state and answered the warning to submit to the dogma of Lutheran ortho-doxy with disdain and indifference. The religious hate of the Social Democrats and the agitation of many teachers for religionless, or at least confessionless schools, are still today the continuing results of this church-political reaction.[7]

Thrändorf goes on to cite the following pertinent comment from a church publication. "For a half century after the old rationalism vanished from our seminaries, our people has been confessionally instructed by church-trained orthodox teachers and it has continually become more unchurchly, more irreligious, and social democratic." It

4*

would of course be wrong to lay all the responsibility on the religious instruction in the schools for this increased secularization of society. But it should be noted that it did not occur because of a lack of religious instruction, for practically every German received such training in the schools. Nor must it be assumed that the growth of social democracy was necessarily a manifestation of the failure of this religious instruction, in fact, some might hold that it was the result of true religious values and insights inculcated in pupils by truly inspired teachers of religion. A sense of social obligation might well be the modern response to ethical religious stimuli. This was, however, not the general view, and to many the growth of more radical political views was a clear reason why something must be done about the method and content of religious instruction. Too often it was thought that a man who had religion would surely not be a socialist.

Others wanted changes because, as Thrändorf phrased it, "the prevailing religious instruction kills the religious interests of children." Whether this was true or not is debatable, for the newer methods when introduced did not bring a religious revival. A few of the very practical problems involved in the teaching of religion should, however, be mentioned.

There was always the question of the memory work which the regulations required. The children must have something to take along with them, and this seemed to be a sure way to see that they had it. Memory work is usually an unpleasant task for children, and learning the catechism, hymns, and Bible verses was often simply a matter of drill which students considered an irksome if not a boring assignment. Punishments were meted out as in other subjects if the material was not learned, and there was always the matter of a grade. If no grade was given it tended to lower the standing of the subject in the eyes of the student and made the task of the teacher harder. If students got a poor mark, it might well color their whole future attitude toward religion and the church. If grades were too generous, students again lost respect and it threw out of line a student's general average. There was also the problem of the clever student who had no difficulty acquiring the book learning but by daily conduct showed he cared little about religion. In contrast there was the devout student of upstanding character, eager and willing to participate in religious services, but somewhat slow in book learning. Under these circumstances what was a just mark in "Religion" at the end of the year was a problem which plagued many a teacher of religion. This very practical consideration—for alas, grades are always so considered—was tied to the basic problem of whether religious instruction was chiefly concerned with imparting knowledge, or instilling and awakening religious feeling.

The possibility that disciplinary action, grades, and other technical matters such as compulsory church attendance might inculcate a lasting hatred for religion always cast a shadow over the teaching of religion. What part the religious work should play in promotion to the next grade and in the important final examinations at the Gymnasium was a point that aroused controversy and produced a variety of solutions. There were no Abitur examinations in religion in Mecklenburg-Schwerin, Hesse, Bremen, Hamburg, Saxe-Meinigen, Baden, and Württemberg. Only in Bavaria was there a written examination, whereas in the other states an oral examination was prescribed. The emphasis laid on the examination varied greatly; in Saxe-Weimar, for example, only those pupils were to be examined whose class work received the grade "not sufficient" (*nicht genügend*).[8] As Dr. Kern states in relation to the higher schools of Baden: "The grade in religion constantly received less consideration in questions of promotion, the more one had to fear that an insufficient mark in religion would lead to formal withdrawal from the church."[9] It must always be remembered that there was in fact a fundamental difference between religion and the other subjects. A student might, for instance, acquire a distaste for mathematics in school, certainly not an unusual occurrence, but the consequences for his later life would be less significant than if he derived from his school work a permanent antipathy to religion.

Problems of Reform

From the most orthodox to the most liberal there was general agreement that a reform in religious instruction was desirable, but beyond that, there was no unanimity. One difficulty was that the whole subject of reform of teaching method got involved in the disputes over school organization and clerical supervision. The most radical reformers wanted to do away with the confessional character of the religious instruction, just as they opposed clerical supervision and the organization of schools on confessional lines. Even if some of their suggestions for teaching were pedagogically sound, they were likely to be condemned by upholders of the old order more or less because of guilt by association.

The long-standing criticism agreed to by most people was that there was too much memory work in the instruction in religion. This varied in different states, and there was no uniformity in the selections which were assigned. Even in Prussia itself there was great variation.[10] A study of assignments in Protestant schools showed there were 100

Bible verses common to all parts of Prussia, whereas the total assigned
was probably about 250. Teachers quite naturally had some latitude
in this matter, and teaching plans often listed "additional suggested
assignments." The following Psalms were common to the whole state:
1, 23, 103 (v. 1-4, 8-13, 15-18), 121, 130, 139 (v. 1-4, 7-10, 23-4). Of
the numerous hymns there were thirteen common selections which are
typical of this part of the curriculum:

    1. Ach bleib mit deiner Gnade
    2. Allein Gott in der Höh sei Ehr
    3. Aus tiefer Not
    4. Befiehl du deine Wege
    5. Ein' feste Burg
    6. Jesus meine Zuversicht
    7. Lobe den Herrn den mächtigen König der Ehren
    8. Mir nach, spricht Christus
    9. Nun danket alle Gott
   10. O Haupt voll Blut und Wunden
   11. O Heiliger Geist, kehr bei uns ein
   12. Wer nur den lieben Gott lässt walten
   13. Wie soll ich Dich empfangen

These were in most part long chorales and were only part of the list
learned. The regulations of 1854 had prescribed 30 hymns, those of
1872, 20. This was in line with the general tendency everywhere to
cut down on the required memory material. More practice too was
made of learning only certain verses, and the list of required hymns
was subject to many revisions. Hymns were regularly taught in the
music classes, but there was a growing movement to supplement them
with appropriate folk songs, many of which were more or less of a
religious character.

   The focal point of the agitation over the amount of memorization
was of course the traditional instruction in the catechism. As one
author states: "Learning the catechism by heart is by far the most
difficult memorization work at the Volksschule."[11] The place of the
catechism in the curriculum was also the touchstone of whether
religious instruction was to be on a confessional basis or not. In Bremen
catechism instruction had been eliminated and only general religious
instruction survived. The battle centered on Luther's Small Catechism,
which was used in most Protestant schools, although the Heidelberg
Catechism was used in states of the Reformed persuasion. There had
been numerous attempts to coordinate the two, the so-called *Exponierte
Katechismus*, used in Baden and Bavaria, and the *Rheinische Katechismus*, used in parts of Prussia, being among the most successful.[12]

There were also specially edited school catechisms, and one of these was used in Bavaria. Yet when all these efforts at revision and modernization were made, the general verdict, as Reukauf says, was that Luther's Small Catechism was the one best suited for school use.

The agitation for catechism reform was not restricted to Protestants, and various new Catholic catechisms were published.[13] But controversy over catechetical instruction in Catholic schools was never as pronounced as among the Protestants because of the unity and authority of the Catholic hierarchy and the control it exercised over the content of religious instruction.

Teaching plans had long stressed the need for having the pupils understand the material before they were to be asked to memorize the catechism. Sooner or later, however, in all Protestant schools students were required to learn by heart the five chief parts of the catechism, with Luther's succinct words of explanation. Other catechisms had much the same material. Teachers devoted a large part of the hours of instruction to hearing students recite. For example, to the query, "What is the Fourth Commandment?" the reply was expected: "Honor thy father and thy mother, that it may be well with thee and thou mayest live long on the earth." And then to the searching question, "What is meant by this?" Luther's explanation: "We should fear and love God and not despise our parents and superiors, nor provoke them to anger, but honor, serve, obey, love, and esteem them."

Or again: "What is the Third Article?" "I believe in the Holy Ghost, the Holy Christian Church, the Communion of Saints; the forgiveness of sins; the resurrection of the body; and the life everlasting. Amen." And then again "What is meant by this?" "I believe that I cannot by my own reason or strength believe in Jesus Christ, my Lord, or come to Him; but the Holy Ghost has called me by the Gospel, enlightened me with His gifts and sanctified and preserved me in the true faith; even as He calls, gathers, enlightens and sanctifies the whole Christian Church on earth and preserves it in union with Jesus Christ in the one true faith; in which Christian Church he daily and richly forgives me and all believers all our sins, and at the last day will raise up me and all the dead, and will grant me and all believers in Christ everlasting life. This is most certainly true."[14]

It was at times easy to get the explanations to various Commandments or to the petitions of the Lord's Prayer mixed, or to interchange a phrase from the longer explanations of the Creed. It was this fact rather than the actual length of the assignment that made the memorization difficult, despite the gradual steps by which it was accomplished.

Understanding the material was not sufficiently stressed and all too often the memorization was accomplished only through rather harsh drilling.

The question of when and how the catechism should be taught caused a great deal of discussion. The Prussian regulations of 1872 had stated that only the first three parts, Commandments, Creed, Lord's Prayer, should be taken up in the schools and the last two, dealing with the sacraments of baptism and the Lord's Supper, should be reserved for confirmation class. Exception was made in the following year for Schleswig-Holstein and Hanover, where all five chief parts were to be learned in the elementary school, and this became the general practice for the whole monarchy in 1884.[15] There was nevertheless a tendency to make a distinction between the first three parts, which were usually thought to be more suitable for school, and the last two which were left for church instruction. Thus when pastor and teacher shared the burden of school instruction as was regularly done in South Germany, one of the divisions of labor was likely to be on this basis. The last two parts were always reserved for the more mature students. In those regions where the material on Confession (*Beichte*) was separated out and the catechism divided into six parts, if a distinction was made, it always resulted in a three-three division. The Reformed Heidelberg Catechism, being arranged in only three parts, included the material on the sacraments in the second part, which centered "On Man's Redemption."

The usual practice was to have instruction in the catechism as a special part of the curriculum. The Prussian regulations provided that such separate instruction was to begin only in the higher grades in schools with only one or two teachers, and no sooner than in the middle grades in schools where there were three or more teachers. This meant regularly in about the fourth year, but the tendency of education experts was to delay such instruction even longer. Reukauf in summarizing the views of various writers states that they all agree that parallel instruction in the catechism and Bible history is bad. The material of the catechism should develop out of Bible history, with perhaps only one-half to a year of systematic separate study of the catechism in the highest grades.[16]

This last statement appears to give the keynote of the multitude of reform suggestions. Everybody wished to make more of a unit out of the material which historically made up the religious curriculum. Bible history, Bible verses, hymns, catechism, and even aspects of church history should all be drawn together into a logical plan. How to do this successfully was, of course, the problem.

For many years the catechism had been the center of instruction. To reform meant to alter this and to shift the emphasis to Bible history. Here difficulties arose as to how to apportion the Old and New Testament material. There were a few radicals who wanted to do away with the Old Testament material entirely, but these were never more than a fringe group. Yet the emphasis over the years was no doubt in the direction of presenting more New Testament material; religion at the schools was to be more Christ-centered.

There were perhaps two basic theories about the presentation of religious material centered in Bible history. The old theory was one of concentric circles (*Konzentrischen Kreisen*). In the lower grades some Bible stories were presented very simply with little additional material. As the child matured, this material was repeated in part but also it was broadened out with more application to the child's personal life and to society and more church history was included. This method, of course, was subject to the criticism that it was repetitious and that as a result pupils in the upper grades lost interest. Then too it was at times difficult to change the rather simple convictions of the early instruction. Children obtained fixed ideas, were reluctant to change them, and as a result did not mature religiously.

There was another basic theory, that of historical cultural levels (*Kulturhistorische Stufen*). Tuiskon Ziller (1817–1882) who carried forward the ideas of Herbart, was the great exponent of this school of thought. He did more perhaps than any other man to implement Kant's dictum: "Pedagogy must be made into discipline of study (*Studium*) else one can not expect anything from it." W. Rein, himself one of the important German educationists, pays him the following tribute: "All new studies of importance involving the theory of the curriculum and the theory of how the material is to be presented go back to Herbart and Ziller."[17] Ziller's basic idea was that the history of mankind had developed much as the powers of an individual child developed. A child, therefore, should get material presented to him suitable to his age, starting with prehistory and coming down. Constructive educative material designed to produce upstanding moral and religious characters should be concentrated about certain topics. Ziller would not have any direct religious instruction in the first year, but would concentrate on twelve fairy stories, the second year, Robinson Crusoe, the third, the Story of the Patriarchs, the fourth, the time of Judges, the sixth, the time of the Kings of Israel, the seventh, the life of Christ, the eighth, the history of the apostles and the history of the Reformation. Such a scheme involved no repetition and was supposedly always to be in line with a child's psychological development. One obvious criticism was that the child did not hear of Jesus until too late. For example, one of the exponents of Ziller's ideas wanted a selection of German folk tales in the first year, Robinson Crusoe stories in the second, Thuringian sagas in the third, and the Nibelungen and Gudrun sagas in the fourth. Only in the fifth year would a start be made with Bible material. It was indeed dubious if a precourse in myths and fairy tales was the way to lead children to Christ and through Christ to God. If adhered to strictly, the plan did little to introduce the child to his immediate surroundings, to explain the meaning of Christmas, Easter, and the other religious observances with which he came in contact very early. Actually much of this material was too difficult and less fitted to children than some of the simple Bible stories.[18]

While there were some exponents of the idea that religious instruction should be started with myths and fairy tales, this part of Ziller's theory never was generally accepted. In fact, it became one of the easy targets for the conservatives in defending existing practices. Nevertheless the Historical Cultural School did have influence and eventually, of course, was even given certain official approval in the era of Hitler. The greatest contribution of Ziller and his school was no doubt their constant insistence that material must be adapted to the capabilities of the child. What progress these theories made among the teaching profession is shown by the Zwickau Manifesto of the Saxon teachers in 1908.

The Zwickau Manifesto

The demands of the Saxon teachers may well be considered the climax of the whole movement for liberal reform of religious education in Germany under the Empire. In 1905 the well organized Saxon Teachers' Organization (*Sächsische Lehrerverein*) had inaugurated the discussion of problems concerning religious education. The next year the Lehrerverein asked the church authorities of Saxony to do away with clerical supervision not only of schools but also of religious instruction, to introduce a school Bible consisting of excerpts from the regular Bible, and to approve a new selection of memory material. They also spoke about having help in introducing a program of religious education based on a scientific pedagogical and religious foundation. Meanwhile discussions by teachers at district meetings resulted in the formulation of a report which was placed before the general meeting at Zwickau and there approved. It summarizes so well the views of the advanced wing of the German teachers that it is desirable to give it in full.

(1) Religion is an important subject of instruction and as such is an independent discipline of the Volksschule.

(2) It has the task of making alive in a child the thinking of Jesus.

(3) Teaching plan and method of instruction must be adapted to the spirit of the child, and these must be determined exclusively by the school. Church supervision of religious instruction is to be done away with.

(4) Only that educative material is to be considered in which the child can experience religious and moral life. Religious instruction is, in its most important aspects, instruction in history. At the center must stand the person of Jesus. Outside of the proper Bible material, biographical sketches of proponents of our religious and moral culture in relation to our people in modern times deserve special attention. The experiences of the child must be used in the fullest possible fashion.

(5) The Volksschule must renounce systematic and dogmatic instruction: For the upper forms a fitting basis for a summary of the ethical ideas of the Christian religion can be found in the Ten Commandments, the Sermon on the Mount, and the Lord's Prayer. Luther's catechism cannot be the foundation or point of departure of the religious education of our youth. It is to be valued as a historical religious source and an Evangelical-Lutheran confessional statement.

(6) The memory material in religion is to be revamped according to psychological-pedagogical principles and to be considerably shortened. Compulsion to memorize is to be lessened.

(7) Religious instruction is not to be started as a separate subject of instruction before the third year. So as not to stifle the interest of the child, the number of hours in the lower forms is to be decreased. The prevailing practice of separating religious instruction into Bible history (Bible explanation) and catechism instruction, as well as the arrangement of material according to concentric circles is to be done away with. Likewise examinations in religion and religious marks must be abandoned.

(8) All the religious instruction must be in harmony with the well-established results of scientific investigation and the advanced ethical experiences of our time.

(9) Alongside the reform of religious instruction in the Volksschulen a corresponding reorganization of the religious instruction at the teachers' seminaries is necessary.[19]

The Saxon manifesto, while it contained much that many teachers would support—notably abolition of clerical supervision—was an extreme statement. The influence of the Herbart-Ziller theories as to how the curriculum was to be organized is evident. The complete elimination of the catechism, however, was too revolutionary for most Germans and afforded the opposing forces a good opportunity for attack.

The synod of the Protestant Saxon church was called into special session and in February 1909, with only one dissenting voice, adopted a spirited refutation of the Zwickau Manifesto. The clergy were willing to support the reorganization of the curriculum on a religious-pedagogical basis. But church and school must continue to cooperate in the education of the youth of the country, and the clergy continued to be opposed to merely lay supervision of the schools. They were glad to support the view that the person of Jesus should be the center of instruction, but would have to insist that students learn to know him as their Savior and Redeemer. There was no opposition to a new selection of material and if necessary a lessening of the compulsion to memorize. However they still considered it desirable to have the student take with him into life as rich a treasury of hymns and Bible verses as possible. Although recognizing the need for reform in catechetical instruction the synod insisted that Luther's Small Catechism was irreplaceable. "The church did not want the kind of confessional religious instruction whereby the differences with other faiths and confessions is sharpened. However it did want children to be reared as intelligent living members of the Evanglical-Lutheran church and through this, indeed, to be educated to true tolerance of those who hold to other faiths."[20]

The synod supported the organization of the *Evangelisch-Lutherische Schulverein für das Königreich Sachsen* which came to spearhead the attack against the Zwickau Manifesto. On the national level they had the support of the *Deutsche Evangelische Schulkongress* (founded in 1882), which at a meeting in June 1909 adopted a manifesto condemning the position of the Bremen and Saxon teachers. Meanwhile the Saxon Lehrerverein published proposals for a new selection of memory material in September 1909 and again in January 1910. This led the officers of the *Evangelisch-Lutherische Schulverein* to publish their famous Red Catechism (*Roter Katechismus*).[21] Their pamphlet received this rather startling name because the editors had taken the material of the existing curriculum and put a red line through those parts which would be eliminated under the proposals of the Lehrerverein. The Small Catechism of Luther, even the Ten Commandments and the Creed were entirely red-pencilled; the Lord's Prayer remained only as a Bible verse in the version of Matthew. Bold black type emphasized their conclusion: *With this the foundations of Christianity are eliminated from the school.* The charge of cancellation of all Bible verses that spoke of the Bible as the plumb line of faith, of Jesus Christ as Savior and Redeemer, and of faith as the way to salvation led to this conclusion: *With this the fundamental truths of the Evangelical church are pushed aside.* Without consideration, so the charges continued, of the religious feeling of Christian people, Bible verses and hymns are eliminated that have shown themselves to be well-springs of power and means of solace. *With this the growing generation is robbed of valuable treasures for their whole life.* Many of the hymns which had been omitted were truly among the most familiar and treasured songs of the church, and it is easy to understand why the proposals aroused furor.

There were of course answers to the Red Catechism. For example, the Ten Commandments, the Creed, and the Lord's Prayer were not being eliminated but were to be discussed in Bible history. To which the rejoinder was, that this might be so, but they were no longer to be memorized.[22] All over Germany polemical books and articles about the Zwickau Manifesto appeared. These discussions actually constitute the background for the sharp controversies which arose over religious education in the schools when the Weimar Republic was founded. In 1910 the Saxon government, although urging certain reforms, declared against the Zwickau Manifesto and supported the retention of compulsory instruction on a confessional basis.

The Zwickau Manifesto served the great purpose of stimulating thought on the manifold problems connected with religious education in the schools. Those who were opposed to the Zwickau demands girded themselves for action. They marshalled their forces to maintain confessional instruction, for they considered that its abolition was the first step toward the complete elimination of religion from the schools. As subsequent years were to show, this was something that the mass of the German people did not want. The opponents of the Zwickau Manifesto, however, were forced to heed the handwriting on the wall. Teaching plans were revised and the amount of memory material was cut. More care was used to relate Bible verses and hymns to the rest of the work. The voluminous Spruchbücher made famous in the days of pietism, from which Bible verse on Bible verse was assigned for memorization, were drastically revamped if not abolished. New texts were published. There was in general more orientation toward Christ (*Christozentrische Behandlung*) with less emphasis on the Old Testament and on church history. More care was also taken to carry over into religious instruction general educational techniques that were being used in other fields. Material should be adapted as much as possible to the mentality of the child (*Entwicklungstreuer Unterricht*). Although not always successfully, the attempt was made to pay more attention to the child's level of experience (*Erlebnisunterricht*). A beginning was also made to introduce some project instruction (*Arbeitsunterricht*), to get students to bring materials to class, to write essays, and to participate constructively in the class work.

While instruction remained on a confessional basis, it nevertheless was being broadened and made more general. A ministerial decree of 1901 in Prussia stated:

In the instruction of religion the views of other religious bodies should receive consideration, particularly where children of different confessions are being instructed in common. This is also to be observed when dealing with doctrinal differences. In fact more stress must be put on what unites confessions than on what separates them.[23]

There was general recognition also that there should be less compulsion about religion in schools. The proposal to abolish examinations and grades, for example, aroused no great opposition. It was suggested by churchmen that teachers who were opposed to giving religious instruction or felt they could not give it in line with confessional principles should be excused from teaching religion. Those interested in religious education seemed to realize anew that the really important thing was to have teachers who were themselves Christians with a living faith. "In the end the decisive thing is the personality of the teacher of religion. Erudition and skill in methods are of no avail where youth does not have the certainty that the piety of the teacher is genuine and deep."[24] To quote Jean Paul: "The first rule for anybody who wants to give something is this, that he himself must have it; so nobody can teach religion except he who has it."[25]

During the period of the Empire the entire system of religious instruction from organization and supervision to material and methods came under question. That this debate should be continued when the whole framework of society and government was shaken by World War I was inevitable.

Part Three

The Weimar Republic, 1918–1933

Chapter VII

The REVOLUTION and the
WEIMAR CONSTITUTION

With the start of World War I a temporary party truce was negotiated and all groups united in defense of the nation. Although the Social Democrats proposed a national school law in the Reichstag in 1915, which would have abolished school fees and have established a predominantly secular school system, there was no chance that such a revolutionary proposal would be accepted, and no serious effort was made in this direction. More important and urgent problems were at hand, and up to the end of the war no significant changes were made in regard to the German schools.

Politically, however, the party truce did not hold throughout the war. Soon there developed within the Social Democratic party a small group, led at first by Karl Liebknecht, Rosa Luxemburg, and Franz Mehring, who refused to be bound by the party caucus and voted against additional war credits. Differences within the party grew and came to a head in the Reichstag budget debate of March 1916. The result was that the dissident group who refused to vote military credits withdrew, and at first constituted themselves as the *Sozialdemokratische Arbeitsgemeinschaft* in order to protect their right to sit on committees. In the spring of 1917, after unsatisfactory consultations with the Social Democratic majority, the dissidents formed the Independent Social Democratic party.[1] Within this party itself there was a small left-wing group known as the Spartacus Union which centered about Liebknecht and Luxemburg. This splinter group, which took its name from the Roman leader of a slave rebellion, eventually formed the nucleus of the German Communist party.

The end of the war thus found the Social Democrats split into three major factions, each of which in turn harbored right and left-wing elements. Yet it was these division-ridden Socialists who, as the leading opposition group in the Reichstag, had to undertake the government when the old regime collapsed. On November 9, 1918, Prince Max of Baden, the last imperial chancellor, offered his position to Friedrich Ebert, leader of the Majority Socialists. The latter recruited a coalition government of three Socialists (Ebert, Scheidemann, Landsberg) and three Independent Socialists (Haase, Dittmann, Barth). This government, known as the Council of the People's Commissioners (*Rat der Volksbeauftragten*), was approved by a general meeting of the Berlin Workers' and Soldiers' Councils and also found general acceptance throughout the Reich. The Socialist ministers, however, constituted only a sort of upper revolutionary crust, for within each of the ministries and in the various governmental departments representatives of other political parties and members of the old civil service continued to hold office.

The new government had to rule by decree, and its chief task was to maintain a semblance of order in the turmoil of demobilization. The food situation was critical and chaos threatened if the entire economy of the nation were to be upset by revolutionary action. The Majority Socialists, pledged to establish a democratic government on parliamentary lines, found themselves forced to cooperate more and more with nonsocialist groups of the center and right. Necessity forced them to establish a working arrangement with certain leaders of the old army.

On November 25 a conference of representatives of the state governments met in Berlin and agreed to the early election of a National Assembly, which was to decide the basis of the new government. Representatives of Workers' and Soldiers' Councils, meeting in Berlin on December 16, approved this decision, setting January 19 as the day for the election. At this meeting, however, basic differences between Majority Socialists and Independent Socialists came to light. The left wing of the latter party introduced a motion to make the council (Soviet) system the basis for the new constitution. This motion was overwhelmingly defeated. The Independent Socialists thereupon decided not to participate in the election of a Central Council to which the government for the time being was to be responsible. The result was that the three Independent Socialist members of the government, although they continued to serve, were without the support of their own party organization. Before long an incident arose which led them to resign.

The People's Marine Division, about one-thousand strong, had been in the vanguard of the revolution and since November had been quartered in the old royal palace. The actions of many of its members had been so far from exemplary that the government decided to shift their quarters. The sailors objected and, needing Christmas spending money, demanded eighty thousand marks as payment for agreeing to evacuate. They captured the military governor of Berlin and were about to detain others, when Ebert turned to loyal troop formations for aid. This alliance between the government and "the generals" to annihilate a "worthy revolutionary detachment" aroused opposition among the Berlin workers. The Independent Socialists had not been present when the decision to call in troops was made, and to underline their opposition to the whole episode resigned from the government on December 29. The Spartacus Union, in order to clarify the situation, now demanded a party congress of the Independent Socialist party. When this was refused, the Spartacists broke with the Independent Socialists and on December 31, 1918, constituted themselves the Communist party of Germany. With this defection of the left wing the government was reconstituted with only Majority Socialist members. Unable to rely on support from the left, the Majority Socialists had to soft-pedal some of their doctrines in order to win the support of the Center and of the liberal Democratic party. This was of great significance in regard to the future regulation of church and school affairs.

New School Legislation in the States

Beset by a multitude of problems of its own, the national government was content in these first months of the new order to let the states continue their historic regulation of the schools. The new governments in Prussia, Bavaria, and Saxony were at first Socialist coalitions similar to the national government, while in Württemberg, Baden, and Hesse, Liberals and Centrists also shared in the portfolios. Despite this fact, in all the states the real power lay in the hands of the Socialists.[2]

The state governments early began to issue decrees in regard to schools. In Prussia, Adolf Hoffmann, an Independent Socialist, and Konrad Haenisch, a more moderate Majority Socialist, jointly headed the ministry of education (*Kultusministerium*). Hoffman, who was known as "Ten-Commandment Hoffmann" because of his pamphlet on the Ten Commandments and the Propertied Class, immediately issued a series of ordinances. On November 15 he decreed that children, on the request of parents or guardians, did not have to attend religion classes in the schools. This order affected notably the children of the dissident religious groups.[3] Local clerical school inspection was abolished on November 27. Two days later a more revolutionary set of directives was issued. (1) Prayers were to be stopped at the opening and closing of the school day. (2) There was henceforth to be no compulsory attendance of pupils at church services or any religious services. (3) Religion was no longer to be a subject for examination. (4) No teacher was under obligation to teach religion, attend any service, or supervise children at services. (5) No child was obligated to attend religious instruction. Parents or guardians were to decide for children under fourteen years of age; for older children, who had reached their majority in religious matters, the general laws were to prevail. (6) Homework in religion classes—particularly the memorizing of catechism passages, Bible verses, hymns, and Bible stories—was not to be assigned. Hoffmann was careful to point out that his decrees only applied to the schools, and that instruction given by the churches, where there was voluntary participation, was under no restriction.[4]

The decrees aroused much excitement, not only in Prussia but all over Germany. People regarded them as first steps towards the removal of all religious instruction from the schools. The banning of school prayers was especially resented, and there can be no denial that a clean sweep was being made of many age-old customs. On December 16 Cardinal von Hartmann made a formal protest in the name of the Prussian episcopate. Protestant leaders also objected and protest petitions were submitted to the government. In Berlin 60,000 people gathered in a street demonstration before the ministry of education, and similar demonstrations were held in many of the larger cities.[5] The ministry, now headed by Haenisch alone, capitulated and on January 9, 1919, issued a regulation stating that, in view of the opposition raised in many sections of Prussia, the enforcement of the decrees would be postponed until a definite decision was made by the Prussian National Assembly. The November 29 decrees were rescinded on April 1, 1919, and new regulations were restricted to the question of freeing pupils and teachers from religious instruction if they did not wish to participate.[6]

In Saxony, where agitation over the Zwickau theses had not completely subsided, the Socialist government began to implement much of that program. On December 6, it was decreed that children of dissidents no longer had to take part in the religious instruction of one of the recognized church groups. This aroused no objection on the part of church authorities. It was otherwise when the government decreed that, from January 1919 on, Bible history was to be restricted to two hours in the lower four grades of the Volksschule and catechism instruction was to be abolished entirely from these grades. On December 12, children, without regard to social status or denominational allegiance, were ordered to attend a common Volksschule. This abolition of confessional schools was a direct challenge to the churches. A large joint Evangelical and Catholic protest meeting was held in Dresden, December 29, 1918, and many other protest meetings took place. The teachers' organization came out in favor of the policy of the Saxon government, but at the same time advocated continuing religious instruction, which was to be nondenominational and controlled by the state. In a manifesto on March 30, 1919, labelled the *Leipziger Thesen*, the teachers called for the establishment of secular Volksschulen and demanded that the schools, not the church, should determine the content, teaching plan, and method of instruction in the religion classes. In spite of the opposition of all the other political parties and widespread opposition among the populace, the Socialists enacted a transitional law on July 22, 1919, which abolished religious instruction in the Volksschulen and required instruction in ethics only during the last two years.[7]

In Bavaria the Socialist minister of education abolished clerical inspection on December 16, and on January 10, 1919, began a system of classes in ethics without religious content. It was not until February 20 that a decree was issued proclaiming education a state matter, and the giving of religious instruction an affair of the churches. No teacher was to be compelled to give religious instruction nor was a student to be compelled to take it. Provisions were simplified for withdrawal of children from religious instruction. The churches did not like the fact that children could be withdrawn from religious instruction, while both children and parents remained within the churches. The Archbishop of Munich used a ready weapon at hand, decreeing that any person who withdrew his or her children from religious instruction was to be denied the sacraments and a Christian burial. A battle also developed over maintaining the "Christian character" of the Simultanschulen. The Democrats and Social Democrats wanted to appoint Jews to the faculties of these schools, but the Center party and Bavarian People's party defeated the proposal. The ordinance on Simultanschulen of August 1, 1919, gave parents a voice in deciding the type of school to be erected in a given locality. This decree, however, was only implemented in four cities—Munich, Nürnberg, Weissenburg, and Selb.[8] This Socialist-instituted right of parents to decide on type of school later came to be considered a "God-given natural right" by Catholic parties.

There was no particular conflict over schools in Württemberg or Baden. In Hesse there were statements to the effect that no one had to teach religion against his will and that the state controlled the schools. Confessional schools were continued in Oldenburg, and in Brunswick some measures were enacted to ease the compulsory attendance laws. The Thuringian states also ended compulsory attendance and abolished clerical inspection. In Gotha in August 1919 ordinances very similar to those issued by Adolf Hoffman in Prussia were enacted. On December 10, 1918, the Workers' and Soldiers' Council of Hamburg abolished religious instruction in all public schools. Bremen had long been notorious for its radical teaching body and for the extent to which churches had been excluded from influencing religious instruction. Here too the Workers' and Sailors' Government abolished religious instruction in the schools on January 7, 1919, a measure which was confirmed by a later government on March 2 and 7, 1919.[9]

The School Issue and the Election of the National Assembly

The agitation over the school decrees issued by the Socialist ministers in the various states played a vital part in the elections of the National Assembly. Church leaders made vigorous appeals for the maintenance of the traditional religious instruction in the schools and for the protection of the churches. The doctrinaire position of the Socialist parties was well known. They stood for the separation of church and state and the establishment of a secular common school (*Einheitsschule*); they were opposed in varying degrees to religious instruction in the school. Nevertheless, in this period the Socialists tended to glide over the school issue in their pronouncements, for they realized that the vast majority of Germans favored the retention of religious instruction in the schools. The Center party and Bavarian People's party demanded a confessional school. The German Democratic party came out boldly for Simultanschulen and for common religious instruction along with religious instruction given by the churches. The German People's party called for religious instruction in the schools, these to be organized on a Simultan or confessional basis according to the wishes of the parents. The German National party demanded confessional schools with regular religious instruction.[10]

The first part of January was a confused period in Germany. Riots broke out in Berlin and the government had to resort to the use of troops. The Communist party had decided not to participate in the elections but nevertheless carried on agitation. On January 15 Rosa Luxemburg and Karl Liebknecht were arrested and met their death at the hands of officers of one of the Free Corps. These formations of ex-soldiers were beginning to exercise great influence, and the government had agreements with some of their leaders. Yet the election itself went off peacefully enough. Under the new election law all men and women over twenty years of age could vote, and proportional representation was instituted. The results showed a victory for the parties favoring the revolution, although the Socialists who had been in the vanguard of the movement did not receive a majority. On the whole it was a vote for moderation as is shown by the small number of seats won by the extreme parties. The results, moving from left to right were: Independent Socialists 22; Majority Socialists 165; Democrats 74, Center 89, German People's party 22, German National party 42; various smaller parties 9.

It was clear that a coalition government would have to be formed. The Majority Socialists made a bid to the Independents but were rebuffed. "There can be no question of the Independent Socialists entering the Government," so ran the reply, "until the present tyranny has been abolished, and until all the members of the Government not only make profession of their intention to secure the democratic and socialist achievements of the Revolution against the middle classes and against a military autocracy, but also give practical proof of their determination to give effect to these professions." [11] The Socialists had to turn to the middle-class parties for aid and soon came to an agreement with the Democrats and Center. These parties were united by the necessity of establishing a democratic parliamentary republic. But on other questions there were sharp divergencies. In cultural matters the Democrats were closer to the Socialists, on economic questions they were closer to the Center. In regard to education the Socialists demanded the secular school, the Democrats, the Simultanschule, and the Center, the confessional school. Clearly some compromise would have to be made, for there was no definite majority for any one system.

Drafting the Constitution

Immediately after the election the national government published a proposed constitution. It had been prepared at the request of the government by Dr. Hugo Preuss, a professor of constitutional law, who had been made state secretary of the interior. Preuss' draft called for the establishment of a unitary state and had little to say specifically about education. It aroused the opposition of the state governments, which succeeded in getting a committee drawn from the several states to consider the constitutional project. The result of their deliberations was a draft establishing a greater measure of federalism. But even in this draft there was only one general article devoted to education, which placed all educational institutions under the supervision (Aufsicht) of the state. This project, somewhat modified by the government, was laid before the National Assembly when it met at Weimar, in February 1919. [12]

In the plenary debate it was soon clear that the school clauses would cause difficulties. The Socialists wanted more power for the

Reich over schools. Dr. Schücking of the Democratic party maintained that the school clauses were entirely unsatisfactory. He wanted uniform laws in regard to compulsory attendance, school terms, and school examinations. Even the more conservative parties were not opposed to giving the national government substantial power over the schools, for through national legislation they hoped to forestall the radical tendencies of certain state governments. Thus through national laws the Center party, for example, might safeguard Catholic school policy in states where politically the Center party was not even represented. Dr. Delbrück of the German National party was a strong advocate of such national legislation in order to curb "the most unheard-of actions by various state governments." The representative of the People's party, Dr. Heinze, demanded the safeguarding of religious instruction and wanted "to lay down in the constitution that our children will, as we wish, grow up in the future with religious education." [13]

After the plenary debate the whole constitution was turned over to a committee, and a subcommittee was named to study the educational clauses. Here it was readily agreed that the Reich government should have the right to prescribe by law fundamental principles in regard to (1) the rights and duties of religious associations and (2) education, inclusive of the universities. There was also no great difficulty about reaching an agreement that clerical inspection should give way to that "carried on by full-time and pedagogically-trained officials." Differences arose over whether religion should be taught in the schools. The Socialists were opposed to this but were not prepared to make a real issue of it, since they realized that undoubtedly the majority of the people, including many within their own party, wanted the retention of regular classes in religion. They would have preferred to leave religious instruction entirely in the hands of the churches, with classes held outside the school building. However, since all the other parties except the Independent Socialists opposed them on this issue, the Socialists were willing to accept religion as part of the regular curriculum of the schools. Even this left plenty of opportunity for disagreement on the content, nature, and supervision of such instruction. Gröber, the representative of the Center party, wanted the churches to have the *Leitung* of the religious instruction. A struggle developed over phraseology and the words *Leitung, Aufsicht, Gestaltung* were debated back and forth. Even the Socialist representative admitted that, if there was to be religious instruction in the schools, the church would have to have some influence over it. In the end none of these troublesome words were used, and it was agreed that "religious instruction shall be given in harmony with the fundamental principles of the

religious association concerned without prejudice to the right of super-
vision by the state."[14] Anschütz, the foremost commentator on the
German constitution, holds that this meant that instruction had to be
given along positive confessional lines (*in konfessioneller Positivität und
Gebundenheit*). It did not exclude the right of a state to give the church
Aufsicht over the religious program as in the case of Prussia, or
Besorgung und Überwachung as in the case of Baden.[15]

There were differences over the continuation of private schools,
but the real struggle came over how the schools were to be organized.
For a time this issue even threatened to disrupt the assembly. If the
Socialists could not achieve their secular schools they favored the
creation of a Simultanschule system and in this they had the support
of the Democrats and of the German People's party. Actually this
meant that about two-thirds of the assembly preferred the Simultanschule. The Center party, however, steadfastly insisted on confessional
schools, and they had the support of conservative Protestant groups
who were anxious to protect the Protestant confessional schools. The
issue was also clouded by the fact that the Einheitsschule, advocated
for years by school reformers, was on the whole very popular. That
Germany was at long last to have a "common" school system appealed
to many, but actually the term "Einheitsschule" meant different things
to different people. Did it mean that all children had to attend the same
schools, that confessional schools were excluded, or simply that there
was to be a uniform integrated school system? Because the word was so
ambiguous the constitutional drafters avoided the term and in the end
agreed that "the public school system was to be developed as an
organic whole."[16] This is the opening provision of Article 146 which,
as a whole, incorporates the most important compromise reached by
the National Assembly on the education issue. It was agreed upon only
after intense strife in the last plenary debate, and is the culmination of
much previous negotiation highlighted by two so-called School Compromises.

The School Compromises

Between the close of the second reading in the constitutional committee on June 18 and the beginning of the second plenary discussion
in the National Assembly on July 2, an important change in the political
situation occurred. The German government was called upon to sign
the Treaty of Versailles. The Democratic party refused to share in this
responsibility and withdrew from the government. This left the Social
Democrats and Center to carry on alone. Gröber, the leader of the
Center, approached Ebert and made clear the necessity of reaching an

agreement on the school question. It was a matter of conscience to the Center party, and unless a solution could be found the Center party would also withdraw from the government. He proposed that parents should decide in each parish if schools should be organized on a confessional or nonconfessional basis. The Socialists, with a dagger at their back, had to make concessions. They agreed to the Center's proposal on the condition that secular schools be put on an equal plane with the confessional and Simultan schools. The Center found it hard to agree to this, for they still wanted all German schools to be on a Christian basis. Yet it had already been agreed upon that children could be withdrawn from religious instruction. Obviously it might even be advantageous to have these children in separate schools where they would not contaminate the rest. The result was the following formula, which constitutes the most important portion of the First School Compromise: [17]

If and how far the Volksschulen within a municipality are to be organized for all confessions in common, or to be separated according to confession, or to be without confession (secular) is to be decided by those entitled to determine the education of the children (*Erziehungsberechtigten*) so far as it is possible to reconcile this with an ordered school system. Details are to be regulated by Reich law which is to be enacted in the near future. Until the issuance of this law, existing regulations remain in force. [18]

The essence of this compromise was that confessional, Simultan, or secular schools were placed on a par and that parents and guardians were to decide which type was to be established. Both Catholic and Protestant church officials were strong supporters of the right of the parents to decide questions of school organization. This was indeed a democratic procedure and as such could not well be opposed by the Social Democrats, who on the whole were more democratic than socialist. The compromise also mentions for the first time the very important provision that, until the enactment of the new Reich law, existing regulations were to prevail. This eventually became Article 174 of the Constitution and for years perpetuated the *status quo*, for a broad national educational law was never enacted until the time of Hitler.

This compromise was adopted in the plenary session on the second reading of the constitution only because most of the members of the Democratic party were away at a party congress. It aroused an immediate reaction. The Prussian and also the German teachers' organizations came out strongly against it. Haenisch, the Prussian minister of education, called a meeting of the ministers of education of the various states. At this meeting it became clear that the ministers of Prussia, Württemberg, Baden, Hesse, Saxony, Saxony-Weimar, Brunswick,

Mecklenburg-Strelitz, Mecklenburg-Schwerin, Lippe-Detmold, Anhalt, Saxony-Altenburg, and Bremen were opposed to the compromise as written and obviously a majority could not be obtained for it in the third reading. If no new solution was worked out, it would be necessary to return to the original committee version, and this the Center party considered impossible. The Socialists and Center thereupon began negotiations afresh with the Democratic party, and the result was what is generally known as the Second School Compromise. It differed from the first principally in that the interdenominational (*Simultan*) school was made the norm-school type (*Regelschule*), while confessional and secular schools were to be established only at the request of parents and guardians.[19] Many ambiguities still existed and many difficulties were overcome only by postponing their actual decision for a future Reich law.

The school provisions were the last big hurdle for the National Assembly. On July 31, 1919, the constitution was adopted by a vote of 262 to 75. The Majority Socialists, Center, and Democrats voted for it, while the German People's party, the German National party, the Independent Socialists and certain stray individualists opposed it. On August 11 the constitution was proclaimed and went into effect three days later.

The Constitutional Provisions Affecting Religious Education

The new constitution had far more to say about schools than the old Imperial Constitution; it provided a basis for the development of a uniform German school system if the people should prove prepared to act in this direction. First of all, Article 10 gave the national government power to enact normative legislation in regard to education, and the rights and duties of religious associations. In the section of the constitution on community life there was inserted Article 120, which stated: "The education of their children for physical, intellectual, and social efficiency (*Tüchtigkeit*) is the highest duty and natural right of parents, whose activities shall be supervised by the political community."

At first sight this clause seems innocuous, but it had several important implications. Chiefly it was directed against the extreme Socialist demand for "community upbringing" (*Gemeinschaftserziehung*), but it was also aimed at the Catholic theory that parents' rights over their children's education were outside the sphere of the state. While the article emphasizes the duty of parents to educate their children, it states in clear language that this is a civic duty, which lies within the supervision of the state. Neither here nor elsewhere did the Weimar

Constitution accept the Catholic teaching in regard to the divine right of parents over education.[20]

Section IV of the constitution was devoted entirely to education and schools. Here it was stated specifically that "the education of youth shall be provided through public institutions" and that the Reich, the states, and the municipalities were to cooperate in their organization (Article 143). The state was to supervise education, and the controversial ecclesiastical supervision of former eras was abolished. Teacher training was to be uniformly regulated according to the principles which apply generally to higher education. With this a demand on the part of elementary teachers that they, too, should receive their training at universities or equivalent institutions was satisfied. Education was to be free, which was no innovation for the elementary schools, although the provision of free school supplies at elementary and also at continuation schools (*Fortbildungsschulen*) was new, as was the provision that the Reich, states, and municipalities should provide public funds to enable children of parents in poor circumstances to attend middle and higher schools. Universal compulsory education was to prevail, and this was to be given primarily at an eight-year elementary school, followed by the continuation school up to the completion of the eighteenth year. The first four years of the elementary school were to constitute a common foundation school (*gemeinsame Grundschule*) and had to be attended by every one. This meant that the old preparatory schools (Vorschulen) which were conducted by many Gymnasiums and private schools were to be discontinued. On the basis of this four-year foundation school the middle and higher schools were to be organized into an organic whole.

Admission to a particular foundation school was to be governed by the child's ability and aptitude and not by the economic and social position or the religious confession of his parents. The next clause, however, introduced an important modification of this provision. It stated:

Nevertheless, within the municipalities (*Gemeinden*), upon the request of those persons having the right to determine education, elementary schools of their own religious belief (*Bekenntnis*) or of their philosophy of life (*Weltanschauung*) shall be established, provided that an organized school system in the sense of Paragraph 1 [establishing the *Grundschule*] is not thereby interfered with. The wishes of those persons having the right to determine education shall be considered as far as possible. Detailed regulations shall be prescribed by state legislation on the basis of a national law.[21]

This clause which enabled parents and guardians to request the establishment of confessional or secular schools must be read in conjunction with Article 174 which states:

Until the promulgation of a national [school] law provided for in Article 146, Paragraph 2, the existing legal status shall continue. The law shall give special consideration to parts of the Reich in which schools legally exist that are not divided according to religious beliefs.

This article had the effect of maintaining the *status quo* in the states and preventing further radical enactments by the various state governments. In practice it meant that secular schools could not be legally established until the new school law was passed, while confessional and interdenominational schools, since they already existed, were to be continued as heretofore. The article specifically attempted to assure the continued legal existence of the old Simultanschule areas, a safeguard which had previously been inserted at various times in Prussian legislation. Effort was made to have this article bind the legal situation as of November 9, 1918, but this was defeated, and technically it did not cover the measures enacted in the states between that date and the adoption of the constitution. The courts did, however, later overrule some of these measures as contrary to the principles of the constitution.

The continued existence of private schools was also subject to much debate.[22] Henceforth, as was already the case in most states, they must have the approval of the state and were subject to state laws. Approval for such schools, however, had to be granted "if the standard of the private schools in their curricula and equipment, as well as in the scientific training of their teachers, does not fall below that of the public schools, and if no discrimination against pupils on account of the economic standing of their parents is fostered." Private elementary schools were to be established only if "there is in the municipality no public elementary school of their religious belief or of their *Weltanschauung*, or if the educational administration recognizes a special pedagogical interest." Private, like public, preparatory schools (Vorschulen) connected with higher schools were abolished. Specialized (music, trade, etc.) private schools were to be continued as under existing law. With these provisions the Center party definitely protected the continuation of the various schools run by monastic orders, among which the higher schools for girls were the most important.

The constitution thus not only made possible the continuation of confessional public schools and church-run private schools, but in Article 149 stated:

Religious instruction shall be part of the regular school curriculum with the exception of nonsectarian (secular) schools. Such instruction shall be regulated by the school laws. Religious instruction shall be given in harmony with the fundamental principles of the religious association concerned without prejudice to the right of supervision by the state.

This made it obligatory to have religion classes as part of the regular teaching plan of all public and private elementary and higher schools. The one exception was to be the secular school, which could be established after the enactment of the Reich school law foreseen in Article 146. Moreover this instruction, which was under supervision of the state, had to be in accordance with the denominational tenets of the respective churches concerned. Nothing was said as to who was to pass judgment on the orthodoxy of the instruction. Obviously, this article meant that in the future as in the past there would have to be cooperation between state and church officials in regard to religious instruction.

Provision was further made that:

Teachers shall give religious instruction and conduct church ceremonies only upon a declaration of their willingness to do so; participation in religious instruction and in church celebrations and acts shall depend upon a declaration of willingness by those who control the religious education of the child.

This provision, with other sections of the constitution protecting the rights of civil servants, was meant to prevent discrimination against teachers who refused to teach religion or to participate in the accustomed religious services. It said nothing about the need for religious teachers to receive the *missio canonica* of the Catholic church or approval by Protestant church officials. Here existing state practices continued. It was also generally interpreted that children would attend religion classes unless they were specifically withdrawn at the request of the parents or guardians. In Hamburg the regulation worked the other way and parents had to present authorization to have their children enrolled in the religion classes. This was changed in 1933, and henceforth here, as generally in the Reich, children attended religion classes unless their withdrawal was especially requested. Administrative officials had some justification for considering that enrollment in a school where religion was a regular subject of instruction, and religion services were held, implied attendance at such classes and services, unless parents made a special request that children be excused. In Prussia a ministerial decree of June 1928 directed school officials to notify the proper denominational church authorities of any Evangelical, Catholic, or Jewish pupils for whom regular religious instruction was not provided. Names of pupils who had withdrawn from religious instruction, or as a result of specific declaration were attending religious instruction of another confession, were, however, not to be included on the list.[23]

Teachers who had expressed their unwillingness to give religious instruction or participate in the school religious services were not to be disciplined. Their eligibility for appointment, however, was often affected by such action, and an obligation to appoint did not exist. It was a disputed point whether they could be employed at confessional schools where instruction was to be in the spirit of the confession. Religion was under the constitution to be a regular subject of instruction and in the multitude of single-teacher schools it was necessary to have a teacher who was willing to give religious instruction, lead the school prayers, and so on. The right of teachers to withdraw from participation in the religious life of a school was a fundamental freedom, but one which was greatly restricted by the realities of school administration.

Although the constitution proclaimed that all inhabitants of the Reich should enjoy complete liberty of belief and conscience and provided specifically that there was no state church, it is obvious from all the provisions in regard to religious education that, with the exception of the Socialist party leaders, there was no desire to bring about a radical separation of church and state. Even in regard to the universities, which were state institutions, it was stated: "Theological faculties in institutions of higher learning shall be maintained." Attempts had been made to restrict this provision to "existing faculties" but the word existing was deleted.[24] States were to be permitted to establish new faculties if they wished, and these were not necessarily to be restricted to the two dominant Christian confessions.

The most significant innovations of the Weimar Constitution were the establishment of a uniform foundation school, the provision that the Reich government might enact normative legislation in regard to education, and thirdly, the recognition that the state governments needed some limitations placed upon them in regard to the regulation of their respective school systems. The national guarantee of religious freedom and other personal rights led to a relaxation of pressures on both teachers and pupils in the matter of religious education. The provision that the Simultanschule should be the normal type of school and that the confessional and secular schools would have to depend on the right of the parents to request them was indeed revolutionary. But this provision lost its significance because of the restrictions incorporated in Article 174, which bound the existing situation until the passage of a national school law. Clerical school inspection was finally ended, and supervision and administration of the schools remained exclusively in the province of the state governments. Despite the early attempts of Socialist reformers, the Weimar Constitution did not break sharply with the past, but did continue the process of liberalizing the course of religious education. This was to be equally true of the school legislation of the new national and state governments which were established under its aegis.

Chapter VIII

The NATIONAL GOVERNMENT and EDUCATION under the WEIMAR REPUBLIC

The political parties all favored giving the national government more power over education, hoping in this way to establish or to safeguard—whichever it might be—their particular educational philosophies in the various states. The Socialists were doctrinaire supporters of a centralized government and held fast to this view, although they were well aware that depriving the states of complete educational autonomy would result in curtailing certain educational "reforms" that they favored and which had already been made in states like Saxony and Thuringia, where Socialists commanded a majority. These losses would, however, be offset by gains made throughout the nation in securing guarantees for Simultan and secular schools and in freeing children and teachers, on request, from religious instruction. There was also the alluring possibility that through a future federal law fundamental changes could be made in the church-controlled educational legislation of states like Bavaria. The more conservative parties in like fashion saw in national legislation the opportunity to guarantee religious instruction in schools throughout the nation. They were anxious to block the action of those states that tended to omit regular religious instruction, and at the same time through general national legislation to obtain privileges in new territories. The Center party particularly desired to secure a status for Catholic confessional schools in some of the North German states and in those areas where Simultanschulen prevailed. Everyone looked forward hopefully, although with different expectations, to the new school laws called for by the Weimar Constitution.

Establishment of the Foundation School

The first major national education measure, the law defining the foundation school (*Grundschule*) of April 28, 1920, aroused no great opposition. Part of the school compromise had been the agreement that the middle and secondary school system should be developed on the basis of a foundation school common to all. The law now merely stated that the first four years of the Volksschule should be organized as the foundation school, and that the provisions of the constitution (Article 146, paragraph 2, and Article 174) safeguarding the confessional schools should apply to these schools. From the foundation school the pupils were either to continue on in the Volksschule or transfer to the middle or secondary schools. The preparatory schools, many of them run in connection with higher schools, were to be gradually closed. New classes were not to be entered in these schools after 1920–1921, which meant that they would be dissolved by 1924–25. In the case of some private schools, where early closing would cause hardships, the term was extended to the beginning of the school year 1929–30. Private instruction and "family schools" were to be permitted only in exceptional cases. The law did not apply for obvious reasons to the education of children who were blind, deaf and dumb, defective in speech, weak-minded, or chronically sick.

A year after the enactment of the law the Reich minister of the interior issued (July 18, 1921) a short pronouncement on "Guiding Principles for Determination of the Aim and for the Inner Organization of the Foundation School." The first paragraph states:

These suggestions are to be regarded as a stimulus to the uniform organization of the foundation school. In other respects, however, with regard to the inner organization of the foundation school, to its problems of method and curriculum the states maintain their full freedom and independence.[1]

Here appears another reason why this national law ran into little opposition: the states were permitted to determine the regulations in respect to the foundation schools.

The national regulations dealt only with generalizations and had nothing to say about religious instruction, yet, under the federal constitution, this had to be a regular part of the curriculum. The fact that the national law prescribed religious instruction was impressed on all state governments in November 1920 by a decision of the Federal Court. This decision declared unconstitutional the laws abolishing religious instruction in the schools of Saxony, Hamburg, and Bremen.[2] Religion again was being universally taught in all the schools of the Reich.[3]

The Law on Religious Education of Children

Since there were to be religion classes in the schools, and these were to be taught in accordance with the doctrines of the churches, it

was obviously necessary to determine what particular classes in religion
a child should attend. Where schools were organized on a confessional
basis it was also necessary to know whether a child should be enrolled
in a Protestant or Catholic school. Heretofore there had been great
diversity among the German states in determining in disputed cases
whether a child should be brought up as a Protestant or Catholic. This
question also caused great difficulty when a family moved from one
state to another and encountered different regulations. Clearly if there
was ever to be a uniform school system this was a preliminary issue
which needed attention. It was this problem which the Law concerning
the Religious Education of Children of July 15, 1921, attempted to
solve. The law begins by stating that:

The voluntary agreement of the parents determines the religious education
of the child. . . . This agreement is revocable at any time and is annulled
by the death of one parent. . . . However, while the marriage is in force,
it can be decided by neither parent without the consent of the other that
the child shall be trained in another faith than the common faith at the
time of marriage or in another faith than hitherto, or that the child shall be
excused from religious instruction. If this consent is not given, then the
mediation or decision of the Court of Wards may be called in. . . . Before
a decision is made the parents as well as relatives and the teachers of the
child, if necessary, are to be heard if this can be done without too great
delay or immoderate expense. . . . The child is to be heard if it is ten years
old.

After the death of one parent the other decides; in case of divorce, if
one parent is declared guilty, the other decides; if both are declared
guilty, the father decides for a son over six years of age, the mother in
other cases. Agreements concerning the religious education of the child
(such as required by the Catholic church in cases of mixed marriages)
are without civil validity. In the case of illegitimate children the
mother decides; in the case of adoptive children that have the same
legal position as legitimate children, the adoptive parents decide.
Guardians with the consent of the court decide in the case of orphans,
but a guardian cannot change a decision already reached in regard to
the religious education of the child. After reaching the age of twelve a
child cannot without its own consent be educated in a different religion
from the one in which it has until then been reared; after the age of
fourteen the child decides itself what religion it wishes to embrace. All
disputes are to be settled by the Court of Wards.

Parents can reach their decision in regard to education before or
after the birth of a child, but in any case the decision has to be made
before the time for compulsory school attendance is at hand. Further,

5*

the agreement does not have to be the same for all children of one marriage. A distinction is also made between religious education (*Erziehung*) and participation in religious instruction in the schools. Parents might, for example, decide to bring up their child in the Evangelical religion, but withdraw him from the religion classes in the school. They might be motivated to such action by many reasons such as their disapproval of a particular teacher, or their objection to the liberalism or fundamentalism of the instruction.

With this national law all the special laws and regulations in the various states regarding mixed marriages and the education of children were swept aside. It was a long-needed reform. While the Catholic church might have wished for a change in one or two sections, its basic demands in respect to the right of parents to determine the education of their children were amply protected. Any evidence of the free agreement of the parents was to be sufficient, and there were no restrictions in regard to special forms or declarations. There was fear in both Protestant and Catholic circles that the provision of the law giving fourteen-year-olds the right to decide in regard to their religious affiliation might lead to increased withdrawals from religion classes in the schools. This did not prove to be the case.[4]

Attempts to Enact a National School Law

In the same year, 1921, a draft for the proposed national school law, projected in Article 146 of the constitution, was also brought before the Reichstag. Such a measure had been discussed in a national school conference held in 1920, but no solution had been reached there on the ticklish problem of how the schools were to be organized.[5] The draft of the law soon bogged down in committee over the problem of finding a formula for confessional schools, since the Social Democrats wanted to incorporate in the same paragraph their program for secular schools. The Center and other supporters of the confessional schools wanted it stated that all instruction at confessional schools should be in the spirit of the confession (*im Geiste des Bekenntnisses*) and that nothing should be taught contrary to the doctrinal and ethical teachings of the church. Finally a formula was agreed upon to the effect that confessional schools were to be Evangelical, Catholic, or Jewish; customary religious practices were to be continued in the schools; general textbooks were to be adapted to a particular type of school; and teachers were to be educated by the states, the churches being given an opportunity to bring their influence to bear. Further the states were to decide when the law was to go into effect.

At this point in the discussions a change of cabinet took place and in the new Cuno government the Social Democrats exercised somewhat more influence. On December 4, 1923, the Reichstag committee after 160 meetings and discussions postponed any further work. This was the situation when the Reichstag was dissolved in the spring of 1924. There were urgent matters before the electorate, growing out of the French attempt to collect reparations by occupying the Ruhr. The new Reichstag was again somewhat more conservative and on the whole more favorable to confessional schools. This was likewise true of the Reichstag elected on December 7, 1924, after a new dissolution.

By September 1925 the government had prepared a new draft of a national school law. When it was published in the press, it immediately aroused the opposition of important teachers' organizations and of various educational leaders. The proposed law dealt rather favorably with confessional schools and provided detailed regulations in regard to them. It was charged that the Simultanschule which was to be the normal type of school under the constitution did not receive sufficient safeguards. Many Protestants found themselves opposed to the proposed law, for they believed it would give the Catholic church too great an influence over education. The Organization of German National Jews came out against the law with the slogan: "Away with the confessional school as with the secular (*religionslosen*) schools. We want a school that is conducted in a religious, not a confessional spirit, and in a German spirit." [6] With the Communists, Social Democrats, Democrats, and German People's party opposed to the law and only the Center and German Nationalists supporting it, the measure was never even brought before the Reichstag.

The government set about drafting a new law. One draft inspired by Minister Külz was never published, but in 1927 the draft sponsored by Minister von Keudell received cabinet approval and was turned over to the Reichsrat. This upper chamber of the German parliament was composed of representatives of the various states and in political alignment did not always coincide with the Reichstag.

The new draft favored the interdenominational (*Gemeinschaft*) school. The use of the term "Gemeinschaftsschulen" to designate the interdenominational schools in contrast to confessional schools became more general in these years and gradually replaced the older term "Simultanschulen." Although the terms were commonly used interchangeably, strictly speaking, the Gemeinschaftsschulen were held to include all religious groups, while the Simultanschulen (despite the frequent presence of Jewish pupils or pupils adhering to other *Weltanschauungen*) were always organized on a Christian (Catholic, Lutheran, Reformed) basis. [7] The Gemeinschaftsschule did not please the Bavarian government. Baden also objected to the law because under it the churches in Baden would no longer have control over religious instruction in the schools. There was in fact an attempt in this law to be more precise about supervision of religious instruction in the schools, and these provisions aroused the opposition of the churches as well as of some teachers' organizations. The influential National German Teachers' Organization was opposed to the law for a variety of reasons, but mainly because it was considered that the law was not in accord with the constitution.[8] In the end the Reichsrat defeated the measure 37–31. Bavaria led the opposition, with the Prussian government delegation voting for the law, while most of the representatives from the Prussian provinces were against it.

Although rebuffed by the upper chamber, the cabinet introduced the measure in the Reichstag. Here endless discussions developed in the committee on educational affairs. Difficulties arose as to whether curriculum plans should be adapted to confessional schools, and also over provisions in regard to opening new schools. No progress had been made before difficulties arose in the cabinet over other matters and parliament was again dissolved in April 1928. New elections brought a shift to the left, and for the first time since 1920 a Socialist was again Chancellor of Germany. Chancellor Müller had difficulties enough in keeping his coalition together without attempting to push through a school law.

The attempts to pass a national school law always shattered because of differences centering on the problems connected with religious education. Other factors, of course, entered into the picture. Foremost was the political diversity within Germany which was only partially the result of educational and church differences. Basic was also the deep-rooted determination in many state governments to retain the regulation of education as a function of the states and not of the nation. Financial matters were also a consideration. Here it was not so much the task of raising new revenue as a question of distributing costs between nation and states. According to the state tax law (*Landessteuergesetz*) of March 30, 1920, whenever the national government put new burdens on the state and municipalities, the Reich was to assume some portion of the financial responsibility.[9] The reluctance of the national government to assume more financial burdens was reflected in the third tax ordinance of February 14, 1924, which provided that schools should be left to the administration of the states. In this connection it is well, however, to recall that the Weimar Constitution never intended to nationalize the schools in the sense of taking them away from the states. The real reason for the failure to enact general education laws was the difficulty involved in state participation in religious education in a religiously divided population. These difficulties were augmented by the fact that a significant segment of the population was opposed to religious education of any kind.

Regulation of Teacher Training

In addition to the law which was to regulate the status of different school types (Article 146, paragraph II, and Article 174) the Weimar Constitution definitely called for one other national educational law. Article 143, paragraph II stated: "The training of teachers shall be uniformly regulated for the Reich according to the principles which apply to higher education." By this provision the drafters of the constitution had tried to meet an old and pressing demand on the part of the Volksschule teachers and of pedagogical theorists. Hitherto the general pattern of preparation for elementary school teachers had been graduation from a Volksschule, three years' study at a preparatory institution, and then three years at a Normal School (*Lehrerseminar*). This differentiated the Volksschule teachers from all other professional groups, who received their training at the historic secondary schools and the universities. The elementary school teachers were thus cut off from the general cultural stream of professional education and too easily restricted to curricula concerned largely with methods of teaching. Secondary school instructors had long been required to graduate from a secondary school and attend a university and this was more or less the ideal now sought for all teachers. It should be noted, however, that the constitution avoided definitely prescribing attendance at a secondary school or university, and provided only that all teachers should be trained "according to the principles which apply generally to higher education."

Differences of opinion soon arose as to what this phrase meant. Could special independent teacher-training institutions be continued, or must they be run in connection with a university? Since secondary and higher education were on a nondenominational basis did this mean that schools devoted to teacher training likewise had to be on such a basis? Some commentators, especially in view of the fact that the Simultanschule was to be the normal school type, held this to be the case. Other commentators, going back to the debates in the National Assembly, maintained that this was never meant to be the rule.[10] The upholders of confessional schools steadily argued that it was necessary to have teachers trained in confessional teachers' institutes, if they were to be expected later to teach at confessional schools "in the spirit of the confession."

It was clear that any Reich law attempting to regulate teacher training would arouse much controversy. It would also require federal funds, and this was the deciding factor. By decisions of the Reich cabinet of January 12, 1923, and January 7, 1924, the draft law on reform of teacher education was withheld until the regulation of financial relations between the national and state governments had been settled. Later attempts in the Reichstag to bring the problem before the House always failed.

With the failure of the Reich to enact normative legislation, the states were left to deal with the problem of teacher training as they wished. According to the solutions reached, they can be separated into three general groups. First there were those states that, stimulated by the provisions of the national constitution, prescribed attendance at secondary schools and universities or at special institutes associated with the universities. Saxony, Thuringia, Hesse, Brunswick, Anhalt, Lippe, and Hamburg belonged to this group.[11] Secondly there were the states that required graduation from a nine-year higher school (Gymnasium, Realschule, Aufbauschule, etc.) followed by attendance for two years at a professional training institution. In Prussia this was regulated by ordinance and the old preparatory institutions (*Präparändenanstalten*) were closed. This meant that the existing teachers' institutes came to an end as their students finished their courses. The new two-year training course, which was on the university level in so far as admission requirements were concerned, was given at pedagogical academies, some of which were organized on an interdenominational and some on a confessional basis. Baden had similar provisions and established three *Lehrerbildungsanstalten*, a Catholic one at Freiburg, a Protestant one at Heidelberg, and an interdenominational one at Karlsruhe. Mecklenburg-Schwerin established a two-year pedagogical institute at Rostock which had entrance requirements similar to those of the universities. Oldenburg made similar arrangements, and in 1929 the Landtag ordered that teacher-training institutes were to be organized on an interdenominational basis. A third group of states, led by Bavaria and Württemberg, retained their old established systems (*Lehrerseminare*), and were content with modernizing the curriculum. In Bavaria the confessional organization of the teacher-training institutions was safeguarded by the Bavarian concordat with the papacy and the agreements with the Protestant churches which were concluded in 1925.

International Agreements and Education

While the national government had power to enact normative legislation in regard to the schools, and was expressly charged to do so in two instances (school types; teacher-education), it had no ordinance power. The several memoranda issued by the federal minister of the interior touching on educational matters were only of an explanatory nature. The possibility, however, also existed that the national government might enter into international agreements which would affect educational matters. This the government did in concluding the German–Polish Convention for Upper Silesia on May 15, 1922. By this convention certain limitations were placed on the Prussian government in administering the educational system in its portion of Upper Silesia, and reciprocal rights were obtained for the German minority in Polish-held Upper Silesia.

Under certain conditions minority schools in which the language of instruction was to be the minority language were to be established and religion too was to be considered. "If at least 40 of these children belong to the same denomination or religion, a minority school of this denominational or religious character shall be established on application." Since Upper Silesia had traditionally been confessional school territory this followed former practice. The convention further prescribed that on demand of "persons legally responsible for the education of at least eighteen pupils of an elementary school who are nationals of the state and belong to a linguistic minority, minority language classes shall be established as soon as possible for these pupils. In the same circumstances, if at least 12 of these pupils belong to the same denomination or religion, minority religious courses for these pupils shall be established on application." [12] The Upper Silesian Convention, of course, did not apply to all Germany and there were some other provinces with small Polish minorities. These too were now given more liberal treatment.

Establishing different regulations for language in general and for use in religious instruction was a distinction that had often been made by the Prussian administration before the war. Under the Prussian regulations of the Kulturkampf period, religious instruction in Polish had been permitted for the first four years, but after this it was to be in German, although Polish could be used in so far as it was necessary to explain the material. [13] While Polish disappeared as the regular language of instruction from the elementary schools, it long continued to be used in religion classes. By administrative action of school officials Polish religious instruction was curtailed in some districts more than in others and there never was a uniform policy for all Prussian territories. In 1906 there was a wave of protest, and a children's strike against increased Germanization of religious instruction was organized. The government countered by coercive measures, and the

principle of religious instruction in the German language was asserted.
In practice, however, Polish continued to be used for religious instruction in many schools, particularly in the lower classes. During the war
"religious instruction in the Polish language was given a little more
scope again in the schools."[14] One of the first decrees (November 30,
1918) of the Socialist minister of education in Prussia stated: "The
ministry is in agreement that, in the future, Polish-speaking children
shall be given religious instruction in Polish during the first three
school years, if this is desired by their parents." By a decree of December 30, 1918, this was extended to instruction in the middle and higher
grades. It was even extended on December 29, 1920, to the Wendish-
speaking children in the districts of Liegnitz and Frankfurt an der
Oder.[15]

The protection of minorities also became involved in the question
of concluding a Reich concordat with the Papacy. In the early twenties
there were some within Germany who thought the Vatican was not
doing its part in protecting the rights of German minorities in various
states of Europe. They advocated the conclusion of a concordat which
would settle church and school questions not only for Germany but
also for German minorities abroad.[16] The Vatican was of course
interested in protecting the right of Catholics to worship and receive
an education in their mother tongue, but could not be drawn into all
the nationality conflicts of the period. It nevertheless desired very much
to conclude a concordat with Germany, just as it sought to conclude
concordats with other European states.

It was in 1921—the year which brought the first attempt to pass
a national school law—that Reich Chancellor Wirth requested the
foreign office to prepare a draft agreement with the Vatican. President
Ebert, although a Social Democrat, favored this proposal and at various
times until his death supported the negotiation of a concordat with the
Vatican. This was in line with Ebert's basic philosophy of a more
centralized state, for a Reich concordat would have put an end to the
possibility that the various German states might make their own
separate arrangements with the papacy. While the foreign office was
charged with preparing the treaty, the ministry of the interior, which
had control of school affairs, was opposed to a concordat. Premier
Braun of Prussia also submitted a memorandum to the federal government in which he stated that under no circumstances should the
schools, which were subject to state regulation, be made the subject of
an agreement with a foreign power. The project, however, was kept
alive because of foreign-policy considerations. It was not set aside until
Cuno became chancellor in November 1922, when the difficult economic

and political problems of the day sidetracked cultural questions. In October 1924 Chancellor Marx, however, again ordered preparatory negotiations for a Reich concordat.[17] Meanwhile the papacy had scored a triumph by successfully concluding a concordat with Bavaria in the previous March. Negotiations for this agreement started as early as February 1920 and were completed in March 1924.[18]

As soon as the Protestant church authorities of Bavaria heard of the concordat they brought pressure on the Bavarian government to conclude a similar agreement with them. It was necessary to negotiate two such state treaties, one with the Evangelical-Lutheran Church of Bavaria right of the Rhine (e.g. Bavaria proper) and one with the United Protestant Evangelical Christian Church of the Palatinate. These agreements were concluded by November, and for the most part ran parallel to the concordat. Not only equity but political expediency demanded such treaties with the Protestant churches, for the concordat had to be approved by the Bavarian parliament. The Protestants on the whole did not like the concordat, but realized that it was a golden opportunity to obtain favorable agreements for themselves. Absolute parity with Catholicism was, and still is, the dominant motivation of Protestant action in Bavaria. For the first time the Bavarian government now recognized the two Protestant churches as entities with which it negotiated as an equal. The state treaties were to go into effect only after ratification by church and state authorities.[19]

By the concordat and the state treaties the churches of Bavaria were guaranteed freedom of public worship. Schools were to be organized on a confessional basis, and religious instruction in the schools was to be in the spirit of the confession and given by teachers who were adequately trained to give such instruction. This latter requirement was usually interpreted to mean that the teacher-training institutes must also be organized on confessional lines, although it was not specifically so stated.[20] Religion was to be a regular subject of instruction at all elementary, middle, and higher schools. Catholic teachers of religion had to receive the *missio canonica* from their diocesan bishop; Protestant teachers had to present evidence that they had been adequately trained to give religious instruction in accordance with the teachings of the Evangelical-Lutheran church and must be approved by the governing officials (*Landeskirchenrat*) of the church. Safeguards were inserted to prevent members of Catholic orders or Protestant deacon or deaconess organizations from being discriminated against as teachers. While the agreements said nothing specifically about clerical supervision of the schools, all contained an identical clause in regard to religious instruction, which stated: "The supervision and conduct

(*Beaufsichtigung und Leitung*) of religious instruction at the elementary, middle, and higher schools is guaranteed to the churches." This was a recognition of existing practice, and no attempt was made to define exactly what the statement meant. The right to establish private schools was accorded both churches, and they were also given assurances in regard to the theological faculties at the universities.

The Bavarian agreements actually did little more than formulate existing practices. Their importance consisted in the fact that they guaranteed the continuation of the confessional schools and in this and other provisions assured the churches a continued influence over the school system. They gave expression to a different spirit and climate of opinion from the more secular regulations and practices of many other German states in the postwar decade.

Many commentators hold that at least some of the provisions of the concordat, notably those in respect to appointment of teachers and church supervision of religious education, were contrary to the Weimar Constitution.[21] The question of the constitutionality of the agreement was raised in the Reichstag, but the minister in answering the interpellation boldly asserted that the Bavarian concordat was in full harmony with the constitution. Catholic forces in general henceforth never were willing to surrender any of the provisions of the Bavarian treaty for the sake of an agreement on the national level.

Shortly after the ratification of the Bavarian agreement in 1925, the able Papal Nuncio Pacelli transferred his residence from Munich to Berlin, and the dormant negotiations with the national government were quickened.[22] In 1927, Marx again headed the cabinet with Keudell as minister of interior. They sought not only to enact a national education law, but attempted anew to conclude a concordat. Issues were debated back and forth. To have concluded a concordat would have meant settling by treaty many things in relation to the schools which the Reichstag could not even agree to settle by legislation. Both the national education law and the concordat failed to achieve Reichstag approval, and for that matter public opinion was also against the measures. There were no further serious attempts by the foreign ministry after 1927 to conclude a concordat until the time of Hitler.[23]

Instead of a national agreement, the Vatican had to be content to sign a rather innocuous concordat with Prussia on June 14, 1929, which was concerned with establishing diocesan boundaries and regulating appointments of the higher clergy. It did not touch on school questions, except for providing for the continuance of Catholic faculties of theology at the universities.[24] The Prussian concordat was followed by a similar one with Baden on October 12, 1932. The Baden agreement did touch slightly on school matters, providing that Catholic religious instruction should be, as stated in Article 149 of the Weimar Constitution, a regular subject of instruction in the schools. This religious instruction was to be given in conformity with the doctrines of the Catholic church. The state likewise agreed to maintain in the future those school rights which the Catholic church now possessed, according to existing laws.[25]

Although the Bavarian, Prussian, and Baden concordats applied only to these states, they did influence directly or indirectly the whole nation. They were specifically confirmed in the Reich concordat later concluded by Hitler and were reaffirmed in post-World-War-II legislation.

Chapter IX

The SCHOOLS Under
The WEIMAR REPUBLIC

Under the Weimar Constitution the Reich, states, and municipalities were to cooperate in the organization of the schools. Everybody
expected the enactment of a broad federal education act, and the
states, after the first flush of revolutionary decrees, did not rush enactment of educational laws of their own. They were in most cases content
to patch their educational systems. Finances were also a fundamental
consideration, for reform measures usually demand increased expendi-
tures. It is not therefore surprising that the dominant issues of the
prewar period continued in somewhat altered form to be the issues of
the day. As in the period of the Empire, the main problems relative to
religious education were the organization of the schools, the supervision
of instruction, and the reorganization of the curriculum.

Organization of the Schools

The states were bound by the provisions of the Weimar Constitution, but just what these meant was none too clear. To be sure, under
the constitution the interdenominational elementary school was to be
the normative school type, with confessional and secular schools optional
at the request of parents. This left room, however, for discussion of the
meaning of these terms, while the safeguards for Simultanschulen were
variously read. The freedom of teachers and parents to withdraw from
religious instruction meant that the *status quo* could hardly answer until
such time as a national school law was passed. As time went on and no
national school law was forthcoming, the school systems developed
some new characteristics, while continuing to show a strong confessional
tinge.

Discussion at first arose over the question: were the interdenominational schools to be Simultan in the old sense, that is, based on the
two leading Christian confessions, or did they also have to consider

other philosophies of life on a par with these two? The new popular term "Gemeinschaftsschulen" added confusion to the scene. These were usually considered to be schools where other religions and philosophies were on an equal footing with the Evangelical and Catholic. No one questioned that religious instruction had to be given in schools of this type, but did all instruction there have to be on a Christian basis as was generally the case in the Simultanschulen? Could instructors who did not belong to the two leading confessions be freely appointed to those schools? If this were done, would it be contrary to Article 174, which was designed to maintain the existing legal status? The Republic thus brought to the old debate of confessional or interconfessional schools a debate over types of interconfessional schools. This, however, was largely a question of terminology—a new word replacing an old one—for in practice there was no real distinction between the two, and it depended on local usage which term was used.[1] Even before the war, teachers of other than the two major confessions had been appointed at some Simultanschulen, and a few exceptional so-called Christian-Jewish Simultanschulen already were in existence.

The federal constitution attempted to establish some safeguards for the continuance of Simultanschulen where they already existed. No mention of particular territories was made, but the historic Simultan territories were usually considered to be Baden, Hesse, and the Prussian territories of Nassau and Frankfurt am Main-Hanau. In addition such schools were permitted as an exceptional type in other sections of Prussia and in Bavaria. The Republic thus brought about at least the legal extension of Simultan school territory. Saxony by a decree of December 18, 1918, and a law of July 22, 1919, abolished confessional schools and established the Simultanschule throughout the state. Although charges were made that this change was contrary to the federal constitution, the courts did not uphold this contention, and the schools remained on a nonconfessional basis. This shift of legal status brought little change in religious instruction except in certain cities, for Saxony is overwhelmingly Protestant, and the great majority of schools remained populated by one confession as heretofore. The new state of Thuringia, resulting from a union of smaller states, enacted a law that new schools must be organized on a Simultan basis, although existing confessional schools could continue. To these states, either because of practice or legal provision, might be added as Simultan school territories Anhalt, Hamburg, Bremen, Lübeck, and Schaumburg-Lippe.[2]

Confessional schools were the regular school type in Prussia and Bavaria, and without exception prevailed in Württemberg and Oldenburg. They also predominated in Brunswick, Mecklenburg-Schwerin,

Mecklenburg-Strelitz and Lippe, although here again there was some dispute as to just how the schools were to be classified.

To divide Germany into Simultan or confessional school territory in this way actually distorts the picture, for a Simultanschule located in a territory inhabited by only one confession is to all intents and purposes a confessional school. Thus, while the schools of the Hanseatic cities were technically nondenominational, the population was so overwhelmingly Protestant that provision was made only for Protestant religious instruction. Catholic children as a rule attended private Catholic schools, which, however, received a subsidy from public funds. Likewise in Baden, the classic Simultan school territory, many regions were so predominantly Catholic or Protestant that schools were often attended and staffed by members of only one confession. In practice these might be more properly classed as confessional schools than many so-called confessional schools in Bavaria or Prussia that had a relatively large religious minority in attendance. At a confessional school in Prussia, if there were twelve members of a religious minority in the school, special religion classes had to be arranged for them, which, of course, was supposed to be one of the main earmarks of a Simultanschule. In practice schools often shifted from one type to another. Private schools, particularly Catholic schools, tended to draw pupils from public Simultanschulen, which, of course, actually changed the nature of these schools. Also to be taken into consideration is the fact that, particularly in many Protestant schools, "the confessional character had been so watered down that one would have to characterize the prevailing *Weltanschauung* in them as a sort of modernism."[3] There was little of the spirit of the confession in their teaching and these schools were closer to being secular than confessional.

Under Article 146 of the Weimar Constitution "upon the request of those persons having the right to education, elementary schools of their own religious belief or of their *Weltanschauung*" were to be established if this did not jeopardize a well-ordered school system. Schools based on a philosophy of life (*Weltanschauung*) were regularly referred to as secular schools (*weltliche Schulen*). In a later provision (Article 149) religious instruction was made a regular part of the school curriculum, except in the secular schools. The latter term was no doubt a translation of the French *école laïque*.[4] Objection was raised to this designation, since the German word "weltlich" has a connotation of being materialistic and nonspiritual (*nicht geistlich*), while these schools were expected to give moral and ethical instruction in lieu of the classes in religion. In any case, under Article 174, they could not be legally organized until the Reich school law was passed. To get around this difficulty Prussian ordinances in 1920 permitted school authorities to group the many children that had been withdrawn from religious instruction into special classes or special school systems. The classes or schools were still to be considered as confessional schools, and were to use the same curriculum plan as heretofore. Religion classes were to be reestablished at any time at the wish of the parents. Only teachers who had volunteered were to be appointed to these schools, and children should be enrolled only with the consent of their parents. Furthermore such classes or schools were not to be designated as secular schools (weltliche Schulen), Evangelical Schools without Religious Instruction (*Evangelische Schulen ohne Religionsunterricht*), or Religion-less Assembled Classes (*Religionslose Sammelklassen*). Nevertheless the term *Sammelschulen* (assembled schools) came to be attached to them, although they were still commonly called weltliche Schulen. These were the only exceptions to the general rule that religion was taught in all the elementary schools of Germany.

Questions were soon raised in the Prussian parliament as to the constitutionality of such schools.[5] The matter hinged on whether existing Prussian law had permitted such an arrangement at the time when the federal constitution went into effect. It was held that, since pupils could be withdrawn from religious instruction even before 1919, there was no reason why they could not be grouped in special classes or schools now. Administratively it was advantageous, and the church authorities raised no serious objections to the procedure, for it prevented the formation of antireligious cells in the confessional schools. The number of such schools was not large, but it steadily increased. In Prussia there were 1644 assembled classes (Sammelklassen) in June 1925, and 1927 in October 1926; in May 1927, there were 249 assembled schools (Sammelschulen) and 289 in May 1931.[6] These Sammelschulen were scattered throughout Prussia, but were chiefly concentrated in Berlin and the industrial centers of the Rhineland and Westphalia. Similar arrangements also existed in practice in Hamburg, Bremen, Brunswick, Hesse, and Saxony, but this was not official. Outside of Prussia, there was only one such Sammelschule listed officially in Hesse and five in Brunswick in 1932.[7]

In practice under the Weimar Republic there were thus three public-school types; confessional, interdenominational (Simultan or Gemeinschaft), and secular (weltliche; Sammel). The school pattern for Prussia and for Germany as a whole is indicated by Table 1. How confessionalized this public elementary-school system was in practice is indicated by a summary of pupil attendance at these schools in the same year.[8]

Students	Total	Evangelical Confessional Schools	Catholic Confessional Schools	Simultan-schulen	Sammel-schulen
Evangelical	4,560,527	3,365,357	24,351	1,141,867	28,952
Catholic	2,702,004	64,097	2,294,546	337,022	6,339

The confessional nature of the elementary schools also was manifest in the teaching body. Of the 190,371 teachers, 120,870 were Evangelical, 63,352 Catholic, 69 belonged to other Christian denominations, 306 were Jewish, 95 belonged to other religions, and 2,067 were without religious affiliation. No data on religious affiliation of the 3,612 teachers of Hamburg was available. These figures would indicate that the minority groups were proportionately well represented in the teaching body.

Private schools continued to exist under the Republic, and the direct prohibition of private preparatory schools in the constitution was never strictly enforced.[9] There were over 2,000 private schools, many of them of a specialized nature. Of these 661 served the purposes of the elementary school (*Volksschulziel*). They were attended in 1931–32 by 16,637 Evangelicals, 16,929 Catholics, 259 other Christians, 5,888 Jews, 21 belonging to other religions, and 256 without religion. These figures indicate that Catholics and Jews patronized private schools far above their ratio in the population as a whole.

In most states the organizational form of middle and higher schools was not so clearly defined either by law or ordinance as in the case of elementary schools. There were some recognized confessional higher schools (usually old foundations) but on the whole higher schools were organized on an interdenominational basis.[10] One reason why they were not confessionalized more frequently was that in these schools instruction was departmentalized. It was consequently impossible to erect small confessional higher schools in the same fashion as confessional elementary schools. But here too legal classification did not necessarily present the correct picture. On May 1, 1927, out of 1,173 Prussian higher schools, 50 had less than one percent of children of a minority confession, while 467 had one to ten percent. This meant that 517 (44 percent) of the schools were so uniformly attended by children of one confession that they had a minority of less than ten percent. Schools having a minority of less than 25 percent would cover about three-fourths of all the public higher schools in Prussia.[11] This was a result of the fact that the population in the various parts of Prussia was fairly uniform in religious persuasion, the long-lasting aftermath of the Reformation settlements (Peace of Augsburg, 1555, Treaty of Westphalia, 1648) which permitted a prince to determine the religion of his

Table 1.   Number of elementary schools, 1931–1932

States and Prussian provinces	Total	Evang-elical	Catho-lic	Jewish	Simul-tan	Secu-lar
Prussia						
City of Berlin	645	481	57	—	54	53
East Prussia	3,357	2,902	417	—	38	—
Brandenburg	3,001	2,940	42	—	12	7
Pomerania	2,643	2,608	22	—	11	2
Posen-West Prussia	483	292	125	1	65	—
Lower Silesia	3,294	2,266	967	—	33	28
Upper Silesia	1,205	232	958	3	12	—
Saxony	2,812	2,582	193	—	18	19
Schleswig-Holstein	1,594	1,574	13	1	4	2
Hanover	3,636	3,145	469	7	6	9
Westphalia	3,287	1,432	1,716	17	42	80
Hesse-Nassau	2,379	1,277	247	41	813	1
Rhine	5,025	1,418	3,383	24	112	88
Hohenzollern	118	3	114	1	—	—
Total[a]	33,479	23,152	8,723	95	1,220	289
Bavaria[a]	7,615	2,002	5,382	—	231	—
Saxony	2,105	4	28	—	2,073	—
Württemberg	2,299	1,404	889	2	4	—
Baden	1,709	—	—	—	1,709	—
Thuringia	1,559	—	2	—	1,556	1
Hesse	997	26	27	—	944	—
Hamburg	246	—	—	—	246	—
Mecklenburg-Schwerin	1,037	1,037	—	—	—	—
Oldenburg	752	552	198	—	2	—
Brunswick	429	420	4	—	—	5
Anhalt	236	236	—	—	—	—
Bremen	80	—	—	—	80	—
Lippe	143	—	3	—	140	—
Lübeck	40	—	—	—	40	—
Mecklenburg-Strelitz	187	187	—	—	—	—
Schaumburg-Lippe	46	—	—	—	46	—
Total: Germany[a]	52,959	29,020	15,256	97	8,291	295

Source: *Statistisches Jahrbuch*, 1932, p. 421.

[a]Does not include Saar territory.

state. Then too, students often had a chance to select their higher school and paid attention to the predominant confessional orientation of certain schools. These figures, however, do indicate that higher schools were not so interdenominational in fact as they were in theory.

Under the Republic as formerly, there were periodic complaints that one denomination or another did not receive its proper share of teaching positions at the higher schools. Protestants, for example, pointed out that the seventeen Gymnasiums in Baden were attended by 2,007 Evangelical, 2,893 Catholic, 123 Jewish and 59 "other" students, whereas Protestant teachers numbered only 103 to 241 Catholics and 13 "others," and the ratio of Protestant to Catholic directors was five to twelve. Similar conditions were said to prevail in the Realgymnasien, Realschulen, Oberrealschulen, Mädchenrealschulen, and Aufbauschulen.[12]

While the public higher schools were at least nominally interdenominational the picture is also blurred by the fact that many private schools in fact received public funds. Thus in Prussia one hundred private higher schools for girls received support from states or cities. These were mostly organized on confessional lines. In contrast to private girls' schools, higher private boys' schools received few public funds. "Saxony, Württemberg, Baden, and Hesse, as well as a number of the smaller states, in general paid no subsidies, or at least not any worth mentioning, to private schools."[13]

Supervision of the Schools

The abolition of clerical supervision of the elementary schools was one of the reforms which aroused no opposition. In fact state supervision had been the rule for more than a century, although the state had regularly made use of clergymen for this function. The Weimar Constitution now prohibited this by stating that supervision of the schools must be carried on by technically trained officials mainly occupied with this duty. The entire school system was to be under the supervision of the state, and this, of course, included private schools. So far as the national constitution went, there was no prescription that Catholic or Evangelical schools should be supervised by officials belonging to their own particular denomination. All schools were subject to the same state supervision. Whether "state" in this instance meant the national or state governments was not clear, but in lieu of a definite provision it was taken to mean that the customary practice of having each state supervise its own educational system would continue. The state was permitted to require the municipalities to share in this supervision. There was no doubt that classes in religion were subject to this over-all state supervision.

These seemingly direct provisions on school supervision did not exclude the churches from exercising considerable influence over schools in some of the states. Traditionally, and often by legal provision, resident clergy were members of the local school boards, and this was not changed.[14] Influence exerted in this way was, however, on a different plane from the inspection and supervision of classroom instruction formerly conducted by clergymen as state officials. This old practice was everywhere abolished.

The constitution, however, provided that religion was to be a regular subject of instruction, and such instruction had to be in harmony with the fundamental principles of the religious association concerned. Here the question arose as to who should decide if this condition was fulfilled. The obligation was placed on the state, but the state was not responsible to the churches in this regard. Commentators, nevertheless, agree that, provided the states' supervisory rights were maintained, the churches should be given the privilege of assuring themselves as to the content and nature of the instruction given.[15] There was great variation among the states as to how this was to be done. Usually it involved consultation in regard to textbooks and curriculum, the right of clergy, on proper notification, to visit classes in religion, and to file charges with the proper authorities against certain teachers who in their opinion were not giving proper instruction. In Saxony and in the three old Hanseatic towns (as formerly) the clergy did not have the right to visit schools. There was no obligation in the national constitution that Catholic teachers of religion were to have the *missio canonica* from their bishop. Prussia, as in the past, refused to give legal recognition to this demand by the Catholic church, but in practice paid heed to the wishes of the hierarchy. The *missio canonica* was required in Bavaria under the terms of the Concordat of 1925 and was also legally recognized in Baden, Württemberg, and Hesse.[16]

It must be noted that while supervision was to be in the hands of technically trained state employees both lay teachers and ministers gave religious instruction. On the whole the clergy were more active in the Volksschulen in southern Germany—Bavaria, Baden, Württemberg, Hesse, than in the north. Often the pastor instructed the two highest grades while the teacher taught the lower grades, or the teacher taught Bible history and the pastor the catechism. The close relationship of confirmation (communion) instruction, regularly given by the clergy, to the school classes in religion should also be noted. Here again the churches had an entree into the schools. Pastors, too, were often called upon to give religious instruction to scattered minorities. In predominantly Protestant sections of Prussia, for example, one Catholic parish might well serve a number of villages all of which had Protestant confessional schools, and, since no lay Catholic teacher was available, the priest had to give all the religious instruction.

As to the amount of influence accorded the churches over the conduct of religious instruction in the elementary schools, the states can be separated into four groups.[17]

(1) Regions where classes in religion were organized by the states, but the giving, supervision, and in a certain sense inspection of instruction, was essentially left to the churches (*Erteilung, Überwachung, Beaufsichtigung*): Bavaria; Baden; Württemberg and Oldenburg for Catholic religious instruction.

(2) Regions where the state retained in its hands religious instruction, but gave to the churches a varying degree of influence, according to their officials differing rights of observation (*Einsichtsnahme*): Württemberg for Protestant instruction; Hesse, Mecklenburg-Schwerin, Mecklenburg-Strelitz, Province of Hesse-Nassau, and the rest of Prussia except for Schleswig-Holstein.

(3) Regions where the church had no right of observation, but special committees were constituted to serve as a tie between church and state: Thuringia; Oldenburg for Protestant instruction; Province of Schleswig-Holstein.

(4) Regions where the churches had no share in the giving or supervision of religious instruction: Saxony; Brunswick; Lippe, Schaumburg-Lippe; Bremen; Hamburg; Lübeck.

The Weimar Constitution made it clear that the schools belonged to the state, not to the churches. On the other hand it did not seek to separate church and state completely, and there was no thought of denying the churches all influence over education. It was left to the states to work out how much influence the churches should have, and this was largely determined by custom, tradition, and existing laws. There can be no question, however, that the influence of the churches was lessened during the Republic. The slow progress of increased secularization of the German schools, which has been manifest since medieval times, continued.

The Religious Curriculum

The nature and content of the religious curriculum had been the subject of much study and criticism in the years preceding the war. In fact it was a perennial problem which naturally carried over into the Republic. The national constitution, as has been pointed out, gave ground for much future dispute, but it also ended some controversies. It was settled that henceforth there was to be religious instruction in the schools, and, secondly, that it was to be in harmony with the principles of the religious association concerned. This largely ended the debate over organizing general religious instruction which children of all denominations might attend. As had been generally true in the past, Catholic and Evangelical students were henceforth to be instructed separately.

The number of hours devoted to religious instruction varied in the several states. In Prussia, for example, the regulations of 1921 required two hours the first year and three hours weekly the second, third, and fourth year. This schedule was changed in 1923. After that date religion was to be part of the integral instruction of the first year without special religion-class hours, and in the next grades it was to be four hours a week, which was also the time allotted in the upper grades of the Volksschule. The allotment of time in Prussia represents the average maximum among the states. Saxony, on the other hand, which in 1923 reduced class hours in religion to two a week, represents the minimum. When the Saxon parliament voted to do away with religious instruction entirely in the first two years, the officials refused to do so because such action would have been contrary to the national constitution. At the higher schools in Prussia, except in a few cases, two hours a week was prescribed for all grades and this was average for higher schools throughout Germany, a few states increasing the hours in certain grades.

According to the constitution, religion was to be a part of the curriculum of all schools except the secular schools, which seemed to mean that it was to be taught in the vocational and trade schools.[18] This was somewhat of an innovation, for previously it was not always taught at these schools, and by a ministerial decree of 1897 Prussia had refused to make religion at such schools a compulsory subject. Clergy of both confessions were, however, given the right to give instruction at these schools, if they so desired. In spite of agitation on the part of church authorities that religion should now be made a regular subject of instruction at vocational schools, the Prussian government refused to order this. As heretofore the matter was left to local regulation. Where religious instruction was given, it was estimated that about sixty percent of the students took it, and in some cities like Bonn, Cologne, Essen, the percentage increased to over ninety.[19] In Bavaria, one hour a week of religious instruction for three years was part of the regular curriculum of these schools; in Baden, it was two hours a week, and it was introduced for some schools in Württemberg. In all other states, as in Prussia, it was not a regular part of the teaching plan.

Attention was also paid to the organization and content of the religion classes. This was a part of the general revision of school curricula. State education departments issued new suggestions and elaborate curriculum plans were drawn up specifying what material should be covered in each class. Prussia, for example, issued new instructions for courses of study for the foundation school on March 16, 1921, for the upper four years of the Volksschulen on October 15, 1922, for the middle schools on June 1, 1925, and for the higher schools on October 31, 1924, and April 6, 1925.[20] In Thuringia new teaching plans were completed in 1925 by the state ministry with the cooperation of the teachers' organization. In Bavaria the churches worked out detailed curriculum plans, which, after being approved by the state ministry of education and culture, went into effect. The Protestant Church drew up such a teaching plan in 1923, revised it in 1926, and gave it a thorough overhauling in 1933.[21] Other states also revised their curricula, and there was no lack of effort to improve the quality of instruction.

Yet there was a limit as to what could be done. One author, writing on reform of Catholic religious instruction, explained it in this fashion :

It is of course impossible that a revision of Catholic religious instruction will be able to cause the "material to give out new tones" (*stofflich neu zu tönen vermag*). Dogmatically, ethically and philosophically, the religious treasure for instruction is established and untouchable. The material is always given, only the exploitation through new ways of application, presentation and use is subject to reform and the only way open to the schools.[22]

The traditional subjects of the Protestant religious curriculum remained : Bible history, catechism, Bible verses, hymnody, and church history including the explanation of church ritual and practices. On the whole, however, there was a shift towards more integral instruction, especially in the lower grades. Bible history, catechism material, Bible verses and songs were all to be part of one religious instruction and not divided into special periods for each subject. The tendency was to shift separate instruction in the catechism to the higher grades in the Volksschulen. In Bavaria, this was to start in the fifth grade; in Prussia, in the seventh or eighth. Bremen had abolished separate instruction in the catechism before the war, and this practice was continued. Saxony and Thuringia also abolished it, which led to continual protests from the churches. Much of the catechetical material, however, was included in the general instruction. In Saxony it was specifically decreed that the

Ten Commandments, Creed, and Lord's Prayer were to be learned, and in Thuringia the Ten Commandments were to be explained in the fifth and sixth year.[23] The catechism naturally remained the center of confirmation instruction, and in many regions of Germany the first three parts of Luther's catechism were taught in school and the last two only in the confirmation classes.

The new regulations invariably point out that care should be taken not to burden the pupils with excessive memory work, although memorization was by no means ended. One writer on reform of religious instruction says: "Short Bible verses are bells which you hang in the souls of children in their early days, in order that later, amid the storm winds of life, they may begin to ring."[24] The number of hymns to be learned was cut down, and the Bible verses to be memorized were carefully selected. Yet when all the trimming was done, the average German child who took religious instruction still memorized considerable material—catechism selections, Bible verses, songs, and prayers—during his school years. Much of this was accomplished through daily use of prayer, song, or Bible verse in the school, and it was not all a matter of mere assignments for memorization.

The trend toward more activity instruction, which was manifest in other subjects, did not bypass the religious classes. There was particular opportunity for this in the lower grades, where it could be centered largely around the great festivals of the church. It was, however, not restricted to the lower grades, and the Prussian regulations for Evangelical religion in the secondary schools state boldly:

Religious instruction is like all other instruction, activity instruction. It is associated with that which has been unconsciously experienced, shows how to use sources, makes voluntary home activities of the pupils valuable for all by discussion in the class. Its form is chiefly conversational; at important points it also affords room for lectures by the teacher. The pupil has to work out for himself the heroes of religion through use of the Bible and church history sources, and out of contact with them to sense that which cannot be worked out. The teacher, important as is his personality, is only a means to this end. Free "activity groups" for delving into important historical problems or burning life problems will be desired by many pupils in the upper section.[25]

The regulations also stress that religious instruction should work "hand in hand with the other core subjects." Maybe this was not always done "in the spirit of the confession," but it served to bring home to students that religion was not something to be isolated from other intellectual disciplines.

New textbooks appeared, often in attractive format, with well chosen illustrations and pictures. The old controversy whether the regular Bible or a school Bible, made up of selected portions, should be used was not entirely stilled, and decisions varied in different states of Germany and for different grades. That there were portions of the Old Testament which would hardly add to the piety and decorum of religious instruction and which inquisitive youngsters might discover and pass from hand to hand was one of the chief arguments for the use of the school Bible.

The schools on the whole continued the use of opening and closing prayers, which raised some problems when religious minorities were present. At Simultanschulen care was taken to have the general services of such a character that they would not arouse religious sensibilities. In Saxony, school prayers had been abolished in the first blush of revolutionary fervor, but it was not until 1923 that the Saxon government attempted to enforce the ban in Catholic schools. This aroused such lively protest that, on January 10, 1924, the edict against school prayers was rescinded, and Evangelical schools were placed on the same basis as Catholic schools in respect to special school religious services.[26] These were customarily morning and evening prayers, periods of meditation (*Andacht*), school communion services, school Masses, and at times regular formal church services. Pupils who had been withdrawn from religious instruction were not required to attend such services. On the other hand those who participated in the classes in religion could also be required to attend school religious services, for an integral relationship between the two was always assumed. This obligation also could be extended to services, even if they were held in the church and not in the school building, so long as they were held for the school as a group. Children of one faith could not be required to attend services of another faith. This, for example, excused Protestant pupils in Catholic confessional schools from participating in religious processions or attending requiem Masses. Under the federal constitution school authorities could exercise no compulsion for attendance at ordinary church festivities or services. Pupils, however, under ministerial regulation were regularly excused from school on high church festivals of their denomination. This applied of course to all, but affected particularly Jewish and Catholic children, since their church festivals, not covered by standard vacations, were the most numerous. Altar boys were also on proper notification to be excused for special church services. In general, school participation in religious observances was determined by local custom, and there was little attempt to alter this under the Republic.[27] Teachers who had not withdrawn themselves from religious instruction could be required to attend school religious services and exercise customary supervision over the students.

Regulations and practices varied in regard to providing substitute instruction for those students who had been withdrawn from religion classes. In Bavaria, they had to attend another class either as participants or listeners during the hour when they would have been attending religious class. In some places they were freed from any substitute instruction but usually they attended an elective class. In Sammelschulen, classes in moral instruction (*Moralunterricht*) were regularly organized, and in Thuringia instruction in ethics (*Lebenskundlicher Unterricht*) was an elective subject in all public schools. The nature and content of this instruction varied greatly. Usually referred to as moral instruction it was also often known as "attitude (*Gesinnung*), free-religious, nondenominational, religious-historical, ethical instruction, all terms for concepts that up to a point are identical, yet at times have a different content. A common principle was the attempt to establish an ethic on a recognizable foundation and to do away with all dogma." [28] To some *Moralunterricht* was but the further development of non-confessional religious instruction as developed by Rousseau and the Philanthropists, and advocated by men like Diesterweg in the nineteenth century. It was general religious instruction, not Christianity as taught in catechisms. The Prussian regulation of March 13, 1920, phrased it as follows: "Since this is a subject of instruction in which we have had practically no experience, the utmost freedom will be given in the selection of material." [29] One thing was clear in the federal constitution: such ethical instruction could not be considered the regular religious instruction to be held in the confessional or Simultanschulen, for this had to be in harmony with the principles of the religious bodies concerned.

In Bavaria and Württemberg regulations covering private instruction governed such *Moralunterricht*. In Prussia, Thuringia, Anhalt, Brunswick, Hamburg, and Baden, it was to be organized according to certain state regulations, but participation of teachers and pupils was to be voluntary. In Saxony and Hesse, however, such instruction was compulsory for all children who had been withdrawn from religion classes, and state regulations prescribed the general nature of the course. Support for such instruction came all the way from atheistic free-thinking associations of various kinds, and from Social Democrats who favored it as a replacement for religious instruction on confessional lines, to some very devout Christians who considered this to be the only kind of religious instruction which the state was qualified to offer.

6+ R.E.I.G.S.

Jewish Education

Under the Republic the German educational system remained definitely on a Christian basis. This was in no small part due to the provisions of Article 174 which has been cited so often. Until the passage of a national school law the existing legal status was to continue, and this meant that the schools would be Christian. Nevertheless there were many other provisions of the constitution which in practice placed Jewish education on an equal basis. Above all, various states enacted more liberal legislation.

Article 137 of the federal constitution, dealing with the organization of religious associations, brought some new freedoms to Jews. Formerly they had been united as cult or synagogue congregations, but now they could unite in *ad hoc* associations for special purposes such as supporting schools. They had the same right as others to organize private schools, and Jewish children could attend any public school. The general laws on the foundation school and religious education applied to them as it did to all Germans. Although the right to establish public Jewish confessional schools was assumed, it never materialized for the whole Reich because of the failure to pass a national education law.

Under law and practice as it existed before 1919, such public Jewish confessional schools could be established in Bavaria, Prussia, and Württemberg—all confirmed confessional school states. In Simultan lands like Baden no special Jewish schools existed. Here Jewish children attended the regular schools, and the law stated that, if they constituted a minority of 40, a Jewish teacher should be appointed who would take care of their religious instruction and might teach certain selected subjects. In practice such appointments were made when there was a minority of fifteen. Technically these schools remained either Catholic or Protestant Simultanschulen, but at times in practice they were referred to as Christian-Jewish Simultanschulen. This was true, for example, in Frankfurt am Main. In states which after World War I established the Gemeinschaftsschule, the Jews were on an equal footing with the two predominant Christian bodies.

The provisions of the federal constitution protecting civil servants did something to enhance the position of Jewish teachers. However, their employment was a concern of the states. In Bavaria, Prussia, and Württemberg, they could not be appointed to Christian confessional schools. In spite of this prohibition it was done, as a rare exception, for the purpose of caring for minorities. According to Prussian regulations, commissioning of Jewish teachers went from case to case. To an inquiry of the Frankfurt school authorities in 1922, the Prussian ministry definitely stated that Jewish instructors could not be appointed at Simultanschulen that were not attended by Jewish pupils.[30] At Christian Simultanschulen attended by a Jewish minority, however, a few Jewish teachers were often appointed. This was the regular practice in Baden, Hesse, Saxony, Hamburg, Anhalt, and Thuringia. Most Jewish teachers were employed in private schools. A school census of December 4, 1929, in Frankfurt am Main, for example, showed 20 Jewish teachers in public schools, while 52 were in various kinds of private institutions.

In general, Jews under the Republic were given more right to share in supervision of Jewish schools and of Jewish education. In Bavaria Jewish schools had formerly been under school inspectors who were rabbis. These schools were now placed under parent-school committees, which also included the rabbi of the district. Rabbis, as representatives of a religious body, also had the right to institute and control the nature, content and method of Jewish religious instruction. Throughout Germany Jewish representation on local school authorities was the rule if the number of Jewish pupils warranted it. Since most of the schools were set up on a Christian basis, Jews did not achieve the position of state inspectors.

The federal constitution made religion a regular subject for all Jewish schools, public or private. Jewish religious instruction at other schools depended on state law. Here prewar practices were liberalized, and the states now bore more of the cost of instruction. It had formerly been the regular practice to make the synagogue congregation responsible for the religious education of Jewish children. This continued to be the practice in some areas, and was regularly done where the Jewish students constituted only a very small minority. This latter practice was also the rule for small Protestant or Evangelical minorities. In Prussia, if the minority numbered twelve at a public school, the local school authorities had the choice of either providing the instruction or paying an appropriate subsidy to the synagogue which carried on the religious education. In 1923–24 the Prussian state for the first time included in its budget a subsidy for financially weak synagogue congregations. The 1927 budget contained a 400,000 mark subsidy for Jewish religious education, which was administered by central Jewish organizations. This was of course in addition to public aid from municipalities. In Bavaria the state paid the teachers, if the minority was large enough, in the same way as teachers of Christian minorities were treated. Hesse paid the cost if the minority in a school numbered ten, and many municipalities made public funds available for Jewish instruction. In Württemberg the maintenance of religious education was the duty of the Jewish religious group. The state paid a subsidy to the central organization of Jewish congregations and the latter dispensed compensation much as it paid the salaries of rabbis. In Thuringia the state carried the cost for two hours of instruction a week, which was in practice given by officials of the synagogues. It can be safely said that throughout Germany, where the Jewish minority was large enough, public funds—either state or municipal—were contributed to help defray the cost of religious education for Jewish pupils attending public schools.

Aside from various general directives it had been customary for states not to issue curriculum plans for Jewish instruction, for that was left to the synagogues to work out. This practice continued under the Republic, although there was a development in the direction of more state instructions and suggestions. Thus in Prussia in April 1926 the ministry of education submitted to provincial authorities guiding principles for Jewish religious instruction (*Richtlinien für den jüdischen Religionsunterricht*). It provided "that schools, at which Jewish religious instruction was given, were to work out individual plans on the basis of these directives and submit them to provincial authorities. The different confessional beliefs of each congregation were thereby to be taken into consideration." [31] A little later the Prussian Association of Orthodox Synagogue Congregations drew up a suggested teaching plan which the ministry passed on to provincial authorities as a guide for judging the individual teaching plans of the different schools. This was not unlike the Christian religion curriculum, except for the addition of instruction in Hebrew. [32] The Hebrew requirement was one of the reasons why it was difficult to provide Jewish religious instruction at the Volksschulen and why it was often left entirely to the synagogues. On the other hand in those secondary schools where Hebrew was an elective subject, the requirement did much to keep Hebrew a part of the curriculum, which was pleasing to both Catholic and Protestant church authorities, who desired it taught to their candidates for the ministry.

In the matter of examinations, Jewish religious instruction under the Republic came to be placed on a par with Christian instruction. This was of some importance, for it could at times affect a student's all-important general standing, and it also gave official school support to what was often in reality private instruction by synagogue officials. In Prussia, for example, in March 1917 it was decreed that those students who had participated in Jewish religious instruction at higher schools should have their marks noted on their regular school records and also in the important final Abitur examinations. This policy was continued after the Revolution, and in November 1926 a decree ordained that the examination regulation applicable to students who had participated in Christian religious instruction should also be applied to Jewish religious instruction. The teacher who had given regular Jewish religious instruction in the highest classes was to be a member of the final examination committee.[33] Equality in examination and evaluation of grades indicates perhaps as well as anything the relatively equal status which Jewish religious education had achieved before the days of Hitler.

In the last analysis Jewish religious education in the public schools, however, always had to contend with the fact that historically German schools were organized on a Christian basis. As a minority Jews had as favorable and at time even more favorable treatment than many of the small Christian minorities, for the laws did not give the latter special consideration. That Jews should favor Simultanschulen over confessional schools was only natural, for in them their position was generally more nearly equal. Likewise it is easily understandable why many Jews were willing to support a completely secular school system, since religion would thereby be left entirely to the religious bodies, a system under which in the main the Jews had been operating for years. Many Jewish religious leaders, however, like Catholic and Protestant churchmen, eyed with approval their own public confessional schools; for in them they really had an opportunity, if care was taken, to give orthodox instruction. Actually, under the Republic, Jewish education moved many steps forward and achieved a satisfactory position of freedom and equality, considering always that the state undertook to teach denominational religion in its schools, and that Jews constituted a widely scattered minority.

Surveying the period of the Weimar Republic as a whole it can be said that religion continued to exert an important influence over the German school system. There was no radical break in historical development. Old controversies and old efforts at reform continued. There are few issues for which one cannot find parallels in early periods. Nevertheless in the more liberal and democratic atmosphere changes progressed at an accelerated tempo, and in general there was less compulsion connected with religious instruction. Techniques of religious instruction did not stand still, and these too were influenced by changing religious concepts. The general emphasis on equality and the trend towards a more social gospel, which manifested itself in the churches, also found its way into the schools. To many upholders of the "good old religion," this at times verged on blasphemy. The age-old controversy over the orthodoxy of instruction did not disappear under the Republic, and there can be no question that frequently religious instruction was largely ethical and secular in character. On the other hand the old core of the religious curriculum was still being taught, and children continued to come directly under the influence of their pastors, priests, and rabbis through confirmation instruction, which, while apart from the schools, was nevertheless closely integrated with them. Traditional religious values were no doubt being upheld more by the schools than by German society as a whole.

Part Four

The Third Reich, 1933–1945

Chapter X

The EARLY YEARS, 1933–1935

When Hitler became chancellor on January 30, 1933, he took over a German educational system which was still shaped by the particularism of Germany's past history. He had long proclaimed the necessity of establishing a strong united German state, and it was clear that he was bent on a policy of centralization. His policy of *Gleichschaltung*, designed to imbue all German institutions with National Socialist principles and to coordinate everything into a unified whole, was, however, in itself anything but uniform. The new government used one method here, another there. Sometimes a few judicious appointments or a rigged election would be enough to win over important professional organizations; sometimes laws had to be enacted as in the case of the reorganization of state governments; then again in many instances a variety of administrative measures were relied upon. New policies were likely to be inaugurated in different sections of Germany at different times. To attempt a uniform national regulation, Hitler himself said, meant being restricted by the territory which was the least advanced from the National Socialist point of view, while by territorial regulation the administrative heads could proceed step by step according to the degree to which the people of the district were prepared to accept the new political orientation.[1]

This piecemeal practice was followed particularly in dealing with the churches and schools. Hitler was aided by the fact that many measures which he favored in regard to schools had already been accepted in parts of Germany and consequently aroused opposition only in certain sections. Then too some of the measures had long been advocated by certain political parties and even by professional educators. Thus when he undertook to convert all confessional schools into interdenominational schools (Gemeinschaftsschulen) he was undertaking a "reform" which many Germans (notably in socialist and liberal circles, and in professional teachers' groups) had long advocated. In fact he was only establishing what under the Weimar Constitution was intended to be the normative school type.

The scattered references in *Mein Kampf* to religion, particularly if read without benefit of hindsight, did not presage a particularly alarming future for the churches or schools. Summarizing these references a well-informed commentator concludes that "it may appear from such a summary that there was greater justification than has sometimes been realized for those who thought National Socialism and the Christian churches could come to an agreement and could cooperate in the national reconstruction." [2]

Indeed, at first, Hitler's policy seemed to be directed against the liberal secularism of the postwar period. Even the unalterable National Socialist party program adopted in 1920 seemed reassuring to the Christian churches, if not to the Jews. Among other things, Article 24 proclaimed: "The party, as such, stands for positive Christianity, but does not bind itself in the matter of creed to any particular confession." Again in the speech to the Reichstag on March 23, 1933, in which Hitler announced the policy of his government, he continued his conciliatory tactics.

The Government, being resolved to undertake the political and moral purification of our public life, are creating and securing the conditions necessary for a really profound revival of religious life. . . . The National Government regard the two Christian Confessions as the weightiest factors for the maintenance of our nationality. They will respect agreements concluded between them and the federal states. Their rights are not to be infringed. But the Government hope and expect that the work on the national and moral regeneration of our nation which they have made their task will, on the other hand, be treated with the same respect. They will adopt an attitude of objective justice towards all Confessions. But they cannot permit that the fact of belonging to a certain Confession or a certain race should constitute a release from general legal obligations or even a licence for the commission with impunity or the toleration of crimes. *The National Government will allow and secure to the Christian Confessions the influence which is their due both in the school and in education.* It will be the Government's care to maintain honest cooperation between Church and State; the struggle against materialistic views and for a real national community is just as much in the interest of the German nation as in that of the welfare of our Christian faith. The Government of the Reich, who regard Christianity as the unshakable foundation of the morals and moral code of the nation, attach the greatest value to friendly relations with the Holy See and are endeavoring to develop them. [3]

Hitler's statements were naturally well received by the churchmen, and indeed they seemed to be in accord with party action. At this time

National Socialists flocked to church services and many who had left the church rejoined. Not to belong to a church was tantamount to being a Social Democrat or Communist, of which no good Nazi would wish to be suspect. The government had concretely shown its religious orientation by providing on February 25, 1933, for the gradual abolition of the 295 secular schools (Sammelschulen). No new pupils were to be taken in, and, as the classes finished, the schools were to be dissolved and the teachers reassigned according to their present or previous confessional connections.[4] Furthermore the classes in moral or ethical instruction which had been instituted in some elementary schools for those pupils who had been withdrawn from religious instruction were abolished. Another happy augury in the eyes of many was a declaration issued on March 28, 1933, by the Bavarian ministry of education on the religious and national attitude of teachers at the Bavarian schools which proclaimed the motto: "Unsere Religion heisst Christus; Unsere Politik heisst Deutschland."[5] (Our religion is Christ; Our politics is Germany.) Instruction in all schools of Bavaria was to start and end with prayer, and in general religion was to be stressed. Similar ordinances were issued by most of the other state governments. To the churchmen this all seemed a striking contrast to the time of the Revolution of 1918, when many of the new governments started out by taking action against school prayers and the traditional role of religion in the schools. An example of this contrast may be found in the practice in Hamburg, where after 1920 it had been the rule that pupils had to make application for religious instruction. This procedure was reversed in 1933, and all students took religion in the schools unless they specifically applied to be exempted from these classes.

Conclusion of the Concordat

It was in this period that finally a national concordat was concluded with the Vatican. In no country in the world, outside of the purely Catholic countries, did the Catholic church have a better position than under the Weimar Republic in Germany. Catholic private schools, some aided by public funds, were permitted, and the freedom of the monastic orders, who largely staffed such schools, was guaranteed in the constitution. There were Catholic confessional schools, staffed by Catholic teachers and attended by Catholic pupils, which were supported by the state entirely. In all public schools the state provided for Catholic religious instruction if there was a sufficient number of Catholic students. The church also had full freedom to organize youth organizations. All these privileges as well as some additional ones the Vatican was anxious to safeguard in a written agreement.

It was Franz von Papen, Vice Chancellor in Hitler's first cabinet, who was the key person in the negotiation of the Reich concordat. An ardent Catholic, he had become well acquainted with Pacelli, then secretary of state for the Vatican and later Pope Pius XII, while the latter was nuncio at Berlin. During his stay in Germany Cardinal Pacelli had obtained a broad understanding of the situation in Germany, and particularly of the bitter conflict over the proposed national school law. He was still eager to conclude a concordat with the Reich and received favorably the advances made by von Papen on his visit to Rome at Easter time in 1933. An audience was arranged with the Pope, and von Papen writes in his memoirs:

His Holiness welcomed my wife and myself most graciously and remarked how pleased he was that the German Government now had at its head a man uncompromisingly opposed to communism and Russian nihilism in all its forms. Indeed, the atmosphere was so cordial that I was able to settle the details of a draft agreement at a speed quite unusual in Vatican affairs and I was soon on my way back to Berlin.[6]

The draft for a concordat drawn up by Minister Delbrück in 1921 was used as a basis for discussion.

Von Papen found "surprising readiness" on Hitler's part to accept his proposals, and he notes: "This was particularly remarkable as the concordat conceded complete freedom to confessional schools throughout the country. Only those who had lived through the ceaseless struggle to obtain this concession can realize what a victory it represented in the mind of Germany's Catholics." The Vatican appointed the Archbishop of Freiburg, Dr. Groeber, to represent its interests and Hitler authorized von Papen to bypass the normal channels, that is, the German foreign office and the German ambassador to the Holy See. When the more radical elements of the Nazi party heard of the proposed treaty, they tried to stop it. After all there had been no Reich concordat with the papacy since the Reformation, and the events of the past decade showed clearly that the people of the country were opposed to such an agreement. Concessions made in the agreement also in part ran counter to announced National Socialist policy on educational matters. Hitler, however, felt that "his reconstruction plans could only be carried out in an atmosphere of harmony in religious matters." Mussolini also urged the conclusion of the concordat and counselled: "The signing of this agreement with the Vatican will establish the credit of your government abroad for the first time."[7] On July 8 the final text was drafted and on July 20, 1933, it was signed in a formal ceremony in the Papal Secretariat. Under provisions of the Enabling

Act passed by the Reichstag on March 23, 1933, Hitler was empowered to conclude international agreements on matters of Reich jurisdiction without submitting them to parliament for approval. This provision cleared the way for the concordat negotiations, since it meant that the vexed question of types of school would not be referred to the Reichstag. On September 10, 1933, ratifications were exchanged and the concordat went into effect.

The concordat guaranteed to Catholics freedom of worship within Germany and the right of the church to regulate its own affairs. It specifically confirmed and gave new legal sanction to the existing concordats with Bavaria (1924), Prussia (1929), and Baden (1932). Clergy were to be German nationals, must have obtained a graduation certificate (*Reifezeugnis*) from a higher school, and must have studied at least three years at a German university, a German theological seminary, or a papal college in Rome. Bishops were to be appointed only after consultation with state officials and were to take a special loyalty oath, the text of which was laid down in the treaty. Although it was a change in practice for Germany, it was in line with provisions of concordats concluded with other European states when the Vatican agreed to forbid secular and regular clergy to be members of a political party or engage in party activity.[8] Provisions were also made in respect to diocesan organization within Germany, and the right of the church to levy church taxes on its membership was confirmed. All these and other provisions in regard to church affairs were not unique. But the provisions in regard to education constituted an important innovation, for they guaranteed to the Catholic church in all Germany certain educational privileges which it had hitherto exercised in only certain German states.

It was not the articles in regard to the continuance of Catholic faculties at the universities or the erection of theological seminaries which went beyond the provisions of the Weimar Constitution and the more specific regulations of some of the state concordats. Rather it was in regard to the regular school curriculum that the concordat made more definite stipulations than had before existed. Whereas the constitution provided that religious instruction should be part of the regular school curriculum and should be given in harmony with the fundamental principles of the religious association concerned, the concordat states specifically: "The Catholic religious instruction in the elementary schools, middle schools, and higher schools is a regular subject of instruction and will be given in accordance with the fundamental doctrines of the Catholic church." The church then agreed that in "religious instruction the education to patriotic, civic, and social consciousness, grounded in the spirit of Christian doctrinal and ethical law, would be particularly stressed, just as was done in other instruction." Curriculum plans and textbooks for religious instruction were to be decided upon in consultation with church authorities. Church officials also had the right in conjunction with school authorities to determine if the instruction was in accord with the teachings and standards of the church. The latter provisions were important, for they gave the church rights which it was denied in many of the German states.

Catholic teachers of religion were to be appointed only after agreement between the bishop and the state governments. This ended the long controversy whether the religion teachers had to have the *missio canonica* (permission to teach religion classes) from the bishop, a demand that Prussia and most of the other German states had consistently refused to acknowledge. Moreover if a bishop declared a man no longer fit to give religious instruction the state was no longer to employ him for this purpose.

The continuance and new erection of confessional schools was guaranteed. Moreover throughout Germany in municipalities where parents, or those exercising rights over education, petitioned for the erection of a confessional school, the petition was to be granted, if the number of pupils was large enough to establish a school without jeopardizing a well-ordered school system. Von Papen underlines this in his memoirs, saying this was easily the most important provision of the concordat. Catholic forces had tried to get this provision into the Weimar Constitution, and again in the three national school laws which during the twenties failed of enactment in the Reichstag. Now confessional schools could be established in even the old Simultan school lands, and no attention was paid to the second clause of Article 174 of the constitution which was intended to protect these territories from the confessional-school system. At all Catholic confessional schools only teachers who were members of the Catholic church and gave promise of meeting the special requirements of a confessional school were to be appointed. Special provision was to be made for the training of such teachers, which in practice meant teacher-training institutes established along denominational lines.

The concordat further guaranteed the church's right to erect private schools and the right of monastic orders to teach and engage in other charitable activities. These provisions, however, were largely a confirmation of provisions already in the Weimar Constitution.

By the concordat the Catholic church obtained a written safeguard for four great Catholic school principles: (1) the peaceful cooperation of church and state in the school, with the protection of the independence of each, (2) installation and support of religious instruction in the schools, (3) freedom for confessional schools, (4) freedom for Catholic private schools. Schröteler, a Jesuit educational specialist, after analyzing how these four principles were met by the concordat, concludes:

One must therefore say that in the Reich concordat the demands which the church has always made for a blessed giving of religious instruction have been fulfilled, and the church norms have largely been met. Herewith the foundation is laid, that the great and strong powers that are incorporated in the Catholic religion for the good of the individual as for the entire nation can be set to work effectively and without friction. . . . If we in conclusion survey once more all the school provisions of the Reich concordat, one must conclude that the great fundamental demands of the Catholic school-ideal, as it is laid down in canon law and in the education encyclicals, have been fulfilled in their essential points. If these provisions are carried out in the spirit of friendliness and in the will for cooperation out of which the Reich concordat came into being, then one must say with a joyful heart that the concordat has laid the legal foundation for a genuine and lasting school peace in the German *Länder*.[9]

This apparently successful attempt of the church to safeguard its position did not work out as planned, for Hitler did not honor the spirit of the concordat and violated many of its provisions. Yet it did serve a purpose, and Pius XII stated in 1945: "Without the legal protection afforded by the concordat the subsequent persecution of the Church might have taken even more violent forms. The basis of Catholic belief and enough of its institutions had remained intact to permit their survival and resurgence after the war."[10] That the Pope was correct in his views is confirmed by Hitler's later irritation at having made the agreement and his determination to abolish it after the end of the war.[11]

Administrative Reorganization

Under the Weimar Republic national education affairs were administered as a separate bureau under the minister of the interior. The Nazis merged this bureau with the Prussian ministry of education, and on May 1, 1934, established a separate ministry with the imposing title, Reich and Prussian Ministry of Science, Education and Culture (*Reichs- und Preussisches Ministerium für Wissenschaft, Erziehung und Volksbildung*). While this new ministry exercised legislative power for the whole country, in Prussia it had both legislative and executive authority. In the other states the local ministers or departments acted as regional executives of the Reich ministry. Since the Reich ministry did not have its own corps of inspectors, the old system of state and provincial supervision continued to operate at the regional level.[12] Bernhard Rust, who headed the national ministry, thus held a dual office, and it is not always easy to say in examining his various ordinances and statements whether they applied only to Prussia or to the whole Reich. Another practice adds to the difficulty of tracing the shifting educational program. Instead of publishing administrative orders so that every one might ascertain what policy was being followed, time and time again directives were issued with the admonition not to make them public. These orders were then passed on in mimeographed form to various subordinate school authorities. The national, state, or local official journals (*Amtsblätter*), of course, do not carry these decrees, and it is impossible to say with certainty who actually received these secret orders.[13] In addition many directives and interpretations conveyed by telephone never appeared in official publications. On such off-the-record material the dictatorship battened.

It should also be noted that different officials at various administrative levels pursued their duties with varying zeal. Very often regional party officials (*Gauleiter*) pushed a policy which went beyond the views of the central authorities; at times they failed to enforce such action as was demanded. While some officials became overly inquisitive and officious, there were at the same time many who developed an uncanny ability not to see things, as they were unwilling to interfere with traditional practices. Even within the same state governments, different officials followed different policies. For example in Württemberg, where the conflict over religion in the schools became particularly acute, Bishop Wurm, the intrepid head of the Evangelical church, wrote to the national educational ministry in 1939: "The *Reichsstatthalter* would not place any difficulties in the way of the wish of the church in the schools, but the *Kultusminister* is a man of a different stripe."[14]

It was indeed Kultusminister Mergenthaler, enjoying the special protection of Party Leader Bormann, who inaugurated restrictive measures in Württemberg which went much further than any attempted in neighboring Bavaria or Baden. Yet in spite of the great diversity in practice, there is discernible an overall pattern.

After the conclusion of the concordat the government for a time continued its cautious policy towards the churches and the schools. Some restrictive measures against Jews were taken, but these were mild indeed compared to what was to follow. On September 9, 1933, a ministerial decree issued in Berlin forbade the introduction of new school texts in all subjects until the decisions on the school reforms had been reached.[15] This incidentally did not preclude the introduction of new ideas into teaching, for on the previous day a decree had provided that principles of heredity, racial science, racial hygiene, and population policies should be taught in the upper-school classes. This was to be done mostly in biology, but additional time if needed might be taken from mathematics and foreign languages, and racial ideas were also to be stressed in German, history, and geography classes.[16] Significantly, no mention was made of the religion hours, although it was obvious that much of the new ideological material would conflict with the subjects traditionally presented in these classes.

Indeed, concern was manifested about the quality of the religious instruction. Complaints had reached the ministry in Berlin that children, whose parents had been influenced by Marxism, were keeping them from attending religion classes, and consequently these children did not have sufficient background for confirmation instruction. Rust called the attention of the Prussian provincial authorities to this and asked them, if possible, to start special courses or to make other arrangements to remedy this deficiency. No special state funds, however, were made available for this purpose. Likewise by a decree of January 24, 1934, it was ordered that teachers who had withdrawn from the church could not resume religious instruction until a year after rejoining the church. Even then, before receiving final authorization to give religious instruction they would have to undergo a trial period of six months.[17] One of the first decrees issued by Rust as Reichsminister of Education (May 15, 1934) stated that the new national law on holidays did not affect the ordinances of school authoities according to which, by regional custom, there was to be no instruction on religious holidays, even if they were not public holidays. Schools of different confessions might continue their special holidays.[18] This lenient position in regard to observance of special religious holidays by the schools was gradually to be abandoned, and it became one of the controversial issues between the church authorities and the government. As late as the spring of 1935, however, the Reichsminister granted to the Protestant Inner Mission Society and the Catholic Caritas Society permission to take up house-to-house collections and asked instructors of religion in the schools to explain the significance of the fine work of these societies.[19] Within a few months this benevolent policy was to be radically altered.

Chapter XI

NATIONAL SOCIALIST REORGANIZATION of the SCHOOL SYSTEM, 1935–1939

The spring of 1935 found Hitler flexing his muscles. In January the Saar plebiscite had gone in his favor, in March the reintroduction of compulsory military service in Germany brought only protests; and in June he scored a point by concluding a naval agreement with Great Britain. German economy was humming, and the time seemed appropriate to tackle some of the unsolved cultural problems. Göring in a message to district officials on July 8, 1935, sounded the new keynote. The era of friendly gestures was at an end. He blasted the political activity of the Catholic church.

The times in which the will and the might of the state were not sufficient to protect the church from atheistic influences are past. For the church, therefore, all cause disappears for extending its activity beyond the religious realm and for attempting to uphold or renew political influences. It cannot call upon God against this state, a monstrosity which we experience every Sunday in open or concealed ways, nor can it be permitted to organize its own political power under the pretext that it must parry threatening dangers from the state. . . . It has applied those abbreviations which have entered into the flesh and blood of all Germans, like H. J. (*Hitler Jugend*) to the Heart of Jesus (*Herz Jesu*); BDM (*Bund Deutscher Mädel*) to League of Daughters of Mary (*Bund der Marienmädchen*) and applied the German Greeting (*Deutscher Gruss*) to Jesus Christ.[1]

The import of this directive was later stated in the official school journal of the district of Wiesbaden to be:

Fundamentally it is determined that we must demand of the clergy as far as they are in the state service as teachers of religion, that they withhold themselves from every negative action against national socialism not only during their classes but at all times. Like every other state employee they

162

must take a positive attitude and place themselves with their whole personality behind the National Socialist state. Only then can the clergy be entrusted with helping the religious education of the youth.[2]

The ire of the Nazis, after their former sweetness and light, may be attributed largely to the issue of the coordination of Protestant churches in Germany. Hitler had attempted to force on the German Protestant churches a constitution and a Reich bishop who did not have the support of many of the church leaders. The complex character of this struggle, involving Reich Bishop Müller and his German Christian Movement, cannot be discussed here. Suffice it to say that by 1935 it was clear that the original attempt to coordinate the Protestant churches in Germany had failed. On July 19 a new Reich ministry for church affairs was created with Kerrl as its head. An energetic attempt to solve the church question was to be made. At the same time the churches were to be put in their proper place and their influence curtailed. One of the most obvious means of attack was to obstruct the historical cooperation between church and state in educational affairs.

On July 9, and August 19, 1935, Reichsminister Rust issued decrees applicable to public and private schools in all Germany, stating that students at higher and middle schools did not have to attend morning prayers, school services, school masses, or other religious observances either on weekdays or Sundays, whether such services were held in school buildings or in neighboring churches.[3] This did not abolish these services but made them voluntary and forbade a school to use any compulsion in regard to them. It was now the task of the parents and church to see that children attended these services. An official explanation of the law pointed out that this met an often-made request of parents to determine themselves what service their children should attend and to take their children with them to church. It was also true that it gave them an opportunity to take their children with them on an excursion without having them marked absent from such services by school authorities. It should be noted that this decree did not apply to elementary schools.

Gradually in both higher and elementary schools morning exercises of a secular character began to replace the traditional prayers. As the Gemeinschaftsschule came to replace the confessional school, the authorities also took steps to see that services were purged of their purely confessional aspects. This meant of course elimination of such things as supplications to saints and the Virgin Mary, and at times even the abolition of the Lord's Prayer, since Protestants and Catholics customarily used different versions of it. Likewise the Catholic practice of crossing oneself and the Protestant custom of folding hands in prayer were in places forbidden.[4] There were great variations among the states and in the various communities of Germany. In some the opening and closing prayers were abandoned in practice if not by governmental decree, in others they lost their religious nature and became patriotic manifestations, while in other cases they remained much as they had always been. Distinction should also be made between the opening and closing prayers and special school-church services. Thus in Bavaria the former were not touched, but in 1938 the school authorities decreed that the arranging of church services was a duty of the churches and that in the future no church services were to be arranged by the schools.[5] A national decree in 1939 stated that as school-church services in the sense of the decree of July 9, 1935, had been abolished, any existing agreements with the churches were to be done away with.[6]

A secret agreement of a later date, which Minister Rust sent to the district presidents on April 21, 1941, summarizes the situation very well and is worth quoting.

In re: School Prayers and School Meditations (*Andachten*).

In the schools, particularly in the Volksschulen, the old custom remains in part that before the beginning and after the close of instruction a prayer is spoken. This custom rests in its historical origin on the ties between school and church that today are a thing of the past. The National Socialist school, out of the experiences of the national community, will find new forms for the spiritual strengthening of the work of the school. In the exchange of the German greeting and a meditation on a word of the Führer there are possibilities that are more in accord with the present life of the school than the traditional prayer. In the transition from the earlier traditional practice to the new form, consideration must nevertheless be given to the opinion of the local population. I therefore desist at present from issuing generally binding regulations. The fundamental principle of freedom of conscience, demands, however, that in classes attended by members of different confessions or philosophical associations (*Weltanschauungsgemeinschaften*) no prayer with a confessional content is to be used.

The customary meditations at higher schools have to a large extent been freed from the traditional church meditations. Here also at present I refrain from issuing definite regulations in order to further the development of more timely forms. I expect nevertheless that the morning meditations will no longer be held along confessional lines, but that they will be given a form in accordance with the education goals of national socialism.

I ask you to inform the schools of this in an appropriate manner. This ordinance is not to be made public.[7]

Another matter closely related to school prayers and religious services was the elimination of the cross from schoolrooms which was noted as early as October 1935 in some localities.[8] The Nazi antireligion campaign, however, really got under way with a decree in Oldenburg on November 4, 1936. This decree began by stating that public buildings, including schools, belonged to all the people and were not to be dedicated or blessed by religious services. Furthermore, as in other public buildings, schools were not to be adorned by crucifixes or pictures of Luther. Such religious symbols were to be removed. This led to energetic protests by parents in some localities, and often the cross remained in the schoolroom. The attempt to "remove the cross" spread to other regions, Westphalia, Rhenish Palatinate, and finally in 1941 came an active campaign in Bavaria. Here again there was no clean sweep, and in many places the crucifix remained in the schools, although the party and government officials frowned on the practice.[9]

The first of a series of restrictions on the giving of examinations and marks in religion was also begun at this time. Even under the Empire religion was not always an examination subject for the final examinations at the higher schools. Reichsminister Rust on September 24, 1935, abolished the compulsory written examinations at higher schools for men, and on October 22 this was extended to schools for women.[10] Since the decree also applied to teachers' academies it indirectly had an effect on the future supply of teachers of religion. This measure concerned Bavaria particularly, for here the examination in religion had maintained itself longer than in most of the other states. In the official report on religious instruction at higher schools of the Bavarian Church for 1935–36 it was stated that the omission of the final examination (*Reifeprüfung*) was welcomed by many teachers, since they could have more discussion with their students and did not have to spend so much time in preparing for examinations. Others objected, for they thought it would lead to a decline in the prestige of religion classes.[11]

The year 1935 also brought the start of two major school campaigns which were to extend over the following years. One was designed to curtail the use of clergy in the schools; the second aimed at the elimination of private schools and the conversion of all public schools into Gemeinschaftsschulen. Confessional schools were to be abolished.

Curtailment of Clerical Instruction in the Schools

The employment of clergy to give religious instruction in the schools was not alike in the various sections of Germany, the practice being most prevalent in the south. Clergy giving such instruction were, in their capacity as teachers, employees of the state and had to abide by the general laws applicable to civil servants. Thus, for example, in accord with the law on the reorganization of the civil service, the Protestant, Catholic, and Jewish clergy who gave instruction in the Frankfurt school system had to sign the following statement in the summer of 1933: "I declare herewith in accordance with regulations that I have not publicly made any statements either orally or in writing against National Socialism and its Führer." [12] Such general declarations had, however, to be signed by all teachers and so were not discriminatory.

In September 1935 the district presidents in Prussia ordered the heads of various schools to observe if the clergy teaching in the schools were supporting the Hitler Youth Organization in proper fashion. Above all they were not to recruit members for church organizations in their classes. [13] Clergy who were not showing the proper enthusiasm were to be reported, and the district president would decide if they were to be dismissed. Neither the procedure for granting permission to clergy to give instruction nor the procedure for withdrawal of such permission had ever been carefully defined. This was now done, and by November 1935 things had moved so far that every clergyman who wanted permission to give religious instruction for the first time, or was to assume a new post, had to receive the approval to teach from the district president. This meant filling out forms for himself, and if married for his wife, which gave, among numerous other details, their racial background. Permission was not to be granted unless the clergyman was willing "to put his whole personality behind the National Socialist state." School authorities were cautioned to watch the activity of the clergy who were giving instruction, and characteristically they were warned that this directive "was not to be published in whole or in part in the press." [14]

Complaints soon came in from church authorities that permission to give instruction was being delayed. Also apparently too much hearsay evidence was being transmitted to the district president, who sent out an order that if the right to teach religion was to be withdrawn he would have to be presented with concrete evidence. [15] Later a simple statement by a Gauleiter that a man was not reliable was considered sufficient evidence.

In a secret ordinance of October 7, 1935, circulated by Rust to district administrative officials in Prussia, the general policy was laid down that in all schools the regular religious instruction was to be given if possible by teachers who had qualified by passing the prescribed examinations. Clerics were to be entrusted with instruction only to the extent that qualified lay personnel was not available.[16] The implementation of this order took some time. A check was now made on how many clergy were actually giving instruction in the schools. Thus, in a report to district headquarters by the Frankfurt Schulamt on April 18, 1936, it was disclosed that 13 Protestant clergy were giving instruction at 13 schools, and 31 Catholic clergy at 26 schools. On June 25, 1936, the Reichsminister ordered that all clergy who were engaged in working with any confessional youth organization were no longer to be permitted to teach.[17] This eliminated a considerable number of Catholic clergy as they, on the order of their bishops (relying on provisions of the Concordat of 1933), refused to give up their duties with the confessional youth organizations. Parents, to the irritation of officials, were informed by the clergy why they were being displaced at the school, but the practice went on.

On March 18, 1937, Reichsminister Rust, in accordance with the general law on payment of salaries (*Angestelltentarifvertrag*), ordered that all persons permanently employed at the schools had to take the following oath to the Führer. "I swear that I will be true and obedient to the Führer of the German Reich and Nation, Adolf Hitler, and will fulfill my official duties conscientiously and selflessly." Others who did not hold salaried positions but, like many clerics, had certain duties in the schools, had to promise and affirm with handclasp: "I pledge myself to fulfill my official duties conscientiously and selflessly, and to obey the laws and ordinances of the National Socialist state."[18] Various interpretations were given to the oath, and in most cases (outside of Württemberg) the taking of this oath of loyalty to the state caused no particular difficulty.

But the net gradually tightened around the clergy teaching in the schools. On July 7, 1937, Rust confirmed his previous ordinance with a decree that religious instruction was, if possible, to be given only by lay instructors. School authorities were to report to him by November 1 on the possibility of replacing all clergy in the schools of Prussia.[19] Again no uniform regulations were issued, but in Frankfurt for example, after November 1, 1937, clergy ceased to give religious instruction in the Frankfurt school system. This left the clergy only the right of visitation, and immediately they began to make more use of this old custom.[20] It was not long, however, before the state began to restrict this privilege as well.

While the clergy in Prussia had to receive the approval of the district president to give religious instruction as early as 1935–36, it was not until 1938 that this practice was established in Bavaria. Here it was incorporated in a new law on school supervision, which was published, and there was no secrecy about the requirement. The clerical applicant had to submit the usual papers on qualifications and ancestry, but there were significant differences from the procedure in Prussia. Whereas in Prussia the church authorities were not consulted, the Bavarian law provided in Article 44 that:

III. School authorities examine the papers and submit them to the district president. He determines if there are considerations which weigh against granting the applicant permission to teach, consults with the higher church authorities, and then makes the decision.

IV. Before a negative decision is made the applicant is to be heard. Reasons are to be given for such a decision and a copy is to be sent to the higher church authorities, to the other district presidents and to the minister of education and religion. Permission to teach can be denied for a limited period.[21]

All clergy who had been teaching in the school were to be permitted to continue to teach, although they had to submit their papers before January 1, 1939.

Under this more circumscribed procedure the clergy fared much better. Out of about 1,200 active Protestant clergy in Bavaria only 98 had the right to teach taken away.[22] This power was at times used as a form of punishment, as for instance in the case of a certain minister who was not permitted to teach religion in the school for a year, because he had held church services on Ascension Day when this was forbidden by the government (1941).[23] At the end of the year the authorities were only too glad to permit this courageous soul to resume his teaching duties, as in the interim other ministers from neighboring villages had at great inconvenience and cost been obliged to take over his teaching load. Secular Catholic clergy were of course under the same restrictions as Protestants, but most of them too were able to continue their duties in Bavaria. In fact, the teaching burden placed on the Catholic secular clergy increased with the elimination from the schools of Bavaria of teachers belonging to monastic orders. Between January 1, 1937, and the middle of 1938, 1,200 of the 1,676 Catholic sisters teaching in the public schools of Bavaria were dismissed. The work of others in kindergartens, children's rest homes and similar institutions, was curtailed. In addition the government began to close many of the private schools run by monastic orders and so further decreased clerical influence on education.[24]

The campaign against Protestant ministers and Catholic secular clergy was not particularly severe in Baden, but what it lacked in intensity there and in Bavaria was made up for in Württemberg. Here over 700 out of the some 1,200 active Protestant clergy were deprived of the privilege of teaching in the schools, mostly because they refused to take the oath to the Führer. In this state Kultusminister Mergenthaler was an ardent Nazi, who had made several pronouncements to the effect that racial questions should be stressed in religion classes, and some sections of the Old Testament eliminated.[25] The church officials had protested and in a statement to authorities in Berlin made certain clarifications and interpretations in regard to the oath. With these observations made, the heads of the church advised the clergy to take the oath, asking them to make special reservations in regard to freedom to teach Old Testament material. Mergenthaler, however, advised the school authorities that there would be no restrictions or reservations to an oath. It thus became a matter for local officials to decide whether they wished to take cognizance of the statements made by the church authorities as reservations, or whether they were willing to accept the oath or affirmation made by the individual minister. This whole conflict coincided with an attempt by Mergenthaler to substitute secular ethical instruction for the traditional religion classes.

Since traditionally clergy gave much of the religious instruction in the Württemberg schools, the regular religious instruction there was subjected to real curtailment. The Reich ministry in Berlin expressed its regrets to the Württemberg church authorities that these unwished-for conditions had arisen but declared that they were unable to do anything about it![26] Here as in other parts of Germany the pastors started to organize instruction groups in the churches and to extend the period of confirmation instruction from one to two years. As the pastors were eliminated from the schools, the regular religion classes, which still had to be held, frequently became nothing more than classes in National Socialist ideology. However, this was by no means always the case, and often instruction continued in traditional fashion. Even in Württemberg, where the situation was acute, the churches undertook a campaign not to have the parents withdraw their children from religion classes, which indicates that not all was lost to the new order.

Resignation of Lay Teachers as Instructors of Religion

While the government carried on its campaign to turn over all religious instruction in the schools to lay teachers, it was caught in its own crossfire, for it was not as yet ready to abolish such classes entirely. On June 26, 1936, Rust issued an ordinance based on a general Nazi decree of October 13, 1933, which stated that no National Socialist should be penalized in any way because of his religious belief. This was, of course, actually nothing but a reaffirmation of a fundamental right proclaimed by the Weimar Constitution. As before, no pupil or teacher was to be forced to take part in religious services. But as the campaign to coordinate the churches ran into difficulty, and it no longer was a mark of good party standing to take part in church affairs, teachers began to express their unwillingness to continue to give religious instruction. This movement was countenanced by many Nazi authorities and was directly encouraged by the National Socialist Teachers' Organization. In East Prussia this organization was particularly active and in printed declarations chided teachers who continued to give religious instruction with lack of loyalty to the Führer. In the beginning of November 1938, as an aftermath of the assassination of a German diplomat by a Polish Jew in the German embassy in Paris, the teachers' organization promoted a wave of resignations from religious instruction. This was done on the theory that teachers now no longer could be expected to teach the Bible, that "Book of the Jews." As a result of this mass exodus from religious instruction Minister Rust on November 17, 1938, issued an ordinance which stated:

According to my ordinance of June 26, 1936, it is left to the conscience of every teacher if he wants to give instruction in religion, or if he wishes to declare that he is unable to do so. Because of the fundamental principle of freedom of conscience it follows that no disadvantage can result either from giving or relinquishing religious instruction.[27]

Church authorities, while recognizing Rust's more moderate position, protested against the action of the teachers and called upon the national ministry for church affairs to stop the wholesale voluntary withdrawal from religious instruction. Whether it was a result of this protest or not, Reichsminister Rust took a further step to halt the withdrawals. On December 7, 1938, he issued another statement:

By my ordinance of July 1, 1937, I decreed that the regular religious instruction in the schools should as a rule be given by lay teachers. For the National Socialist teacher who on the basis of this ordinance has declared himself ready to give religious instruction, there can be no fear that anything will be demanded of him in giving religious instruction, especially in the presentation of Judaism, which is contrary to the fundamentals of National Socialism. Relinquishment of religious instruction by a teacher is consequently, as far as National Socialism is concerned, only justified when actually serious conscientious objections exist in line with my ordinance of June 26, 1936.

In numerous recent declarations relinquishing religious instruction, as I gather from recent reports which have come to me, reasons were many times advanced which are not in line with this position. I ask therefore that a copy of this ordinance be communicated to all teachers. Teachers, who since November 1, 1938, have made such declarations of relinquishment, are to be asked to consider them in view of the above fundamental principles and to deliver to the proper school authorities a new binding declaration.

By January 15, 1939, it is to be reported to me when and if any difficulties have been made manifest in the giving of religious instruction. I reserve announcement of curriculum directives for religious instruction. This ordinance is being issued in consultation with the Führer's deputy. It is not to be published.[28]

For all ardent Nazi teachers to give up religious instruction was not in the over-all interest of the party, which was not as yet ready to ban religion classes from the schools, but merely sought to control them. Then, too, in many sections of Germany, as the teachers refused to teach religion, the clergy stepped into the breach and took over the classes, particularly in Bavaria and Baden. This, of course, laid a tremendous additional burden on the clergy and necessitated consolidation of classes.[29] While the orthodoxy and perhaps even the quality of instruction may have been strengthened, nothing like as systematic training as heretofore could be given under these conditions. More and more was left to confirmation instruction, and this was greatly expanded throughout Germany.

There were other indirect results from this withdrawal of lay teachers from religion classes. No longer were these teachers expected to lead school prayers and meditations, and often these religious observances disappeared completely from the schools. Giving up religious instruction by lay teachers also helped to break up the remaining joint school and church positions to be found in many regions. The National Socialists were intent on completing this process and on September 7, 1938, a Prussian law provided that as of October 1, 1938, all such school and church positions were to be considered as separated.[30] Provision was made to compensate for the various payments in kind which teachers had formerly received because of their church duties. There is, however, a reverse side to this picture. In practice the existence of joint school and church positions often tended to make teachers loath to withdraw from religious instruction lest such withdrawal jeopardize the receipt of extra compensation for performing various church duties. Certainly all the dispute and uncertainty about the teaching of the regular religion classes in the schools did impair friendly relations between the local clergy and the school teachers.

Further Curtailment of Old Practices

There were other pinpricks, all designed to lessen the influence of the clergy over religious education. Under an ordinance of 1929, school

authorities in Prussia at the beginning of each school year informed
the proper church authorities of the names of pupils who could not be
supplied with regular classroom instruction in religion. These were
usually scattered members of religious minorities, attending confessional schools in predominantly Catholic or Protestant regions. Customarily the churches arranged to supply instruction for these pupils
in one fashion or another. On February 14, 1938, this practice was
stopped, and the list of names was not to be sent to the church authorities. Here again it was specifically stated that the ordinance was not
to be published in the official journal of the ministry.[31]

At this time, too, the state took steps to cut down on the number
of religious holidays. Reformation Day, All Souls' Day, and Corpus
Christi Day (except in some predominantly Catholic regions) were no
longer legally recognized, and teachers and pupils were not given time
off to attend church services. Group participation of schools or classes
in religious processions was forbidden by an ordinance of October 26,
1938. Privately, teachers and pupils could take part, but in order to
make sure that there would be no sign of school participation, teachers
were specifically warned not to supervise children or youth groups on
such occasions. This measure hit the Catholic church most directly and
particularly affected the traditional Corpus Christi Day processions. In
Frankfurt, for example, authorities in 1939 refused to permit Catholics
to erect procession altars on Corpus Christi Day in the portals of certain
schools as had hitherto been the custom.

Measures were also introduced to facilitate the withdrawal of
students from religious instruction. Henceforth a simple notification
to the head of the school would suffice. By a decree of January 18, 1939,
Minister Rust ordered that pupils withdrawing from religious instruction should be excused at once, and not be forced to wait until the end
of the term. The following April, instructions were issued that henceforth religion classes should be held during the first or last period (so-
called *Eckstunden*) of the morning, so that pupils not taking religion
could be excused from school during this period.[32] This of course eased
a problem of school administration, but at the same time was an
attraction calculated to appeal to pupils. Now, as in earlier times, the
churches did not like this arrangement, and indeed it often proved
inconvenient for those members of the clergy who still gave this
instruction.

The Campaign against Confessional Schools

A principle of the Weimar Constitution, which had been reinforced
by the Concordat of 1933, was the right of parents to determine the

type of school their children were to attend. The National Socialist state was supposed at first to be in favor of confessional schools. As late as 1935, Reich Education Minister Rust declared at a party rally in Kurmark, "We have agreed in a concordat to confessional schools. What we have promised we keep."[33] In spite of these promises, in 1935–36, the Nazis aggressively set about persuading parents to demand the Gemeinschaftsschule.[34] All the arguments for this type of school that had been advanced in Germany for years were now brought out in full force. A new organization, the *Deutsche Schulgemeinde*, was formed to support the battle against the confessional schools. A placard, which this organization distributed in 1936 at the time of school enrollment in Munich, illustrates well the standard arguments.

> Why the *Deutsche Gemeinschaftsschule*?

because	the purpose of the national life, the maintenance of the nation and the development of a community and unitary mentality can be achieved through it
because	it brings about common interest also in the field of education
because	as a Christian school it provides for separate religious instruction for the two confessions, but does not tolerate in other subjects of instruction a separation according to confessional points of view
because	it makes possible a well-integrated school system and thereby promises to provide the best educational and instructional results
because	it will avoid having a large number of pupils in many classes
because	it will make it possible for a child to attend the closest school
because	the construction of new school buildings can only be undertaken for *Gemeinschaftsschulen*

> Therefore German Parents the slogan on February 2, 1936 is: *Deutsche Gemeinschaftsschule*
>
> *Deutsche Schulgemeinde*[35]

The proponents of the new order always emphasized that a shift away from confessional schools did not mean the end of religion in the schools, for religion was to remain a regular part of the curriculum. Much emphasis was also laid on the argument that schools should serve to unite Germans and no longer separate the children according to confessions. In fact, the term "German School" (*Deutsche Schule*) was often used instead of "Gemeinschaftsschule" in persuading parents to desert the traditional confessional schools. When parents enrolled their children for the first time they had to designate the type of school desired. In Munich in February 1935, only 64 percent of the pupils were enrolled for confessional schools instead of the usual 84 percent.[36] This showed clearly in what direction the wind was blowing.

Everywhere the school authorities began "to consult parents" as to what type of school they wanted. Pressure was exerted in many ways. People were coerced into signing petitions through fear of losing jobs. Political pressure was brought, and one of the most telling arguments was: "The Führer wants the Gemeinschaftsschule! He who is against the Gemeinschaftsschule is against the Führer and therefore an enemy of the state."[37] Election results were doctored, and all too often the consultation of parents was pure farce. In Würzburg, for example, not just the persons legally entitled to give a decision on the education of pupils were consulted, but large mass meetings of the whole citizenry were held. Speeches lasted until 12:30 A.M., and then the presiding officer announced: "In the name of this assembly I address to the Bürgermeister the request that the Gemeinschaftsschule be instituted in Würzburg. In approval of this we will all arise and call 'Sieg Heil dem Führer.'"[38] The ever-present band immediately struck up a loud march, which drowned out the voices of any who might have wished to protest the proceedings.

After 1938 the official journal of the Reich ministry of education no longer carried the statistics on school types. The following summary tells the story of the beginning of this campaign, which in the end eliminated all confessional elementary schools from Germany.[39]

Type of School	1936	1937	1938
Interconfessional	8,766	12,441	17,150
Evangelical confessional	28,308	26,204	24,261
Catholic confessional	15,231	13,025	9,639
Jewish confessional	65	69	68

Both Protestant and Catholic church circles in the traditional confessional-school states were much disturbed by the elimination of the confessional school. They considered it an attack on the Christian basis of the German school system, and the faithful were admonished "not to let them take away your Christian schools." To the Catholics the abolition of confessional schools was not only contrary to the Concordat of 1933 but was a direct violation of canon law. Canon 1374 states:

Catholic children are not allowed to attend non-Catholic, neutral, or mixed schools. It is the province of the bishop of the diocese alone, in accordance with the direction of the apostolic chair, to determine under what circumstances and through the application of what safeguards for the avoidance of danger to faith, attendance at such schools can be permitted.

That this canon is a clear prohibition of attendance at non-Catholic schools is confirmed by an examination of the precise prescriptions under which exceptions to the rule may be permitted.[40] That there has, however, been a liberal interpretation of the canon in practice is manifest from the history of education in Germany, France, and above all in the United States. Yet in his famous educational encyclical "Divini illius Magistri" of December 31, 1929, Pope Pius XI reaffirmed this canon and in explanation of the forbidden school types added:

To these belong all schools that without differentiation are equally open to Catholics and non-Catholics. Attendance at such schools can at best be tolerated, and it is the province of the bishop alone to decide if, out of consideration for special local and current conditions and with the observance of certain precautionary measures, this toleration is in order. For Catholics such a mixed school is not permitted (even if it is the only school, and attendance is generally prescribed) wherein, to be sure, separate religious instruction is given, but all other subjects are taught by non-Catholic teachers for all students together, Catholic and non-Catholic.

The Nazi-sponsored campaign for Gemeinschaftsschulen not only violated these specific provisions of canon law and the encyclical of 1929, but also ran counter to other provisions of Catholic law and teaching which outlined the Catholic school ideal. It was fundamental that the whole educational process should be imbued with Catholic spirit. In this connection the statement of Pope Leo XIII is frequently quoted: "It is not only necessary that children are given religious instruction in certain definite hours, but all the other instruction must be inspired with the breath of religious Christian spirit."[41]

That many Germans considered the interdenominational school just as Christian as a confessional school naturally weakened the force of the argument for the continuance of confessional schools. Yet the church authorities quite rightly feared for the future and recognized that the whole movement for the Gemeinschaftsschule was an effort to lessen and eventually to eliminate the influence of the church on education. That the way the government conducted the campaign against confessional schools was contrary to agreements with the churches is clear, although the Nazis had a technical way of making everything appear legal. Actually in many places the change in school form brought no radical departures, for in solidly Catholic or Protestant sections the schools continued to be staffed as before. In cities where populations were more mixed it did lead to some reorganization. No longer did a child have to pass by a school of an opposite confession and walk blocks further to reach his own confessional school. The Nazis also took care to see that at the interdenominational schools, both on the elementary and higher levels, Catholics and Protestants were actually interspersed. The old practice of grouping Protestant and Catholic pupils into separate classes, which had prevailed in many so-called interdenominational schools "because of scheduling difficulties," was stopped. This change from a confessional to an interconfessional type of school did not eliminate religious instruction; regular hours for religion continued to be an integral part of the school curriculum.

Liquidation of Private Schools

While the campaign was under way to organize all public schools as Gemeinschaftsschulen, the Nazi officials began the process of liquidating the private schools. On December 28, 1936, Reichsminister Rust ordered the provincial authorities of Prussia (and asked authorities in the other states as well) to examine all private schools. As a rule they were to be permitted only when they served a special purpose. Since private schools in Germany always needed the approval of the government, here was an opening, and it was a relatively simple matter to discover a pretext for withholding this approval. This "examination" of private schools continued into the following years. On April 6, 1939, Rust ordered that the directors of all those higher schools that remained must belong to the *Reichsgemeinschaft der deutschen Privatschulen*. At the same time the states were called upon to report how many such private schools there would be on April 1, 1940.[42]

As the Catholics had the best developed private-school system, they were the hardest hit by these measures. Three private girls' schools were closed in Württemberg by Kultusminister Mergenthaler, and an appeal was made to the courts. The schools pleaded that the action of the minister was contrary to the Concordat of 1933, but the court ruled against them, maintaining that National Socialist law permitted private schools only in those places at which public schools of a similar nature with adequate facilities were not available. Such facilities were available in this instance. The Catholic church had only the same rights as others to have private schools, and therefore the closing of the schools was not contrary to the concordat.[43] In 1937, children of civil-servant officials in Bavaria were forbidden to attend monastic schools, and soon measures were taken to close many of these institutions. The movement gathered momentum until, in the spring of 1938, the Bavarian education ministry ordered the closing or gradual elimination of 84 monastic schools, 64 run by nuns and 20 by male orders. Among the institutions closed were some which were designated primarily for the education of future priests.

The closing of monastic schools was paralleled by the elimination of members of religious orders as teachers in the public schools. Concurrently a general campaign of defamation of Catholic orders was under way. A few isolated cases of moral dereliction on the part of monks in private schools were discovered. At the same time charges were brought against a few clergy and nuns for attempts to smuggle currency out of the country. Some of the Nazi charges were probably true, but they were blown up beyond all reason in a violent propaganda campaign.[44]

The various attacks on monastic orders did much to center attention on the persecution of the Catholic church in the Third Reich. Other churches and associations were also subjected to the attack on private schools, but were affected less because they did not have monastic orders or an extensive private-school system. In Württemberg the seizure of four old private schools (1941) which served primarily as preparatory institutions for Protestant ministers aroused much opposition. At first the establishment of private Jewish schools was encouraged as a means of taking the Jewish pupils out of the public schools, but these were all destroyed in the holocaust of the final years of the regime.

Special National Socialist Schools

Private schools were never completely eliminated, for those schools which served very special purposes (notably for the physically handicapped) were permitted to continue.[45] The Nazis even established private schools of their own. In 1933 they began to set up special *Nationalpolitische Erziehungsanstalten* (NPEA or *Napola*), which were boarding schools designed to educate a future reservoir of good National Socialists. These schools were directly under the minister of education and in the Greater Germany of 1943 there were 37 of them, including three for girls. Their curriculum approximated that of the German *Oberschule*, with, however, more emphasis on sports and physical training. Religion in the beginning was even a formal part of the curriculum, although it was obviously permeated with National Socialist ideas. Yet the radical German Faith Movement, which turned completely away from Christianity, remained outside the school system, and the students were still prepared for confirmation, which was held in the school chapel. This was followed by a party ceremony at which the students were promoted to the upper division of the school.[46]

In 1937 the so-called Adolf Hitler schools were started as special training institutions for the future governing elite. There were ten of these in 1943, and the expectation was that there should be one in each *Gau* (district). Above these were to be established student communities to be known as *Ordensburgen* and finally a party university (*Hohe Schule der Partei*). These higher echelons of the party's private-school system were never actually realized.[47]

Higher Schools

In this period when, by a variety of measures on various fronts, the Nazis were pushing their basic policy of establishing a uniform German elementary-school system that would be entirely under their domination, they enacted important legislation affecting secondary education. For years there had been debate on the organization of German secondary education. The strangle-hold of the Gymnasium had been challenged during the reign of William II. Under the Republic new secondary-school types had been introduced but it had never been possible to enact general legislation such as reformers had long advocated. The field was more than ready to be mowed when the Nazis moved in. The German school system was in need of simplification and greater unity. By a decree of March 20, 1937, the eight main types of secondary schools were reduced to three. The chief type was to be the eight-year Oberschule, branching off in the upper grades into a science–mathematics line (home economics line in girls' schools), and a language line in the last three years. The old Gymnasiums were permitted in limited numbers, although their curriculum was now standardized at eight instead of nine years for the whole Reich. Both the Oberschule and Gymnasium were built upon the universal four-year foundation school. The third general type of secondary school was to be a six-year *Aufbauschule* based on six years of elementary school. These were to be located primarily in rural areas, and were designed to give rural children the opportunity to prepare for university study. It was difficult for pupils to change from one type of school to another, once the choice had been made.[48]

In all the secondary schools religion remained a regular part of the curriculum although the hours were curtailed. Practice had varied in different sections of Germany under the Republic but it had usually been two hours a week in all years. This was now reduced to one hour a week in the last four years. This curtailment led to protests by church leaders, but in comparison to other issues with which they were faced this was a minor restriction.

Chapter XII

The WAR YEARS, 1939–1945

The outbreak of World War II on September 1, 1939, brought at least a partial truce in the state's conflict with the churches. This was only natural with the inevitable emphasis on national unity which a war brings. Amnesties were granted to many pastors and pending prosecutions were forgotten.[1] Foreign Minister Ribbentrop even had a friendly interview with the Pope in March 1940, although he refused to be drawn into a discussion on the problem of confessional schools in Germany. A month later Hitler himself went out of the way to thank the Catholic Archbishop of Breslau, Cardinal Dr. Bertram, who, as chairman of the Fulda Bishops' Conference, had sent birthday greetings and assurances of loyalty from the Catholics of Germany to the present state and its government. On July 24, 1940, the minister of the interior notified all the higher administrative officials that Hitler wanted, so far as possible, all measures avoided that might disturb the relationship of the state and party to the churches.[2]

It was, however, soon evident that the party and government had not changed their basic position on church and school affairs. Inaugurated policies were not rescinded, and under the guise of emergency war measures the policy of restricting the influence of the churches on education was to be furthered.

Shortage of Teachers

One of the most immediate effects of the war was the calling to the colors of many teachers. This was the more marked because of the great predominance of male teachers in the grade schools; in 1938 there were 131,229 men as compared to 47,981 women full-time teachers in the public elementary schools.[3] Substitutes were not always available, and instruction in almost every subject at times had to be curtailed. It was perhaps inevitable that school administrators would do their best to keep "reading, writing, and arithmetic" going, but all too often religion was considered an expendable subject. This did not always meet with governmental approval, as is indicated by the following order of a district official in Wiesbaden on March 11, 1940.

From a report which is before me, I see that instruction in religion has been entirely discontinued at some schools for a period of weeks. Such conditions cannot be continued and do not meet with my approval.

Curtailment of instruction made necessary by the mobilization of teachers must be extended in equal fashion to all subjects and of course also to religion. A complete cancellation of religious instruction under these conditions nevertheless is not permissible. If in the future religion classes must be omitted because of the sudden drafting of a teacher, I request you to provide as soon as possible for a regular substitute.[4]

No doubt all district officials were not as solicitous as this one in regard to keeping the religion classes going, but everywhere religion was maintained officially as part of the curriculum. Local conditions, and particularly the interest of district officials, were the deciding factors. The hours of religious instruction were apparently cut most radically in Saxony, and in general were curtailed more in North and East Germany than in the South.

In those sections of Germany where ministers still gave religious instruction in the schools, they shouldered an ever-increasing teaching load. This resulted not only from the shortage of available lay teachers of religion, but also because many of the clergy were called to the service.

The impact of mobilization on the church can be illustrated by citing the situation in Württemberg, where, out of 1,253 Protestant ministers, 759 were called to the service, usually as regular combat soldiers. These were mostly young men, of course, and the preaching and teaching load carried by the older men who remained was a heavy tax on their strength. Church authorities were concerned with the problem and issued instructions as to how ministers could unite classes and where to cut instruction, since there simply was not enough time to go around.[5]

Such mobilization of the clergy cast its shadow on the postwar years, for, out of 759 ministers called to the colors in Württemberg alone, 184 were killed, 35 were officially reported as missing, and 20 were still missing without any official word as of February 19, 1949. In addition 130 theological students were killed and 27 were among the missing.

Often religious instruction, particularly in the lower grades in the larger schools, was given by women teachers. These classes went on

much as usual during the war. Through its policy of insisting that
Catholic lay teachers receive the *missio canonica*, the Catholic church
had a direct tie with lay teachers which the Protestant churches did
not have. No figures are available but it would seem to be a safe
generalization that proportionately more Protestant than Catholic lay
teachers withdrew from giving religious instruction.

Training of teachers in teachers' institutes was also curtailed.
After 1939, when teaching posts in religion became vacant, no re-
appointments were made, and in the teacher-training institutions
opened after 1941 there was no opportunity to prepare for teaching
religion.[6]

A matter closely related to teaching personnel was the right of
church authorities to visit the classes in religion. In the Frankfurt school
system, for example, the Protestant church officials had long given up
this practice. Catholic officials had, however, continued to visit, and
when the clergy were denied the right to teach in the schools, the
Catholic authorities began inspecting more frequently. On January 13,
1942, district officials in a very secret ordinance laid down new procedures for such visitations. Only the dean (*Dekan*), not his representative, could visit classes. Proper notification had to be given school
officials, and the visit was to be in the presence of a school official who,
as representative of the National Socialist state, was entitled to pre-
cedence. Further, all deans had to obtain new credentials. If he was
involved in giving additional religion classes in the parish his credentials
were automatically not to be approved. This held also if he was unable
to receive clearance from the district party officials in respect to his
political attitudes. Thus Dr. Jakob Herr, the Catholic head of the
Frankfurt Catholic parishes, after having served for 23 years as a
regular visitor of schools, was in 1942 denied the right to do so. In spite
of his repeated requests he was never informed of the ground of his
dismissal. The archives show, however, that the local Gauleiter had
found it impossible to say that the prelate was positively oriented
towards the National Socialist state. Here at least the Gauleiter was
speaking the truth.[7]

In spite of repeated requests from subordinate officials, Reichsminister Rust refused to abolish the right of clergy to visit religion
classes. The practice continued to the end despite obstacles, and in
Bavaria, for example, the Protestant church authorities in May 1944
ordered that every elementary-school class where religion was given
should be visited officially at least once every four years, with spot
visitations in between.[8]

The first important war measure directly affecting religion classes came in March 1940. Because of the shortage of teachers and the pressure to provide more time for instruction in the sciences, all instruction in religion was ended at the higher schools during the last four years and reduced to one hour a week in the fourth year. This measure was extended to the middle schools in April 1941. Henceforth religious instruction would cover only the period of compulsory school instruction, which by a national law of July 1938 had been set at eight years for all Germany.[9] This brought students to what was traditionally the age of confirmation in Protestant communities. By this time most of them were fourteen years of age, when, according to German law predating the Nazi era and Protestant church tradition, children reached the age of majority in religious matters.

One of the immediate results of this curtailment of hours was that both Protestant and Catholic clergy attempted to gather the upper-grade pupils into voluntary study groups which met in the parish buildings. This was a difficult procedure and was on the whole not very successful. State officials moreover looked askance at the practice and Reichsminister Rust issued an ordinance that school authorities must in no way support this outside instruction. No teacher was to take part in it. If any teachers felt that they did not have enough to do they should be assigned additional class hours or more war work.[10] The curtailment of hours of religious instruction in higher and middle schools was a factor in the rapid spread of a movement throughout Germany to extend the period of confirmation instruction from one to two years.

In line with this general policy of limiting religious instruction in schools to the first eight years of a child's schooling, the Nazis in 1940 also abolished classes in religion at vocational schools.[11] Such instruction had not been customary in most of Germany, but the new policy did bring changes, particularly in Württemberg and Bavaria.

In order to bring more uniformity in the school system after the annexation of Austria and the Sudetenland, it was decided to adopt the intermediate school system (*Bürgerschulen*) of these regions for Germany. At these new so-called *Hauptschulen*, which were to be attended only by selected pupils from grades five to eight, the emphasis was to be on practical education and religion was to be allotted only one hour a week.[12] The decree establishing these schools was issued on April 28, 1941, but because of war conditions not many of these schools actually came into being. The Nazis did not see fit to abolish religious instruction entirely, but one hour a week for grades five to eight marks the minimum that had ever been officially allotted to religion in regularly established German lower schools. In spite of a special ordinance of Reichsminister Rust ordering the establishment of religion classes at the Hauptschulen, such instruction was omitted from the 51 Hauptschulen in Württemberg, which aroused a protest from church authorities.[13]

Abolition of Grades in Religion Classes

State officials now undertook to solve in a half-way fashion another problem which had often been debated in the past. It was the old question of examination and marks in religion. This issue had become more acute as the traditional position of religious instruction in the schools was challenged by the Nazis. Church authorities were of course aware of the situation. In the summary church report on religious instruction at the higher schools of Bavaria for 1937–38 there is a severe criticism of the grades that were being given. Understanding was expressed for the practice of teachers who were generous in their grades in order to win over pupils and keep them from withdrawing from religious instruction class. "It cannot, however, be approved," so the report continued, "when at many schools only the two top marks seem to exist. With such practice religion instructors bring their instruction into disrepute and pupils get an idea of dishonesty about religion classes."[14] On February 2, 1941, Minister Rust issued an ordinance regulating uniformly the printing of report cards for all Germany. This carried a line, "Evangelical-Catholic Religion." Three months later he issued another ordinance stating that this line should be omitted. Where confessional religious instruction was still given at schools and up to then had been graded, the grades henceforth should be given on a separate form which he prescribed.[15]

The removal of a place for a grade in religion on the regular report cards indicates a definite decline in the importance placed on religion as a regular subject of instruction by school authorities. In Bavaria at least the Protestant church immediately countered by having the ministers inform their congregations of the new procedure. Parents were told to be sure to save the religion report-cards, as evidence of attendance at religion classes might be of importance for future admission to confirmation classes and for permission to act as sponsors at baptisms. For the time being the report for attendance at religious instruction in the last class was to be presented when pupils announced themselves for pre-confirmation or confirmation instruction.[16] A realization of how traditional and important confirmation is in Germany is necessary in order to understand the significance of this counter measure by the Protestant church.

The Closing Years

As the bombing of Germany grew heavier, the school system became increasingly disorganized because of destroyed buildings, relocation of schools, the evacuation of children and, of course, shortages of all kinds. Reichsminister Rust on August 23, 1943, issued a directive that children of evacuees were to have the same amount of religious instruction as they had in their home locality (*Heimatsort*), and this was to be given by regular teachers. In practice, however, it was impossible to carry out such a policy, even if there had been good will on the part of the officials.[17] On June 20, 1944, the district president at Wiesbaden issued regulations in regard to religious instruction for transferred schools and refugee camps. Religion was to be taught by official teachers in the scope of the regular teaching plans. If teachers were not available the district president was to be notified only when there was a demand for religious instruction. An increase of religion hours could not be considered. Teachers from other sections had to follow regulations of this district, and under no circumstances were clergy to be permitted to give instruction in any school building or in the camps. So-called traveling clergy who sought to minister to the evacuees in no instance were to instruct in the schools. Teachers were likewise forbidden to give extracurricular religious instruction.[18]

This ordinance shows again how varied conditions were. Teachers from other sections of Germany accustomed to other practices had to follow the regulations of this district. Here clergy were to give no instruction whatever, while in Bavaria, Baden, and the district of Hohenzollern, the clergy were responsible for a larger proportion of religious instruction than ever before.

Hitler always maintained that agreements like the Concordat of 1933 did not apply to the regions which he annexed to Germany. In the territories taken from Poland he attempted to introduce a radical separation of church and state. Churches were no longer to be considered public law corporations.[19] All schools were organized as Gemeinschaftsschulen, and private schools were dissolved. Monastic orders were denied the privilege of teaching, and were subject to more severe restrictions. Clergy could not teach in the schools, and confessional religious instruction was not permitted there. In some districts all religious instruction was stopped. The Polish minorities suffered particularly. Both Catholics and Protestants protested vigorously, and the new church policy in the Polish districts of Warthegau and Wartheland never was fully implemented before the turning tide of the war transformed confusion into turmoil.

Chapter XIII

METHOD and CONTENT of RELIGIOUS INSTRUCTION, 1933–1945

The account thus far of Hitler's Germany has dealt mostly with how the organization and administration of schools affected religious education. There remains to be examined the quality and orthodoxy of the instruction that was given. This was, of course, a perennial problem in Germany, but never was it more acute than in the Third Reich.

The general spirit of National Socialism, which came to permeate the entire school system, had much that was unchristian about it, and affected religious instruction adversely. Side by side with classes in religion students were taught Nazi racial concepts and theories of eugenics that obviously were in conflict with Christian principles. Just as in the past there were people who could reconcile Christianity and slavery, or damn democracy as being contrary to true religion, so now there were people who could reconcile their religious instruction with Nazi ideology. Surely there were many instructors now, just as there had been in earlier periods, who taught anything but religion in their classes, and these teachers often used Bible stories as a basis for government propaganda. There were also many who introduced a few Nazi ideas into their classes, while otherwise continuing to teach Bible history and catechism more or less on traditional lines. A perfunctory and formal "Heil Hitler" at the beginning of a class or observance of some Nazi holidays did not necessarily vitiate all religious instruction in the prescribed religion classes. It is well to remember that what constitutes sound religious instruction is something on which Christians with their many divisions and viewpoints find it hard to agree.

Curriculum Plans and Textbooks

Although curriculum plans were issued by Reichsminster Rust in other subjects, he never issued any for religion. In his pronouncements

7*

these were always "reserved for the future." This was because such
general directives were always blocked by Bormann, the Führer's
deputy, and by Rosenberg, deputy of the Führer for supervision of
spiritual and ideological training of the National Socialist party. In
February 1940 the question of new curriculum plans again was raised.
This time Bormann had heard rumors that Reich Bishop Müller of the
German Christians was spreading the word that Rosenberg had asked
him to work out curriculum plans for religious instruction in the schools.
Alarmed by this prospect, Bormann wrote Rosenberg a long letter
urging that the party should not depart from the policy followed up to
this time. It was impossible to draw up curriculum plans which would
suit the churches and which could at the same time be approved by
the party; there could not be a synthesis between National Socialism
and Christianity. If a curriculum for Protestant instruction were drawn
up, it would inevitably have to be followed by a Catholic one. These
instructional guides would of necessity differ fundamentally from each
other, and yet both Catholics and Protestants would claim their curriculum was the authentic interpretation of Article 24 (positive Christianity) of the party platform. Bormann continued:

On the other hand I too am of the opinion that it is not possible to cancel
religious instruction in the schools without replacing it with something better
for the ethical instruction of youth.

Religious instruction, as it is given today in the schools, includes not just
instruction in Christian doctrine, the story of creation, and of immortality,
but alongside of this the children receive an explanation of the Ten Commandments, which for most of the citizenry represent the only remaining
guide for ethical conduct and an orderly life in the community. If the
children are deprived of this instruction, without replacing it with something better, then according to my opinion there would be ground for the
charge that the degeneration of youth, which many hold to be true today,
was to be traced back to the fact that religious instruction was no longer
given in the schools. . . .

Bormann proposed the preparation of a small catechism-like presentation of National Socialist ethical concepts. This was not to be made a
text in the schools, although eventually they might adopt it "as the
schools had taken over the catechism from the church."

With regard to religious instruction in the schools it seems to me that the
existing conditions do not need to be changed. No National Socialist teacher,
according to the clearcut directives of the Deputy of the Führer, must be
accused in any way, if he is prepared to teach the Christian religion in the
schools. The content of the religious instruction should continue to be

determined by the curriculum plans that the churches themselves drew up in former years. In the circular of the Deputy of the Führer Number 3/39 of 4 January, 1939, it is expressly stated that teachers of religion are not by any means to make their own choice of Biblical material for religious instruction, but are obliged to give instruction on all the Biblical subjects. They are to abstain from all reinterpreting, analyzing, or paraphrasing, as has been attempted several times by certain church groups. Pupils should be given a total picture of Biblical instruction material.

Teachers of course are entitled to represent this material as constituting Biblical thought and not as German or National Socialist. If in certain areas they call attention to certain comparisons, this is not contrary to the circular letter, but is part of their duty as teachers. The churches cannot complain about such religious instruction.[1]

The meeting of all the *Reichsleiter* to discuss the problem of curriculum plans never took place, and no national plans for religious instruction ever appeared. Neither did many states or districts issue such plans, most authorities restricting themselves to making pointed suggestions.[2] The old teaching plans of the pre-Nazi era continued *de jure* in effect, but *de facto* they were variously interpreted and instructors often paid no attention to them. Although this had to some extent always been the case, it is no doubt true that the official plans were bypassed more during the Nazi era than in previous periods. This bypassing even received official sanction. A directive on the giving of Protestant instruction in the District of Wiesbaden in April 1935 called attention to the usefulness of plans worked out earlier, but stated that these needed revision. "What material is to receive less attention, I must leave to the individual teacher, whereby I rely on his sense of responsibility and entrust to him the duty of teaching Biblical Christianity and the preservation of the doctrinal values of the Reformation."[3] It was the duty of the teachers to pay attention to the core selection of the Biblical material, hymns, and catechism, and particularly to a systematic explanation of the first part of the catechism (Ten Commandments). Curtailment of hours, of course, also made it impossible to adhere closely to the old plans. When the religion classes were abolished in the last four years of the higher schools, the Bavarian Protestant church authorities ordered that the material be compressed for the use of the lower grades, so that the basic curriculum would remain.

The Old Testament material as provided in the regular teaching plans was most frequently eliminated or perverted. This met with the approval of Nazi officials, but not of most churchmen. Even the suggested teaching plan drawn up by the group of German Christians that cooperated most closely with the Nazi regime did not entirely omit reference to the Old Testament.[4] In Württemberg, Kultusminister Mergenthaler issued an ordinance that made the selection of Old Testament material contingent upon its accord with German ethical conceptions. This order became involved in the oath question, and church authorities protested that the Old Testament was being squeezed out of the curriculum. In Thuringia at the end of 1936 the Old Testament was practically eliminated from the teaching plans.[5] How much Old Testament material should be taught in the schools had long been a subject of controversy. Here again the Nazis were but pushing a movement which some pedagogical experts had urged as a reform for years.

Not only was the amount of Old Testament material cut; all too often it was made to serve National Socialist ends. Teachers were encouraged to use it as a means of "unmasking the Jews," and by careful selection of incidents a derogatory interpretation could be made. The following quotation will indicate the tenor of some of this material.

Now some people come and ask: Why should I tell the children of the lying and deceiving nature of the Jews? How a son deceived his dying father, how a wanton woman bore false witness against Joseph; how Joseph mulcted the Egyptians, how daughters committed incest with their own father, how Sodom and Gomorra were a foul nest of the worst kind, how the Jews slandered their prophets, how again and again they forsook God— is this not informative? Is this not a way of getting to know the Jews? Of teaching God's patience and final anger? Is it not worth while to observe how this chosen people has dissipated its right to be the elect?[6]

To the author of the above diatribe the Old Testament could only be understood as a product of a detestable spirit which he attached to the Jewish race.

That there are certain passages in the Old Testament that do not lend themselves to instruction in elementary schools had for years been used as an argument for an edited "School Bible." A rash of books, pamphlets, and articles now appeared which attacked the use of the Old Testament. Many teachers believed that the only honorable thing to do was to throw it out of religion classes altogether. The Old Testament was for theologians and people who were studying to be teachers, but not for school children. Instead teachers should concentrate on the New Testament and the life of Christ.

This call for more emphasis on the New Testament was also an old one in German educational circles. But here too the Nazis were inclined to make it serve their purposes. They were fond of picturing Jesus as a hero and leader; they stressed his denunciation of hypocrisy and sanctimony, his action against the Pharisees, the difficulty of following him, and the fact that while God was a good father he also damned to hell.[7] Or as another writer put it:

As Führer Jesus leads us to God; as a Warrior He fought against God's enemies; as a Hero He is the fighter for God's rule over the hearts of men and the whole world. And as He, as the sole glorious Messenger of the Father, fought and battled; as He leads us and can lead us no other person on earth can lead and direct us.[8]

This author outlined the following selections from the New Testament:

I. The Power of Jesus' message:
   Mark 1:21f.; Matthew 7:28f.
   Luke 12:49; Jesus the world revolutionist.
II. Jesus calls you to follow Him:
   Mark 1:16–20; 2:14
   Luke 9:57–62; Jesus' call is radical; He demands the total person
   Mark 10:17–27
   Matthew 10 – Usually designated as the call to missionary activity (Aussendungsrede); we say command to march (Marschbefehl)
   Matthew 10:28 – Away with fear of death
III. Sharp separation from the Jews and the Jewish religion:
   Mark 2:21–22; – "No man putteth new wine into old bottles"
   Mark 2:23; 3:6; Luke 13:10–17; 14:1–6. – Against the Sabbatarianism of the Jews; the son of God and love are lords of the Sabbath
   Mark 7:1–16 – Against purification prescriptions
   Matthew 5:17–48; 7:1–5; – Chief part of the Sermon on the Mount; against the Jewish idea of God
   Mark 11:15–17; – Cleansing of the Temple
   John 8:44; Jews are children of the devil.

Here certainly is evidence that the Bible is so rich in its content that by unscrupulous selection and devious implications or interpretations it can be called upon to justify the most diverse doctrines. "In religion, what damned error but some sober brow will bless it, and approve it with a text. . . ?"[9]

Not only was Jesus pictured as the Führer but it was of course easy to carry this analogy over to the hierarchy of the church. Thus a Catholic writer in the early years of National Socialism wrote enthusiastically: "The religious Führer is Christ. His deputy is the Pope whose helpers are the bishops and priests. Sub-leaders (*Unterführer*) are the parents and teachers."[10] This man, so permeated with Nazi doctrine, even prophesied that the teachers of the future would be Führers of the Hitler Youth and the Storm Troops.

The Nazi-minded teachers also were inclined to accept the views of those education experts who, at the turn of the century, had advocated the use of fairy stories and myths in the religion classes for beginners. A committee for religious instruction drew up a plan which contained much of this for the first years and only in the upper grades concentrated on the life of Jesus, emphasizing: (a) Jesus as an heroic herald of God, (b) Jesus tests himself again, begins to teach and wins converts, (c) Jesus in battle with the legalistic religion of the Jews, (d) Jesus' desires to remain true to his calling and continues to teach, (e) Jesus' death, (f) what one recounts of the resurrected Jesus.[11] This particular teaching plan contained nothing about the Old Testament and is typical of the more extreme position taken by some innovators.

While such teaching plans were never officially adopted, it is impossible to say how much they influenced various teachers. Teaching, particularly on the elementary level, is rather conventional and neither methods nor content change rapidly. Furthermore these radical teaching proposals were matched by the pamphlets and writings of more conservative-minded men. The Protestant Confessing church was well aware of its obligations in this respect, and the Catholic church was able to prevent any radical innovations in Catholic religious instruction.

Another factor which helped preserve a measure of traditional instruction was that there were few changes in the textbooks used in religion classes. To change texts is an expensive matter, and German schools were, and still are, particularly conservative in this respect. Catechisms, selections of Bible verses, collections of hymns, and even many of the important Bible stories cannot be changed much through getting out new textbooks and the Nazis did not rush to undertake this task. This is not to say there were no new books introduced or alterations made in new editions of old texts, but only that there was no widespread introduction of new teaching material.[12] The old practice of having churches approve the books used for religious instruction was still observed for the most part. Interpretation and explanation was in the last analysis the important thing, and this depended on the personal bent of the instructor.

On the whole the traditional subjects of Bible history, catechism, Bible verses, hymns, and church history continued to be taught. The old question of the suitability of the catechism was raised, and since it was an earmark of confessional instruction it lost favor. Where the Lutheran catechism was retained, the practice was quite general of reserving the last two parts, Baptism and the Lord's Supper, for Confirmation instruction. Even the catechism was not immune when it came to the subtle infiltration of Nazi theories, if a teacher wished to use it in this way. What was more natural than to point to Hitler's Aryan laws when discussing the conclusion to the Commandments as given in Luther's Catechism? [13]

I the Lord thy God am a jealous God, visiting the iniquity of the fathers upon the children unto the third and fourth generation of them that hate Me; and showing mercy unto thousands of them that love Me and keep My commandments.

Indeed a catechism was but a concise formulation of doctrinal belief, serving the same purpose as the compact twenty-five points of the National Socialist party platform. If separate instruction in the catechism was omitted, much of the material—Ten Commandments, Lord's Prayer, Creed—was incorporated into Bible history. Such integrated instruction had long been practiced and was strongly advocated in some educational circles.

The churches often objected that hymns were being ousted from the schools. Confessional hymns were forbidden along with confessional prayers when Gemeinschaftsschulen were introduced. Hymns also received less emphasis in the regular periods of singing instruction, and secular songs came to have a far more important place in the life of the school than heretofore.

Changes made in religion textbooks under the Nazis were often minor. One of the books used in church history in the schools was Schuster and Franke, *Bibelkunde, Helden und Werke der Kirche* (14 ed; Leipzig, 1936). When the American authorities after World War II undertook to purge Nazi textbooks, they gave this book a conditional classification, after removal of certain passages.[14] They eliminated the following quotation from Strabo in respect to the Jewish diaspora of early times: "The Jews have penetrated into every town and it is not easy to find a village which does not shelter these people and that is not dominated by them" (p. 51). The American authorities also demanded the elimination of a section (pp. 192–196) on the struggle against "Christianity and Church in Marxism and Bolshevism"; another section (pp. 198–200) on "The Victory of National Socialism as the Savior of German Faith," which included quotations from Hitler's speech of March 31, 1933, and an analysis of the Protestant Church Constitution of July 11, 1933; and an excerpt of a letter (p. 268) from a soldier who had been killed, extolling comradeship. There were, of course, other books which the Americans censored more severely, but the above example illustrates the continued use of much standard and orthodox material in the religion classes during the Nazi period.

Ideological versus Religious Instruction in Württemberg

In Württemberg, when numerous ministers were denied permission to teach religion in the schools because of difficulties over the oath to the Führer, many religion classes came into the hands of teachers who were prepared to teach a Nazi version of religion. Parents in certain parishes thereupon made use of the right to withdraw their children from religion classes, and made other provision for their religious training. Local Nazi authorities countered this step by ordering that all children withdrawn from religious instruction had to attend special ideological classes (*Weltanschauungsunterricht*). There was plenty of precedent for such action, for it was a practice dating back to the days of the Empire and even earlier, that if a child did not attend the regular religion classes he had to receive an equivalent ethical instruction. The Nazi officials, however, soon advanced a step farther, and in the Ulm district an unsigned memorandum dated November 22, 1938, was circulated among all teachers urging them to recruit students for these ideological classes. When church authorities protested to the responsible officials no one knew anything about the memorandum.[15] It was soon clear that Kultusminister Mergenthaler was behind the whole movement. In a speech on January 14, 1939, at a meeting of schoolmen he declared that the New Testament was also to be taught in accordance with racial principles, and that the aim was to replace religion classes by the new *Weltanschauungsunterricht*. The people were not yet sufficiently prepared for this program, but this was the goal to be sought.

Throughout Württemberg a campaign was now launched by party and school leaders to influence parents to withdraw children from religion classes. This led to a whole series of protests to Reichsminister Rust and to local Württemberg authorities. Bishop Wurm, who had more than once challenged Hitler's policy towards the churches, urged parents not to withdraw their children from religion classes in order to enroll them in the *Weltanschauungsunterricht*. Although threatened with arrest, pastors read his letters from the pulpits, and the regime had to cancel the police measures, for they could not well arrest most of the ministers in Württemberg.

When on August 15, 1939, Reichsminister Rust issued an ordinance which ended the so-called undenominational religious instruction in the schools of Saxony, Württemberg church authorities were encouraged, for it seemed to be direct recognition by Reich authorities that religious instruction should be on denominational lines. The Reich governor of Württemberg, undoubtedly as part of the policy of truce with the churches because of the war, did issue an ordinance on September 16, 1939, which seemed to indicate that the position of the church in the controversy would be given consideration. But the situation there in fact remained unchanged and when it came time to enroll for the 1940 school year Kultusminister Mergenthaler launched a new campaign to influence parents to enroll their children for the *Weltanschauungsunterricht*. Bishop Wurm protested to Minister Rust and to Marshal Göring, who in addition to filling many other positions was head of the Reich Defense Council. The counterattack by the churchmen and their protests seemingly produced no results, and the *Weltanschauungsunterricht* in Württemberg continued. Yet their opposition did have an effect, as is clear from Reichsminister Rust's statement to the ministry of education in Saxony on June 7, 1940.

I cannot approve the plans which you have submitted for the introduction of *Weltanschauungsunterricht* in the schools of Saxony. During the war I consider such attempts as undesirable. There is also no cause for extending to another state, the attempt which has been made in Württemberg and which I approved at that time because of special reasons.[16]

Here is again an excellent illustration of how the Nazis varied their policies in different sections of Germany and were content to advance in piecemeal fashion. Nazi-minded officials in Württemberg continued their campaign to get parents to enroll their children for the *Weltanschauungsunterricht*, but with diminishing results.[17] In some schools this ideological instruction was inserted in the classes in German or history without a special attack on Christian belief. This did not satisfy the church leaders, for it was clear from the regularly published material for the *Weltanschauungsunterricht* that its goal was an attack against Christian points of view. School authorities, without asking parents, made the *Weltanschauungsunterricht* a compulsory subject of instruction in certain school types, such as the Aufbauschule and the Hauptschule. Faced with this situation the church authorities decided that they would accept these children for confirmation instruction, since parents had not been consulted and the children were compelled to attend these classes.

In all other instances the church-directors must expect that Evangelical parents will hold fast to their right to an Evangelical religious instruction for their children, and if they have enrolled their children in the *Weltanschauungsunterricht* they will rescind such enrollment at the end of the school year. It is not bearable that Evangelical parents send their children at the same time to the anti-Christian *Weltanschauungsunterricht* and to confirmation instruction. The highest authority in these matters, the Reich education ministry has specifically guaranteed freedom of conscience and the church's freedom of instruction.[18]

The conflict in Württemberg over religious instruction in the schools was one of the most pronounced in all Germany. Only here was there a concerted attempt to replace the regular religion classes by a substitute instruction in "ethics." This was far from being a success, and religious instruction was not eliminated from all the Württemberg schools. The Catholic church in Württemberg was less involved than the Protestant in this particular conflict. Catholic parents were more accustomed to adhere to the admonitions of the church in educational questions than were many of the Protestants, and they kept their children in Catholic classes in religion. The Catholics were also more united, for in Württemberg there were adherents of the so-called German Christians, who sniped at the policy and directives of the regular Protestant church authorities under the leadership of Bishop Wurm.

There can be no doubt that where it was not eliminated entirely, the quality of religious instruction suffered in many schools during the Nazi regime. This was the inevitable result of the general de-emphasis of religious education sponsored by the Nazi officials, and the stress placed on certain National Socialist principles and ideas. On the other hand it should be remembered that in many schools, especially in rural areas, religious instruction was given by the same teachers who had taught under the Republic, using the same texts and following accustomed patterns of instruction. A good number of these were earnest, devoted Christian teachers. Many reports indicate that very often the quality of their teaching was relatively satisfactory to the churches. Catholic lay teachers had, of course, received the direct authorization of the church (*missio canonica*) and they continued as a whole to instruct according to the principles of the church. These Catholic lay teachers undoubtedly were not always so able as some of the monastic or secular clergy who were removed from the schools, and this substitution naturally resulted in some deterioration of religious instruction. In Bavaria, Baden, and in some other sections where the clergy never ceased teaching, the instruction was as orthodox as the cleric himself. But even here the quality must have suffered because of the great increase in teaching-load and the shortage of time.

Where the churchmen were particularly dissatisfied with the situation in the schools, they began to hold religion classes of their own outside of school hours. The state would not permit these classes to be held in school buildings, but otherwise did not forbid them. In this connection mention should be made of the activities of the group of Protestant churchmen and churches that withdrew from the Nazi-dominated church organization. Known as the Confessing church (*Bekennende Kirche*), this organization, of which Dr. Niemoeller was a leader, developed its own school commissions, began training lay teachers, drew up new teaching plans and teaching material.[19] The financial and other restrictions placed upon this body by the Nazis, combined with internal dissension, diminished the effectiveness of this movement. Throughout the Nazi period children continued to be confirmed, and there can be little doubt that in many instances the quality of confirmation instruction was greatly improved. Here is where the churchmen still had a free hand and they made the most of it. Special confirmation instruction plays a greater role in the Protestant than in the Catholic church, and in many sections of Germany the Protestants lengthened the period of such instruction from one to two years. While this was apart from the regular school religion classes, it indicated a healthy renewed realization on the part of the church of its responsibility for the religious instruction of youth.

Chapter XIV

JEWISH EDUCATION
in the THIRD REICH

Since the German school system was definitely established on a Christian basis, Jewish education was always a thing apart and, in reality, constitutes a separate topic in the history of German education. Historically the Jewish community was held to bear the chief responsibility for the education of Jews, and the state simply assisted. The amount of control increased over the years and with it the amount of state assistance. By the time Hitler became chancellor in January 1933, Jewish schools and Jewish religious instruction had come to have a status similar if not exactly equal to that of the Christian confessions.[1]

Conditions of course varied in the different states. In some places schools receiving much of their support from the state were classed as Jewish Community schools, in others they were classed as public schools. Statistics as to numbers must therefore be interpreted, but it is clear that the Jews had a well developed private-school system, their own public Jewish confessional schools in some states, and were always free to attend the Christian *Simultan* or confessional schools if they wished.[2] Where their numbers were sufficient in the latter schools, public authorities provided funds for Jewish religious instruction. In both public and private Jewish schools religion was of course a regular subject of instruction.

It is impossible to separate measures which affected Jewish education in general and those which applied directly to religious education. The whole educational picture was, of course, also affected by the broad complex of sordid measures which were taken against the Jews in the Third Reich. All these cannot be discussed here, nor will it be possible to give a complete history of Jewish education, for that would involve a discussion of such topics, among others, as the shift to more vocational training, the dissolution of Jewish Communities, and the effect of the destruction of the synagogues not only on Jewish religious life but on Jewish education. It had taken many years for Jewish education to become a regular part of the German educational system, yet in the few years of the Third Reich it was once again set apart.

Preparatory Restrictions, 1933–1935

On April 7, 1933, Hitler promulgated a law for the reorganization of the civil service, which contained an Aryan paragraph. Non-Aryan civil servants could be pensioned off, unless they were officials before August 1, 1914, fought at the front for the Central Powers during World War I, or were fathers or sons of persons who had been killed in that conflict. By supplementary ordinance it was decreed that this law did not apply to religious corporations, and it was specifically stated: "The law does not apply to Jewish teachers employed at public Jewish schools, or those who, on the basis of legal provisions, give religious instruction at other public schools. The same is true for Jewish honorary officials, who were named to these offices on the basis of special legal provisions."[3]

In a law of April 25, 1933, directed at the overcrowding of German schools and universities, it was provided that at no higher school or in any faculty should the number of non-Aryan Germans as defined in the civil-service law, exceed the number of Aryan Germans. This law did not apply to elementary schools, which were considered compulsory schools. Here again, as was customary in Germany, ordinances amplified the original law, and it was decreed that non-Aryans were to be limited to 1.5 percent of the entering classes at higher schools and the universities, and in no case were they to exceed 5 percent of the total student body.[4] Foreign Jews were not to be counted in the quota, and the restrictions applied to both public and private schools, with the obvious exception of Jewish private schools. With this legislation Germany returned to an old anti-Semitic technique, one which had been long practiced in imperial Russia and unofficially at many American colleges and universities.

Except for this law on overcrowding at German higher schools and universities, all the old laws remained in effect. New measures were to be anticipated, and in Frankfurt, for example, it was ordered that, until all things were settled, (1) no Jewish instructor should teach German or history, (2) be a class leader for more than four years, or (3) be appointed a class leader in classes where there were no Jews or only a very small number of them.[5] When some one suggested putting all Jews in one school, the authorities stated this could not be done because there was no legal provision for doing so.[6]

Since Jewish teachers were under the same general regulations as their Christian colleagues, in the summer of 1933 they had to sign a declaration that neither by written or spoken word had they said anything publicly against National Socialism and its Führer.[7] This requirement held also for rabbis who were giving religious instruction at the schools on a part-time basis. It was generally considered a form requirement and apparently caused no great difficulty. In line with previous regulations, on September 15, 1933, it was ordered that no Jew could receive permission to give private instruction, unless he had given such instruction before 1914, had been a front-line soldier, or had lost a father or son in World War I.[8] Measures were taken in many places, however, to dismiss Jewish teachers. On October 9, 1933, for example, the directors of the Jewish Community in Frankfurt protested to the school authorities that the Jewish women teachers at the city elementary schools had been given their notices. They wanted Jewish religious instruction continued under paragraph 40 of the School Law of 1906. The school authorities replied that they would try as much as possible to give consideration to Jewish religious instruction in the curriculum. At present there were two men giving such instruction. Each one had twenty hours of teaching, and would be excused from other classes. In one school a regular teacher gave the religious instruction. The dismissals took place, and in January 1934 except for the teachers at the purely Jewish schools, there were only two Jewish instructors in the Frankfurt elementary schools.[9]

Not only were Jewish teachers dismissed but in a decree of December 18, 1933, rabbis were removed from local school committees in Prussia.[10] Hitherto under Article 44 of the Prussian law of 1906, whenever there were 20 Jewish elementary-school pupils, the rabbi with the longest service was added to the school committee. This provision paralleled one for adding Catholic or Protestant clergy to the local committees. Jews were now left without representatives on the local school committee unless by chance a lay representative won one of the other seats.

On June 17, 1933, the minister in Berlin issued a notice effective in all Prussia that Jews could be excused from classes on Saturday if they wished. Further, if Jewish pupils did attend Saturday classes, on the request of parents they should be excused from writing and drawing assignments. Schools were not to be responsible for any missed work because of such excuses. In March 1934 Reichsminister Rust issued an ordinance on this subject applicable to the whole Reich.[11] Jews and Adventists could on request be excused from all Saturday classes or just for the hour of services. This time, however, it was ordered that if they chose to attend classes they had to take part in all regular instruction including drawing, writing, hand work, and activity instruction. The order also established uniform practice for Jewish holidays. Henceforth Jewish pupils could be excused two days at New Year's (Rosh Hashana) ; one day at the Feast of Atonement (Yom Kippur), two days at the beginning and at the end of the Feast of Tabernacles (Sukkoth) ; two days at the beginning and end of Passover (Pesach) and two days at the Feast of Weeks or Pentecost (Shabnoth).

At schools Jewish children were not to be forced to use the "German Greeting" but also it was not to be denied to them. There apparently was never an attempt made to enforce instruction in National Socialist racial theories at purely Jewish schools. This in itself set Jewish education apart from German education. On the other hand instruction in National Socialist ideology in non-Jewish schools could not be hindered by consideration of other points of view. School directors were to decide from instance to instance when Jewish students were to be excused from certain classes and school ceremonies. By orders issued in August and September 1934, classes in National Socialist education in Prussia were put on Saturday, and so Jewish students could be conveniently freed from them.[12]

Jewish pupils, if attending Christian schools, could always be excused from the regular religious classes and services. At purely Jewish schools they had their own religious practices. Although aimed primarily at the Christian schools, Minister Rust's decree of July 9, 1935, to the effect that henceforth at higher schools no compulsion on the part of school officials might be exercised in regard to attendance of teachers and pupils at religious services, also affected purely Jewish schools, for Jewish public and private schools were of course subject to the regular school legislation of the period.

Increased Isolation, 1935–1938

Just as the summer of 1935 had brought the inauguration of new restrictive measures on the Christian churches and on Christian education in the schools, it brought also a more aggressive anti-Semitic policy. At the Party Congress at Nürnberg in September, Hitler suddenly called a meeting of the Reichstag which went through the formality of passing a "Law for the Protection of German Blood and Honor" and a "Reich Citizenship Law." Under these laws and the important supplementary decrees of November 14, Jews were denied German citizenship, and placed under many restrictions.[13] Furthermore a Jew was defined as a person who was descended from three or four Jewish grandparents, or a person descended from two Jewish grandparents, provided he professed the Jewish faith or was married to a Jew. Persons with two racially full Jewish grandparents were classed as *Mischlinge* of the first degree, those with one such grandparent as Mischlinge of the second degree. Such "mixed offspring," could with special permission marry Aryans and were at times freed from other restrictions placed on Jews.

The introduction of racial criteria increased the number of persons officially classed as Jews within the Reich, but it is not known by how many, for there never had been a count on this basis before, and there was none made until 1939. The total number of Jews by religion in 1933 (including the Jews of the Saar) was 502,799. Following the great emigration of the next years, by 1939 there were in the old Reich only 233,646 racial Jews. Of these 213,930 (91.5 percent) were of Jewish faith, which would indicate that in the first six years of the Third Reich there had been a decrease of 288,869 Jews according to religious classification. Of the racial Jews 19,716 (8.5 percent) were not of Jewish faith and were divided as follows: Lutherans 10,461; Roman Catholics 3,025; other Christian denominations 320; deists 2,859; no religion 2,712; no designation 339. Of the 52,005 Mischlinge of the first degree, only 5,177 (9.9 percent) were Jews by religion; of the 32,669 Mischlinge of the second degree, only 392 (1.16 percent) were of Jewish faith. Thus only about 10 percent of children of mixed marriages were brought up as Jews, the rest being affiliated with Christian denominations.[14] There were thus full racial Jews who were Christians and also Mischlinge who were Christians, and the Nazis in their ordinances sometimes distinguished between the groups. Most of the children of these Christian non-Aryans were of course attending Christian religion classes in the schools. Forcing these children out of the Christian schools into purely Jewish schools raised new problems.

A few days before the enactment of the Nürnberg laws, Minister Rust, on September 10, 1935, issued a directive on racial separation in public schools.[15] He had discovered that Jewish children were still attending public German schools. Starting with the school year of 1936 there was to be as complete a separation of races as possible, and administrative authorities were to report to him by November 14 on the situation in their districts. At the higher schools he would deal with the situation by cutting the percentage quotas. At the compulsory elementary schools (*Pflichtschulen*) this was another matter. He did not want private Jewish schools, but expected to erect public Jewish schools wherever twenty children were available. He wanted to know how many such schools would be necessary and invited suggestions in regard to them. He anticipated that the Jewish parents would bear the burden of the schools, with the state and community furnishing subsidies. Mischlinge of the second degree (one-quarter Jews) were not to be affected by the separation of races.

Thus at a time when the campaign against Christian confessional schools was being launched, Rust decided to erect Jewish confessional schools. The policy of separation was soon underway, although it was not uniformly carried out. By December 1935 all the Jewish children not in the purely Jewish schools in Frankfurt were concentrated in two public schools. This, of course, made it necessary for some pupils to travel considerable distances, and a rabbi made the request, which was turned down, that they be given free transportation on the streetcars.[16] Another directive is at hand of July 2, 1937, which indicates that this policy of having public elementary Jewish schools was carried out in the next years. If it was not possible to have a completely separate Jewish school, classes of Jewish students gathered from several districts (Sammelklassen) were attached to regular schools and taught by Jewish teachers. Jews could attend only elective schools (middle, higher, vocational) according to the law on overcrowding of higher schools. Mischlinge could attend any of the elective schools, for it was held that, by the Nürnberg laws, they did not come under the quota restrictions, although in case of overcrowding others were to be given preference. Mischlinge could also take the important Abitur examinations.

One of the first actions of the Jews after Hitler had come to power was to form in April 1933 a National Organization of German Jews (*Reichsvertretung der Juden in Deutschland*).[17] This national organization, a coordinating body for the various Jewish organizations, did much to aid the founding of the new Jewish schools, for the state did not assume all the burden. Here again it is hard to distinguish between what was a public or private school, particularly if viewed from the American conception of what constitutes a public school. Thus the *Israelitische Volksschule* in Frankfurt, a private school, received funds from the Jewish Community, from the city, and from the state. In 1937 the Frankfurt school authorities proposed that the city and state raise their subsidies to 15,000 RM and the state officials agreed to do so for one year.[18]

In spite of many handicaps, there was built up in the years 1935–38 an effective Jewish educational system. Many of the elementary schools added a ninth year devoted chiefly to vocational training, and this aspect of education was greatly expanded through many special establishments designed to prepare youth for emigration.[19] Under a Nazi directive, racial studies (*Rassenkunde*) became a part of the program of the Jewish schools.[20] This was used to good advantage by the teachers, and Jewish children became more conscious of their Jewish

inheritance. It has been estimated that "there were in Germany in the
first half of 1938: 68 public Jewish primary schools, 72 private Jewish
primary schools, which with the intermediate and high schools totaled
about 160 Jewish schools of all grades. They were attended by 20,029
Jewish primary pupils and about 5,000 Jewish higher school pupils.
The Central Committee (Reichsvertretung) supported these schools
according to their needs without discriminating on the basis of religious
or philosophical orientation."[21] What proportion of private Jewish
funds, as compared to "public" communal and state funds went to
support the various schools it is impossible to say.

Alongside the policy of segregating Jewish children there also went
a policy of eliminating Jewish religious instruction from the public
schools. The latter would quite naturally have been the result of the
former, but the two did not always coincide, for in some places special
Jewish classes continued as annexes of the regular elementary schools.
It was also a separate question in the higher schools, for here, under the
quota system, there were always in these years a few Jewish students
to be found.

One of the first ordinances aimed directly at Jewish religious
instruction was apparently issued in Württemberg and it came well
before the Nürnberg Laws.[22] Here Minister Mergenthaler, who was
noted for his zeal in furthering National Socialist educational aims, on
May 7, 1934, issued an ordinance ending Jewish religious instruction
as a regular part of the curriculum at the public elementary and higher
schools. The Jewish community organization could henceforth arrange
to give such instruction privately to Jewish students but no public
funds were to be allotted for this purpose.

It was not until July 31, 1936, that Bavaria took measures comparable to those in Württemberg. On that date regular Jewish religious
instruction was barred from all Bavarian schools. It could be given
privately, but there were henceforth to be no grades in Jewish religious
instruction entered on the report cards. Nor could state or local public
funds be spent for Jewish religious instruction. A supplementary decree
of November made it clear that private religious instruction could not
be given in school buildings, except in schools attended only by Jewish
pupils or in elementary schools which had special Jewish classes attached
to them.[23]

Although the above decree applied only to Bavaria it was reprinted
in the official journal of the Reichsministerium at Berlin, and its policy
was apparently followed throughout Germany. At least in 1936 Jewish
religious instruction ceased to be a regular subject of instruction at
public elementary schools so far as the Frankfurt school authorities

were concerned, which is indicative that the policy was being followed in Prussia.[24]

The small number of Jewish students at the higher schools made it difficult, of course, to keep regular religion classes going, and without a will to maintain them on the part of the authorities, they naturally were soon discontinued. By February 24, 1936, according to a report to Minister Rust, Jewish religious instruction was no longer given at any of the higher schools in Prussia. In September 1936 the ban on religious instruction was extended to middle schools. Rooms in school buildings at higher and middle schools were no longer to be made available for private Jewish religious instruction.[25]

Another measure affecting Jewish religious instruction more or less directly was the elimination of Hebrew from the curriculum of the higher schools. One of the first decrees banning it was apparently issued in Bavaria on December 21, 1936. This was followed at once by a decree by Minister Rust who ordered that starting with the school year 1937–38 no Hebrew was to be taught at the Gymnasiums. It was to be left for the universities to provide for future Oriental scholars. The Christian churches, however, were not of this opinion. They objected to the cancellation of Hebrew, and soon began to provide future ministerial candidates privately with instruction in Hebrew. This apparently met with some success, for a decree of August 14, 1941, pointed out that no recruiting should be permitted at higher schools for instruction in Hebrew, Aramaic, or Greek. Schoolrooms were not to be made available for such instruction, even if it was free and was given by church authorities.[26]

These regulations affecting Hebrew instruction at Gymnasiums did not affect Hebrew instruction at purely Jewish schools. In fact the increased emigration to Palestine after 1933 led to a renewed interest in studying Hebrew. It has been estimated that in 1934 there were some 15,000 students of Hebrew in Germany.[27] A seminary for Hebrew teachers was founded at the end of 1935 with 30 students. The number of students of Hebrew declined after this, in part because of the shortage of teachers and other reasons, but largely because of the great decline of the Jewish school population due to emigration.

Just as the Nazis did not meddle with Hebrew instruction at Jewish schools, neither did they attempt to interfere with or determine the content of Jewish religious instruction. In this regard the Jews were more fortunate than the Christian churches, although it should be recalled that even in respect to Christian instruction the Nazis never officially attempted to draw up specific curriculum plans. They relied upon more devious ways to infiltrate their ideas into religion classes.

Final Liquidation, 1938–1945

Immediately after the successful annexation of Austria the German government began to prepare further measures against the Jews. Existing German anti-Jewish legislation was introduced into Austria practically at one fell swoop. By a decree of March 28, 1938, Jewish Communities throughout the enlarged German state were deprived of their status as public-law corporations (*Körperschaften des öffentlichen Rechts*).[28] The communities were henceforth to be voluntary civil-law associations, and Jews no longer automatically became community members but had specifically to enter their names. The new Jewish associations no longer had the right to levy communal taxes and have the state agencies collect them; the property of the Community was no longer exempt from state taxes. This decree was one of a long series of discriminatory tax measures, and of course handicapped the Jewish Communities in carrying on their collective activities. Minister Rust realized this and in a secret directive asked all district presidents to note how the Jewish schools were affected by the new measure and to report any difficulties to him.[29]

To name a few of the other decrees which followed in rapid succession will indicate that Hitler's anti-Semitism was being activated with a vengeance. On April 26, 1938, appeared a "Decree Regarding the Registration of Jewish Property"; on June 1, 1938, all Jewish schools were excluded from tax exemption; on July 6, 1938, a law further limited the economic activities of Jews; July–September 1938, a series of decrees completed the elimination of Jews from professions; and on August 17, 1938, a decree restricted Jews to a limited number of names of "Jewish origin."[30] The first of these measures were a cause for and the later ones a reaction to the international conference which had been called on the initiative of President Roosevelt to consider the problem of involuntary emigration from Germany. Thirty-one countries were represented at this conference which met at Evian, France, from July 6 to July 15, 1938.[31]

Germany did not cooperate with the Evian conference in making more liberal economic provisions for Jewish emigrants. On the other hand the Nazi officials were glad to have Jews leave the country under the severe economic restrictions which they imposed. At times they resorted to deportation, which entailed even greater hardships. On November 7, 1938, Herschel Grynszpan, the son of a Polish-Jewish deportee, shot and seriously wounded Ernst vom Rath, third secretary of the German embassy in Paris.[32] Two days later the victim died, and his death was made the occasion of a violent pogrom throughout

Germany. Preparations had long been made for such an occasion. Nowhere did the police intervene. Synagogues were put to the torch, except in those places where the fire might damage gentile property. Jewish stores were smashed and looted, and many Jews suffered physical violence and arrest.

On November 12 a meeting of important Nazi leaders was held under the chairmanship of Field Marshal Göring to survey the damage and to see "that the Jewish question be now, once and for all, coordinated and solved one way or another." Göring as head of the Four Year Plan was not happy over all the economic destruction. He was particularly concerned that Jewish firms would receive insurance payments from German Aryan firms for damage done. He could have cancelled the insurance payments, but since the German companies had reinsured with foreign concerns he did not want these foreign companies to escape making their payments. Glass breakage alone was estimated at $6,000,000, and Germany had to import practically all its glass from Belgium. In one night Germans had broken about half of a whole year's production of the Belgian glass industry. Discussion ranged far and wide and all the remarks and decisions cannot be considered here. One observation by Goebbels, however, is pertinent and requires quotation:

I think it is imperative to give the Jews certain public parks, not the best ones—and tell them: "You may sit on these benches," these benches shall be marked "For Jews only." Besides they have no business in German parks. Furthermore, Jewish children are still allowed in German schools. That's impossible. It is out of the question that any boy should sit beside a Jewish boy in a German Gymnasium and receive lessons in German history. Jews ought to be eliminated completely from German schools; they may take care of their own education in their own communities.[33]

Whether the conference reached any formal decision on Goebbels' proposal is not recorded, but three days later on November 15 Minister Rust issued an ordinance which echoed the propaganda minister's words.

After the ruthless murder in Paris, no German teacher can any longer be expected to give instruction to Jewish pupils. It is also self-evident that German students find it unbearable to sit in the same classrooms with Jews. Racial segregation in schools has been carried out in general during the past years, but a small number of Jewish pupils have remained who can no longer be permitted to attend schools with German boys and girls. Subject to additional regulations, I order that immediately:

(1) Jews are forbidden to attend German schools. They are permitted to attend only Jewish schools. Insofar as it has not yet happened all

Jewish boys and girls still attending German schools are to be dismissed immediately.

(2) Who is Jewish is to be determined according to Paragraph 5 of First Decree of the Reich Citizenship Law . . . of November 14, 1953.

(3) This regulation extends to all schools under my supervision including compulsory continuation schools (*Pflichtschulen*).[34]

With this decree the complete isolation of Jews from the German elementary and higher schools was inaugurated. It did not specifically apply to Mischlinge, and these were not always removed from the elementary schools. It did affect particularly those racial Jews who were Christians and had thus far been permitted in general to attend the regular German schools. These now were forced to attend the Jewish schools. In Frankfurt am Main they were sent to the venerable Philanthropin school and figures for May 1939 list 3 Evangelical, 1 Catholic and 12 Deists (*Gottgläubig*) as being in attendance there.[35] In Berlin, the Confessing church organized a family school (*Familienschule Oranienstrasse*) which at one time had as many as one hundred Protestant and Catholic non-Aryan pupils. Eventually the *Reichsvereinigung der Juden in Deutschland* had to take over official sponsorship of the school, although the Confessing church retained active connection with it.[36]

Rust's November 15 decree was only the start. On December 8 he ordered that the permission which had occasionally been granted to Jewish professors and others, who had been dismissed from the universities, to continue to use libraries and other facilities for their private research, should be withdrawn.[37] In a further secret decree of December 17, 1938, he pointed out that Jewish children could not be left without all instruction, and school authorities were to try to keep arrangements going. If, however, it was not possible to get special rooms for "collected classes" these would have to be dissolved, for it was impossible to instruct Jews in the same building with other German pupils. Jewish teachers who had heretofore received salaries from public authorities would continue to do so. Jewish teachers who had been taken into protective custody were going to be released by the police. Although he anticipated the future ending of state subsidies to private Jewish schools, this was not officially done until March 7, 1939.[38] Even this decree, however, did not necessarily end subsidies to Jewish private schools from local public funds.

With all Jewish students in special Jewish schools, Rust undertook to make the Jewish Community more responsible for them. In an ordinance of August 14, 1939 (amplifying the citizenship law of July 4, 1939), he pointed out that it was a compulsory duty of the Reichsvereinigung der Juden in Deutschland to establish elementary Jewish schools only.[39] The establishment of middle, higher, and vocational schools was optional according to need and available funds. The Jewish elementary schools were classed as private schools, could have special curriculum plans, and might teach Hebrew. Teacher academies were to be permitted only so far as it was necessary to train Jewish teachers. Under the citizenship law of July 4 all publicly employed teachers at Jewish schools were retired as of June 30, 1939. These retired Jewish teachers could be employed in the schools established by the Reichs-vereinigung, and if they refused to serve, their pensions would be stopped. By September 30, 1939, the Reichsvereinigung was to take over all public and private Jewish schools. Former public-school buildings could be rented by them.

With this decree the segregation of Jews into a separate school system under the supervision of the Jewish Community was virtually complete. With war conditions and continued enforcement of anti-Semitic measures it became more and more difficult to maintain these schools. The constant decrease in the number of pupils necessitated the closing of many of them. What had happened can be illustrated by some figures from the Frankfurt schools.[40] In January 1934 there were two private Jewish elementary schools with 1,092 pupils and in addition there were 548 children scattered through thirty-six other schools. In May 1937 there were 1,125 pupils in the two schools and 109 in three classes annexed to German elementary schools. By August 1941 the two elementary schools together had 700 pupils and had been placed in one building. Because of the departure (*Abwanderung*) of so many Jews during October and November of 1941, the number of pupils declined to 450 by February 1942, and the Reichsvereinigung for reasons of economy decided to combine the two Frankfurt Jewish elementary schools into one which was to be called the "Private Jewish *Volksschule* in Frankfurt am Main." Even this school had to find new quarters, for the army confiscated its old building for a hospital.

The Nazis did not leave private instruction untouched. As early as October 15, 1936, they had forbidden Jewish teachers to give private instruction to "Germans." The decree of April 4, 1941, requiring the concentration of Jewish schools in big cities, added that authorization for private instruction of Jewish children was no longer to be given. Apparently this ordinance was never completely effective and a year later (January 23, 1942) a final decree stated: "Giving of private instruction to Jewish children is permitted only in special cases with the permission of the supervisory authorities."[41]

With the inauguration of the final terror which ultimately reduced

the total Jewish population of Germany to about 19,000, the German
Jewish educational system came to an end. The death-knell ordinance
of Minister Rust was issued on June 20, 1942.[42]

To the District President of Wiesbaden:

In view of the development of the resettlement (*Aussiedlung*) of Jews in
recent times the minister of interior . . . in agreement with the Reichsvereinigung der Juden in Deutschland has directed that all Jewish schools
should be closed by June 30, 1942. Their members are to be informed that
starting July 1, 1942, all schooling of Jewish children by paid or unpaid
teachers is forbidden. I inform you of this. The ordinance is not to be made
public.

As authorized.

(Signed) Holfelder

As a result of this order Jewish schools were closed throughout the
Reich. But some problems remained. What was to be done with the
Mischlinge, those unfortunates who were neither fish nor fowl, neither
Jew nor gentile? On July 2, 1942, Rust issued a long decree, the content
of which may be summarized as follows:

(1) Mischlinge of the first degree are no longer to be admitted to Hauptschulen, middle, or higher schools. In exceptional cases they may with
my permission attend full-time and advanced vocational schools
(*Berufsfach- und Fachschulen*).
(2) Mischlinge of the second degree can attend all the above schools as long
as there is room and it does not cause disadvantages to pupils of German
or related blood.
(3) Mischlinge of first degree who are in the seventh class can stay until
they have finished their final examinations (*Reifeprüfung*).
(4) Mischlinge of first degree in fifth and sixth classes at middle schools
can attend until they receive their certificate of graduation from the
middle school or until promotion to the seventh grade of higher schools.
(5) Mischlinge of first degree in classes one to four at middle or higher
schools or in comparable classes at a Hauptschule must leave when they
have completed their compulsory school attendance.
(6) Mischlinge of first degree who are in attendance at full-time or advanced
vocational schools can finish their courses.

A further ordinance of September 9, 1942, cleared up some ambiguities
and specifically stated that Mischlinge of the first degree were to attend
the regular elementary schools, but not the more advanced elective
schools. They might also attend kindergarten.[43]

All these picayune gradations were of course difficult to administer,
and many a school authority closed his eyes when it came to applying
the regulations. Cognizance of this situation was finally taken in Berlin

when, in an ordinance of April 5, 1944, it was admitted that there was no uniformity in testing the ancestry of Mischlinge of the first degree for purposes of enforcing the ordinance of July 1942.[44] Henceforth for the duration of the war no genealogical papers were to be required. Instead parents or guardians were simply to make a declaration that to the best of their knowledge the child was not descended from Jewish parents or grandparents. At elementary schools and compulsory classes of vocational schools not even this declaration was to be required, on the basis that Jewish Mischlinge were subject to compulsory education. For the exclusion of Jews no declaration would be necessary as the few scattered Jewish children were known.

With this final ordinance in regard to Mischlinge the history of Jewish education in the Third Reich is complete. Under Hitler's leadership the Germans put the clock back in many places, but nowhere more than in their treatment of Jews and Jewish education. It would be necessary to go back centuries and would require much research to discover—if it were possible—when there was not a single Jew in the regular Christian school system of Germany. This status the Nazis achieved almost overnight. But not only were the Jews isolated from the regular German schools; the separate Jewish educational system, which for a time was encouraged, was itself dissolved when the Nazis forbade all schooling of Jewish pupils by either paid or unpaid teachers.

Part Five

The Post-World War II Era

Chapter XV

The PERIOD of
FOUR POWER CONTROL

The end of the war (May 7–8, 1945) brought the complete collapse of the German government, and all authority passed to the allies. They divided most of Germany into four zones of occupation under the control of the Soviet Union, the United Kingdom, the United States, and France. The territories east of the Oder-Neisse rivers were not included in this arrangement, but were set apart and placed under direct Russian or Polish administration, pending the conclusion of a peace treaty. Similarly in the west an enlarged Saar territory was formed, which France controlled until 1957. An Allied Control Council was established in Berlin, which was divided into four occupation sectors, and although territorially situated within the Russian occupation zone Berlin was not a part of any zone. The Allied Control Council was given power over matters affecting all Germany, and it was expected that it would establish general policies which would then be implemented by each of the occupying powers. Pressure of time and circumstances, as well as ideological differences and governmental practices, had the result that the military governments of each of the powers tackled problems in their own way in their respective zones.

By the time the fighting was over most German schools had ceased to function, and the whole school system was in chaos.[1] The occupying powers ordered all schools closed, which was not a radical thing to do, as summer vacation was at hand, and for many other reasons it would have been impossible to put the schools in running order immediately. Equipment had deteriorated because of the shortages of the war years and many buildings had been destroyed. As of 1947 a survey in Württemberg-Baden showed that, out of 1511 school buildings, 65 had been destroyed, 53 partially destroyed, and 87 had been requisitioned for the housing of refugees, for use as hospitals, and for army occupation purposes. Soviet authorities stated that 4.3 percent of the school buildings in their occupation zone were destroyed and 17 percent severely damaged. Cities were especially hard hit. In Dresden, Leipzig, and Chemnitz alone, 205 school buildings were destroyed and 28 severely damaged. Munich suffered the destruction of one-third of its school buildings.[2]

Although in many of the smaller towns and rural areas the school buildings remained unscathed, they were totally inadequate because of the high birth rate in the late thirties and the great influx of evacuees, refugees, and expellees. The school problem did not lessen as people who had been evacuated returned to their old homes. The allied policy of expelling Germans from the territory east of the Oder-Neisse line, from Czechoslovakia, and from other countries in Southeastern Europe continued to swell the school population. What this meant for the overburdened school facilities is shown by the fact that in West Germany on September 13, 1950, there were 1,163,300 expellees from the above

Table 2. Geographical distribution of Protestants and Catholics in Germany (percent of population)

Area	1939		1946	
	Protestant	Catholic	Protestant	Catholic
Germany	60.6	33.3	59.7	35.0
German Federal Republic (West Germany)	49.2	45.8	50.2	45.8
German Democratic Republic (East Germany)	86.8	6.1	81.6	12.2
Berlin	70.0	11.3	71.4	10.9
Saarland	25.6	71.7	24.2	73.8

Sources: *KJ*, 1951, p. 397; *KH*, 1944-1951, pp. 219-238. Statistics of 1939 and 1946 are adapted to territories later formed into the German Federal Republic and the German Democratic Republic. The census of September 9, 1950 showed a slight shift in the Federal Republic: Protestant 51.2 percent; Catholics 45.2 percent.

territories between the ages of 6 and 14, and 503,500 between 14 and 18. To these should be added the children among the many "refugees" who fled to the west from East Berlin and the Russian occupation zone. The refugees totaled 1,550,000 by 1950, and the number increased rapidly in the next years. These displaced people were not settled uniformly in all lands of West Germany, but their number was sufficient everywhere to complicate school problems.[3]

The Russian zone, of course, also received its full share of expellees. According to censuses taken in 1950, there were 4,100,000 expellees out of a population of 17,600,000 in East Germany and 7,876,000 out of 47,696,000 in West Germany. This mass migration changed the religious complexion of Germany. Table 2 covers only the initial stages of this migration, but already indicates changes in religion in the main territorial divisions. Such a table, however, scarcely reflects the effect in individual communities.[4]

Of the total number of expellees in West Germany in 1950, 53 percent were Protestant and 45.2 Catholic, 0.1 percent Jewish, 1.5 percent belonged to other religious bodies, and 0.1 percent did not designate themselves as having any religious affiliation.[5] A breakdown of the religious affiliation of the expellees in East Germany is not available but there must have been a substantial Catholic group among them as Table 2 indicates. These displaced people all brought different educational traditions and practices to the territories where they settled. The resulting mixture of religious denominations meant that in many formerly purely Catholic or Protestant villages there came to be a substantial religious minority. Especially large groups of Protestant displaced persons settled in the predominantly Catholic lands of North Rhine-Westphalia, Rhineland-Palatinate, Baden and Württemberg-Hohenzollern, while the predominantly Protestant lands of Hesse and Württemberg-Baden received a high percentage of Catholics.[6] This new intermixture of denominations proved to be a serious complicating factor when schools began to function again and the churches demanded the reestablishment of the old confessional-school system.

Denazification

Added to these difficulties was the great shortage of teachers. Many had been killed during the war, and normal numbers of new teachers had not been trained. The allies also launched on a policy of denazification which bore heavily upon the teachers. The Nazis had been zealous in forcing the teachers to join the National Socialist Teachers' Organization, as well as other ancillary party groups and even the party itself. The teachers, as is customary in most countries, had been given numerous petty jobs to do in community affairs, and it is not surprising that many of them were caught by the first sweeping denazification decrees. In the United States zone in 1946 more than half the former schoolteachers were eliminated.[7] By comparison the French military government tackled the problem more expeditiously and left more former teachers free to carry on in the schools of the

French zone. The Russians are reported to have dismissed 80 percent of the teachers.[8] On the other hand the states could draw upon the supply of teachers among the expellees. This was done particularly in the British and American zones. For example in Württemberg-Baden at Volksschulen and higher schools 24 percent of the teachers were expellees, in Upper Bavaria 33 percent and in Hanover 32 percent.[9] One effect of the denazification procedure was that former clergy, particularly members of the Roman Catholic religious orders, came at first to have a disproportionate share of the teaching positions. They were not members of the long list of proscribed organizations and early had the privilege of teaching restored to them. Everywhere short cuts were devised to train a new supply of teachers.

Not only the teaching staff was denazified but the curriculum as well. Textbooks all had to be reviewed by the occupation authorities and cleared for use in the schools. The texts formerly used in religious classes fared very well in this examination. By August 1946 the education and religious-affairs branch of the United States Military Government had examined 66 volumes, approved 44 of them, had given conditional approval to 21, and had disapproved only 1.[10] Most of the conditionally approved books had only a few objectionable passages and after these were removed could again be used. Thus Otto Dietz's *Die Biblische Geschichte* (Munich, 1932, and later editions) drew this comment.[11]

Over-emphasis on part played by Jews in the condemnation and crucifixion of Christ, which makes a sweeping generalization of what was only a segment of Jews. Matthew, Mark and Luke, in telling of these events, refer to the mob as "das Volk" or "der ganze Haufe," terms which would be more suitable instead of "die Juden" (St. John does use term "die Juden").

This book was given approved standing in 1948 after corrections had been carried out satisfactorily.

Herman Ebert's *Lehrbuch der katholischen Religionslehre I* (MS, place and date of publication not given) was censored in 1945 with this comment:

An explanation of the Ten Commandments for teaching purposes in higher Catholic institutions of learning; references to Communism, Socialism, Soviet Russia are politically onesided, undemocratic, historically untrue and do not belong in a book of this kind.

A different type of objection is indicated in the comment on Jakob Schumacher and Hubert Lindemann's *Hilfsbuch für den katholischen Religionsunterricht in den mittleren Klassen höherer Lehranstalten II:*

Kirchengeschichte in Zeit- und Lebensbildern (25 ed., Freiburg im Breisgau, 1936).

Guidebook for religious instruction in Catholic schools; treatment of historical events not always objective, e.g. the Queens Mary and Elizabeth of England, the causes of the French Revolution, etc. Deletion of Hitler's Concordat with Rome and of praise of Mussolini's cooperation with the Church required.

Religious Education in the Laws of the Four Zones

This brief introduction indicates the nature of some of the problems which confronted the occupying powers as they set about getting the schools ready to open. In November 1945, the coordinating committee of the four occupying powers adopted the following resolution:

In matters concerning denominational [confessional] schools drawing on public funds, religious instruction in German schools, and schools which are maintained and directed by various religious organizations, the appropriate allied authority should establish in each zone a provisional regulation adapted to local traditions, taking into account the wishes of the German population in so far as these wishes can be determined, and conforming to the general directions governing the control of education. In any case, no school drawing on public funds should refuse to children the possibility of receiving religious instruction, and no school drawing on public funds should make it compulsory for a child to attend classes of religious instruction.[12]

This resolution came relatively late and zone authorities had already been forced to act. Schools had to be opened without too much delay, and often decisions were made which more logically should have followed the establishment of the new governments. Many of these early decisions restricted the freedom of occupational authorities later in pushing educational reforms, for practices once approved—even if only provisionally—were hard to reverse.

Policies varied in the four occupation zones. In the British and American zones the military government authorities intervened on the whole less than did their French and Russian counterparts.[13] In general in the western zones there was a tendency to return the schools, particularly as regards church-school relations, to the status existing prior to 1933 when Hitler took over. An early American directive specifically stated that so far as possible questions concerning denominational control of German schools and religious instruction in German schools were to be left to the decision of appropriate German authorities.[14] In all four zones regulation of education was made a function of the new German states (*Länder*) established by the four powers. In some cases

8*

these states coincided fairly closely with old territorial units; others were made up of portions of several former government areas. The result is that today, as formerly, Germany not only has a different educational system for each state, but within the various states a variety of provisions exists, carried over from previous regimes. Legally the German educational system consists of a tremendous complex of constitutional, treaty, and legislative provisions, which are overlaid with ordinances accumulated over the years. Many rights and privileges are jealously guarded by special interests or by local communities. During the Nazi era the privileges which the churches had long exercised in relation to the schools had largely been set aside. These changes were in large part never confirmed by legislation, which meant that there were no legal handicaps to nullifying them. Once the war was over the churches, backed by large sections of the population, were determined to restore many of the old practices. It also seemed to many a logical and practical way to achieve denazification, although in some cases it was a step backward, in view of trends in educational legislation over the past century.

In general the Germans agreed with the occupying powers on the need for school reform. It was no new problem, and they had been discussing it for years. But the Germans traditionally move slowly in this respect. For example the education law heralded by the Prussian Constitution of 1850 was not passed until 1906, and even then it was not complete, while the general-education law promised by the Reich Constitution of 1919 was never passed. Hitler did inaugurate important educational changes, many of which leading educational reformers had long advocated. People who stressed similar plans after World War II were placed in the unenviable position of advocating things which the "devil" had blessed.

The occupying powers had to provide a legal basis for the various German governmental agencies which carried on the day-to-day affairs. True to their belief in the value of unwritten constitutions the British did not push the formulation of written formal constitutions in the states of their zone. They issued directives as need arose and encouraged the state governments to deal with problems through ordinary rather than constituent legislation.

In the American, French, and Russian zones written constitutions were drawn up as the various states were organized. All these constitutions contain statements on individual rights including provisions in regard to education and religion. Many of the educational clauses were taken over almost word for word from the Weimar Constitution, or in the case of Bavaria from the concordat which the Bavarian government had concluded with the Vatican in 1924–25. The Bavarian constitution, which was approved by American authorities, contains an article, quite apart from the education sections, which states: "The state treaties formerly concluded, especially the treaties with the Christian churches of 24 January 1925, remain in force." [15] This article of the constitution in itself virtually restored to Bavaria her old system of confessional schools and publicly subsidized private (church) schools.

Whether or not the concordat which Hitler had made with the Vatican retained its validity for all Germany at the close of the war was a vital question so far as school legislation was concerned. The Allied Powers considered this question and "it was decided that, in view of the Nazis' complete disregard of their agreement and their flagrant breach of its terms, the concordat could only be considered as being in abeyance. This did not imply, however, that it could not be revived or held to be binding on a responsible German government or its guardians." [16] The four-power decision was interpreted in various ways in the four zones. Nowhere did the powers undertake to implement the provisions of the concordat. In the American zone the view was taken that:

The terms of the Concordat of 1933 remain technically binding and will be respected unless declared inoperative in whole or in part by the Allied Military Authority.

The terms of the Concordats between the Holy See and Bavaria (1924), Prussia (1929), and Baden (1932) which are confirmed by Article 2 of the Concordat of 1933, will be respected by Military Government unless the appropriate section of the 1933 Concordat is declared inoperative by the Allied Control Authority. [17]

In the Russian zone no attention was paid to Hitler's concordat. Here the formulation of state constitutions was preceded by the adoption of a Soviet-sponsored "Law for the Democratization of the German School." [18] This law was passed in almost identical form in all the states of the zone between May 22 and June 2, 1946. It is not surprising, therefore, that the educational provisions of the constitutions formulated later are virtually the same throughout the Russian zone.

With the exception of Bremen, which did not give final approval to its constitution until October 1947, all the other states of the United States, French and Russian zones had adopted their constitutions by June of that year. [19] It is to the provisions of these new constitutions that one must look first of all to find what are the fundamental principles regulating church-school relations in most of Germany today. A consideration of these provisions, however, is best postponed to the later chapters where the West and East German school systems are discussed separately.

Further Four Power Directives

Once the constitutions were drawn up education laws had to be formulated to implement the provisions. New study plans had to be set up, regulations enacted to determine how parents should make their choice as to school types, finances arranged, and many other matters regulated. There had of course been suggestions and directives issued earlier, but in January 1947 the American authorities formulated what they called "Guiding Principles for Evaluation of Educational Programs" and sent them to the four ministers of education of the states of the American zone. These were later changed a little but they form the essential points of Directive No. 54, issued by the four occupying powers on June 25, 1947. These "Basic Principles for the Democratization of Education in Germany," issued by the four powers, omit the American points on religious education which stated: "where the constitutions permit the establishment of interdenominational and denominational [confessional] schools side by side, the school law should safeguard their educational standards with regard to grading, staff, equipment, and the like." [20] Directive 54 emphasized the provision for free compulsory education, training for international understanding, the need for teacher training to take place in a university or in a pedagogical institution of university rank, and the "participation of the people in the reform and organization as well as in the administration of the educational system."

In October 1947 the Allied Control Council adopted another less important directive entitled *Basic Principles for Adult Education in Germany*. [21] However, Directive 54 and the Education Law for Berlin, which was adopted by the Berlin City Council on November 13, 1947, and approved by the Allied Council (June 22, 1948), together constituted the most important educational legislation which was achieved on a quadripartite level.

The Berlin School Law

In 1933 practically all schools in Berlin were organized on confessional lines; of these 515 were Protestant, and 54 were Catholic. There were a few Jewish schools and a somewhat greater number (28) of secular schools. Under Hitler, the secular as well as the Jewish schools were abolished, while the confessional schools were all converted into interdenominational schools.

On June 11, 1945, exactly a month before the western powers occupied their respective sectors of Berlin, the Berlin *Magistrat*, which had been established by Marshal Zhukov, apparently on his order issued "Regulations for Reopening the Schools of Berlin." Point 8 stated: "Parents are at liberty to have their children receive religious instruction in the schools. It is, however, to be given in additional or opening and closing hours (*zusätzliche oder Eckstunde*) by clergy or teachers commissioned by the church."[22]

This brief order seemed clear enough but actually led to many interpretations particularly as to time of instruction. An ordinance of September 26, 1945, is indicative of this and of the generally critical attitude of the Berlin authorities of that time towards religion in the schools.

Giving of religious instruction is not a concern of the schools, but is entirely a matter for the churches. They can authorize clergy or teachers, or other suited persons to give this instruction. (1) Religious instruction as a purely church affair takes place outside of the real period of teaching and is independent of the teaching plan of the school. (2) The hours of religious instruction are not school hours and cannot be counted among the required number of teaching hours of the teachers who participate in giving such instruction. Payment is made directly by the churches. . . . (3) Children under 14 years of age, who are to take part in religious instruction, are to be reported directly to the churches by the parents without the cooperation of the schools. Children from 14 years of age report personally themselves. These notifications can be withdrawn at any time. As the churches have sufficient means of contacting parents, there can be no question of furnishing school address lists, or of handing out church questionnaires or enrollment papers (*Werbezettel*) in the school, nor is the religious instruction to be considered in school reports.[23]

This ordinance was protested by church authorities, but it set the conditions according to which the new religious education program had to get under way. It was definitely to be carried out by the churches (*im Auftrage der Kirche*) although it was not yet clear to either church or civil authorities what this involved. Obviously it was not to be religious education as formerly carried on in the schools. To emphasize the difference the Protestant church leaders soon adopted the phrase *Christenlehre* (Christian teaching). The term is not unknown among Catholics, although they have in general retained the old phrase *Religionsunterricht*.

By October 1945 religious instruction was being carried out in thirteen of the twenty districts of Berlin.[24] In these districts from 85 to 100 percent of the Protestant parents enrolled their children for instruction, and the percentage was certainly no less for Catholics. Some school

principals were cooperative and sympathetic, but others raised difficulties and made it almost impossible for the churches to organize
classes. On October 15, 1945, the civil administration of Berlin drew up
new regulations which definitely stated that, "Religious instruction is
to be given in addition, outside of regular teaching hours." [25] Under
this provision the difficulty of organizing religion classes was greatly
increased; in fact, it was made virtually impossible where schools were
operated on a shift basis. The Allied Military Government (*Kommandantur*) was always favorable to the principle that religion should be
taught in the schools to all children whose parents desired it. In an
order of April 4, 1946, the Kommandantur overrode the Berlin civil
administration, decreeing that religious hours should be normal classroom hours. Yet disputes over when the classes could be held continued, and with few exceptions religion classes were pushed to the
"Eckstunden" or even outside the regular school day.

In the same order of April 4, 1946, the interallied Kommandantur
also demanded that a new written enrollment for religious instruction
should be carried out in all schools. This was the third time within a
year that parents were called upon to state whether they wanted their
children to take religious instruction. The churches rightly regarded
this as a referendum and made an all-out effort to contact all parents. [26]
The lack of personnel, the shortage of necessary supplies, the size of
the parishes (sometimes numbering over 20,000 souls), the fact that
school districts and parish districts were not the same, that no good
mailing lists were available in view of the mass destruction of living
quarters, that schools did not cooperate in furnishing lists of pupils,
and that people constantly shifted dwellings, all this made it a difficult
campaign to carry out. Nevertheless it was eminently successful. In
spite of difficulties and hindrances created by some officials, 86 percent
of the Protestant children in all the various kinds of schools registered
for religious instruction. In the next few years the number of children
participating in this program, if anything, increased.

The conflicts of church and state under Hitler had in many ways
prepared the churches for the emergency which now faced them. The
Protestants established a "Chamber of Education and Instruction"
(*Kammer für Erziehung und Unterricht*) which has become one of the
most important offices of the Berlin Protestant church. [27] This Chamber
was placed under the direction of Pastor Hans Lokies of the Gossner
Mission Society. Even before the end of the war, he had begun training
religion teachers, and he now assembled a group of dedicated men to
direct the training of the many teachers who were needed. Ten to
twelve-week training courses were established in which laymen were

trained as catechists (*Katecheten*) to give religious instruction in the schools. Men and women from all walks of life volunteered for this task. Many of them had a basic religious knowledge from their school days, but there were others who had had little contact with religion and church, but to whom the catastrophes of the period had brought an eagerness for religious truth and a willingness to serve. As Gerhardt Giese, one of the leading men in the Chamber of Education, wrote in 1955: "Today we would not like to be without all those catechists who through our courses were first brought to Christ and the churches." [28] Some of these training courses were held at night, but as early as 1945 full-time courses during which catechists lived and studied at a school (*Internatskurse*) were established. These courses were extended, and by 1948 regular two-year seminary programs had been established. Later a half year of practice teaching became an integral part of the training of all catechists in West Berlin.

These specially trained lay religious workers and teachers have in the postwar period become a notable addition to the personnel of the churches. They exist in both West and East Germany, but are particularly significant in the latter and in Berlin, because here they must carry practically the whole burden of religious instruction in the schools. Also of great help to the church in Berlin, especially in the early days, was the fact that many regular teachers voluntarily taught religion classes in addition to their regular teaching load of thirty hours a week. [29] Pastors, deaconesses, and other church personnel also stepped into the breach and helped with the instruction in the schools. Pastors were particularly active in the higher schools where instruction was traditionally given by trained theologians. Restricting instruction to opening and closing hours made it particularly difficult for clergy to work in the schools, for they often had other commitments. Since 1946 the number of hours of instruction given by Protestant pastors in the Berlin schools has decreased, although church authorities have ordered that four weekly hours of instruction are part of a pastor's duty. In Berlin at the beginning of the school year 1948–49 Protestant instruction was being given by 715 catechists (57,451 hours), 526 regular teachers (4,973 hours), and 308 church personnel (6,173 hours). [30]

The Catholic church also established its special school bureau at diocesan headquarters and has worked out its educational program not unlike that carried on by the Protestant churches. The fact that Catholics are less numerous, and often in former times had pupils come to church buildings for instruction, perhaps made the problem of providing schoolrooms less acute for them. Secular clergy, catechists, regular teachers, and other church helpers (*Seelsorgehelferinnen*) shared the burden of instruction. Although some of the latter were members of orders, a relatively small amount of religious teaching in Berlin schools since 1945 has been done by members of a monastic order. They have been more active in the Catholic private schools.

Financing their program was far more difficult for Protestants than for Catholics, partly because their numbers made the program more extensive, and secondly, because the Catholic church could draw more quickly and directly on outside help. By October 1945 the Catholic church in Berlin was already able to pay all its teachers. The Protestants had to resort to various makeshifts. In each district of the city committees were appointed which were to assume responsibility for financing religious instruction. Some of these were active, others not. Always the burden returned to the *Erziehungskammer* and to the central church authorities. The regular church taxes were not enough to keep the churches functioning properly and could only be raised with the consent of the four powers.[31] There was nothing else to do but to rely on the methods through which funds for missionary activities had always been raised. Church collections, special monthly church offerings, sponsorship of certain schools by church groups and other similar devices were resorted to. Finally in 1946 Pastor Lokies and his colleagues hit upon the idea of having a special Education Sunday, to be followed by an organized house-to-house canvass. This plan produced results and became the chief source of revenue in the next years. Gifts also were received from foreign churches. The Lutheran World Federation was especially helpful in financing the training program for the catechists. In spite of all financial efforts salaries remained low, and the instruction program could be carried on only through the faith, devotion, and sacrifice of those participating in it.

In October 1946 elections were held in Berlin which resulted in a leftist majority. The new chamber undertook to draw up an education law, which, as usual, led to much heated discussion and debate. Although their school ideals were not identical, Protestant and Catholic church authorities cooperated closely in the attempt to prevent complete secularization of the school system. In spite of this their efforts were not very successful, and the law as finally adopted did not meet with their approval. Actually the law was largely a formulation of existing Berlin practices so far as religion was concerned. In the preamble it was stated that the aim of the schools was to educate to tolerance and democratic peaceful living. To this end education was to be based on "classical antiquity, Christianity, and those social movements which have led to humanism, freedom, and democracy, that is, on the whole cultural inheritance of humanity, including the German inheritance."[32]

The law provided for only one common school type (*Einheitsschule*), with an eight-year elementary and four-year higher school.

Religious instruction could be given in the schools, but it was left entirely to the religious and ideological societies, and it was to be given by clergy or teachers of religion who were authorized and paid by the societies. Regular teachers had the right to give religious instruction on the side according to the laws which governed this type of extra employment. No advantage or disadvantage was to accrue to teachers from either giving or not giving such instruction. Only those pupils were to receive religious instruction whose parents had made a written request to this effect. While this law continued the existing Berlin practice, it was contrary to historical custom, for formerly, as in West Germany today, a child received religious instruction unless specifically withdrawn from religion classes by the parents.[33] School authorities in Berlin had to set aside for those wanting such instruction two hours each week, which were to be either the first or last class hours of the day. Rooms with heat and light were to be provided free by the school authorities. Pupils not receiving religious instruction were to be given no other instruction in those hours when the religion classes met. This avoided the possibility of pressure from the school authorities either to the advantage or disadvantage of those receiving religious instruction. The important point, however, was that the religion hours, while restricted to the opening or closing hours, were to be part of the regular school program and not shunted to before or after regular school hours.

At first it was the intention to abolish all private schools in Berlin, but at the request of the American representative, the four-power Kommandantur changed the provision of the law so as to permit each confession and other interested groups to establish at least one private school.[34] Since Berlin's schools had always been predominantly Protestant and organized on confessional lines, the Protestants had never established a private-school system in the city. It was for them not simply a matter of reopening old schools closed by Hitler; they had to start from the beginning and they were slow getting under way. The Berlin school authorities resisted the establishment of private schools, and as the Russians withdrew from the Control Authority, it was impossible to get the necessary four-power approval. When Protestant churchmen finally started five elementary schools in 1948, they were challenged by the Berlin school authorities. Finally on August 22, 1949, the administration of West Berlin and the three Western Powers consented to the establishment of these five Protestant elementary schools and one Gymnasium.[35]

De facto *End of Four Power Control*

Legally the status of religious instruction in the Berlin schools was more in line with developments in the Soviet zone than in the western zones. Administratively, however, authorities in West Berlin took a more friendly attitude toward the religion classes which were organized than did the authorities of East Berlin. These differences became more marked as the rift between the Western Powers and Russia widened. On July 18, 1948, the Western Powers, having failed to reach an agreement with Soviet officials, introduced a much needed currency reform in the three Western zones. Russia countered with the blockade of Berlin which was soon extended to a general blockade between the Eastern and Western zones of occupation. On November 30, 1948, a separate government (*Magistrat*) was established for the Russian Sector of East Berlin. The Berlin blockade was broken by a sensational airlift of supplies which the Germans aptly called *Die Luftbrücke* (the air bridge). It was not until May 12, 1949, that the blockade between the Western and Soviet zones (including Berlin) was ended. By that time the Parliamentary Council at Bonn had already adopted the final draft of a basic law for Western Germany which henceforth was officially to be known as the Federal Republic of Germany. The Russian zone in turn was proclaimed the German Democratic Republic on October 7, 1949. The era of four-power government was ended *de facto* if not *de jure*. Already showing basic divergencies the school systems of East and West Germany were now free to develop without regard to four-power control. Although political unity had ended, the unity of the churches remained and this has not been without significance for the maintenance of religious instruction in the schools.

Chapter XVI

RELIGIOUS EDUCATION in the FEDERAL REPUBLIC of GERMANY

The boundaries of the states organized by the Western Powers in their occupation zones usually coincided with old administrative frontiers, but sometimes nothing more historic than an Autobahn served as a demarcation line. The break-up of historic Prussia had far-reaching effects, but of almost equal significance was the division of Baden and Württemberg, and the separation of the Palatinate from Bavaria. Laws went with the territory, and this meant diversity in most states in regard to educational regulations. In this connection the religious diversity of the population of each state was also important. Table 3, in which the statistics for 1939 have been adapted to the present territory of the states, shows that in the main the religious pattern of Germany has not changed greatly. However, such a table cannot show the infinitely more diversified picture within small localities.

State Constitutions and Religious Education

In most of West Germany the tendency was to wipe out changes introduced under Hitler and to restore the schools to their pre-Nazi status. This was particularly true in regard to the organization of the schools and the place of religion in education. In January 1946 the British issued a temporary directive effective in their zone, which provided that parents could ask for a confessional school if they wished.[1] Regularly in the following years parents were consulted as to type of schools, and the school systems which thus came into being were later written into the constitutions and the school laws. The result is that in North Rhine-Westphalia and Lower Saxony both confessional and interdenominational (Gemeinschaftsschulen) prevail. In some districts of Lower Saxony there are only interdenominational schools, while in the

Table 3. Religious affiliation in the Federal Republic of Germany

State	Year	Protestant		Catholic		Jewish		Other		Type of School
		Number	Per-cent	Number	Per-cent	Number	Per-cent	Number	Per-cent	
British Zone										
Schleswig-Holstein	1939	1,417,838	89.2	68,299	4.3	594	0.0	102,263	6.5	Interdenominational
	1946	2,277,596	87.9	176,188	6.8	485	.0	137,965	5.3	
	1950	2,282,532	88.0	154,857	6.0	195	.0	157,064	6.0	
Lower Saxony	1939	3,566,404	78.6	745,918	16.4	6,199	.1	220,911	4.9	Confessional and interdenominational (varies in districts)
	1946	4,828,803	76.6	1,208,847	19.2	1,963	.0	260,440	4.2	
	1950	5,245,001	77.2	1,277,637	18.8	997	.0	273,744	4.0	
North Rhine-Westphalia	1939	4,415,301	37.0	6,775,102	56.7	28,535	.2	726,159	6.1	Confessional and interdenominational
	1946	4,579,536	39.0	6,604,551	56.2	2,912	.0	561,405	4.8	
	1950	5,412,717	41.1	7,231,707	54.8	2,311	.0	549,441	4.1	
Hamburg	1939	1,357,158	79.3	101,484	5.9	8,438	.5	244,797	14.3	Interdenominational
	1946	1,140,553	80.3	91,961	6.5	961	.1	187,396	13.1	
	1950	1,265,695	78.8	104,486	6.5	936	.1	234,489	14.6	
U.S. Zone										
Bremen	1939	471,666	83.8	49,199	8.7	788	0.1	41,262	7.4	Interdenominational
	1946	417,286	85.3	43,464	8.9	127	.0	28,548	5.8	
	1950	474,142	84.8	49,721	8.9	106	.0	34,650	6.3	
Hesse	1939	2,398,977	69.0	896,172	25.7	23,670	.7	160,307	4.6	Interdenominational
	1946	2,532,615	63.4	1,301,540	32.6	2,949	.1	158,574	3.9	
	1950	2,773,002	64.2	1,391,707	32.2	2,142	.0	156,950	3.6	
Württemberg-Baden	1939	2,042,240	63.5	1,020,638	31.7	10,747	.3	143,716	4.5	Interdenominational
	1946	2,108,734	58.5	1,360,524	37.7	2,165	.1	135,881	3.7	
	1950	2,315,525	59.2	1,478,756	37.9	1,153	.0	112,414	2.9	
Bavaria	1939	1,749,595	24.9	5,149,878	73.2	14,668	.2	123,451	1.7	Confessional and interdenominational
	1946	2,325,663	26.5	6,271,648	71.3	22,770	.3	169,569	1.9	
	1950	2,421,360	26.5	6,556,217	71.8	8,595	.1	139,881	1.6	

French Zone

						Others				
Rhineland-Palatinate	1939	1,161,189	39.2	1,723,564	58.2	7,298	0.2	70,059	2.4	Confessional and interdenominational
	1946	1,089,098	39.6	1,614,866	58.6	348	.0	49,257	1.8	
	1950	1,224,541	40.8	1,734,425	57.7	387	.0	45,399	1.5	Interdenominational
Baden	1939	306,597	24.9	892,344	72.6	2,411	.2	28,344	2.3	
	1946	309,089	26.0	855,667	71.9	183	.0	25,902	2.1	
	1950	379,238	28.3	935,770	69.9	183	.0	24,438	1.8	Confessional and interdenominational
Württemberg-Hohenzollern (incl. Lindau)	1939	455,869	42.4	595,283	55.3	828	.1	23,873	2.2	
	1946	478,349	43.1	605,198	54.6	150	.0	25,071	2.3	
	1950	565,041	45.5	660,899	53.2	111	.0	16,153	1.3	
Baden-Württemberg	1950	3,260,627	50.7	3,030,744	47.2	1,442	0.0	137,412	2.1	Confessional and interdenominational
Saarland	1939	211,816	25.7	589,526	71.5			22,636	2.8	Confessional
	1946	209,905	24.7	626,142	73.5			15,568	1.8	
	1951	242,132	25.3	701,570	73.4	439	.1	11,005	1.2	

Sources: *KJ*, 1951, pp.408–416; 1954, p. 385; *SJ*, 1956, p. 43. The column "others" includes those belonging to the Evangelical Free churches and members of other religious denominations, as well as those without religious affiliation. In the Schleswig-Holstein figures two corrections have been made in the "others" column from the totals as given in *KJ*, 1951, p. 408. The Evangelical Free churches number 1.15 percent of the Protestants in Schleswig-Holstein; 1.5 percent in Lower Saxony; 2.81 percent in North Rhine-Westphalia; 1.27 percent in Hamburg; 0.99 percent in Bremen; 1.52 percent in Hesse; 3.58 percent in Württemberg-Baden; 1.38 percent in Bavaria; 1.52 percent in Rhineland-Palatinate; 1.54 percent in Baden; and 3.94 percent in Württemberg-Hohenzollern. In 1952 Württemberg-Baden, Württemberg-Hohenzollern, and Baden joined to form a new southwest state known as Baden-Württemberg. In the figures for the new state taken from *SJ*, 1956, p.43, the Evangelical Free Church and the Catholics-Independent-from-Rome are included under Protestants.

district of Oldenburg legally only confessional schools exist. In Schleswig-Holstein and Hamburg only interdenominational public schools are permitted.

The constitutions drawn up in the states of the American and French zones usually make reference to a religious purpose, and many of them state specifically that the schools are to be organized on a Christian basis. Two of the states of the French zone (Württemberg-Hohenzollern and Rhineland-Palatinate) and one of the American zone (Bavaria) provided for confessional as well as interdenominational schools, the parents and legal guardians having the right to request either form. In these states confessional schools became the prevailing type, while in Saarland only confessional schools were permitted. One state of the French zone (Baden) and three of the American zone (Württemberg-Baden, Hesse, and Bremen) provided for only interdenominational schools, for in these states this type of school organization had long prevailed. Bremen, with its predominantly Protestant population, was historically organized on a confessional basis, but it had for years been interdenominational in practice.

Private schools were permitted in all states of West Germany upon receiving approval of the state authorities. This was to be given if these schools equalled the standards of the public schools. Such denominational private schools provide a good opportunity for experiment, are a safeguard against the encroaching power of the state, and also are considered essential as a last resort of the denominations in case the state-supported confessional schools should be entirely replaced by an interdenominational system.

In West Germany the strong Catholic-dominated Christian Democratic Union (CDU) favors confessional schools, while the other leading German party, the Social Democrats (SPD), favors the interdenominational form. In this the Socialists are supported by the Free Democrats. While the parties differ in their position on type of school, none is opposed to having religion taught in the school. In fact only the Communists are opposed to such instruction. This is a reversal for the Social Democrats, for until after World War I they generally stood for the abolition of religious instruction from the curriculum. This modification of their program means that there is general agreement in favor of religion as a subject of instruction in the schools.

It is therefore not astonishing that the constitutions and laws in West Germany provide that religion is to be a regular subject of instruction in all elementary and higher schools and even in vocational schools. Parents and guardians may withdraw a child from religious instruction, although in Bavaria, Baden, and Rhineland-Palatinate, pupils who do not take religion are to receive instruction in generally recognized principles of morality. The school law of 1954 in Lower Saxony provides that after the fifth year "comparative religion" (*Religionskundlicher Unterricht*) is to be a regular subject of instruction for those who do not take part in the religion classes. This is to be instruction about religion, but in no particular religion; it is to cover the important religions of the world, particularly Christianity and Judaism, and to discuss personalities who, without confessional ties, have contributed to ethical progress. "From such instruction pupils will learn that all great religions, in spite of differences in doctrine and cult, are one in furthering such ethical principles as humanity and love of neighbors."[2] Bremen, in accordance with long-established practice in its schools, makes provision only for nonconfessional instruction in Bible history on a general Christian basis. The constitution of Bremen goes on to state:

Instruction in Bible history will be given only by teachers who have stated their willingness to do so. Those entitled to determine the education of the child will decide as to the participation of the child in this instruction. Churches, religious, and *Weltanschauung* associations have the right to instruct outside of school hours those children whose parents or guardians (*Erziehungsberechtigte*) desire it.[3]

In all other states of West Germany religious instruction, whether given in confessional or interdenominational schools, is to be given in accordance with the principles of the religious denomination. To insure this the constitution and laws contain various provisions. Church authorities are given the right to participate in drawing up teaching plans, to approve textbooks, and to visit classes in religion. This is in no way to place in jeopardy the general state supervision of the schools. Clerical supervision as practiced in the nineteenth century remains legally abolished. Everywhere schools are under supervision of the state, and lay inspectors are employed, the church having only certain rights to inquire into the work of the religion classes.[4] In most states the constitutions provide that the authorization of the church is required for teachers who give religious instruction. This is a constitutional approval (in Hesse it was by way of explanatory ordinance) of what the Catholic church has always insisted upon—that no one should teach religion without possessing or receiving the *missio canonica* from the church. That the Protestant churches are now also to make this authorization (*Vokation, Placet*—whatever it is termed) is a new thing. It is a measure definitely aimed at preventing the religious instruction from getting into the hands of skeptics. Provisions are also made in the fundamental laws that teachers should be adequately trained in religion.

The Federal Constitution and Religious Education

At the meeting of the Parliamentary Council which met in Bonn in 1948–49 to draw up a basic statute for West Germany, schools were a hotly debated issue. The Catholic church wanted to see the right to establish confessional schools throughout West Germany written into the constitution. This had not been granted by the Weimar Constitution of 1919, but the Catholics maintained that it had been accorded to them in the Concordat of 1933. They demanded the insertion of an article in the constitution which would specifically recognize agreements which the churches had made with the German governments.[5] The case for the confessional school system also rests on the recognition of the right of parents to determine the education of their children. This has often been interpreted to mean that parents should have the right to decide what type of school should be established in their communities. Neither of these points is specifically covered by the Bonn Constitution. A considerable number of Protestants are as ardent supporters of confessional schools as are the Catholics, but this constitutional battle was largely waged by the Catholic bishops. The Catholics were still bound by the encyclical of Pope Pius XI of December 31, 1929, on Christian Education of the Youth (*Divini illius Magistri*) in which he made it a matter of conscience to demand a Catholic school. The official yearbook of the Protestant church states in reference to the conflict over confessional and interdenominational schools: "The responsible men of the Evangelical church showed themselves fundamentally disposed to approve a Christian interdenominational school, but it was made impossible for them to do so by the demands of the Roman Catholic church for Catholic confessional schools."[6] It was felt that if Catholics by demanding confessional schools withdrew into their own schools, then the Protestants, being left to themselves, would do well to avail themselves of the denominational privileges which go with a confessional school system.

While the constitution of the Federal Republic does not determine types of schools it does contain some provisions on religious education which fall in line with those of the old Weimar Republic. Private schools, particularly of a denominational character, are to be allowed if they meet certain standards set by the states. Religion is to be a regular subject of instruction in all public schools, except for such purely secular (*Bekenntnisfreie*) schools as may be established.[7] This instruction is to be given according to the principles of the religious denomination, without prejudice to the state's right of supervision. Parents may withdraw their children from religious instruction, and no teacher is to be placed under the obligation of giving religious instruction. These provisions in general correspond to the state constitutions, and there is even a limiting clause (Article 141) which states that the paragraph making religion a regular part of the curriculum would not apply in a state where another regulation by state law existed on January 1, 1949. This would cover Bremen's limitation of religious instruction to Bible history on a nondenominational basis and would also cover Berlin and the East zone, should they ever be joined to West Germany under the present federal constitution.

Later Constitutional and Legal Developments

After the adoption of the Bonn Constitution various legislative problems remained. The states of the British zone had still to adopt constitutions, all the states had to formulate comprehensive education laws, and in southwestern Germany there was a manifest desire for unification and a rearrangement of state boundaries. One of the most hotly debated issues affecting the solution of each of these problems was the old question of whether schools were to be organized on a confessional or interdenominational basis. In the background of all these problems was the decisive question as to whether the Concordat of 1933 with its all-important educational provisions was still valid in Germany.

The constitutional debate in North Rhine-Westphalia was particularly bitter on the school issue. Here Protestants number about forty percent of the population, but some seventy percent of them had consistently voted after 1946, to send their children to Protestant confessional schools. Among the Protestant teachers, on the other hand, it was estimated that about seventy percent were for the Gemeinschaftsschule.[8] The Social Democrats, strongly organized in this state, were for making the Gemeinschaftsschule the normal school form. Most of North Rhine-Westphalia was traditionally confessional school territory, although there were sections that had formerly been part of the state of Lippe which supported interdenominational schools. In the end the decision was in favor of continuing a mixed confessional and interdenominational school system, with the right of parents to decide to which school they would send their children.

A basically similar decision was reached in Lower Saxony by an indirect route. The school problem was not treated in detail in the constitution. Instead the already existing situation was confirmed in the former lands of Hanover, Oldenburg, Brunswick, and Schaumburg-Lippe, which have been united into the new state of Lower Saxony. The failure to solve the school issues in the constitution of Lower

Saxony made the enactment of a school law all the more urgent there
The law, passed in 1954, favored the interdenominational schools, but
permitted confessional schools. In Article 31, however, the law specifically maintained the status of schools as they were established in 1919
in Oldenburg, which means that in this one district of Lower Saxony
there can be only one type of school, the confessional.[9]

In Hamburg and Schleswig-Holstein it was definitely stated that
the public schools as Gemeinschaftsschulen gather together all pupils
without considering their confession or *Weltanschauung*. In accordance
with the federal constitution, these constitutions, like the older state
constitutions, provide for religion as a regular but not compulsory
subject of instruction in all public schools except purely secular schools.
In the words of the Hamburg law:

Religion is a regular but not compulsory subject of instruction. Without
prejudice to state supervision it will be given in conformity with the doctrines of the Religious Associations (*Religionsgemeinschaften*) in the spirit
of toleration and respect towards all confessions and *Weltanschauungen*.[10]

In the negotiations leading to the formation of the new southwest
state of Baden-Württemberg through a union of Baden, Württemberg-
Baden, and Württemberg-Hohenzollern, the school articles were the
ones that aroused most debate and sharpest differences.[11] The Christian-
Democrats wanted to insert in the new constitution a clause specifically
recognizing the validity of the Reich Concordat of 1933. This was rejected in the responsible committee by a vote of 13 to 11 with one
abstention. The same committee by a vote of 14 to 11 decided that all
public schools should be Christian Gemeinschaftsschulen and rejected
the demand of the Christian Democrats to permit the establishment of
confessional schools. The proposed constitution was submitted to the
plenary assembly on June 6, 1953, but had not been ratified when the
national elections were held on September 6, 1953. The latter election
brought a sweep for Chancellor Adenauer, which meant that his
Christian Democratic party gained ground everywhere. As a result the
government in the new Southwest State, as it was then called, was
reconstituted, representing a large coalition of all the leading parties.
This coalition compromised their differences on disputed articles of the
proposed constitution.

Among these differences the school compromise was most important. Here the basic decision was to continue the *status quo*. The rights
and duties resulting from agreements with the Catholic and Protestant
churches remain untouched by the constitution. This provision was
definitely recognized as bypassing the vexed question of the legality

of the Reich Concordat of 1933. On this point no agreement could be reached. The constitution of Baden-Württemberg calls for a Christian-oriented training, and religion is to be a regular subject of instruction at public schools.

It is to be given according to the doctrines of the religious associations, without prejudice of the supervisory rights of the state, by people commissioned and supervised by the churches. Participation in religious instruction and at religious school exercises is subject to the decision of parents and legal guardians (*Erziehungsberechtigte*), participation in giving religious instruction is left to the decision of the teachers.[12]

As to types of schools the constitution simply states:

The types of Volksschulen remain in the different parts of the state as determined by laws and regulations that were valid on December 9, 1951.

The natural right of parents to have a voice in the upbringing and education of their children must be considered in the establishment of educational and school systems. Detailed regulations will be made in a school law which requires a two-thirds majority.

The reference to December 9, 1951, is to the date of the referendum on unification, and so this means that confessional and interdenominational schools will have the status which they had in the three former postwar states. Baden is historically one of the oldest Simultan territories in Germany, and the people in these regions cling tenaciously to the interdenominational school system. This is one reason for the provision that the future school law will need a two-thirds majority.

The Baden-Württemberg school compromise resembles very much the school compromises which lay back of the adoption of the Weimar Constitution. That document envisaged the enactment of a national school law which was never passed, and it seems likely that the proposed state school law in Baden-Württemberg will suffer the same fate. The whole bitterly fought controversy illustrates again how deeply tradition and history underlie the educational system of Germany. The American and French occupation authorities in general followed a conservative educational policy. When the Germans themselves finally had a completely free hand, they could only agree to carry on the traditional systems just as the Allies had done.

In each state the constitutional provisions discussed above were implemented by extending or modifying existing laws and regulations. In most cases detailed education laws were expected, but formulation of these is a difficult task and the Germans did not hurry unduly. In order to bring about more uniformity in educational matters a standing conference of the ministers of education of the German states was established in 1948. This group, which came also to include the "Senator for Education" of West Berlin, gave itself an organizational statute in 1956. The conference has only advisory powers, but when unanimous agreement is reached it usually means that a similar policy or measure will be enacted in each of the states. For example, out of agreements reached by the conference has come the common beginning of the school year on April 1 (Bavaria remains an exception to this), the widespread use of a common designation for middle and higher schools, the common recognition of "leaving" examinations (Abitur) of higher schools, the common recognition of the second teachers' examination, and a common grading system in the schools. It has been stated that between 1947 and 1953 this body had agreed on more measures to unify the German school system than were passed in the whole period of the Weimar Republic, 1920–1932.[13] It is true that often these agreements have dealt with not very vital matters, but it is becoming more and more possible to speak of a German educational system.

School laws have been enacted in Berlin (June 6, 1948), Bremen (April 4, 1949), Hamburg (October 25, 1949), North Rhine-Westphalia (April 2, 1952), Lower Saxony (September 14, 1954), Rhineland-Palatinate (February 4, 1955); laws covering elementary schools (August 8, 1950) and vocational schools (March 25, 1953) in Bavaria; laws on compulsory attendance (December 5, 1955), and school-finances and administration (March 28, 1957) in Schleswig-Holstein; and four laws covering compulsory education (May 7, 1952), private schools (April 27, 1953), finances (July 10, 1953) and miscellaneous matters elaborating school laws (December 22, 1953) in Hesse. Other states besides Hesse and Schleswig-Holstein have also passed compulsory education and finance laws, and in all states detailed ordinances have been issued explaining the laws or implementing existing constitutional provisions, laws and regulations.[14]

German schools are still based on a four-year foundation school (with some exceptions, six years in Bremen, Hamburg, and Berlin), on which follow the upper branch (*Oberstufe*) of the Volksschule, or the middle school, or the various types of higher schools (Gymnasium, Oberschule, etc.). Education is compulsory up to 14 years of age, except in Schleswig-Holstein, Bremen, Hamburg, and Berlin, where the age limit is 15. At present there is a strong movement in the other states to add a ninth year to the Volksschule. After this, if students do not go on in a regular school, they must attend a part-time vocational school until the age of eighteen. Education is free, although in some states fees are still charged in the upper grades of the higher schools and the universities.[15] Everywhere it is under the supervision of the states. Private schools which fulfill public-school functions are everywhere permitted if they meet minimum standards, and many special schools exist, such as kindergartens and schools for the handicapped.

There is no need here to discuss all the educational changes which have been enacted in postwar Western Germany.[16] In regard to religious education there are some matters still to be considered in regard to: (1) types of schools, (2) the recruiting of teachers of religion, (3) teacher training, (4) the conduct and curriculum of the religion classes, and (5) school religious services.

Types of Schools

As has been indicated above, the public schools are either organized on a confessional or Christian-oriented interdenominational basis. Only in Berlin (and East Germany) are the Gemeinschaftsschulen organized without a Christian orientation. The terms used to describe types of school in the constitutions and laws vary: *Schule* in Berlin; *Christliche Schule* in Lower Saxony and former Württemberg-Hohenzollern; *Gemeinschaftsschule* in Bremen, Hamburg, Schleswig-Holstein, and Hesse; *Christliche Gemeinschaftsschule* in former Württemberg-Baden; *Christliche Simultan* in Baden; *Bekenntnis* and *Gemeinschaft* in Bavaria; *Bekenntnis* and *Christliche Simultan* in Rhineland-Palatinate, *Bekenntnis* in the Saar, while North Rhine-Westphalia even uses four terms, *Bekenntnis, Gemeinschaft, Weltanschauung* and *Bekenntnisfrei*. The multiplicity of terms is indicative in itself of how disputed a problem the organization of the schools in post-war Germany has been.

Summarizing in another fashion, there are four states where only interdenominational schools exist: Bremen, Hamburg, Schleswig-Holstein, Hesse; and four states where both confessional and interdenominational schools exist: Lower Saxony, North Rhine-Westphalia, Rhineland-Palatinate and Bavaria. In addition there is Baden-Württemberg, which is divided, the territories of Baden and North Württemberg having only interdenominational schools, while the region formerly known as Württemberg-Hohenzollern, now called *Regierungsbezirk* Tübingen, has both interdenominational and confessional schools. In Lower Saxony which is listed above as having both confessional and interdenominational schools, there is one district (Oldenburg) in which only confessional schools are legal, as is also the case in the Saar. Only in Berlin are the schools without any religious orientation.

In those states where confessional and interdenominational schools are permitted side by side, the opportunity for choice always raises the question of which type of school is to be established. The American authorities in their overall program held that: "The establishment of additional schools in a community for religious or other reasons should be prohibited if the educational standards of the community are thereby lowered."[17] In general German authorities agree to this, but there is no agreement as to "when educational standards of the community are thereby lowered." For example, are educational standards lowered if a one-room confessional school is erected for a religious minority, while the majority attend a well-developed elementary school? Similarly, do two less developed confessional schools perhaps offer educational advantages over one more developed interdenominational school? The constitution of Saarland makes bold to answer this, stating in Article 27: "In connection with [establishment of confessional schools for a minority] it is to be observed that a one-class school guarantees a well-ordered educational school system." The arguments pro and con have resulted in voluminous provisions stating under just what conditions confessional or interdenominational schools may be established. In Lower Saxony parents or guardians of at least 120 children (240 in communities of over 5,000 population) must request a certain school type if it is to be set up; in Bavaria the number is twenty-five. Regulations usually contain provisions aimed at preventing too great a splitting-up of the school system. In Württemberg-Hohenzollern the school law of 1948, for example, provided that: "If in places on the day of voting there are fewer than 100 children of school age belonging to different confessions, and the number of the minority equals one-third, only an interdenominational school is to be established."[18] In Bavaria the confessional school is the normal school type and interdenominational schools can only be established on request of parents and guardians under certain conditions.

Regulations in regard to establishing various types of schools necessarily are detailed and complex. The cornerstone on which they all rest is the right of parents to decide what type of school they want for their children. This is a principle long upheld by the Catholic church as a natural right of parents, and also accepted by the Protestant churches, and one which even the Socialist party has come to agree to because of its essentially democratic character. The consultative right of parents in some educational matters is today a generally accepted principle of German education administration.

In connection with school types, the question of whether all, none, or only part of the provisions of the Concordat of 1933 were valid remained until 1957 an undecided issue. If it were valid, it would mean that the Catholic (and Protestant) churches would have the right to establish confessional schools in all parts of the Federal Republic. Most legal experts held that the concordat was valid,[19] but the political bodies—notably the assemblies which drew up the Bonn Constitution (1949) and the constitution of Baden-Württemberg (1953)—refused to recognize specifically the concordat as such as binding. In neither the Federal Constitution or any of the new state constitutions was the national Concordat of 1933 specifically confirmed, although various constitutions do confirm the three separate state concordats.

On September 9, 1952, when the constitution of Baden-Württemberg was being considered, the Vatican requested the federal government to bring influence to bear so that the provisions in the new constitution would be in agreement with the terms of the Reich Concordat of 1933. This the federal authorities did, asserting that it was necessary to recognize international obligations, and that the proposed establishment of Gemeinschaftsschulen to the exclusion of confessional schools would not be in accordance with the law of the land. The authorities in Baden-Württemberg did not accept this federal interpretation but were able to avoid the issue through the school compromise.

The question of the validity of the concordat, however, would not be stilled. Lower Saxony, after much public and parliamentary debate, on June 24, 1954, finally enacted a general education law. During the months of discussion the federal authorities, at the instance of the papal nuncio, reminded the government of Lower Saxony several times that the Concordat of 1933 was valid for all Germany and that the proposed Lower Saxon school law was contrary to it. While the Lower Saxon authorities refused to admit the latter point, they nevertheless took the position that the concordat was not binding in their state. In introducing the bill for the third reading, Minister President Kopf expressed the wish that the question of the validity of the concordat might be decided by the Federal Constitutional Court.

The continued protests of the Vatican to the effect that the Lower-Saxon Education Law violated the concordat raised for the federal government the question of loyalty in the observance of international agreements. Therefore on March 12, 1955, the federal government brought before the Federal Constitutional Court at Karlsruhe the charge that Lower Saxony had violated its obligations and loyalty to the Republic in enacting its Education Law of 1954.[20] In this action the federal government maintained that the Saxon law favored the Gemeinschaftsschule to such an extent that the right of parents to request confessional schools under Article 23 of the concordat was negated. Bremen and Hesse later joined Lower Saxony in the case

before the court. Bremen took the position that religion was not a compulsory subject in its schools, something which the federal constitution
specifically recognized in Article 141, and enforcement of the provisions
of the concordat in Bremen would be contrary to this constitutional
provision. Hesse charged specifically that the concordat was not valid,
because it had been enacted in an illegal fashion under Hitler's Enabling
Act of 1933.

The legal proceedings aroused much interest throughout Germany,
and it was not until March 26, 1957, that the court finally handed
down its 88-page decision.[21] The verdict, superficially at least, was in
the nature of a compromise. The court held that the concordat was
indeed valid, but that Lower Saxony had not violated its obligations of
loyalty to the Republic, because in school affairs the states are sovereign
and not bound by the provisions of the national concordat. The court
reasoned that the states had in large part decided upon the organization
of their schools, which often departed from the provisions of the concordat, before the federal constitution was enacted on May 23, 1949. If
the fathers of the constitution intended to bind the states to the provisions of the concordat, they should have specifically inserted a clause
to that effect. The essence of the federal character of the Republic rests
in the cultural autonomy of the member states. While maintaining the
validity of the concordat as such, the court thus actually declared its
school clauses invalid, since there was no power to coerce the states in
school matters. The decision recognized the federal government as the
contracting power with the Vatican for some portions of the concordat,
but not for others. This decision, paradoxical as it may seem, was in
line with the historic German practice of letting the various states
regulate educational affairs.

Elementary school types in West Germany in May 1955 numbered
13,460 interdenominational, 5,110 Protestant confessional, 11,356
Catholic confessional, and 14 other schools. While a breakdown confessionally of the 1001 special schools, 806 middle schools, and 1572
higher schools is not available, it may be assumed that they are overwhelmingly interdenominational.[22]

Such an enumeration does not present the complete picture. Many
of the interdenominational schools are in territories where the population, all or nearly all, belongs to only one confession, and these schools
in practice are virtually confessional schools. Now as in years past many
confessional schools are attended by children of other confessions because populations are mixed and there is no other school for them to
go to. In Bavaria, the strongest confessional-school state, 22.7 percent
of the Catholic confessional schools are attended solely by Catholic

Table 4. Protestant and Catholic attendance at confessional and interdenominational schools in three states, 1954–1955

State	Evangelical			Catholic		
	Number of students	Percent in Evangelical confessional schools	Percent in Gemeinschafts-schulen	Number of students	Percent in Catholic confessional schools	Percent in Gemeinschafts-schulen
North Rhine-Westphalia	603,272	65.8	30.4	794,484	95.6	3.6
Rhineland Palatinate	138,235	44.4	52.4	196,819	77.9	20.7
Bavaria	236,101	61.1	20.3	691,355	92.4	3.7

Sources: *KJ*, 1955, pp. 451–458; *KE*, VIII (1955), 175. See also graphic presentations in "Die Konfessionen und Ihre Wirksamkeit in der Welt," *KE*, X (1957), 293–296.

pupils, while 11.9 percent of Protestant schools have only Protestant pupils. Seventeen percent of the Protestant children attend Catholic confessional schools while only one percent of Catholics attend Protestant confessional schools. Out of 19,141 Catholic school classes in Bavaria, 38.2 percent are attended by only Catholic pupils, 15.6 percent have one Protestant, 12.9 percent have two, 19.7 percent have three, and 2.6 percent have more than eleven. That Catholics lay more stress on confessional schools is clearly indicated by the figures in Table 4 which shows attendance in three states which have both confessional and interdenominational schools. Taking West Germany as a whole, about 42 per cent of elementary-school children attend Catholic confessional schools, 41 percent interdenominational schools, and 17 percent Protestant confessional schools. This means that about two-thirds of the number of Protestant elementary-school pupils are in interdenominational schools, while in contrast only about one-eighth of the Catholic pupils are in such schools.

As has always been the case in Germany, Protestants continue to send a greater percentage of their children to higher schools than do Catholics. The ratio of Protestant teachers to Protestant students in all schools is below what it should be, the ratio of Catholic teachers to Catholic students is approximately correct, while the number of teachers without particular confession (*sonstige*) is well above the proper ratio to students who fall in this category.

The right to establish confessional schools in all Germany, while sought by the Catholic church, is actually not a crucial issue because the church has everywhere the right to erect private schools. Permission to erect such schools must be granted if they meet the established standards of the public schools. Private elementary schools, however, can be established only when the authorities recognize that the school fulfills a special pedagogical interest or when a particular kind of confessional, *Weltanschauung*, or interdenominational school is not at hand and parents demand that type. The state has no financial responsibility in regard to these private schools, although in most cases they receive subsidies and indirect aid either from the state or local government authorities. In Hamburg the state is particularly generous to the Catholic private schools which have the benevolent support of the school authorities. All teaching supplies and 90 percent of the salaries of the teachers are paid from public funds. Appointment of teachers is however made by church authorities. There are in Hamburg fourteen fully organized Catholic private Volksschulen, one middle school, and two Gymnasiums, the one for boys being in charge of Jesuits, the one for girls in charge of Sisters of the Sacred Heart.[23]

The Catholic church has by far the largest number of private schools throughout Germany; the Evangelical churches have few in comparison. In recent years the followers of Rudolf Steiner (a leader who founded the Anthroposophy movement during the twenties) have established a number of schools known as *Freie Waldorfschulen* (or Rudolf Steiner Schulen).[24] Only the North Rhine-Westphalia Constitution provides for the establishment of secular (*Weltanschauung*, *Bekenntnisfrei*) schools, and as yet none of these have been established.

Recruiting of Teachers of Religion

The Bonn Constitution, following in this instance almost word for word the Weimar Constitution, provided that not only must religion be a regular subject of instruction in public schools, but it also must be given in accordance with the principles of the religious denominations. The state constitutions usually spelled this condition out even more clearly, and there is no doubt at present that the churches are to be consulted in regard to religious instruction. In fact the churches usually cooperate in formulating the teaching plan in consultation with school authorities and teachers.

A brief quotation from the teaching plan drawn up for Protestant instruction in Bavaria indicates how closely religious teaching is supervised by the churches.

Church instruction in the schools . . . takes place through members of the congregation who have been commissioned with this task by the church and who are ready to carry it out as a matter of personal conviction.

Church instruction in the Volksschulen is carried on by clergy, by catechists, and by teachers, the last under protection of the rights accorded them by state law.[25]

The commissioning of religious instructors had long been done by the Catholic church and the Catholics simply carried on old procedures in regard to granting the *missio canonica*. For the Protestant churches this raised new problems. Who was to grant the authority in a church which held to the basic concept of the priesthood of all believers? Who was to receive the authority? Would special examinations be required? The situation was also complicated by the fact that in some states there was more than one Protestant church organization. Gradually rules and procedures were worked out for granting permission to teach, the permission being usually referred to as *Vokation*.

Teachers who had qualified to teach religion classes before 1945 and desired to teach were usually automatically granted the *Vokation*. New teachers who qualify in religion in their first teacher's examination receive a temporary permit. On qualification in the second examination (representatives of the churches are present at the examinations in some states), the final certificate is usually presented, although in some cases a certain trial period of teaching is required before the final certificate is issued. In Hesse the minister of education notifies the Protestant church authorities of candidates who have qualified. If the church approves the candidate, the certificate is issued by the church, and it may be transmitted to the teacher through regular state educational channels, or, as is most often the rule, the *Vokation* is handed to the teacher by church representatives in a church service. Churches also usually require that the candidate request the issuance of the *Vokation*, which serves to assure acceptance on the part of the candidate and avoids the indignity of a refusal. While the requirement of the *Vokation* caused considerable concern among teachers in the immediate postwar years, this has diminished steadily with the improvement of relations between teachers and church. The Protestant church ordinances for Rhineland-Westphalia and Lippe on the granting of the *Vokation* state specifically the position which Protestant churchmen in general hold.

The Evangelical church takes the position that teachers, who cannot give Evangelical instruction because of matters of conscience, should not be handicapped in their professional rights. The church in case of emergency is prepared to take care of Evangelical instruction through pastors and catechists.[26]

This provision, like many similar statements by churchmen, was meant to indicate that the church did not wish to coerce the teaching profession.

Admittedly, however, church approval of religion instructors raises a problem. Religion must be a subject of instruction in schools, and in one-teacher rural schools, school authorities as well as local clergy and populace usually want a teacher who is willing and able to teach religion and to conduct the religious school services. In schools with several teachers the problem is not so acute. The following statement, however, no doubt voices the opinion of a substantial segment of teachers.

I maintain, that the number of people who can sincerely say that they accept the old confession of Jesus the Lord and Savior, is much smaller than would be necessary to maintain religious instruction as it has heretofore been given. That it still appears to be otherwise is because . . . it is today difficult in several German states to be appointed as a Volksschule teacher if one is not qualified to teach religion. I am of the opinion this situation is unworthy of all interested parties and of the problem itself.[27]

The right to grant permission to teach religion also means the right to deny it or to withdraw the privilege once granted. The churches have in such cases established procedures for the teacher to be heard, and decisions are made by regularly constituted committees, usually made up of clergy and teachers.

Special church-trained lay catechists also receive the *Vokation* or *missio canonica* and in some places participate in giving instruction. Clergymen automatically receive the authorization, but they are not employed as teachers of religion in all sections of Germany. Here custom and the regulations dating back to the Weimar Republic and the Empire are the governing factors. Now as formerly, however, fully trained theologians or teachers that have studied religion and have qualified by examination are the rule at higher schools. Immediately after the war and even at present the teaching load of some ministers, Protestant and Catholic alike, in sections of Bavaria is unbelievably heavy. The writer talked to a number of ministers and priests and found most of them teaching from ten to twenty or more hours a week in addition to their confirmation classes and carrying on all their parish duties.

The method of compensating the church authorities for religious instruction in the schools varies from one state to another, and the regulations are extremely complicated. For instruction at higher schools, but not at elementary schools, the ministers usually personally receive direct compensation. In Bavaria new regulations have recently been adopted.[28] When Bavaria was a kingdom both clergy and teachers were salaried royal employees, and the king expected all clergy to teach in the schools. The present secular state has retained this attitude. An ordinary clergyman is expected to teach six hours, an "exponierter" curate eight, all other vicars twelve hours a week. The state then totals up the number of religion hours given by clergy in the schools, subtracts the number of hours the clergy are obligated to give, and pays the church authorities (Catholic or Protestant) a lump sum for the remaining hours. The individual clergyman receives nothing extra. At higher schools the Protestant church has ruled that a clergyman can "earn" 900 marks "extra," a curate 600 marks. If he earns more, the church deducts the additional sum from his regular salary. Compensation is about 169 marks for an hour a week of instruction throughout the school year. By deducting from salaries the excess income earned by Protestant clergymen teaching at higher schools, the church gained about one-half million marks in 1955. There is, of course, more than a financial reason for this provision, as it tends to deter pastors from teaching too many hours at higher schools to the neglect of their parishes, and it is also an important factor in equalizing salary levels. Teaching at higher schools as compared to elementary schools usually involves more preparation, and some additional compensation is probably justified. In Hesse the state can commission clergy to give instruction up to four hours a week. The churches have also taken some steps to prevent overburdening of the clergy. In the Archdiocese of Cologne Cardinal Frings in 1950 designated twelve to fourteen hours for chaplains and six to seven hours for priests in large cities as the maximum teaching load.[29] Certainly more clergy in Central and North Germany participate now in religious instruction than ever before.

In addition to the training of catechists, church authorities have also taken the initiative in sponsoring study groups where teachers of religion meet to discuss their problems and are given aid by expert leaders. By attending these study courses teachers immediately after the war could obtain the right to give religious instruction. In fact teachers who have received permission to teach religion are expected to attend various church-sponsored study groups and conferences. Very often they also have their own professional organizations. As more qualified lay teachers become available the teaching load of the clergy will no doubt be lessened, but in most places where they are now teaching the clergy have no intention of permitting themselves to be crowded out of the schoolroom altogether. They desire to share in the religious instruction to insure its orthodoxy. Clergy are *ipso facto* not necessarily good teachers, but at present more attention than ever before is given to pedagogy and school problems in the training of clergy. In Hesse-Nassau since 1954 ministerial candidates, after their first examination, work for two months in an elementary school under the direction of a teacher. Before receiving their theoretical pedagogical training they are thus made acquainted with the practical problems of the schools where they in the future will have to teach religion classes. Although the time allotted is short, the reports have been that this has been a most helpful training experience. It is also evidence of the better relations that have developed between clergy and teachers, that there have been more teachers willing to undertake such supervision than there have been ministerial candidates.[30] The Catholic church is also providing more pedagogical training in its education for the priesthood. Since 1952, the *Deutsches Institut für Wissenschaftliche Pädagogik* at Münster has organized each semester a special fifteen-day session for priests who desire to perfect their instructional techniques.[31]

Although it is not a matter of granting the *missio canonica* or *Vokation*, there is a somewhat related problem which should be mentioned. This is the question of appointing teachers to confessional schools. It has usually been considered an earmark of those schools that all instruction is carried on in the spirit of the confession. The North Rhine-Westphalia Constitution (Article 12), for example, provides: "In confessional schools, children of Catholic or children of Evangelical belief are brought up and instructed in the spirit of their confession." The Bavarian Constitution, unlike most of the other constitutions, states (Article 135) baldly: "In the confessional schools only such teachers will be employed as are qualified and willing to instruct and educate according to the principles of the denomination concerned." This, of course, raises problems as to whether a teacher is doing this, and narrow interpretations are likely to impinge on the rights of teachers guaranteed to them by the state as civil servants. The Protestant churches make much less of all instruction "being in the spirit of the confession" than the Catholic church does.

Even at interdenominational schools the question of religious affiliation presents itself, although on a broader plane. This is illustrated by an incident in Baden, where, in 1949, the minister of education refused to reinstate, after denazification, seventeen teachers who were without confession. The minister maintained that the Baden schools were Christian interdenominational (Simultan) and a Christian belief was necessary as a qualification for teachers. The Socialist party as a matter of principle protested, but the High Court of Baden refused to recognize their protest.[32] In practice no great difficulties arise in matters of appointment on account of religious affiliation, but it can only be expected that there will be occasional incidents, if schools are legally organized not only on a Christian but also on a denominational basis. The problem also involves the use of Jewish teachers, but this is less acute than formerly, since there are so few Jews left in Germany today who aspire to be teachers.

Teacher-Training Institutes

The constitutions have little to say on the education of teachers. In the first years after the war it was necessary to resort to all kinds of short cuts, but more recently real advances have been made. Through the efforts of the Permanent Conference of the Ministers of Education, the education of elementary-school teachers has been raised again to a university level. This meets with a long-time demand of teachers' organizations. With a few exceptions candidates for admission to teacher training must have graduated from a higher school. The training courses last four to six semesters and take place in institutions bearing various names such as *Pädagogische Hochschule* or *Pädagogisches Institut*. All are state institutions except in Bavaria, which has also some private confessional institutes. In Hamburg the institute is closely connected with the university. There are 23 Catholic, 10 Protestant, and 25 Simultan teachers' institutes in Western Germany.[33] Of the latter, eight are in Lower Saxony, and while officially Simultan, two of them are overwhelmingly Catholic and six overwhelmingly Protestant. Several of the confessional institutes in other states also have one or two guest students of another confession, but the confessional lines in teachers' institutes are usually rather strictly followed. Berlin, Bremen, Hamburg, Hesse, Lower Saxony, and Schleswig-Holstein have only Simultan training schools, while Bavaria, Baden-Württemberg, and North Rhine-Westphalia have both confessional and Simultan training schools. Rhineland-Palatinate has only confessional teachers' institutes, and its constitution is most emphatic in upholding the confessional training system, stating:

Teachers are trained in special training schools which are separated according to denominations and must be permeated with the spirit of the denomination involved. The same holds true for the dining hall and dormitories attached to these training schools. (Article 36.)

In Württemberg-Hohenzollern teacher training was given in two stages, students attending first interdenominational and then confessional institutes. This system was continued for this region when the new state of Baden-Württemberg was established. Saarland has one teacher-training institute with independent Protestant and Catholic divisions.

The big argument for confessional institutes is that teachers cannot be expected to teach at confessional schools in the spirit of the confession if they are not trained in a similar school. On the other hand higher schools and universities traditionally have been organized in Germany on an interdenominational basis, and many feel that this is a sound basis for teachers' institutes, if instruction in schools is to be in a democratic spirit of toleration towards all. In all institutes candidates can, if they wish, receive the necessary preparation to qualify for religious instruction in the schools.

Conduct and Curriculum of Religion Classes

In regard to the number of hours given over to religious instruction there has been in general a return to old established practices. This means in most states four hours a week in the elementary schools (except for two in Schleswig-Holstein, Bremen and Hamburg, three in Hesse and Baden-Württemberg), two hours a week in middle and higher schools, and one hour a week in the vocational schools, where religion is now generally taught. In terms of overall instruction it means about 15.4 percent of the hours in the first four years of the Volksschule, 12.8 percent in the last four grades, and 5 to 6 percent in the various grades of the higher school.[34] In this connection, however, it should be borne in mind that religious education is not restricted to these formal hours in religion. There are the school religious services, the learning and singing of hymns in music hours, and above all confirmation instruction in the churches which is more or less correlated with the school work.

It should be pointed out that it is not always possible to maintain the full number of religion hours, or to provide separate instruction for each grade. This is true because religious instruction has to be on a denominational basis, and often in school systems the minorities are not numerous enough to form religion classes in each grade. It is also an inevitable result of the lack of teachers and the fact that in some sections of Germany the clergy still bear the brunt of religious instruction in the schools. It is often the case in Germany, as elsewhere, that a clergyman will have charge of several congregations in neighboring villages, each of which has a school. Even if the regulations and curriculum plans call for two to four hours of instruction a week, it would be a physical impossibility to have four hours for each grade separately. Classes have to be thrown together and at times even have to be curtailed. Herein lies a practical reason why German authorities did not take kindly to the suggestion of some American advisers that they adopt a series of graded textbooks for religion.

The churches have found it particularly difficult to staff the religion classes at vocational schools. Numbers alone constitute a problem, and moreover this is a whole new field of religious education, for formerly in many regions there was no religious education in vocational schools. In 1955 there were 4,229 vocational schools in the Federal Republic, attended by 2,228,567 students.[35] To this may be added the 1,250 more specialized full-time vocational schools (Berufsfachschulen) with 146,439 students. Since students in the regular vocational schools are usually employed as apprentices for most of the week, there is little time for study. Instruction must necessarily be largely in the form of lectures, and only if the classes are small enough can there be discussion groups. In most regions one hour a week is the normally allotted time, but it has not been possible to meet even this schedule in many places. For example, in Lower Saxony, ordinances of December 1953 provide that where religious instruction has not as yet been established at vocational schools Protestant and Catholic clergy may lecture once a month on religious topics.[36] In some cases an hour of church instruction on Sunday (*Christenlehre*) is recognized as fulfilling the assignment.

In most cases textbooks which had been used during the Weimar Republic continued to be used in the Hitler epoch. Therefore few were banned under denazification procedures, and at first old texts remained in use after the war. German church and educational leaders, however, have given much attention to new books, and some well-illustrated and freshly-edited texts have appeared. Of particular importance was the issuance in 1955, after some twenty years of careful study, of a new Catholic catechism known as the Catechism of the Bishoprics of Germany. It is divided into four chief parts: (1) Of God and our Salvation. (2) Of the Church and the Sacraments. (3) Of Life according to the Ten Commandments. (4) Of Ultimate things (*Von den letzten Dingen*). The usual questions and answers have been completely worked over, and the whole catechism is characterized by a new spirit of reverence and religiosity. Whereas the catechism of Canisius, which set the standard for several centuries, was in many ways directed against Protestantism, and the catechism of Deharbe, issued in 1847, which dominated the next decades, was directed against modernism and materialism, the new catechism was drawn up as a positive statement of faith and of the salvation of man through Christ.[37]

Now, as in past periods of German history, religious instruction has been under close scrutiny. After the experiences of the past decades, when religion classes were retained but often lost vitality or any real religious content, there has been a general attempt to restore more

9*

"orthodoxy" and more actual "religion" to the curriculum. This movement was given support by the frank recognition in the federal and state constitutions that instruction must be in line with the doctrines of the confessions. Hence comes the general recognition of the duty of the churches to commission instructors in religion and to help supervise what is taught in the classes. The old demand for general Christian religious instruction on a nondenominational basis in the schools has been pretty well stilled. Only in the city of Bremen, in accordance with long practice, is there nondenominational instruction in Bible history, with all denominational (catechism) instruction left to the churches. It is worth noting that the Catholic church has forbidden Catholic children or teachers in the Bremen schools to participate in the regular Bible history classes.

Another expression of this new concern over the content of instruction is the growing use among the Protestants, particularly in North Germany, of the term *Evangelische Unterweisung* rather than *Religionsunterricht*. It is again a distinction in German terminology which is almost impossible to translate. Dictionaries translate both *Unterweisung* and *Unterricht*, with the word instruction, but the former term has a connotation of directing and informing, particularly in regard to matters of doctrine. One could perhaps translate *Evangelische Unterweisung* as "evangelical indoctrination," using the term in its best sense. There is no doubt that the expression is meant to convey greater emphasis on Christian attitudes in the Protestant evangelical sense. To quote Kittel:

Evangelische Unterweisung, so our newly placed task is named—never again *Religionsunterricht!* We know now that every supraconfessional (*überkonfessionelle*) instruction in truth will become less than confessional, that every supra-Christian instruction in truth less than Christian. "Religion in general" in spite of its sentimental and wordy commendations, we know is without substance. We turn ourselves resolutely to the tasks which have been placed before us, since we have again come to realize that the Gospel of Jesus Christ is the Word of God.[38]

Asked by a newspaperman why the Evangelical church presently used the term *Unterweisung* and not *Religionsunterricht*, Oberkirchenrat Osterloh explained it in this fashion:

According to the fundamental teachings of the Evangelical church religious instruction in the schools fulfills on its part the charge which the church has obtained from its Lord to spread and teach the Gospel. This *Evangelische Unterweisung* is therefore not just knowledge about religion and also not so much a matter of imparting knowledge; it is witness of the living

God who upholds and directs his flock. This concept is emphasized when in the church reference is made to *Evangelische Unterweisung* and not to *Religionsunterricht*.[39]

There is also another consideration in regard to the use of the new term *Evangelische Unterweisung*. This term emphasizes the idea that the religious instruction in the schools is to be the result of a rich new cooperation between churches and teachers. "In order," writes Gerhardt Giese, "that religious instruction as *Evangelische Unterweisung*— or as we say here in Berlin *Christenlehre* (Christian teaching)—can really become 'Church in the School' it is necessary to have a real coordination of church and state in school affairs."[40] A necessary part of this program consists in persuading the teachers that there is no intention on the part of the Protestant churchmen, through their new rights in relation to religious education, to resort to bygone practices of clerical supervision in the schools. A new order calls for new terminology, and the use of the term *Evangelische Unterweisung* is spreading. It is at least descriptive of the present efforts to pour new spirit and content into old forms and practices.[41]

Whatever the terminology used to describe religious instruction in the schools, the basic religious curriculum is different from the old mainly in emphasis and method. While formal teaching of the catechism in school has been considerably restricted, Bible history, learning of Bible verses and hymns, the significance of the church year, introduction into the life of the church, and, in the upper grades, the broad outline of church history constitute now, as formerly, the core of religious instruction. How these materials are to be interrelated has always been a problem and remains one. The modern trend for more integrated instruction has continued. The various divisions of religious instruction are less compartmentalized than ever before. Nevertheless the custom that Bible history should be taught by teachers, and the catechism, or at least the last two parts, by the clergy, still prevails in many sections. A division of labor along these lines is particularly true among Catholics. Among Protestants the emphasis on the catechism comes in the upper grades and is chiefly outside the schools in confirmation instruction.

New teaching plans have appeared in various states which have been worked out by school and church authorities, the latter no doubt having a dominant influence. The plan for Evangelical instruction in Bavaria which indicates maximum and minimum norms is a good example of how material has been interrelated and how it has been arranged around the great festivals of the church year.[42] There is, no doubt, less memory work than in times past, but it has not been abolished. A child still learns, if perhaps in less obtrusive assignments, some portions of the catechism, a core selection of Bible verses, and a substantial number of the great hymns of the church. The difference between curriculum plans and actual accomplishments may be great, but it seems clear that the curriculum is such that no German child runs the risk of growing up religiously illiterate for want of an opportunity to learn about his religion.

The teachers of religion have not stood aside from general pedagogical advances and they, like others, employ activity instruction, visual aids, and various new educational techniques.[43] The teaching of religion has its own particular problems, and to compare it with other subjects such as mathematics, history, or the languages, would be a mistake. Now as in times past, the teachers of religion are expected not only to be concerned with imparting a certain amount of knowledge, but with the far more difficult problem of arousing and nurturing a true religious spirit and belief in God. If a pupil acquires a distaste for religion because of too heavy assignments or bad grades the whole purpose of the instruction is defeated. Here too the problem of discipline arises. Often in order to win over classes, to get their confidence and give them proper insight into religious values, a teacher permits somewhat more freedom in the religion hour. There is much discussion and raising of questions by students in the present-day class in religion. It is true that pupils sometimes take advantage of this freedom. In times past it was charged that a teacher drove the catechism and other memory material into the child's head by pounding his back. Happily this procedure is now a memory associated by some with the good old days. Discipline problems also arise because the religion teachers often come to a school only for a few classes; they are guest instructors and have no standing which comes from teaching something beside an "elective course," for no child is required to take religion. Then too there can be no doubt that many pastors and, particularly in recent years, catechists are not good disciplinarians in the usual pedagogical sense. While discipline in religion classes has its own peculiar aspects which are omnipresent, nevertheless on the whole it is not an alarming problem in the German schools.[44]

With religion a regular subject of instruction, grades in religion, which Hitler had abolished, have generally been restored. But restoration of grades has only revived some of the old problems. Few pupils indeed ever fail in religion, which again raises difficulties in relation to other subjects in the curriculum. Too often the instructor solves the problem by what passes in teachers' parlance as "a neutral grade." At higher schools the issue is particularly important because it becomes involved in the general average. In 1951 the minister of justice and education in Rhineland-Palatinate called a conference of teachers of religion at higher schools of both confessions, for the purpose of settling the problem of giving grades in religion. They came to the conclusion that the grade must represent only intellectual accomplishment; it must not be influenced "by the disposition, attitude, character, or 'churchliness' (*Kirchlichkeit*) of the student." It was realized that this would require an educational campaign to make the parents and public aware of the exact nature of the grade in religion. In Bremen, Hamburg (and West Berlin) only notice of participation is entered on students' records; elsewhere grades are entered as in other subjects. In practice no uniformity exists in Germany today as to the role of religion in the important final Abitur examinations at higher schools.[45]

The generally favorable climate of opinion which prevails in the Federal Republic in regard to religious education in the schools is manifest in the importance given to religious services and devotions. These had been largely abolished or drastically altered under the Nazi regime. Now some of the state constitutions even mention these services specifically, and today religious devotions are generally a part of German school life. No teacher or pupil is required to take part in them. In practice nonparticipation at a confessional school is a rare occurrence, and indeed it is so at all schools considering the total number of students and teachers. No doubt more is made of these services at confessional schools than at interdenominational schools, but they are by no means lacking in the latter. In Catholic confessional schools, especially higher schools, occasional school Masses and corporate Communion are customary in some regions. Among Protestants particularly there has again been a shift in terminology not unlike the change from *Unterricht* to *Unterweisung*. Now the term School Church Service (*Schulgottesdienst*) is being stressed instead of the older term School Meditation (*Schulandacht*) which had fallen into disrepute in many areas.[46] These school church services are usually held for children when they start school, at the beginning and end of the school year, in connection with school and church holidays, and in many areas they are even held weekly. This is often the case in the higher schools. Everywhere the school systems again pay attention to the important church festivals and these are usually school holidays. Crosses, crucifixes, and religious pictures, which the Nazis did their best to remove from school buildings, are again in evidence.

The nature of the religious exercises vary in the different types of schools and also according to the custom of the region. Here also the leadership of the teachers and headmasters is important. Usually there are short daily devotions. These may consist of only a short morning prayer, or may be extended by a song, reading of scripture passages, recitation of weekly Bible verses or other religious material. In inter-denominational schools these are of course without denominational slant.

It would be wrong to give the impression that these religious school observances raise no problems. These have long existed and the Germans have learned to live with them. Although teachers are sup-posed not to have to participate in school devotions, it becomes diffi-cult for them not to. The same is true for students. What are they to do while the services are being held? Not to participate sets them noticeably apart and this is exactly what most children seek to avoid. There is also the problem of religious minorities in confessional schools. Services too are likely to become perfunctory and instead of awakening religious feeling to deaden it. On the other hand there is much that can be said for them, if the purpose of teaching religion in the schools is to awaken the religious perceptions of a child. At least these services give public expression to what the people have written into their fundamental laws: that the schools are, with due respect and tolerance for representatives of other *Weltanschauungen,* to be organized on a Christian basis, and are to teach reverence for God in the spirit of Christian brotherhood.

Chapter XVII

RELIGIOUS EDUCATION in the GERMAN DEMOCRATIC REPUBLIC

Whereas West Germany was divided among three occupying powers, East Germany was under the sole control of Soviet Russia, subject only, as all the powers were supposed to be, to four-power control. This meant that from the beginning there was one rather than three policies in East Germany, and with one power directing affairs, the groundwork was laid from the start for the establishment of a centralized unitary state. Although initially there was a facade of traditional federalism, power and control remained with the central government. Each of the five states that were set up was formed out of a central core of territory that, under the Empire and the Weimar Republic, had its own state administration. Here as in West Germany the school systems were based on varying state laws, customs, and traditions. Short shrift was made of these.

In one respect, however, there was already a basic unity in East Germany, which over the years had resulted in a more uniform school system than could be developed in West and South Germany. East Germany was overwhelmingly Protestant. Some of the formerly predominantly Catholic sections, such as part of Silesia, were now placed under Polish administration. As expellees, some of the Catholics from beyond the Oder-Neisse line or from Czechoslovakia settled in East Germany, but most were scattered throughout the whole of Germany. Nevertheless, for the first time since the Reformation the number of Catholics in Thuringia, Anhalt, and Mecklenburg was more than ten percent. Table 5 shows the religious pattern of the various states on October 10, 1946, and on August 31, 1950.

Political parties in East Germany were not organized on religious lines to the extent that they were in the Western zones. Above all there was no traditionally strong Catholic party with its tenacious views on educational matters. The successors to the Center party, the Christian Democrats and some smaller conservative parties, favored the confessional-school system, but they were a small minority. On the school question as on other issues they were outmaneuvered. Parties of the left were now dominant,[1] and they had long opposed confessional schools. These parties were intent on carrying through reforms which advanced (especially Socialist) schoolmen had long advocated: the creation of a centralized unified school system, the removal of religion from the schools, and the complete secularization of the school system. While in the West both German authorities and the Control Powers turned back from the Hitlerian school reforms to 1933 and began building on old foundations, in the East they carried forward the changes in the school system which Hitler had begun. This was done, of course, to the accompaniment of many proclamations about rooting out Nazi influences from the schools and converting them into truly democratic institutions. The Nazis had eliminated many socialist and liberal school-men, and under the postwar policy of denazification these were among the first to receive positions of key responsibility in the Soviet Zone. Contrary to practice in the Western zones, the clergy were kept at a distance. The new officials, animated with a passion for liquidating reactionary forces, now had the opportunity to carry out reforms they long had advocated. As so often, however, the unleashed reform genie conjured up unforeseen changes and results.

State Constitutions and Religious Education

On July 27, 1945, the Soviet Military Administration created a German Central Administration for People's Education, and gave its president, Paul Wandel, the functions of an education minister for the whole zone. Under his direction a "Law for the Democratization of German Schools" was drawn up and was adopted in the spring of 1946 in almost identical form by each of the states. This brief law established the basis of all future educational developments in East Germany. It is so important that its main provisions should be summarized.[2]

(1) The task of the German democratic schools is to educate youth to be independent and responsible people, who are capable and willing to undertake service for the good of the nation. The pupils are to be inculcated with a truly democratic spirit of peaceful international cooperation.
(2) Schooling of the youth is exclusively a concern of the state. All private schools of every kind are forbidden. Religious instruction is a concern of

Table 5. *Religious affiliation in the German Democratic Republic*

States	Total Population	Protestants		Catholics		Jews		Others (inc. Weltan-schauung)		No Affiliation	
		Total	Per cent	Total	Per cent	Total	Per cent	Total	Per cent	Total	Per cent
Brandenburg											
1946	2,527,492	2,171,353	85.9	232,199	9.2	424	0	120,157	4.8	3,359	0.1
1950	2,579,675	2,188,351	84.8	224,193	8.7	297	0	162,508	6.3	4,326	.2
Mecklenburg											
1946	2,139,640	1,784,911	83.4	305,950	14.3	153	0	46,767	2.2	1,859	.1
1950	2,027,124	1,730,386	85.4	225,882	11.1	91	0	67,351	3.3	3,414	.2
Saxony-Anhalt											
1946	4,160,539	3,337,650	80.2	633,440	15.2	435	0	185,074	4.5	3,936	.1
1950	4,071,856	3,255,547	80.0	549,268	13.5	215	0	259,645	6.4	7,181	.2
Thuringia											
1946	2,927,497	2,254,709	77.0	488,902	16.7	428	0	176,787	6.1	6,671	.2
1950	2,837,641	2,186,744	77.1	428,594	15.1	228	0	219,095	7.7	2,980	.1
Saxony											
1946	5,558,566	4,659,129	83.8	450,012	8.1	654	0	441,193	8.0	7,578	.1
1950	5,682,802	4,626,691	81.4	472,155	8.3	503	0	574,567	10.1	8,836	.2
East Germany[a]											
1946	17,313,734	14,207,752	82.1	2,110,507	12.2	2,094	0	969,978	5.6	23,403	1.0
1950	17,199,098	13,987,719	81.3	1,900,092	11.0	1,334	0	1,283,166	7.5	26,789	.2
East Berlin[b]											
1946	1,174,582	830,384	70.7	122,808	10.4	2,535	.2	215,579	18.4	3,276	.3
1950	1,189,100[c]										

Sources: For 1946, *SJ*, 1956, p. 535; for 1950, *Statistisches Jahrbuch der Deutschen Demokratischen Republik*, I (1955), 9, 33. The German Democratic Republic lists *Apostolisch, Neuapostolisch, Adventisten, Methodisten, Baptisten* separately, and these figures have been added to those listed as *Evangelisch* to give comparable figures to those for 1946. In addition to Catholics, figures on Catholics-Independent-from-Rome (*Romfreie Katholiken*) are given: Brandenburg 729; Mecklenburg 728; Saxony-Anhalt 2,069; Thuringia 1,743; Saxony 2,350.

a Including 133,327 war prisoners and inhabitants of transient camps.

b Without 1,397 war prisoners and inhabitants of transient camps.

c Statistics on religious affiliation of population of East Berlin (*Gross-Berlin, demokratischer Sektor*) for 1950 are not available.

the churches. It can be given at their expense and by their representatives. Education at public schools is coeducational.

(3) The democratic unified school (Einheitsschule) comprises the whole educational system from the kindergarten to the university:

a. Preliminary branch (Kindergarten): 3–6 years.

b. Foundation School: 6–14 years, obligatory.

c. Upper branch: 14–18 years, part-time vocational (Beruf) school is obligatory for all who do not attend another school: Fachschule, Oberschule.

(4) Curriculum plans must be approved by the German Central Administration.

(5) Attendance at the foundation school and vocational school is free; scholarships are planned for the needy.

(6) Educational officials of the states are to supervise the schools in conformity with the direction of the German central administration. They charge the district school offices with supervision of the schools. Teachers, representatives of the democratic parties, parents and pupil committees have advisory rights.

(7) The curriculum plan for the foundation school and upper school is as follows: (Here the law specifies how many hours are to be devoted to each subject in each grade. From the fifth grade on there is separate instruction in special subjects, and Russian, French or English was to be started in this grade. Since 1951 Russian has become compulsory and another foreign language may be started in the seventh grade.)

The provisions of this law were faithfully echoed with few insignificant variations in all the state constitutions which were enacted from December 1946 to February 1947. Private schools were abolished, and all public schools were organized on a uniform basis without reference to social strata, sex, or religious confession. The German term *Gemeinschaftsschulen*, which generally has meant that schools are organized on a Christian basis without reference to confession, was carefully avoided. Religion was removed as a subject of instruction and was left entirely to the churches, which had to bear the cost. The right of the churches to give such religious instruction was guaranteed, but no child was to be forced to take it. Brandenburg guaranteed that this religious instruction could be held on school premises; Saxony-Anhalt and Saxony that it could be held on school premises as long as it did not interfere with the regular instruction in the schools; Mecklenburg guaranteed provision of rooms, while Thuringia made no mention of where the religious instruction was to be held. Mecklenburg was unique in having a provision which stated that no person employed in public service needed the approval of his superiors if he wanted to impart religious instruction in his spare time. This evidently was meant to make it possible for some teachers to teach religion on the side if they were inclined to do so.

The Constitution of the German Democratic Republic and Religious Education

In the following years under the guidance and control of the central educational authorities, the administration of educational systems in the various states took on a uniform hue. The creation of the German Democratic Republic in 1949 led to a reformulation of basic law in regard to the educational system. The new constitution provided that while the states were responsible for the establishment and practical operation of the schools, the Democratic Republic would issue uniform legislative directives in regard to the schools. Furthermore in Article 1 the constitution states that "any issue of basic importance for the existence and development of the entire German people shall be resolved by the Republic." In these provisions the supremacy of the central government in educational affairs is proclaimed.

Articles 40 and 44 deal specifically with religious education.

Religious education is a function of the religious associations. The free exercise of this right is guaranteed.

The right of the church to give religious instruction on school premises shall be guaranteed. Religious instruction shall be given by personnel selected by the church. No one shall be forced to give, or be prevented from giving, religious instruction. Parents or their deputies, shall determine whether children shall receive religious education.

Religious liberty is guaranteed and the constitution, in line with general German practice, establishes fourteen as the age when a child reaches its majority in religious matters. But as is usual in constitutions drawn up under Communist domination, the document also openly proclaims that the basic rights conferred are subject to alteration if the interests of the state require it. Here Articles 41 and 49 may be quoted:

Every citizen shall enjoy complete freedom of faith and conscience. The unhindered exercise of religious beliefs shall have the protection of the Republic. Any abuse of establishments created by religious associations, or religious acts or religious education for purposes which are contrary to the principles of the constitution or for purposes of party politics is prohibited. However, the right of religious associations to express an attitude in keeping with their own viewpoints toward issues vital for the public shall be uncontested.

All basic rights shall remain inviolable, except where this constitution authorizes their restriction by law or makes their further development subject to legislative action.

It is clear that under these provisions it would take little interpretation for the government, if it wished, legally to curtail the rights which had been previously guaranteed. In regard to religious education the new constitution did not change the existing situation. The specific guarantee of the right of the church to give religious instruction on school premises confirmed a right granted in most state constitutions, but which had not been lived up to by all local school authorities.

The centralization of the German Democratic Republic continued and reached a new phase when on July 23–24, 1952, a law on further democratization of the Republic was issued. Under this law the five states ceased to exist and were replaced by 14 Provinces (*Bezirke*) and 216 Districts (*Kreise*). Each of these has a representative body, but their powers are strictly limited. The age-old organization of education on state lines—even if in practice it was only for administrative purposes—was now a thing of the past in East Germany.

Types of Schools

The question of confessional or interdenominational schools was never really an issue in East Germany, but a few comments should be made on the types of schools in East Germany as they affect religious education either directly or indirectly. The schools in the German Democratic Republic have been completely secularized and are no longer organized on a Christian basis. In this they differ not only from the schools in West Germany but also from the traditional pattern of the past. Conversely the schools are now based on a communist Marxist ideology. Whereas religion was formerly a required subject and, at least in confessional schools, was to permeate all instruction, so now this is true of *Gesellschaftslehre* (sociology). The latter is largely a Marxist "democratic" ideology, and all instruction is to be permeated with the spirit of communism. Actually the schools have become, to use an old German term, confessional schools of Marxist materialism.

The establishment of a unified school system on an eight-four basis has meant the end of the higher schools as they have hitherto been known in Germany. Now the East German schools resemble the division made in the United States between grade and high school. The last four years, which constitute the secondary school, have a three-year practical branch and a four-year academic branch, which most closely resembles the old Gymnasium. Here a pupil starts Russian in the fifth grade of the foundation school, adds a second language

(English, French, Latin, Polish or Czech) in the ninth grade; in the tenth grade Greek, if he is in the classical-language track, and in the eleventh grade Latin, if he is in the modern-language track.[3] The churches complain that candidates for the ministry no longer receive adequate training in the classical languages in a secondary school. In comparison to what was done previously, it is indeed a scant preparation; in comparison to United States' schools, it is magnificent. The Nazis ended instruction in Hebrew at secondary schools, and this practice has continued. The abolition of all private schools has had its most marked effect on secondary education, in which field they used to be especially strong.

The simplicity of this 8–4 arrangement was, however, soon modified. It was found desirable to have some ten-year schools, to which the old term middle school was later applied. In 1956, a plan was announced which aims by 1965 to extend compulsory education to ten years, whether in middle or higher schools. This will involve considerable changes in the school structure and a more complex system. The state at first prescribed that a certain percentage of the students accepted for admission to middle and higher schools must be children of worker or peasant parentage.[4] Children from certain other groups such as national prize winners, meritorious teachers and doctors, members of the armed forces, people active in political organizations, were also given preference. Under the 1955 regulations, the preference remains, but percentage quotas are no longer prescribed.

East German authorities have made a vigorous effort to eliminate the small one-teacher schools in rural areas.[5] In their place they have established central schools with pupils collected by bus. Since beginners are too young to make the long journey often required, in some places grades one to four are permitted to remain in the old village school. Undoubtedly this centralized school system is a real educational advance, but it has taken children away from their connection with the local parishes and the religious instruction which centered there. If a school principal refuses for some reason to provide rooms for religious instruction in such a centralized school, it is practically impossible for catechists to assemble the pupils from scattered parishes in church rooms even if such rooms were available.[6]

Teacher-training institutes naturally enough are entirely state-controlled and are organized on a uniform basis. Since religion is not taught in the schools, there are no classes in religion at the training institutes, and prospective teachers cannot receive any training in this field. This means that as older teachers are replaced there will be no teachers qualified to teach religion for the church even on the side. The

officials have always opposed such voluntary additional instruction on
the part of the teachers, and although legally permitted it has already
disappeared in practice. All teachers, of course, receive a heavy dose
of training in communist ideology, and the examination in this subject
is one of the most important that the teaching candidates must face.

Participation of parents in the running of the schools, above all
in deciding what type of school is to be established, is one of the pillars
of the school system in West Germany. Such a democratic institution
could not be scorned in East Germany, and the law of 1946 provided
that parents should be consulted. It was not, however, until April 12,
1951, that a law formally provided for the participation of parents'
councils in school affairs. At the same time parent seminars were
instituted, the purpose of which was to enlighten parents on school
policies and obtain their support.[7]

Churchmen criticized the election procedure of this law, stating
that it was apparent that only parents who were "peace loving, progressive, and friends of the Soviet" could get elected to the councils.
Unless it was made possible for parents to be elected who were favorable to the church and opposed to the attacks of the more radical
teachers on Christian beliefs and traditions, the church could not
approve of the councils. As a matter of fact, in the December 1951
elections, where there was chance for a choice, parents who were known
to be close to the church came out very well. There was considerable
opposition in the parents' councils on religious and other grounds to
many measures of the authorities.

On October 15, 1955, a new law on parents' councils replaced the
law of 1951, and new ordinances for election of the councils were issued.
In all schools an election committee is to be formed which nominates
a list of candidates. At a meeting of parents this list is elected or
altered by open ballot. Not only is the membership of the council
(numbering at least five) controlled in this fashion, but the law provides
for four to five ex-officio members with the right to vote: a representative of the Free German Youth (Freie Deutsche Jugend) movement, of
the Democratic Women's League, a teacher, the school principal, and
a representative of the *Patenbetriebe* (special industrial organization to
sponsor schools). Now, more than ever, parents' councils are under
government direction.[8]

Legally the functions of the parents' councils include a rather
attractive list of duties which would further the school systems of most
countries if they were freely and impartially performed. However, the
actual power of parents to influence schools in East Germany is not
to be compared to the *Elternrecht* enjoyed by parents in the Federal

Republic. In regard to parents' rights the German Democratic Republic holds, as in regard to all personal rights, that they are subject to the control of the community, which means the party authorities.

Church-Administered Religious Education

Although laws and regulations establishing a unified school system were enacted relatively soon after the war, it took some time to get the system functioning.[9] As schools were opened local customs and traditions continued to prevail, and one of the oldest of these was that children should receive religious instruction as part of their school training. Everywhere parents continued to enroll their children in religion classes, even though they were no longer part of the official curriculum. Not everywhere could a regular program for religious instruction be worked out, but that was equally true for other subjects. Detailed statistics on the percentage of the total number of pupils in East Germany enrolling for religious instruction are not available. Quite naturally it varied for grades as well as in different sections, and between rural and urban areas. Except for possible spot instances well over a majority, probably seventy-five to one hundred percent of the children, enrolled in the religion classes.[10]

The churches were faced with the tremendous task of providing teachers and teaching materials for this host of willing pupils. Making use of the experience and plans of the Confessing church during the Nazi period, they tried to build a program for the future. As early as 1946 a central Education Chamber (*Erziehungskammer*) for the Protestant church of the East Zone was established in East Berlin. Each of the regional Protestant Evangelical churches has created a bureau for religious education (*Referat für Evangelische Unterweisung*), and these send representatives to the central chamber, whose purpose is not to direct, but to serve as a coordinating and consultative center.[11]

Even before this organization could be formed, however, make-shifts were devised, and a beginning made. In the first years some teachers undertook to teach religion outside their regular hours. There were retired teachers who could be called into service, and also the many teachers who had been summarily dismissed under the denazification procedures. Many of these had been qualified to teach religion, and with sincere encouragement and orientation, the churches were able to use many of them in their programs. A good number of people could be recruited from among the expellees, people who had been in church or school service before being driven out and now were anxious to find employment again. The churches also had a heritage which proved of great value; German adults had almost all received religious training in their school days. They had a foundation on which to build, and the churches found that with short training classes many very acceptable teachers for the schools could be discovered. Most of these catechists, as they came to be called, possess an inner zeal and devotion to the cause which makes up for some of their deficiencies in training. Some devoted their full time to this work, others only part time. As years have passed their preparation has become more systematized and "the training given is hard and modern in every sense of the term".[12] It usually consists of a two-year term at well-staffed seminaries, administered by the various churches. In 1949 the first three-year training course was established in Wittenberg to prepare graduates of the secondary schools for a career as catechists, primarily at the secondary-school level. Another school in nearby Schoenbeck trained catechists for employment at elementary schools and combined this instruction with instruction in organ playing. It was expected that in many places, where the regular teacher no longer taught religion or played the church organ, parishes would welcome graduates of the Schoenbeck school as teachers of religion and as organists.

The great burden of organizing and giving the instruction in the early years fell to the lot of the ministers. They did a truly remarkable job, in spite of a great shortage of ministers in East Germany. In some regions the situation was more acute than in others. In 1950 there were one hundred ministers for 400,000 people in the regional church of Anhalt. At the end of 1951 there were 5,434 ministers in 6,100 Protestant congregations, and about twelve percent of the parishes were without pastors. At the same time the Catholic church was in need of at least 250 Catholic priests. In 1956 Bishop Jaenicke of the regional Protestant Church of Saxony reported to the Synod that there were 576 congregations in the Church of Saxony without pastors. Fourteen women ministers were filling preaching assignments, and the church was making use of many "ministerial helpers"—people who had no professional training at all but because of their age and experience were fitted to preach and teach in congregations. Many of the pastors taught regular religion classes, and there were 649 full-time and more than 1,000 part-time catechists at work in the Church of Saxony. In 1956–57 there were more than 6,000 catechists serving the Protestant churches of the German Democratic Republic.[13]

The Protestant churches in East Germany as in West Germany have resorted to various expedients to recruit more ministers. "Ministerial schools" have been established which accept candidates that have not passed academic examinations. At present, failure in courses on Marxist ideology often trips up candidates at secondary schools.

After fulfillment of their training courses and a period of practical training, these men are ordained. In 1952 Premier Grotewohl proposed to the church authorities that they establish their own theological seminaries, for which he promised financial aid, and that the theological faculties at the state universities be ended. Church authorities, except for Bishop Mitzenheim of Eisenach, objected to the proposals. So far the Protestant theological faculties have been continued at the universities, although some chairs have remained vacant for long periods. There never have been any Catholic faculties at these particular institutions. The training program for theological students at the universities has been extended from four to five years because the students must make up deficiencies in their language preparation, and some of their time is taken up in required courses in political subjects. Candidates for the ministry, in view of their other language requirements, are exempted from taking the usual compulsory courses in Russian. Although the supply of ministerial candidates is totally inadequate, attendance at the theological faculties increased for a time as Table 6 shows.[14] This is due in part to the fact that soon after 1948 it became virtually impossible for students from East Germany to go to West Germany for study.

Table 6.   Student enrollment at Protestant Faculties of East German Universities

University	1946–47	1947–48	1948–49	1949–50	1954–55
East Berlin	83	100	159	197	147
Greifswald	32	31	54	75	75
Halle	73	115	142	131	117
Jena	21	58	108	127	154
Leipzig	65	68	84	175	299
Rostock	19	28	51	77	79
Totals	293	400	598	782	871

Source: *KJ*, 1954, p. 370.

Catholic priests are trained at a Catholic Hochschule in Erfurt and at two seminaries in Neuzelle near Frankfurt an der Oder and the Huysburg, near Halberstadt, where one-year advanced courses are given. All clergy must be citizens of the Democratic Republic and receive their training there, a provision reminiscent of the days of the Kulturkampf.

With more general parish work than the clergy could properly perform, it is not surprising that the churches have turned to lay helpers. In general, efforts have been successful in arousing a new sense of responsibility among the laity. Deacons and other lay officials of the congregations are taking on new tasks. The old criticism that the German Protestant churches are *Pastorenkirchen* (pastor-dominated churches), while probably still true, nevertheless has less substantiation today than ever before. Church lay organizations are more numerous and active than ever in times past.

The burden of the religious-teaching program in the schools has to be borne by the catechists. They have actually become a new professional group (*Stand*) serving the church along with the ministers, deaconesses, organists, and other church officials. Most of them are now full-time career people, the larger number of them being women. The church will always need more part-time catechists, particularly to take care of instruction in less populated areas, or to round out a local program. Here the mother who teaches four or six hours a week is a very important aid. The catechists have not been placed under the direction of local ministers, but are responsible to their own district or provincial supervisors. This dissipates somewhat the danger of resurrecting difficulties between pastors and teachers such as existed in the old days of clerical supervision in the schools. So far most catechists still have too heavy a teaching schedule. There will be some relief in the immediate future, through the decline in school population because of the low birthrate in the postwar years as well as the tremendous exodus to West Germany. By the very nature of their vocation, catechists should be closely connected with some congregation so that religious education is not something separate, but part of the life of the church. What it will mean for the vitality of the whole church to have the aid of this large group of trained people is something which the future holds in store. It is one of the brightest spots in the whole picture of postwar religious developments in Germany.

In such a religious-education program as this, no one working in it could ever become complacent. There are the old problems of lack of discipline in classes, and now and then the old charges are heard: that children do not learn anything, that they do not know basic material when they come up for confirmation instruction. Yet the overall verdict seems to be that instruction is on a high level. The catechists who give it are better trained theologically than many teachers in former times. Chiefly it may be said that they are more dedicated to their work than regular teachers, for whom religion was all too often a side issue. Newly written books are used, and central loan libraries for visual aids have been established. If there is less insistence on memory work, there is much more discussion between teacher and student and stress on developing a sense of religious values.

President Walter Zimmermann, head of the Protestant church's Education Chamber for the German Democratic Republic estimates (1957) that they are reaching eighty percent of the Protestant school children of East Germany.[15] It remains to be seen how the church's recent stand that children who have failed to attend regular *Christenlehre* classes cannot be accepted for confirmation will affect attendance. It is a ruling designed more to emphasize than coerce, for by its very nature the church forgives an errant or negligent member. In most cases up to the age of confirmation there is one hour a week of instruction; in a few congregations or schools, two hours a week. On the other hand there are probably also some scattered places where, because of difficulties over rooms or lack of teaching personnel, no regular instruction at all is being given. No religious instruction takes place at vocational schools, since the state maintains that these do not belong among the common schools (*allegemeinbildende Schulen*). This is in accord with traditional practice in North Germany where even in the days of the Empire religion was not taught at vocational schools. At higher schools, where religion was always part of the curriculum, the state now refuses to recognize any obligation under the constitution to make rooms available for religious instruction. The church challenges this position without much success. It follows that religious education at higher schools is very spotty. The method of selecting pupils for higher schools and the very intensive program of study do not encourage students to take religion on the side. Many of the students come from strata of society in which for generations it was the common assumption that religious training ended with confirmation, that is, elementary school. There is also a lack of competent teachers to instruct at higher schools. A well intentioned but pedagogically poorly trained pastor, who is likely to sermonize instead of teach, is not the man to assign to higher schools. Here the answer may be better pedagogical training of ministers or better still, training of more catechists to an advanced level. The churches do, of course, reach a number of students at both vocational and higher schools through their church-centered youth programs.

Exact figures as to the percentage of Catholic school children receiving regular religious instruction in the Democratic Republic are not available. For the Bishopric of Berlin-Brandenburg (exclusive of the city of Berlin) the following figures can be cited: 22,529 out of 23,030 children were receiving instruction in 1956–57. This was being given largely by the parish priests and by 59 parish helpers (*Seelsorgehelferinnen*).[16]

In addition to the regularly scheduled religion classes organized to replace the former school religion classes, the churches have stepped up other aspects of youth training. Special children's services (*Kindergottesdienste*) have been refurbished. For the latter a much-needed songbook and a service book have been compiled by the Protestants.[17] Numerous activities, particularly discussion and study groups, have been formed. A Protestant church youth organization, *Junge Gemeinde*, has been built up, which had its own paper, the *Stafette*, until its licence was revoked in 1953. It is not surprising that the Junge Gemeinde came under attack by the state-sponsored youth group, the Freie Deutsche Jugend (FDJ). Membership in the latter is supposedly voluntary, but there is a good deal of pressure on young people to join it. Although the aim is no doubt to make FDJ the sole youth organization in East Germany, the Junge Gemeinde has managed to hang on.

Confirmation instruction has been strengthened, and the churches have fought to maintain the significant role which this instruction has always held among the young people. Beside its religious significance confirmation in a measure has symbolized the achievement of having completed grammar school. There always were and still are new clothes, presents, and family festivities connected with the event. It is an occasion which critics of religion have often felt could not be left a monopoly of the churches.

Even before World War I the National Free Thinkers' Association sponsored youth-dedication services as a ceremonial for those children who were not taking confirmation instruction. Hitler took over the idea, and instituted a National Socialist Dedication Service, and a similar attempt has again been made. In November 1954 a "Central Committee for Youth-Dedication Services in the German Democratic Republic" was established. Soon branches sprang up throughout the country, and an active propaganda organization took shape. The dedication services were set for a Sunday in April and were to be preceded by ten double periods of preparation. This was to be in the nature of discussion groups on natural sciences and sociological topics. An attractively illustrated book of essays, entitled *Weltall, Erde, Mensch*, published in the summer of 1954, became the basis of the instruction. This book has been publicly condemned by both Protestant and Catholic church authorities because of its antireligious tone.

The new attempt to provide a secular youth-dedication service was also promptly denounced by the churches. Bishop Dibelius in a statement to the Protestant churches of Brandenburg on November 30, 1954, said: "We are at one with the confirmed supporters of Marxism-Leninism that Christian faith and Marxist *Weltanschauung* stand opposed to each other in an unbridgeable inner opposition. Therefore we insist on a clear differentiation between church confirmation and youth dedication." On the day after Christmas 1954, Wilhelm Weskamm, the Catholic Bishop of Berlin, sharply condemned the youth-dedication service and asked his fellow Catholics, "Can one make a profession of faith to God and at the same time a profession to ungodliness?" As early as 1951, the Lutheran churches in Germany had drawn up an ordinance which stated: "The church must deny confirmation to such children who have taken part in or plan to take part in ceremonies which are in opposition to confirmation." The youth-dedication leaders made little of these objections, saying the children could take part in both a confirmation and youth-dedication service. But to this Protestant and Catholic leaders alike pronounced an emphatic negative. In the words of Bishop Dibelius: "It cannot be 'as well as' but must be 'either or'." This issue creates a greater problem for Protestants than for Catholics, since Catholic confirmation occurs at an earlier age and does not coincide with the end of elementary school, to which the youth-dedication services are joined. Catholic and Protestant, however, are firmly united on the basic principle.[18]

In spite of much ballyhoo and considerable moral and political pressure, most of the children who had taken part in confirmation instruction chose to be confirmed in 1955. The Central Committee stated that 60,000 young people had taken part in the youth-dedication services that year; another friendly source gives the figure as 83,000. Actually these included many who did not come out of the current group of confirmation candidates. The churches estimated that less than one percent of the actual confirmation candidates forsook confirmation for youth dedication.

There were all sorts of pressures brought on parents and children to participate in youth dedication. Rumor was that only children who had taken part in youth-dedication services would be admitted to secondary schools, and that parents who did not cooperate would lose their positions. This sort of rumor—even if it did not materialize into fact—can be most effective, and, as in the Nazi period, the church can be credited with a steadfast resistance seldom found elsewhere. The campaign for youth dedication continued in 1956 and 1957 and undoubtedly gained ground. The sponsors of the campaign have taken increased pains to make the program attractive.[19] Trips to zoos, theaters, various industrial establishments, longer excursions to places of national cultural significance, all add interest. The final dedication service is held in a theater or other prominent hall, and leading men lend their presence to the occasion. There are the usual new clothes and presents for the youngsters. The program consists of speeches, recitation of poetry and mottoes ranging from Goethe to Grotewohl, questions and solemn pledges on the part of the children to uphold the new order, and finally the inevitable handclasp, presentation of a certificate, and a copy of *Weltall, Erde, Mensch,* or of *Unser Deutschland,* a well-illustrated "modern" history of Germany. Most observers estimate that the youth-dedication services gained only slightly and were not outstandingly successful in 1957. Probably about six percent of those who should have been confirmed went to youth-dedication services instead. The number, of course, varies greatly from section to section, and especially between rural and urban areas.[20]

At each of the universities the Protestant church has a special minister for students. These men have organized student congregations and developed a program of activity. They too have worked under handicaps. In the fall of 1955 the order went out that these Protestant student groups could no longer use university lecture rooms and auditoriums for their meetings, nor were they allowed to put up bulletins and posters anywhere on campus.[21]

The financing of the education programs by the churches has not been easy. The state (with the exception of a brief period in the spring of 1953) has continued to pay subsidies to the churches, and the churches have been permitted to levy the customary church taxes. But there are decided limitations on the amount which can be raised in this fashion, for the churches know that opposition to payment of the tax is the most often cited reason for withdrawal from the church. As in times past withdrawal requires either declaration before a court or an officially attested individual declaration. In the spring of 1953 the state stopped the municipal collection of church taxes and ruled that they had to be paid directly to the churches. The latter had great difficulty in getting the information from the state which was necessary for the collection of taxes. This led to such delays that when the levies could finally be made they had to be regrettably heavy. The greatest difficulty came in delivering the tax notices. In tens of thousands of cases the notices were returned as undeliverable, and it was impossible to find out where the people had moved to. Since many of the parishioners cannot be reached, and at the same time the number of withdrawals from the churches has increased—about 20,000 in East Berlin in 1955—the churches have budgetary troubles.[22]

It has been largely through new measures that the educational program has been financed. One of the most important methods in the early postwar years was house-to-house and street collections. Usually there were four of these each year, but in 1953 all house collections were ended, and only two street collections were permitted. In Thuringia the church asked parents to contribute regularly a "Religious Education Penny" (*Christenlehre-Groschen*), to which most parents agreed. The Catholics also collect the Caritas Penny (*Pfennig*). In Brandenburg in 1951, the Church Penny (*Kirchenpfennig*) was increased to one mark, making a total of four marks for the year, in order to put the salaries of the catechists on a sounder basis. In 1955 the practice was generally adopted by the various consistories of dividing church offerings on a certain percentage basis, so much for missions, education, music, and so on. Offerings in the churches have increased, and the people are shouldering the additional burden, formerly borne by the state. Gifts have also come at critical periods from outside churches. The Lutheran World Federation was particularly helpful in establishing schools for the training of catechists. The Catholic Church has also benefited from financial aid from beyond the boundaries of the Democratic Republic.

Church–State Relations

For the churches to replace the religious education which had been carried on for so many years by the schools would have been a difficult task even under the most favorable circumstances. But circumstances and conditions were anything but favorable. To all the disorder caused by war and foreign control was added the consistently unfriendly attitude of public authorities. All was not persecution; just as in the days of Hitler there were variations. Local officials at times were co-operative and lent a willing and helpful hand. This was also true of many regular teachers. As under Nazi, so under Communist totalitarianism, conditions varied in different districts. Yet when all allowances are made, there was always a generally unfriendly attitude on the part of the controlling authorities. Under both the former state constitutions and the national constitution, churches were to have the right to give religious instruction in schoolrooms. Yet often local school authorities denied them this privilege. Protests were ignored or left unanswered. Many of the Protestant churches had no available church rooms, and a campaign was undertaken to remedy this situation. It is estimated, however, that in spite of considerable improvement, forty to fifty percent of the parishes in 1957 still did not have adequate parish halls.[23] Since the Catholic churches had for years been obliged to gather scattered pupils from various schools, they were on the whole better equipped with parish halls than Protestant churches. There were also many restrictions on the buying of paper, which seemed to strike the religious press with undue severity. It took not only effort but ingenuity to provide the necessary teaching materials. A one-volume compendium for general use in Protestant religion classes, which contains hymns, essential Bible stories, the catechism, and material on the church year and church history, has proved most successful.[24]

In general it can be said that the churches encountered increasing difficulties as the split between East and West became sharper. Bishop Dibelius, the head of the Protestant Church of Germany with his headquarters in Berlin, in April 1950 expressed publicly, in a letter both to the clergy and to the church membership, his anxiety over mounting tensions between church and state. Among other things he spoke of deep concern over the teaching of materialistic philosophy in the schools and the general disparagement of religion that went with it. The former Archbishop of Berlin, Cardinal von Preysing, issued similar protests.[25] Here indeed is perhaps the greatest problem which confronts the churches in their teaching program. The schools emphasize learning, science, deride superstition—and then equate religion with superstition. History textbooks have been rewritten which omit customary references to the church or place it in an unfavorable light. In the history of the Reformation Thomas Münzer and the Peasants' Revolt receive as much if not more emphasis than Luther and the other reformers. The situation is well characterized by a protest to the government drawn up at the sixteenth meeting of the Evangelical-Lutheran Synod of Saxony in 1950.

The freedom of conscience which is guaranteed by the constitution is in practice done away with by the fact that in the schools the doctrines of historical and dialectical materialism alone have consideration. . . . The Soviet pedagogy, which is binding for present-day schools, expressly characterizes itself as atheistic. In materialism one deals with a doctrine in which no ground is left for the recognition of the reality of God. From this it is clear, that the schools do not maintain neutrality in questions of belief (*Glauben*), but have become a materialistic-atheistic confessional school, in which actually freedom of conscience (*Glaubensfreiheit*) no longer exists. . . . Freedom of conscience exists in the schools only when instruction in all subjects is such that Christians and non-Christians can participate with equal inner freedom. The prevailing climate of opinion in today's schools, that an educated thinking person must be an atheist and therefore atheism must be the determining factor in the schools, is not only educationally untenable, but it is also a denial of freedom of conscience, and therefore a violation of the constitution.[26]

How antireligious, how antichurch, instruction in schools becomes, depends a great deal on the individual teacher. Yet basically the situation is such today that the churches in East Germany have to deal with a school system that is no longer even neutral in regard to religion.

There is no need here to attempt a detailed account of church-state relations in East Germany. Despite complete ideological disagreement, it appeared that the government, on the one hand, did not want to get involved in an all-out Kulturkampf, and the church, on the other, was anxious to be permitted to continue its work and ministry. On February 17, 1952, the able reporter to the *Christian Century* stated in his regular newsletter from East Germany: "Although relations between Christian ministers and party and police representatives are in general more calm and peaceful than people in the western countries believe them to be, conflicts do occasionally arise." [27] He then went on to report on the arrest of a pastor. The tempo of arrests increased, and soon the newsletters were filled with accounts of arrested ministers and church lay leaders. In the next months (which was also the time of the peace crusade and anti-NATO agitation) an active campaign was launched against the church youth organization Junge Gemeinde. Many students (church officials estimated 3,000) were dismissed from higher schools for refusing to resign from the organization; a good number were arrested. [28] Trials of arrested ministers or students were delayed. The state officials took many other restrictive measures. Funds were withheld, and more handicaps were placed on the churches in raising their regular church taxes. On January 1, 1953, the minister of education ended the use of schoolrooms for religion classes. Requests by church authorities to visit congregations and travel in East Germany were answered only after great delay and at times were refused. Tension mounted, and it looked as if an outright church and state conflict was about to be set off.

The death of Stalin on March 5, 1953, seemed to inaugurate a "new course" in the Democratic Republic as in all the other Russian satellite states. On June 9, 1953, the Politburo of the Central Committee of the SED decided to recommend a series of measures to the East German government, all tending toward a more moderate policy. Pupils dismissed from secondary schools because of their connections with the Junge Gemeinde were to be given an opportunity to take examinations. "Similarly, the dismissals and transfers of teachers ordered in connection with the investigation of secondary schools . . . were to be cancelled." [29] On June 10, 1953, Bishop Dibelius and Premier Grotewohl reached a nine-point agreement designed to relieve the tensions between church and state. This agreement was surprisingly favorable to the church and sharply reversed the state's recent policy. There was to be no further action against the Junge Gemeinde and other church groups; jail sentences against upwards of 100 pastors for opposing the state were to be reviewed and rectified; confiscated church properties were to be returned, and all state subsidies to the church were to be resumed and paid on time; the ministry of education was to work out a plan so that classrooms would again be made available for religion classes; students ejected from schools because of their activity in the Junge Gemeinde were to be readmitted to classes, and discrimination against advanced students for their loyalty to the church or church groups was to be eliminated; the church's right of assembly was recognized, and the regulation requiring advanced notice of church meetings to be submitted to civil authorities was to be reviewed and relaxed.[30]

With the conclusion of this agreement, relations between church and state appeared to be considerably improved. On October 31, 1953 (Reformation Day), the government in agreement with the churches issued an ordinance labelled: "Regulations on the giving of religious instruction in the rooms of the common schools."[31] Again the school principals were categorically told that at the request of the churches they had to provide rooms for religious instruction as provided in Article 44 of the constitution. The appropriate times were to be agreed upon in consultation with representatives of the churches. But what was here stated was practically annulled by other provisions of the ordinance and by later interpretations. Thus the official explanation of the ordinance maintains that rooms need be provided for the churches only if they have no other rooms at their disposal.[32] Section two of the ordinance decrees that the provision of rooms should not hamper regular instruction in any way. If classes start at eight o'clock, no religious hours may be given before that time. In practice this had the effect of denying the churches the first hour of the day, which was a particularly burdensome restriction. Religion hours cannot be scattered throughout the day, but must be given immediately before or after regular instruction. "Care is to be taken that the pupils are not unduly burdened by this instruction." This means, for example, that no religious instruction can be given at the end of a day which has been prolonged by other school tasks. No attempts can be made in the school or its establishments (parents' councils, meetings, seminars) to recruit pupils for religious instruction, nor on the other hand is it permitted to speak against such participation in the schools or in school meetings. Schools are not allowed to furnish lists of students to the churches. Catechists cannot use school bulletin boards, nor can they enter other rooms than the one set aside for their use. If, however, there is an interruption in the class schedule which affects the religion classes, teachers are to be notified and given the opportunity to contact the children. Changes such as removing pictures may not be made in the arrangement of the school room, and no doubt the pictures of many communist leaders beam down on religion classes. Although the ordinance itself is silent as to what constitutes religious instruction, the official commentary points out that this must be limited to the traditional program, such as instruction leading to confirmation or first communion. It cannot be extended to cover provision for school religious services, for giving general religious instruction to young people, or for holding Bible discussion groups for adults. Under this interpretation it naturally follows that no rooms are to be made available for religious instruction at higher schools, a ruling which has been repeatedly protested by the churches. How this ordinance affected the religious instruction given by the churches depended a great deal on how it was administered by local school officials. Certainly it brought no fundamental change for the better.

In May 1954 the Synod of the Protestant Church of Berlin-Brandenburg denounced the new ordinances of March 20 and April 5, 1954.[33] These ordinances stated that teachers were to be considered as officials of the Workers' and Peasants' State, and demanded of them as well as of pupils "definite adherence to the party and its principles in instruction and examinations." In December of 1954, all the Protestant churches of the Democratic Republic again protested to the government on the continued emphasis on communist materialism in the schools. The Catholic church likewise made its opposition to the policies of the government known. These ordinances and the opening rounds of the campaign for youth-dedication services were clear evidence that the so-called "new course" in educational policy had produced no real change in church–state relations.

Disputes and difficulties over providing classrooms continued, public officials maintaining that there was obligation to provide rooms only if church rooms were not available. The church has never accepted this interpretation, although church rooms have under certain circumstances proved more convenient than schoolrooms. A host of children descending on parish rooms throughout the week often disrupts other parish activities and certainly adds to the cost of heating, lighting, and cleaning—things the state must provide in schoolrooms. In 1956–57 about 40 percent of Protestant instruction was still being carried on in schoolrooms, and sixty percent in church rooms.[34] The tendency of school authorities is to make only afternoon hours available for religious instruction, although in East Germany they have not gone so far in this respect as in East Berlin. Constant changes in teaching schedules also add to difficulties if a catechist tries to include children from different school grades in one class. Catechists, without being given the opportunity to defend themselves, are often denied the right to teach at a particular school (*Hausverbot*). At state-supported children's homes or vacation centers religious instruction is either simply forbidden or made impossible by scheduling other programs.[35]

The influence of communist ideology is felt in many ways. The attitude of the higher officials has been consistently unfriendly to the church-sponsored program. In April 1957 Fritz Lange, the minister of education, in a published article declared that the demands made on pupils by religion classes, confirmation instruction, and Bible discussion hours, were leading to an overburdening of pupils.[36] Also the secular program is thoroughly impregnated with Soviet Marxism and shows definite antireligious orientation.

Yet old customs are not easily eradicated. Pupils in some regions still attend special church services at the beginning of the school year, even though this is no longer a school service. In addition to the regular state holidays Reformation Day is a holiday in regions which are predominantly Protestant, and Corpus Christi Day and occasionally All Souls' Day in Catholic areas. This dates back to legislation passed when there were still state governments. In Berlin and Saxony-Anhalt such legislation was not passed, and it is a disputed point whether Reformation Day is a holiday there.[37] Children are of course free to participate in the services of the churches on these days if they wish. On individual petition of parents (group petitions are not allowed) children can be excused from school in order to fulfil their religious obligations on other church holidays, but the attention of parents is called to the consequences of such absence from class. For those who observe Saturday as a day of rest, there is no regular exemption from classes, although excuses are granted on special occasions. Jewish teachers and pupils have the Day of Atonement as a holiday.

While the calendar of the school year is established yearly and regularly recognizes holidays for the main church festivals, such as Christmas, Easter, Ascension Day, Pentecost, and Day of Repentance, no reference is made to their religious significance. Some of the school songbooks have been purged of Christmas carols. A Christmas program recommended for the schools in one of the pedagogical journals centers about a Christmas tree, but makes no mention of the birth of Christ.[38] Although it is unlikely that things are carried to this extreme everywhere in the Democratic Republic, the fact remains that for the first time in history the school system of a whole section of Germany has been completely secularized.

Here, however, a vital point must be made. The school system is secular, but education as a whole has not been completely secularized. The duty and right of the churches to give religious instruction is

recognized. At no time have the East German authorities enacted pro-
hibitions to compare with the complete abolition of religious instruction
which was inaugurated by the Soviets in Russia in the twenties. Everything is done to negate the influence of the church-conducted religious
education, but it has not been abolished.

Chapter XVIII

BERLIN SCHOOL DEVELOPMENTS

The formation of the two German republics made the position of Berlin even more anomalous than it had been heretofore. Although four-power control technically continued, and there were occasional joint meetings of officials at different levels, for all practical purposes Berlin was divided into two sectors, West and East Berlin, each with its own government. The unity of the Berlin school system disappeared as East Berlin came to conform more and more closely to the practices in the Democratic Republic, while West Berlin established contacts with the Federal Republic. West Berlin's senator (minister) of education has regularly participated in the Conference of Ministers of Education of West Germany, and the recommendations of this group have been adopted by West Berlin.[1]

West Berlin

In West Berlin a benevolent attitude toward religious instruction given by the churches soon made itself manifest. On November 24, 1949, Protestant and Catholic representatives had a long discussion with Senator May, the head of West Berlin's educational affairs, on the changes which the churches would like to see inaugurated. A memorandum drawn up by the Protestant leaders, which Catholics also supported, was the basis of discussion and actually outlined the reforms which were subsequently made. The Senator was a Socialist but nevertheless was sympathetic to the program. Results were slow in coming but on November 9, 1950, May issued an ordinance in which he attempted to draw a boundary between the spheres of school and church.[2] Reference was made to the values of Christianity mentioned in the school law of 1948, and this friendly observation followed: "Religious instruction and the educational work of the school have a common goal: to bring up our youth as upright citizens." The ordinance regulated the provision of rooms for religion classes, and by it catechists

278

were given the right to use the teachers' common rooms in their free periods. At the request of catechists rooms were to be made available for special religious services.[3] By these and other provisions of the ordinance the work of the catechists was made much pleasanter.

City elections were held on December 3, 1950, and in these the Christian Democratic Union (CDU) and the Free Democratic Party (FDP) achieved a majority of four. Although the new coalition government included the Socialists, May was replaced by Dr. Joachim Tiburtius (CDU) as senator (minister) of education. Tiburtius was known for his interest in religion and sympathy with the churches. Under his direction further measures favorable to the churches were inaugurated.

Providing sufficient teachers remained a problem in spite of expanded and regularized programs for the training of catechists in both Catholic and Protestant churches. A committee representing the regular teachers, who in addition to their teaching load of 28–30 hours a week taught Protestant religion classes, presented a petition to the Berlin authorities in the spring of 1951.[4] Naturally enough most of the teachers that assumed this burden were those who had taught religion before the war and consequently were getting advanced in years. The task was becoming too much for them, yet they had an interest in seeing the instruction carried on in orderly fashion. They did not want religion to be a regular subject of instruction (*ordentliches Lehrfach*), since this would subject it to state control, but preferred that it should be recognized by the state as a subject in the curriculum (*schulplanmässiges Lehrfach*). This would involve counting the teaching hours in religion as part of the regular teaching load and also as part of the total compulsory hours a student must take as long as his parents had not explicitly asked to have him exempted from religion classes. Along with this they proposed that limiting religion classes to the start or end of the school day (Eckstunden) should be abolished. This plan would mean that the city would pay the teachers, who, it is true, would get no additional payments, but would have the religion hours counted as part of their obligatory classroom hours. To provide for properly qualified religion instructors in the future they asked that a Professorship for Religion be established at the *Pädagogische Hochschule*.

The Berlin authorities did not meet the demands of the petition forthwith, but they were willing to discuss matters with the church representatives. The details of these negotiations and party struggles cannot be traced here, but in the next months most of the points in the petition were conceded.[5]

An important revision of the education law was enacted in May

1951, and went into effect on June 1. It reduced the period of the common foundation school from eight to six years, on which basis was erected a higher school with three main branches: *Praktischer Zweig* (7–9 grades), corresponding to higher division of the old elementary schools; *Technischer Zweig* (7–10 grades), corresponding to former middle schools; *Wissenschaftlicher Zweig* (7–13 grades), corresponding to old Oberschule or Gymnasium with Abitur. The latter in turn has three types according to the stress laid on certain subjects: classical languages, modern languages, or mathematics and sciences. This technical regrouping was welcomed by many churchmen, particularly in Catholic circles, for it restored the old humanistic Gymnasium with its stress on training in ancient languages.

Independently of the revision of the education law, West Berlin in the same year assumed fifty percent of the cost of paying the catechists and this percentage increased until in 1956–57 the city bore seventy-five percent of the cost. The amount paid is based on the hours of instruction and has been raised from time to time.[6] From the total grant to the churches the regular hourly subsidy (3.85 DM in 1956–57) is deducted for every hour of religious instruction taught by the regular teachers. In this fashion, although it is only a matter of bookkeeping, the churches technically still provide for all religious instruction.

The rest of the religious-education budget still has to be raised by the churches. In 1949 the Protestant church of Berlin had followed prevailing practices in the East Zone, instituting the custom of the *Schulgroschen*. This was in Berlin a charge of half a mark per month for a child enrolled in religion classes, with lower rates for a second child, although no child was excluded if the parents were unable to make the payment. It was a troublesome fee to collect and necessitated much paper work for the catechists. With the payment of subsidies by the city the collection of the Schulgroschen was given up by the Protestants in West Berlin, although it is retained by the Catholics. The Protestants still rely heavily on a house-to-house canvass which is held yearly. Income and expenses are, however, a matter for the central church authorities, and are not a concern for any one particular parish or school. The grants to the Catholic church are made on the same basis as to the Protestant. In 1955 this amounted to 337,000 DM, and the remainder (156,000 DM) needed for Catholic instruction had to be raised by the Union of Catholic Parishes (*Gesamtverband der katholischen Kirchengemeinden*).[7]

An ordinance of December 16, 1951, did much to increase the standing of religion classes. Among other provisions it specifically provided that at the time of enrollment the attention of parents and guardians should be called to the availability of religious instruction. This was a most important concession as the failure to follow a similar policy in East Berlin has amply demonstrated. Teaching of religion classes by regular teachers was encouraged by the statement: "Giving of religious instruction in accordance with Paragraph 13 of the school law by teachers of the public schools, who have the confidence of the churches, is especially fitted to make religious instruction fruitful for the whole educational process, and therefore is not to be hindered by the school administrations."[8] The authorities even ordered that for parallel classes the same hours should be set aside for religious instruction, so that pupils could be united in one religion class. This was an important friendly gesture, especially for Catholics, since there are not many Catholic children in some of the Berlin schools.

The revision of the school law on August 5, 1952, was long debated. The Christian Democratic Union and Free Democratic party with a majority of only four seats were prepared to force through sweeping changes, including making religion a regular subject of instruction. To this the Socialists were unalterably opposed, and they had the support of the Protestant Chamber of Education. Under these critical conditions Bishop Dibelius in February 1952 invited representatives of all parties to a conference. Here he stated plainly that a less complete realization of the church program, if agreed to by a substantial majority, was preferable to a full program carried out by means of a parliamentary battle won by only a few votes.[9] Long and tedious negotiations led to understandings among the parties concerned which were not all formally written into the law. In the end the amendments were passed unanimously. Textually there were few changes in the law, but they were significant. Article 13 was amended so that fully employed teachers who give religious instruction are to have these hours counted as part of their teaching load. "From the giving or not giving of religious instruction teachers are to derive neither advantages or disadvantages." The procedure for enrolling pupils for religion classes was also made easier. Most important of all, the provision that the hours made available by school authorities for religious instruction had to be at the beginning or end of the school day was now eliminated from Article 15. This gave more flexibility, and religion hours could henceforth be built into the curriculum. This made it easier for churches to provide instruction, for now a catechist could teach a full schedule of twenty-four hours a week, which was impossible if religious instruction was limited to "corner" hours.[10]

An ordinance of November 3, 1952, defined and extended the above changes in the law. Teachers, if they chose to give religious instruction,

10*

were to do this if possible at their own school. No limit was set to the
hours of such instruction that a teacher might undertake, and in a later
ordinance it was specifically stated that, if teachers had received the
necessary permission from the churches, their availability for religion
classes was not to depend on whether or not they were needed in other
subjects. The November 1952 ordinance stated that funds for instructional material are henceforth to be made available to the church
authorities in a yearly agreement, these funds to be administered by
the churches. The school authorities are also to have at hand a supply
of the necessary forms provided by the churches for requesting religious
instruction on the part of the parents. Such requests for religious
instruction or for withdrawal from religious instruction are as far as
possible to be made at the beginning of the school year. In practice once
the request has been made for religious instruction children continue
to be enrolled in religion classes, unless parents or guardians specifically
in writing withdraw their former request.[11]

That the number of regular teachers giving religion classes continued to decline in spite of the new regulations reflects to some extent
a mistrust on the part of many teachers of possible clerical supervision.[12]
But it was even more the result of the fact that since 1942 no provision
had been made for training teachers in religion at the Berlin teachers'
institutes. Under an arrangement with the city school administration,
representatives of both Protestant and Catholic churches have since
1952–53 given courses at the Pädagogische Hochschule Berlin (Lank-
witz). This was to enable students to obtain the qualification from the
churches to teach religion classes in the schools. So far the students
have not showed much interest in obtaining this qualification, since
religion is not an examination subject in the important state test, and
it is not considered in making appointments to the schools. Beginning
in 1957 a regular appointee (*Dozent*) on the faculty of the Hochschule is
to give instruction in various aspects of Evangelical thought. The
Protestant church officials hope that this may eventually lead to a
regularized program for the qualification of teachers in religion.

West Berlin has also come to take a more friendly attitude towards
private schools and on May 13, 1954, passed a private-school law.[13]
Erection of private schools requires the consent of the city school
administration, but this consent must be granted if the school meets
the necessary standards both as to instruction and the economic and
legal position of the teachers. The schools also may not make a distinction according to the wealth of pupils; that is, sufficient scholarship
funds must be available for an adequate number of pupils of lesser
means. If a teacher transfers from a private to a public school, his years

of teaching at the former are counted towards salary and pension status. Provision is also made for public subsidies to the private schools, and the private schools participate in the programs which provide free books, school meals, and reduced fares on the streetcars. In 1956, about half the expenses of the one private Catholic Gymnasium and the six foundation and higher schools were paid by the city.[14] Similar support is given to the schools which the Protestants have established. One Protestant Gymnasium and five foundation and higher schools were founded in 1948–49 and were developed by adding an additional class each year.[15] Four of these reached their full ten-year program in 1957, while the remaining one is to be developed into a thirteen-year higher school (*Oberschule Wissenschaftlicher Zweig*). It will offer special opportunities for the study of languages: English, Latin, French being taken up in this order, and the first Abitur examinations are to be held at Easter 1961. The fully developed Evangelical Gymnasium graduated its second class in 1957. At this school in 1956 a special five-and-a-half-year program was begun for pupils from the East sector or zone who had completed their eight-year elementary education but were not admitted to the higher schools there. These pupils are to continue their study of Russian and with the addition of Latin and Greek are to have the opportunity of taking the Abitur examination at the classical (*altsprachlich*) Gymnasium. One of the private elementary schools is organized according to the Jena plan, a pedagogical reform movement under which pupils are divided into three age groups instead of by yearly grades. Older pupils are expected to help instruct the younger ones, and pupils remain in one group three years before moving on. These instances illustrate the experimental value of private schools.

The changes in West Berlin legislation have done much to aid the churches in carrying out their programs. More important than any specific measure is the increasingly friendly attitude that has been displayed by the civil authorities and by schoolmen. This is partly the result of developments in the Federal Republic and the natural tendency to bring West Berlin schools into line with these, but the significant factor is the confidence that has been built up between officials connected with the religious school program and the school authorities. The insistence of Bishop Dibelius and other Protestant leaders that religious-education issues must not be permitted to become the focus of a parliamentary battle, decided by a margin of a few votes, has paid rich dividends in good will, particularly on the part of the Socialists. Open support of the Gemeinschaftsschule as established in Berlin, and the fact that Protestant leaders do not aim to make religion a regular school subject have convinced Socialist leaders that their old fears of a church-dominated school system were exaggerated.

The financial grants made by the state have taken the pressure off the churches and have enabled them to extend the training of cate-chists and to provide necessary scholarships for further study. There is still a shortage of personnel, which is felt in Protestant circles especially at the level of the higher schools. In the spring of 1957 Protestants began a program of religious instruction at the vocational schools, where traditionally in Berlin no such instruction was ever given. So far they have received no city grants for this work, but it is expected that funds will be forthcoming.

Starting from scratch both Catholic and Protestant churches have established an efficient working system. In 1955–56, of the 23,030 Catholic pupils in the schools, 22,529 were taking religious instruction.[16] In the school year 1956–57, instruction was being given by 136 priests, 129 regular teachers, 131 catechists and 64 other church personnel, mostly lay women teachers (*Seelsorgehelferinnen*). In principle the Catholic church tries to give one hour of instruction in the schoolroom and another in church rooms. Priests teach an average of ten hours a week. The church authorities are of course grateful for the more favor-able situation as it has developed in West Berlin, but frankly are not satisfied with it. They would prefer to have religious instruction made a regular subject of instruction taken by all pupils unless they are specifically withdrawn from religion classes. As always they would like to have the public schools organized on a confessional basis, although they have not pressed this issue in West Berlin. There are of course also other desiderata, notably in regard to teacher training.

Protestants, because of their very numbers, had to have a far more extensive program. They estimate that they have attained about 85 percent of their goal of having two hours a week of instruction in all classes of the West Berlin schools.[17] In 1954, 71.2 percent of the classes had two hours a week, 28.2 percent one hour a week, and only 0.6 percent of the classes were without instruction. A closer analysis indi-cates that most of the one-hour-a-week classes are concentrated in the upper classes of the higher schools, where the pupils are beyond the age of confirmation. The church has tried to support the religious pro-gram in the schools by stating that children who do not attend the *Christenlehre* cannot be confirmed. In 1956–57, of all the Protestant (Evangelical) pupils in West Berlin schools 94.8 percent were enrolled in religion classes. In elementary schools (1–6 grades) 99 percent were enrolled; in higher schools: practical branch (7–9 grades) 92.4 percent;

technical branch (7–10 grades) 93.6 percent, and in the scientific-humanistic branch (7–13 grades) 85.2 percent. Such overwhelming participation, which has been steadily maintained since 1945, would seem to indicate that Berlin parents want their children to have religious instruction, even if they themselves are not stalwart church-goers.

Of the 53,470 total hours of Protestant religious instruction in West Berlin schools per month in 1956–57, 90.2 percent was being given by 635 catechists; 1.4 percent by 77 pastors; and 8.4 by 427 regular school teachers.

Leaders of the Protestant church, particularly those at the Education Chamber, take pride in what is essentially a new program, fully in the hands of the church (*im Auftrage der Kirche*). While they would oppose a return to state control of religious instruction, they hold that there can be legitimate ties between church and state; that both institutions draw benefits from each other. Under these conditions they are willing to accept subsidies from the state, but they believe that this should never mean total state support of the religious-education program, for fear of diminishing church control over the content of instruction.

To say that the Protestant leaders look favorably on the situation in West Berlin does not mean, however, that they are satisfied with their existing program. They have recently (1956) inaugurated Religious-Philosophical Schoolweeks (*Religions-Philosophische Schul-wochen*) in which school authorities set aside for one week the fifth and sixth hour of the day at one higher school. For an hour an able speaker presents a topic before an audience of students and faculty; the second hour is then devoted to discussion. So far Catholics have cooperated in the program, and it is hoped that these weeks can be continued as a joint affair. The procedure is not unlike Religious Emphasis Week at American colleges, but it is a new thing in Germany.

Teaching plans and texts have been revised, and efforts are constantly being made to improve them. The most important item in the program is recruiting more and better-trained workers in the field. The men in charge of the program would like to have more regular teachers participate in giving religious instruction. A system of in-service-training has been established for catechists which not only gives intellectual stimulus but provides a very necessary opportunity for Christian fellowship. Catechists in many cases still have to teach too many hours a week, and the proper relationship of catechists to church congregations requires constant attention. While it is probably a wise provision that catechists are appointed and supervised by district authorities and are not under the direction of local pastors, it is also desirable for each catechist to have a close connection with some one church. This is usually true, and it may be safely asserted that the catechists have been fully as helpful to the churches in West Berlin as in the German Democratic Republic. This is not only a matter of helping in Sunday children's services (*Kindergottesdienste*), but also in other church programs. The catechists do considerable visiting of parents, a great help to ministers in large city parishes. The fundamental purpose of the newly oriented *Christenlehre* is to make pupils more aware of the gospel message, and to bring them into closer contact with the churches. While this effort is not new, different approaches are being used. In this, as in most things, example is the best teacher; a catechist must have time not only to do his classroom work properly, but also to share in the life of the congregation.

East Berlin

Whereas the position of religious education in the schools of West Berlin continually improved after 1948, the contrary was true in East Berlin. While the school law passed under four-power control remained in effect there—at least has never been repealed—it has been encrusted with a host of ordinances and interpretations. East Berlin also has taken over much of the school legislation of the German Democratic Republic.[18] Just when and to what extent this latter legislation became effective in East Berlin is almost impossible to determine. East Berlin authorities may sometimes recognize a law or interpretation of the German Democratic Republic as valid, but in other cases they may say it does not apply in Berlin, or only part applies. Local school authorities sometimes claim to be following directives which the central office disclaims issuing, and which indeed cannot be found in the official printed directives. Moreover East Berlin has its own laws and ordinances which do not apply in the Democratic Republic. It all adds up to a very confused legal situation, by far the most complicated in Germany. This is one reason for Bishop Dibelius' lament in his report to the Provincial Synod of the Protestant Church of Berlin-Brandenburg in October 1955. "Here is really the place of our sorrow. Nowhere else do we have to struggle with so much opposition and so many difficulties as in East Berlin."[19]

Certain it is that the school law of 1948 has been interpreted in East Berlin in a way to restrict the holding of religion classes in the schools. By that law schoolrooms were to be placed at the disposal of the churches for religious instruction, but school principals under the pretext of shortage of available space and schedule limitations often denied rooms for this purpose. The provision of the law that religion hours were to be confined to "corner" hours constantly raised difficulties. In West Berlin this restriction was relaxed administratively in favor of the churches as early as April 1949, but in East Berlin often not even corner hours were provided, and religious instruction was shunted to before or after school hours. The East Sector officials also took the position that religion should not be taught to children in the ninth grade, since this grade could no longer be considered the elementary school, an interpretation of the law which church officials have steadily contested. Pressure was put on regular teachers to give up voluntary teaching of religion classes, although the 1948 law clearly allowed it. History and current-events instructors were directly forbidden to teach religion; other teachers could not hold such classes in their own schools lest impressions gained in religion classes should affect their judgment of the work of pupils in other classes. In 1952 forty regular teachers were giving evangelical religion classes in the schools of East Berlin; by 1953 the number had diminished to four and in 1956–57 there were none.[20]

Conditions varied from district to district, from school to school, and also from time to time. Protests and requests from church school officials were by no means always without effect. This was particularly true as long as Ernst Wildangel was in charge of the Central Educational Office (*Hauptschulamt*) of East Berlin. Although he was diametrically opposed to their views in educational affairs, the church officials found him to be a man of his word and a person with whom they could deal. After his death (April 11, 1951) difficulties for the church multiplied, partly also as a result of heightened political tension between East and West. More and more restrictions were placed on the work of the catechists, and they were treated as pariahs by many school principals, often being denied the use of school rooms. In the early months of 1953 in East Berlin just as in the Democratic Republic as a whole, relations between the church and the civil officials reached an acute stage.

This tense situation was relieved by the fresh breath of air which swept through Europe on the death of Stalin in March 1953. When an agreement was concluded between the government of the German Democratic Republic and the Protestant church leaders, there were repercussions in East Berlin. Tension there did lessen, but it was soon evident that no great transformation had taken place. Writing of the next months a member of the Protestant Education Chamber stated: "After June 10 [date of agreement] under the development of the 'new course' things did improve in some instances without a fundamental change having been inaugurated."[21] The director of catechists in East

Berlin commented in November: "In the Democratic Sector [East Berlin] the relation of catechists to school principals, teachers and leaders of the Free German Youth Movement, seen as a whole, has not changed essentially since June; even if especially sharp measures against catechists have been rescinded it is not possible to note a generally friendlier attitude on the part of the schools." [22]

On October 31, 1953, East German officials issued an important "Regulation on the Giving of Religious Instruction in the Rooms of the Common Schools." This ordinance the East Berlin officials came to recognize as also effective for East Berlin. While it again stated that rooms were to be available for religion classes, it had provisions which were contrary to the school law of 1948. The school law provides that two corner hours a week are to be made available for religious instruction; the 1953 ordinance, on the other hand, states that religious instruction can be given "immediately before or after the regular instruction of the individual classes." It is not to be given before, if regular instruction starts at eight o'clock; it cannot be built into the teaching plan (*Springstunden*); care must be taken that students are not over-burdened. Another section states: "The appropriate times for instruction will be agreed upon with the representatives of the churches." Certainly here there was opportunity for varied administrative interpretation on the part of school officials. [23]

In the spring of 1955 some schools began to cancel the morning hour for religious instruction, and this practice was extended in the next school year until in January 1956 there were practically no schools left where classes could be held in the morning. [24] Only the final afternoon class hours were left. In November 1955 school principals began cancelling these periods, saying that religion could only be given after the close of regular instruction. Since a number of the afternoons are devoted to sport and other activities, the days thus became limited on which religion could be given. After Christmas 1955 further restrictions were instituted, and it was maintained that religion classes could not be held immediately after the close of instruction. There was no general regulation at this time, and supposedly these measures were undertaken by the "Pedagogical Council" of the school concerned. These bodies advanced all kinds of reasons, such as the necessity of cleaning schoolrooms, overburdening of students, or use of the period immediately after instruction for students who had to stay after school.

In these months catechists, under the strictest possible interpretation of regulations, were often excluded from schools. They were to confine their activities to the room assigned to them, and because, for instance, they had in a school corridor called pupils' attention to

Reformation Day services or to hours of religious instruction, they were denied further entrance to the schools (*Hausverbot*). In one instance a catechist had taken a boy by the shoulders, which was held to be contrary to the regulation forbidding corporal punishment. On January 16, 1956, seventeen catechists were under such restrictions, some for only a district, others for the whole sector.

It is clear that a new turn in policy was pending, but even the churches were hardly prepared for the ordinance (*Fechner Erlass*) issued by the Magistrat of East Berlin on Ash Wednesday, February 15, 1956.[25] Under this decree, which officially was to safeguard the order and stability of the instructional-educational process, all demands, beyond those made by the school on the pupils, can only begin after the end of regular classes, and a period of at least two hours' rest must precede these extra activities. School authorities are to see that no undue demands are placed upon the students. In order to protect the students from accidents, teachers, after the last period of instruction, are to lead the class out of the school building to the gate of the school yard. All persons who give pupils special instruction must be qualified, and must be positively oriented to the State of the Workers and Peasants. The school principal decides as to the qualifications of anyone not a regular school teacher. Such persons must be citizens of the German Democratic Republic, and exceptions to this rule can only be made by the director of education of the Magistrat of East Berlin. Those giving extra instruction are to receive a certificate which has to be renewed quarterly. All such extra instruction must be held at a place designated by the school principal. In addition to these regulations which obviously applied to religion, section five of the ordinance deals specifically with religious instruction.

The director of the school determines in which schoolrooms religious instruction is to be held. Persons giving this instruction are to use only these rooms and are to stay in them only for the designated periods of instruction. Arrangement of schoolrooms cannot be changed about for the purposes of religious instruction. It is not permitted to recruit pupils for religious instruction in the school or its related establishments.

As far as religious instruction is concerned it ends at the latest with the completion of the foundation school (8th grade).

On March 4, 1956, in all Protestant churches of East Berlin a vigorous protest was read from the pulpits.[26] It was pointed out that the ordinance was contrary to the constitution of the German Democratic Republic, as well as to the Berlin school law of 1948. Particular objection was raised to the ruling that pupils could no longer be given instruction at the higher schools, and that pastors and catechists would have to obtain approval and permission from the school principal every three months. Parents were urged to see that their children attended the children's services, the periods of Christian instruction, and the confirmation classes which were held in the church rooms. A similar protest in the form of a Pastoral Letter from the Bishop of Berlin, Dr. Wilhelm Weskamm, was read in all Catholic churches of East Berlin and of the Soviet Zone on April 22.

Meanwhile the Protestant church headquarters on March 2, and the Catholic diocesan office (*Bischöfliches Ordinariat*) on March 5, sent strongly worded unpublished protests to the East Berlin authorities. Attention was called to the fact that the ordinance of February 15 was not only contrary to the Berlin school law of 1948 and the ordinance of October 31, 1953, but also violated provisions of the constitution of the German Democratic Republic. Replies were not forthcoming. A repeated request for an answer sent by Catholic headquarters brought a letter from Oberbürgermeister Ebert to Otto Menschke, an East Zone official who passed it over to the office of the bishopric.[27] Ebert reasoned that under the constitution religious instruction could not be used for unconstitutional or political purposes, and that observation and control were necessary to see that instruction was meeting this standard. The argument that making pupils return to school a second time was a burden, he turned aside by saying it was good for them to have a little exercise.

It is surprising that after the ordinance of February 1956 any religious instruction at all was carried on in connection with the schools. Yet such was the case, for East Berlin authorities have not attempted to enforce the regulations in full. The vigorous protests of the churches, while unanswered, seem to have had some effect. The provision that religious instruction cannot be held until two hours after the last regular class hour is observed so far as school premises are concerned, but not for church buildings. In fact in some instances buses sent by the churches take pupils directly from school buildings to church rooms, where instruction is then given. Catechists receive a purely formal permit to enter school buildings, and there has been no attempt to check their qualifications by municipal authorities. If a school principal ever attempts to visit a religion class, Protestant catechists have been ordered to start a singing lesson and, if the principal insists on staying, to dismiss the pupils.[28] The Catholics stop classes at once without giving the principal a concert. The prohibition of recruiting for religious instruction on school premises is, however, enforced more strictly than ever. This means that churches cannot even find out how many

Protestant or Catholic pupils are at a school. They have no idea how large classes are, or if students know about the availability of religious instruction—when and where classes are held. Not being able to get in contact with entering classes is particularly restrictive. The ordinance, even if not strictly enforced in all particulars, has created additional handicaps, and both Protestant and Catholic programs have suffered from it.

Catholics decided to give instruction one hour a week to the first- and second-year classes in the church rooms immediately following school. This avoided requiring small children to make a second trip to the schools. From the third year to the eighth, there was to be one hour of religious instruction a week in schoolrooms, plus one hour a week in church rooms. For middle and higher schools, instruction was to be held in church rooms once a week for a one-and-one-half-hour period. In 1955–56, out of 7,395 Catholic pupils in East Berlin schools, 6,402 were taking part in instruction.[29] No exact figures are available for 1956–57, but the church official in charge of this work in East Berlin estimated that participation was reduced to about 60 to 80 percent of the previous figure. A certain drop in the total number of pupils participating must be expected, for the school population is declining because of the low postwar birthrate. In 1956–57, the teaching in East Berlin was being done by 66 priests, 47 catechists, and 34 church helpers. A considerable part of this instruction is still being carried on in the schoolrooms.

In 1956–57, 37,661 Protestant pupils in the schools of East Berlin were receiving religious instruction. In the elementary schools, 966 classes had one hour a week, and 898 two hours a week. Of the total weekly hours, 953 were being given in schoolrooms and 1,944 in church rooms. This instruction was being carried on by 187 catechists, 32 pastors and other church helpers.[30] Since it is no longer possible to determine how many Protestant pupils there are in East Berlin schools (either by way of church or school records) percentage figures of those participating in the religious education program cannot be worked out. That the number has declined since 1948 is certain, but it remains a vigorous program. That so much of the instruction is still being given in schoolrooms testifies to the tenacity of the church officials and their determination not to be pushed out of the schools entirely.

There are no subsidies paid by the city of East Berlin to the churches for their education program. House-to-house collections for the church programs are no longer permitted but the churches can still conduct street collections once or twice a year, and both churches collect small fees (Schulgroschen). In 1954–55 the budget for the

Protestant program amounted to about 1,000,000 East Marks, of which 243,000 came from offerings (*Opfergroschen*), 60,000 from fees (Schulgroschen), 435,000 from the City Synod (*Stadtsynodalverband*), and 362,000 from other sources.[31]

All private schools are prohibited in the German Democratic Republic, and with one exception this rule holds for East Berlin as well. Shortly after the close of the war the Catholic church was able to reopen the Maria Theresia Higher School in East Berlin, and this private higher school has been able to maintain a precarious existence. Evangelical church authorities have for years sought permission to open a similar private higher school. After long discussion they were told that they might hand in a petition for a school, and this was done by Bishop Dibelius on November 2, 1949. A year passed without any answer, and on November 8, 1950, a second petition was submitted. In spite of various oral reminders no answer was forthcoming and a third petition in somewhat altered form was submitted on December 12, 1951. Finally a year later on November 9, 1952, the petition was definitely rejected. This brief recital of dates is a good example of communist delaying tactics.

East Berlin is different from West Berlin, as any visitor who makes a casual trip to the "democratic" sector soon realizes. It is not possible to telephone from one sector of Berlin to the other, except via Frankfurt-am-Main. Yet the two parts of the city are not so separate as this seems to indicate. Men pass daily from one part of the city to the other, and the program of religious education in East Berlin is part of that of West Berlin. It is the same program, carried out by churches that are not divided into east and west sections. In West Berlin the program flourishes, thanks to the benevolent civil administration; in East Berlin it suffers and shrinks as a result of the antagonism of the civil authorities. Nevertheless, in both sectors, determined church educators, both Catholic and Protestant, have maintained the principle of religious education, controlled by the church, yet so far as possible connected with the school system.

Chapter XIX

A SURVEY

A review of historical trends may perhaps bring into clearer perspective the question of German religious education in relation to the whole problem of German education. Religious education as it exists today in German schools is rooted deeply in the past. Like education in general it started out as a province of the church, but as the state gradually took over the burden of educating its citizenry, it also came to have considerable control over religious education. The post-World War II period has brought a reversal of this trend, and today churches are again assuming greater obligations in regard to religious education. In West Germany this has been done in friendly cooperation between church and state; in East Germany the state has manifested a negative attitude, and the responsibility for carrying on the program of religious instruction rests solely upon the churches.

During medieval times it was the church, primarily concerned with educating its own clergy, that furnished the centers of education where increasing numbers of laymen also received schooling of varying degrees of excellence. There was little specifically religious instruction, although theological topics were often under discussion. It was the impact of the Reformation which actually established religion as a field of instruction in the schools. This came about gradually during the process of the development of a general education system in Germany. The necessity and desire for religious education was a natural consequence of the doctrine of the universal priesthood of all believers, with its corollary, the personal responsibility of each individual for his own salvation. In order to educate Christians the first sacristan schools were set up, and it followed that in this period the religious curriculum for Evangelical schools was established in its essentials, emphasizing instruction in the catechism, Bible history, memorization of hymns and Bible verses. Catholic schools somewhat later developed instruction in the services and practices of the church. In Catholic schools there has been less departmentalization of religion and greater stress on religious instruction permeating all subjects. The Reformation, by dividing Germany into Protestant and Catholic sections, thus brought about the development of two confessional educational systems. In broad outlines they were not dissimilar, but to this day the diversity of the German school system is largely due to this difference in religious affiliation. Over the years it has provided an educational and political problem.

At the end of the disastrous Thirty Years' War, the Peace of Westphalia (1648) reinforced the principles of the Peace of Augsburg (1555) which gave the prince the power to determine the religion of his state. This patriarchal principle, under which the prince was head of both church and state, resulted in almost complete annexation of schools to the church. Not before the eighteenth and nineteenth centuries were independent school systems established. Each prince created his own legal and educational system, and such systems were not easily changed. Inevitably as territorial consolidations took place through marriage, inheritance, or conquest, Protestant and Catholic lands came under one prince. Economic considerations as well as the rationalism of the period tended toward toleration, and both Catholic and Protestant educational systems were allowed to continue. The Prince of Nassau broke new paths in 1817, when, in an effort to consolidate territories acquired during the French Revolutionary Era, he ruled that Catholics and Protestants should attend the same schools. After an attempt to introduce common religious instruction, which proved impracticable, he permitted separate Protestant and Catholic religion classes to be established in the same school. Thus there came into being the Simultanschule, Christian in character, but interdenominational in organization. This new type of school was a direct challenge to the older schools, all organized on confessional lines. Each school type had its proponents and opponents, and much of the controversy over educational matters in Germany in the late nineteenth and twentieth centuries has centered in this question of school types. The interdenominational school has steadily expanded into new areas and its constant growth is one of the most noteworthy developments in German education in the last century.

The reaction to the revolutionary movements of the first half of the nineteenth century lent a new significance to religious instruction in the schools. Princes, as well as theologians, usually held that there was a close relationship between educating good Christians and good citizens, and in the effort to preserve their thrones, they looked more than ever to religion as an antidote to revolution. The nineteenth century, however, saw the constantly growing secularization of society.

The state was forced to assume more and more obligations, and foremost among these were the steadily mounting financial requirements of the schools. With this came more state control over types of schools, the nature and content of the curriculum, and eventually curtailment of clerical supervision.

When the Empire was formed in 1871, education remained under the control of the various states. Powerful factors, however, were pressing towards unity in the educational system. Territorial consolidation helped to create a national forum for educational matters. The formation of national political parties, which immediately took stands on educational issues, brought school questions into the vortex of national political agitation. The Catholic Center party became the champion of Catholic educational ideals, giving strong support to the confessional school system. The Social Democratic party, firmly opposed to the close connection between throne and altar, had as one of its slogans, "Religion is a private matter." It advocated the abolition of religious instruction in the schools, although this part of its program never had much popular support. The state authorities, with the possible exception of a few brief controversies, never assumed a hostile attitude toward religious education in the schools, maintaining that it was a vital part of the educational process. Neither did the teaching profession as a whole oppose the teaching of religion, merely taking the position that it should be in the hands of professional teachers, free of clerical inspection. They looked to the state to support them in the struggle for emancipation from clerical influence. This movement was particularly strong among the elementary-school teachers, for the teachers at higher schools had long asserted their independent professional status. The development of pedagogy as a distinct intellectual discipline also did much to further the secularization of the school system.

The establishment of the Weimar Republic after World War I inevitably evoked the question of state or national control of education. Neither of the leading parties was opposed to national control, if its particular program could be enacted. But the two coalition leaders, the Center and Social Democratic parties, were on opposite sides of the fence, the one advocating a confessional-school system, the other, in lieu of complete secularisation, at least an interdenominational organization. The only way out of the dilemma was to agree on a compromise, the essence of which was to continue the *status quo* until the national government should regulate educational affairs through the enactment of an education law. Meanwhile the states were to continue to regulate their own educational affairs.

The expected national education law, however, never materialized, because no agreement could be reached on problems centering
about religious education in the schools, chiefly the issue of confessional
versus interdenominational schools. The Weimar Constitution specifically stated that the interdenominational school was to be considered
the "normative" type, but implementation of this principle in a
general law proved baffling politically. The intellectual climate, however, remained tolerant. Even under the Empire students might be
excused from religion classes, and under the Weimar Republic new
regulations made it easier for students or teachers to withdraw from
the regularly scheduled classes, although few took advantage of this
privilege. Jewish educational opportunities were on a par with other
groups, for they had private schools receiving some support from the
state, there were a few public Jewish confessional schools, and there
was provision for separate religious instruction in other public schools
wherever the number of Jewish students warranted it. Though purely
secular schools, where no religious instruction was given, were now
permitted, their number remained insignificant. The Vatican continued
to press for confessional schools and did succeed in arranging a concordat with Bavaria guaranteeing such schools in that state, but could
not achieve one with the national state until after Hitler came to
power.

It is to be expected that the tides and currents of thought should
affect religious education. Through the centuries, passing from pietism
to rationalism, moved by tolerance or scientific criticism, influenced
in turn by conservative or radical persuasions, not only the type of
school, but also the content of the religious curriculum was increasingly
subject to discussion. In the late nineteenth and early twentieth
centuries the religious curriculum did not go untouched by modern
pedagogical thinking. Efforts were made to work out an integrated
program, with less emphasis on memorization. More of the catechetical
material was left to instruction by the clergy either in the schools
or, more often, in confirmation classes. Such reforms were able to
make little headway against the effects of the growing secularization
of society.

The period of National Socialism ended the sort of truce under
which religious education had continued to function. After a first
honeymoon period when the National Socialists concluded a concordat
with the Papacy and attempted to negotiate a settlement with the
Protestant churches, they began to introduce restrictive measures.
Many of these were but a radical enforcement of ideas of fundamental
rights dating from the Weimar period. Here might be classed such

steps as the end, in practice as well as in theory, of the compulsory attendance of pupils at school church services; or again the freedom of a teacher not to teach religion. Basically they wanted to remove all clergy from the schools and with some exceptions, notably Bavaria, Baden, parts of Württemberg and Prussia, they were able to do so. They attempted with some success to bring more uniformity into the school system. This aim was at least one reason given for the virtual elimination of private schools. It also accounts for the successful campaign to convert all confessional schools into interdenominational Gemeinschaftsschulen. Many schoolmen had long favored this, but churchmen were opposed to it because they believed it to be the first step towards the creation of an entirely secular school system from which religious instruction and church influence would be barred. In spite of protestations and assurances they feared, with good reason, that the new Nazi Gemeinschaftsschulen would be far different from the old Simultanschule as it had existed in Baden, Hesse, and other sections.

Although many restrictions were introduced affecting the traditional role and significance of religious instruction, it is also clear that the Nazis did not completely eliminate religion from the schools. Officially and in most sections in practice—aside from some of the extreme situations brought about by war conditions—religion remained a regular part of the school curriculum to the end. The time allotted to it was reduced considerably. The general practice came to be to restrict religious instruction to the years of compulsory full-time school attendance, and hence it was not given in vocational schools. What was taught in the religion classes no doubt often had little to do with good religious instruction, and it was often made to serve Nazi ends, as in times past it had served the monarchy and other special interests. On the other hand not all teaching was of this caliber, and there was a considerable measure of worthy instruction in spite of the Nazis. Such instruction had to contend with the general tenor of education in other fields. Religious education in the schools was probably as orthodox, if not more so, than the climate of religious opinion among the masses of the German population.

The history of Jewish education under the Nazis roughly parallels the general treatment of the Jews in the Third Reich. At first there were restrictions, then general isolation, and finally complete annihilation. Under the Weimar Republic Jewish education could be said to have reached a status of equality. The Nazis ended this and placed responsibility upon the Jews for their own education. Then, as the attempt to exterminate all Jews progressed, even this separate Jewish education system was ended in 1942. While the number of Jews in

Germany has been insignificant since the Nazi holocaust, their former position of equality has been restored, and the same provisions apply to Jewish religious instruction today as to Christian.

At the close of the war, churchmen, perhaps more keenly than any other group, were aware of the dangers toward which Hitler had been heading. They were determined that never again should the state be permitted to have a commanding influence over religious instruction. How this was to be accomplished was a delicate problem, in view of the heritage of close ties between church and state, and the financial dependence of the churches on the state. The division of Germany has led to very different developments in West Germany from those in the Soviet Zone.

While, in general, people and clergy in West Germany were agreed that religion should be separated from the state, there was a trend away from the ideas of secularization so dominant in the twenties. Defeat, loss, turmoil and grief, all brought a renewal of religious interest, and not only the churchmen, but also most of the population felt the need of religious education more than ever. It was generally agreed that the duty of the state was to protect individual liberties, to promote toleration, and to cooperate with the churches. Everywhere in West Germany schools have again been established on a Christian basis, and religious instruction continues to be given in the schools. Moreover it is specifically provided that this instruction is to be given in accordance with the teachings of the church. To this end the churches have been given far-reaching rights and duties in regard to the establishment and supervision of the religious curriculum. More important, it is now definitely recognized that teachers of religion must be approved by Protestant or Catholic church authorities as the case may be. The churches recognize this as an obligation, as well as a welcome opportunity to improve religious instruction in the schools. The churches have made extraordinary efforts to provide qualified religious instructors. Many clergymen have assumed heavy teaching schedules and numerous catechists have been trained to make up for an insufficient number of regular qualified teachers. The general extension of religious education to vocational schools constitutes a major challenge to the churches, but one that has been willingly accepted, for contact with this age-group is recognized as being particularly important.

Church control of religious education in the schools has not been accepted without controversy. Many teachers feared that clerical supervision of the schools might be reestablished. On the whole this spectre has been exorcised by the wise and careful action of churchmen, who have accepted the right to approve teachers' qualification as sufficient guarantee of proper instruction. They do not visit classes and have made a real effort to establish friendly relations and free cooperation with the teachers. The question of whether confessional or interdenominational schools should be established has indeed produced much controversy. The occupying powers on the whole kept their hands off this burning issue. The Catholic church has strongly championed the cause of the confessional-school system. Often it has had the support of Protestant groups, but Protestants as a whole would have accepted the interdenominational system—which indeed has been established in the predominantly Protestant states. An attempt on the part of Catholic groups to write a provision safeguarding the confessional-school system into the national constitution failed, although it does appear in a number of state constitutions. The decision (1957) of the Supreme Court concerning the Concordat of 1933 between the Vatican and Hitler's government reinforces the independence of the individual states in all cultural matters.

In the Soviet-controlled zone of Germany, religious instruction has been dropped from the school program as such, the state only grudgingly providing rooms for religious instruction by church authorities in school buildings, when church facilities are not available. There has been no attempt to control the content of this instruction, but on the other hand all other subjects have been impregnated with concepts of dialectical materialism. The schools have been completely secularized, and they are characterized in general by a critical tone toward religion and the churches. Parents still enroll their children in overwhelming numbers for the church-sponsored religious hours. In the majority of instances, however, because of lack of personnel the churches cannot provide for more than one hour a week of instruction. The state has forbidden religious instruction at other than elementary schools, although churches continue their attempts to keep in contact with students at higher schools, largely through other church programs. Conditions vary somewhat according to the disposition of local authorities.

The traditional socialist attitude toward religious instruction derives, of course, from Marxist doctrine. Whereas separation of church and state in the United States was originally enacted to protect the freedom of the church from the state, the original socialist Marxist concept was that this separation must be carried out in order to protect the state from the church. Separation of church from state in the United States meant a pro-church policy; in socialism under European conditions it meant an anticlerical, antichurch, antireligious policy.

Berlin provides a most vivid example of different interpretations of the same principle. While Berlin remained under four-power control one common school was introduced, in which religion might be given by the churches at their own expense. In West Berlin since the division of 1949, Socialists have departed in varying degrees from the Marxist concept. Separation of church and state, which they still hold vital, is now not so much a matter of radical separation as in a chemical analysis, but is rather a question of drawing the proper line between church and state activities. Drawing such a line is not easy, and no doubt it will be shifted back and forth from time to time. Yet in West Berlin the line has steadily moved over toward more support of the church's religious-education program by the city. This has been done carefully without evoking bitter antagonism or opposition on the part of any political party. The churches give religious instruction in interdenominational schools with the cooperation of the state, which now furnishes most of the funds for that program. There are even a few private confessional schools, partly financed by the state.

In East Berlin, the original law of 1948 has not been officially revoked, but it is constantly violated by new ordinances and provisions hostile to the religious instruction which the churches still manage to carry on in the schools. In contrast to West Berlin, where the city even gives financial support to this instruction, the Magistrat of East Berlin places many obstacles in the way of the churches. Use of school-rooms has been hedged about with such restrictions that it has been greatly reduced. But here as in all of Germany, Catholics and Protestants alike maintain not only German but Christian unity in a divided city, state, and world.

The future of religious education in Germany cannot be predicted yet certain tendencies and possibilities do come to the surface in the course of a study such as this.

Perhaps the most remarkable circumstance to American readers is the obvious fact that religion is not only being taught in West German schools, but is definitely wanted there by the German people. There is still considerable criticism of the material and methods in the lower schools, but here and even more notably in secondary schools great advances have been made. The author visited classes where discussion methods and topics related to daily living brought lively participation by the pupils. There is in West Germany no movement of any weight to remove religious education from the schools, while in East Germany the churches have had remarkable success in keeping the issue before the people, in spite of heavy obstacles.

It is difficult to speak of a tendency throughout West Germany since great variations exist between states, such as between Bavaria and Hesse, for example. Nevertheless it would seem that the idea of the Simultan or interdenominational school is steadily growing stronger. More important is the active part played not only by the Catholic church, but also by the Protestant churches in training qualified teachers for religious education and in supervising study plans. In every field of education the ability of the teacher to awaken the interest of his students in the subject is essential. That the church may succeed in developing such a corps of teachers is the hope of the new programs of religious education in West Germany. The more radical solution of church–state educational problems which has developed in West Berlin may eventually prove useful in other parts of Germany, and is, in itself, a dramatic experiment in cooperation between churches and schools for the religious education of youth.

Note on Bibliography
Bibliography
Notes

NOTE on BIBLIOGRAPHY

The sources for a study of religious education in German schools are so numerous that, at least in certain categories, it seems preferable to point out what the available sources are, rather than to list them by title.

There are, first of all, constitutions, laws, and ordinances, usually recorded in the various official journals issued by (1) the state governments, (2) the lower administrative divisions: provinces, districts, municipalities, and (3) the different national governments after 1871. Since educational affairs were traditionally left to state regulation, national statutes and ordinances play no great role during the Empire, but take on increased significance with the Weimar Republic and the Hitler era, and are all-important in the German Democratic Republic today. On the other hand, state laws and regulations have always been of prime significance. To list all the official Amtsblätter and legal collections of each state in the various periods of German history would require a volume in itself; even to list those consulted would result only in a meaningless table of titles. Official designations and titles, always long in Germany, vary slightly with administrative shifts in government departments or with changes from monarchy to republic to Third Reich and back to republic. To be accurate one would have to list three or four titles for what is in reality one file of an official state gazette. Official journals are always cited in the notes in sufficient detail to enable a reader to recognize their origin easily.

German laws and administrative ordinances applicable to education have had to be available to countless local officials, teachers, and clergy, as well as to many others. To meet this need there have always been collections of the more significant legal school regulations. These collections are actually primary sources, although they are customarily cited under the name of the compiler and will be so listed below. Volume VI of Brauchitsch, *Verwaltungsgesetze für Preussen*, Drews and Lassar, eds. (Berlin, 1933) is such a collection and is most helpful for Prussia during the Weimar Republic. This volume was actually compiled by Walter Landé, perhaps the greatest expert on the Prussian school system in this period. His volume *Religionsunterricht. Sammlung der staatlichen Bestimmungen über Religionsunterricht an Volks-, mittleren und höheren Schulen, religiöse Erziehung, Moralunterricht, Konfirmantenunterricht, usw.* (Berlin, 1929) is most helpful in the more limited field of religious instruction. In Germany, more than in the United States, the practice prevails of editing loose-leaf legal collections which are kept up-to-date through supplements. Homeyer's *Neuordnung des höheren Schulwesens. Sammlung der wichtigsten diesbezüglichen Gesetze, Erlasse, und*

Verfügungen seit Januar 1933, 2 ed. (Berlin, 1940) is most useful for the Nazi era. Important for the Post-World War II period are the volumes edited, with the aid of others, by Paul Seipp, *Schulrecht. Ergänzbare Sammlung der Vorschriften für Schule und Schulverwaltung* (Karlsruhe, Stuttgart, Berlin, 1954–   ). So far collections have been issued for Baden-Württemberg, Bavaria, Berlin, Hesse, Lower Saxony, North Rhine-Westphalia, Rhineland-Palatinate, and Schleswig-Holstein, and others are planned. For the Democratic Republic the loose-leaf *Karteibuch des Schulrechts der Deutschen Demokratischen Republik*, 2 ed. 10 vols., (Berlin, n.d.) is indispensable. Another volume of commentary on East German Schools should be cited here: *Schulrecht und Schulverwaltung in der Deutschen Demokratischen Republik. Herausgegeben im Auftrage des Ministeriums für Volksbildung* (Berlin, 1956).

In addition to the many laws and ordinances from governmental sources there are the regulations, prescriptions, and directives issued by church bodies. Each of the Protestant churches in the various states has its own official journal, and these often contain vital information in respect to religious education in the schools. There are also the official journals of the various Catholic dioceses. However it is useless to list separately all these official church publications. The yearbooks of the churches are helpful in the more modern periods, for they usually contain sections devoted to educational affairs. Here should be named above all the *Kirchliches Jahrbuch für die Evangelische Kirche in Deutschland* (Gütersloh, 1874–   ), usually referred to as "Schneider" after its founder and long-time editor, Johannes Schneider, and *Kirchliches Handbuch. Amtliches statistisches Jahrbuch der katholischen Kirche Deutschlands* (Freiburg, 1909–   ; Cologne, 1933–   ).

The periodical and newspaper literature is endless. There are not only the special pedagogical, religious, and historical journals, but, since education and religion are of concern to the mass of the people, many important articles and reports appear in popular magazines and in the daily press. Today the most significant Protestant periodicals in Germany for religious education are: *Der evangelische Erzieher; Schule und Leben, Zeitschrift für christliche Erziehung und Unterrichtspraxis; Evangelische Unterweisung, Mitteilungsblatt für pädagogische Arbeitsgemeinschaften; Die Christenlehre, Zeitschrift für den katechetischen Dienst*, the last being the magazine for the German Democratic Republic. Catholic periodicals are *Katechetische Blätter: Jugendseelsorger, Zeitschrift für katholische Religionspädagogik und Jugendseelsorge*; and *Der katholische Erzieher*. Articles cited from journals and yearbooks are not listed in the bibliography; such articles are usually cited only once with a complete reference in the appropriate note.

A very few volumes of general value, not cited in the notes, are included in the bibliography. To enable the reader to find the complete bibliographical reference easily for works cited frequently by abbreviated title, the bibliography is arranged alphabetically.

BIBLIOGRAPHY

Adolph, Walter. *Im Schatten des Galgens. Zum Gedächtnis d. Blutzeugen in der nationalsozialistischen Kirchenverfolgung.* Berlin, 1953.

Albrecht, Hellmuth. *Die Stellung des politischen Katholizismus in Deutschland zu den Fragen des Unterrichts und der Erziehung in den Jahren 1848–1850.* Leipzig, 1929.

Allgemeine Deutsche Biographie. 55 vols. and general index. Leipzig, 1875–1912.

Allgemeiner evang.-luth. Schulverein. *Zum Staatsvertrag der evangelisch-lutherischen Landeskirche in Bayern rechts des Rheins mit dem bayerischen Staat.* Dresden, 1925.

Anschütz, Gerhard. *Die Verfassung des Deutschen Reichs vom 11. August 1919. Ein Kommentar für Wissenschaft und Praxis.* 3 ed., Berlin, 1930.

Appens, W. *Die pädagogischen Bewegungen des Jahres 1848.* Jena, 1914.

Arbeitsgemeinschaft für deutschen Religionsunterricht. *Am Urborn deutscher Frömmigkeit. Kernworte deutschen Glaubens. Ein Hilfsbuch für deutschen Religionsunterricht.* Breslau, 1939.

Arndt, Adolf. *Die Verfassungsurkunde für den Preussischen Staat.* Berlin, 1907.

Bachman, Dr. Ph. *Ein Volk, Ein Staat, Eine Schule. Eine Untersuchung zum Schulkampf der Gegenwart, insonderheit über die nationale Bedeutung der Gemeinschaftsschule und der Bekenntnisschule.* 2 ed. Langensalza, 1918.

Bainton, Roland H. *Here I Stand: A Life of Martin Luther.* New York, 1950.

Barnard, Henry. ed. *Memoirs of Eminent Teachers and Educators with Contributions to the History of Education in Germany, Republished from the American Journal of Education.* Hartford, 1878.

Bartels, Friedrich, ed. *Dr. Wilhelm Harnischs Handbuch für das Deutsche Volksschulwesen.* Langensalza, 1893.

Barth, Alfred. *Katechetisches Handbuch zum katholischen Katechismus für die Bistümer Deutschlands.* 3 vols. Stuttgart, 1955.

Barth, Paul. *Die Geschichte der Erziehung in soziologischer und geistesgeschichtlicher Beleuchtung.* 3 and 4 ed. Leipzig, 1920.

Barth, Richard. *Die Krisis im evangelischen Religionsunterricht in Lichte deutschen Christentums.* Weimar, Verlag Deutschen Christen, 1937.

Baumont, Maurice, et al., eds. *The Third Reich.* New York, 1955.

Baynes, Norman. *The Speeches of Adolf Hitler, April 1922–August 1939.* 2 vols. London, 1942.

Becker, Hans-Joachim. *Zur Rechtsproblematik des Reichskonkordats.* Munich, 1956.

Benze, Rudolf. *Erziehungsmächte und Erziehungshoheit im Grossdeutschen Reich als gestaltende Kräfte im Leben des Deutschen.* Leipzig, 1940.

Bergman, Bernhard, ed. *Volksschule heute. Beiträge zur Entfaltung der Richtlinien für die Volksschulen des Landes Nordrhein-Westfalen.* Ratingen bei Düsseldorf, 1956.

308   Bibliography

Bergsträsser, L. *Geschichte der politischen Parteien in Deutschland*. 7 ed., Munich, 1952.

Berlau, A. Joseph. *The German Social Democratic Party 1914–1921*. New York, 1949.

Berndt, Johannes. *Methodik des Unterrichts in der evangelischen Religion*. Leipzig, 1909.

Bibelanstalt Altenberg. *Christenlehre. Ein Buch für die evangelische Jugend*. 5 ed. Berlin, 1952.

Bischöfliche Arbeitsstelle für Schule und Erziehung Köln. *Das Ringen um das sogennante Reichsschulgesetz. Dokumente aus den parlamentarischen Verhandlungen 1919–1927*. Cologne, 1956.

—— *Mit Kelle und Schwert*: Vol. I, *Stellungnahme Roms und des deutschen Episkopates zu den Schulfragen in der Zeit vor 1933*; Vol. II, *Elternrecht und Schule*; Vol. III, *Die katholische Kirche und ihr Schul- und Erziehungsideal*; Vol. IV, *Stimmen des deutschen Episkopates zur Schulfrage in der Zeit des "Dritten Reiches"*. Cologne, 1949.

Bischöfliches Ordinariat Berlin. *Dokumente aus dem Kampf der katholischen Kirche in Bistum Berlin gegen den Nationalsozialismus*. Berlin, 1946.

Blättner, Fritz. *Geschichte der Pädagogik*. 2 ed. Heidelberg, 1953.

Blau, Bruno. *Das Ausnahmerecht für die Juden in Deutschland 1933–1945*. 2 ed. Düsseldorf, 1954.

Bopp, Linus. *Katechetik. Geist und Form des katholischen Religionsunterrichts*. (Part IV, vol. I in *Handbuch der Erziehungswissenschaft*) Munich, 1935.

Brandt, Richard B. *The Philosophy of Schleiermacher. The Development of His Theory of Scientific and Religious Knowledge*. New York, 1941.

Brauchitsch, M. von. *Verwaltungsgesetze für Preussen*. Bill Drews and Gerhard Lassar, eds., introduction by Walter Landé, Berlin, 1933. Vol. VI deals with schools.

Buch, Dr. Günther. *Die Rechtstellung des Lehrers zu Kirche und Staat bei der Erteilung des Religionsunterrichts. Abhandlung und Mitteilungen aus dem Seminar für öffentliches Recht*. Hamburg, 1932.

Buchheim, Hans. *Glaubenskrise im Dritten Reich. Drei Kapitel Nationalsozialistischer Religionspolitik*. Stuttgart, 1953.

Bundesministerium für gesamtdeutsche Fragen. *Das Erziehungswesen der Sowjetzone. Eine Sammlung von Zeugnissen der Sowjetisierung und Russifizierung des mitteldeutschen Schulwesens*. Bonn, 1952.

Bundesvertretung der Studenten an Pädagogischen Hochschulen. *Pädagogischer Studienführer für das Bundesgebiet und West Berlin*. Düsseldorf, 1955.

Burckstümmer, Christian. *Der Religionsunterricht in der Volksschule. Untersuchungen zur Reform der religiösen Jugendunterweisung*. Munich, 1914.

Burger, Tiberius. *Der katholische Religionsunterricht in der Grundschule. Katechetische Skizzen für die Unterstufe der katholischen Volksschulen*. Vol. I, *Das Alte Testament*; Vol. II, *Das Neue Testament*. Munich, 1950.

Castellan, Georges. *D.D.R. Allemagne de l'est*. Paris, 1955.

The Church College. New York: World Council of Christian Education and Sunday School Association, 1951.

The Church of Scotland. *The Church under Communism*. New York, 1953.

Cole, Luella. *A History of Education. Socrates to Montessori*. New York, 1950.

Cölln, Detlef. *Lehrplan für deutschen Religionsunterricht*. Kiel, 1935.

Colodner, Solomon. "Jewish Education in Nazi Germany." Manuscript Ph.D. thesis, Dropsie College, Philadelphia, 1954.

Constitutions of the German Länder. Issued by the Civil Administration Division Office of Military Government [U.S.], Berlin, 1947.

Corsten, Wilhelm, ed. *Kölner Aktenstücke zur Lage der katholischen Kirche in Deutschland, 1933–1945*. Cologne, 1949.

Cramer, Hans, and Adolf Strehler. *Schulreform in Bayern. Arbeitsergebnisse der Stiftung zum Wideraufbau des bayerischen Erziehungs- und Bildungswesens*. Bad Heilbrunn, OBB, 1953.

Danehl, Erich. *Das Landesrecht in Niedersachsen*. Cologne, 1951f. A looseleaf collection.

Deiters, Heinrich. *Die deutsche Schulreform nach dem Weltkriege*. Berlin, 1935.

Deuerlein, Ernst. *Das Reichskonkordat. Beiträge zu Vorgeschichte, Abschluss und Vollzug des Konkordates zwischen dem Heiligen Stuhl und dem Deutschen Reich vom 20. Juli 1933*. Düsseldorf, 1956.

Deutsches Institut für Wissenschaftliche Pädagogik Münster in Westfalen. *Lexikon der Pädagogik der Gegenwart*. 2 vols. Freiburg im Breisgau, 1930.

Deutschland Jahrbuch 1949; 1953. Essen, 1949, 1953.

Dittmer, Hans. *Religionsunterricht auf dem Grunde der Wirklichkeit und neuen Erziehung*. Weimar, 1932.

Documents on German Foreign Policy 1918-1945. From the Archives of the German Foreign Ministry. Washington, 1949– .

Dorst, Werner. *Erziehung, Bildung und Unterricht in der deutschen Demokratischen Schulen. Grundlagen*. Berlin, 1954.

Dreising, Franz. *Das Amt des Küsters in der evangelischen Kirche*. Berlin, 1854.

Eberhard, E. *Die wichtigsten Reformbestrebungen der Gegenwart auf dem Gebiete des Religionsunterrichts in der Volksschule*. Leipzig, 1908.

Ebers, Godehard Josef. *Staat und Kirche im Neuen Deutschland*. Munich, 1930.

Edmunds, L. Francis. *Rudolf Steiner Education – A Brief Exposition*. Ilkeston, Derbys., n.d.

Ellwein, Prof. Lic. *Der Evangelische Religionsunterricht an d.dt. Schule*. Berlin, 1937.

Ellwein, Thomas. *Klerikalismus in der deutschen Politik*. 2 ed. Munich, 1955.

Die Evangelischen Grundschulen in Berlin. Gründungsgeschichte und Bericht über die Schuljahre 1948–50. Berlin, 1951.

Evang.-Luth. Landeskirchenrat. *Lehrpläne für den evangelisch–lutherischen Religionsunterricht an den Volkshauptschulen in Bayern r.d. Rhs*. Munich, 1933.

——— *Lehrpläne für den kirchlichen Unterricht an den Volks- und Berufsschulen*. Munich, 1949.

Fabricius, D. Caius. *Positive Christianity in the Third Reich*. Dresden, 1937.

Feely, Raymond T. *Nazism vs. Religion*. New York, 1940.

Fischer, Hubert. *Einführung in den neuen Katechismus*. Freiburg, 1955.

Fischer, Konrad. *Geschichte des deutschen Volksschullehrerstandes*. 2 vols. Hanover, 1892.

Fleming, Hans. *Religionsunterricht? Moralunterricht? Ein Wort für Eltern und Lehrern*. Berlin, 1918.

Flitner, Wilhelm. *Die vier Quellen des Volksschulgedankens*. Hamburg-Wandsbek, 1949.

Francke, Kuno. *A History of German Literature as Determined by Social Forces.*
New York, 1907.

———— *Personality in German Literature Before Luther.* Cambridge, 1916.

Franz, Georg. *Kulturkampf Staat und Katholische Kirche in Mitteleuropa von
der Säkularisation bis zum Abschluss des Preussischen Kulturkampfes.*
Munich, c. 1955.

Frobenius, Friedrich Otto. *Die Entwicklung des Rechts der religiösen Kindererziehung im deutschen Reich.* Halle-Saale, 1926.

Frör, Kurt. *Das Zeichnen im kirchlichen Unterricht. Ein Arbeitsbuch.* Munich,
1950.

———— *Der kirchliche Unterricht an der Volksschule. Ein Vorbereitungswerk im
Anschluss an den Lehrplan der Evangelisch-Lutherischen Kirche in Bayern.*
Munich, c. 1952. Frör is preparing teaching manuals for all grades.

Funck-Brentano, Frantz. *Luther.* Translated from the French by E. F. Buckley.
London, 1936.

Gawin, Adalbert J. *Die Rechtsnature der Konkordate im Gegensatz zu den evangelischen Staatskirchenverträgen. Nach dem Stande vor dem 7. April, 1933.*
Marburg, 1935.

Geissler, W. *Staat und Kirchen in Preussen.* Dresden, 1931.

Gengnagel, Ludwig. *Mein kirchlicher Lehrauftrag im ersten Schuljahr.* Stuttgart,
1948. The author has teachers' manuals like this one for various school
years.

Giese, Friedrich. *Grundgesetz für die Bundesrepublik Deutschland vom 23 Mai
1949.* 4 ed., Frankfurt am Main, 1955.

———— *Religionsunterricht als Pflichtfach der deutschen Berufsschulen.* Berlin, 1933.

———— *Verfassung des Deutschen Reiches vom 11. August, 1919.* 7 ed., Berlin,
1926.

Giese, Gerhardt. *Deutsche Schulgesetzgebung.* Berlin, c. 1931.

———— *Erziehung und Bildung in der mündigen Welt.* Göttingen, 1957.

———— *Evangelische Erziehung Christenlehre und kirchliche Verkündigung.*
Berlin, 1949.

———— *Die Kirche in der Berliner Schule. Mit drei schulpolitischen Denkschriften
von D. Hans Lokies.* Berlin, 1955.

———— *Die Schulpolitik der Evangelischen Kirche in Berlin.* Reprint from
Mission Draussen und Drinnen. Berlin, 1955.

———— *Staat und Erziehung. Grundzüge einer politischen Pädagogik und Schulpolitik.* Hamburg, 1933.

Goetz, Georg. *Die schulrechtlichen Bestimmungen der neueren und neuesten
europäischen Konkordate in ihrer Beziehung zu jeweiliger staatlichen Schulgesetzgebung.* Regensburg, 1935.

Goldbach, Erwin. *Wege und Irrwege der Berliner Schulpolitik.* Berlin, 1954.

Goldbrunner, Josef. *Katechismusunterricht mit dem Werkheft.* 3 vols. Munich,
1956.

Goodspeed, Edgar J. *How Came the Bible?* New York, 1940.

Grapengeter, Andrew. *Kultusrecht. Sammlung von Gesetzen, Verordnungen und
anderen öffentlich-rechtlichen Vorschriften des Bundes (Reiches) und der
Hansestadt Hamburg auf den Gebieten der Erziehung, Wissenschaft und
Kultur.* Hamburg, 1953– .

*Gründungsgeschichte und erster Jahresbericht des Evangelischen Gymnasiums
Berlin.* Berlin, 1950.

Hahn, Friedrich. *Die evangelische Unterweisung in den Schulen des 16. Jahrhunderts.* Heidelberg, 1957.

Hammelsbeck, Oskar. *Glaube Welt Erziehung.* Mülheim (Ruhr), 1954.

Hammerstein, L.v. *Das Preussische Schulmonopol mit besonderen Rücksicht auf die Gymnasien.* Freiburg im Breisgau, 1893.

Hansen, Heinrich. *Über Memoriern und Memorierstoff auf dem Gebiete des Religionsunterrichts. Ein Beitrag zur Reform des Religionsunterrichts.* Berlin, 1909.

Haugg, Werner. *Die Schule in Nordrhein-Westfalen.* Vol. I, *Der weltanschauliche Charakter der Volksschule (Dritter Abschnitt des Schulgesetzes);* Vol II, *Uber Erziehung und Unterricht (Erster Abschnitt des Schulgesetzes);* Vol. III, *Vom Elternrecht zur Schulpflegschaft (Zweiter Abschnitt des Schulgesetzes);* Vol. IV, *Die Private Schule (Fünfter Abschnitt des Schulgesetzes);* Vol. V, *Der Religionsunterricht in den Schulen (Vierter Abschnitt des Schulgesetzes);* Vol. VI, *Schulgesetze in Nordrhein-Westfalen (Textausgabe).* Düsseldorf, 1953–54.

Heckel, Hans. *Deutsches Privatschulrecht.* Berlin, 1955.

———— and Paul Seipp, *Schulrechtskunde. Ein Handbuch für Lehrer, Eltern und Schulverwaltung. Ein Studienbuch für die Lehrerbildung.* Berlin, 1957.

Hehlmann, Wilhelm. *Pädagogisches Wörterbuch.* 3 ed., Stuttgart, 1942.

Heilmann, Friedrich, and Horst Birnbaum. *Gesetze und Verordnungen für die Schule der Deutschen Demokratischen Republik.* Berlin, 1955.

Henselmann, P. *Schule und evangelische Kirche in Preussen. Zusammenstellung der wichtigsten gesetzlichen Bestimmungen und Verordnungen.* 2 ed. Langensalza, 1928.

Heppe, H. *Geschichte des deutschen Volksschulwesens.* 5 vols. 1858–60.

Herborner Arbeitskreis für evangelische Jugendunterweisung. *Wort und Zeugnis.* Vol. I, *Evangelische Kinderbüchlein,* Vol. II, *Biblische Geschichte;* Vol. III, *Bilder aus der Kirchengeschichte für die evangelische Jugend in Hessen;* Vol IV, *Evangelische Kirchengeschichte für Mittel- (Real) Schulen und für die Mittelstufe der Höheren Schulen;* Vol. V, *Grundlinien der Kirchengeschichte in evangelischer Sicht für die Oberstufe der Höheren Schulen und für Studierende;* Vol. VI, *Quellenbuch zur Kirchengeschichte und Kirchenkunde;* Vol. VII, *Zeittafel zur Kirchengeschichte.* Frankfurt am Main, 1952–54. Various textbooks prepared under the auspices of the Protestant church in Hesse and Nassau.

Herman, Stewart W. *Report from Christian Europe.* New York, 1953.

Hermann, Gotthilf. *Religionsfreiheit. Eine Quellensammlung mit zahlr. amtl, Dokumenten. (Teil 1: Amtliche Dokumente. Worte führender Männer).* 5 ed. Zwickau, 1936.

Hermelink, Heinrich. *Geschichte der Evangelischen Kirche in Württemberg von der Reformation bis zum Gegenwart.* Stuttgart, 1949.

———— *Kirche im Kampf. Dokumente des Widerstands und des Aufbaus in der Evangelischen Kirche Deutschlands von 1933 bis 1945.* Tübingen and Stuttgart, 1950.

Hertz, Frederick. *The Development of the German Public Mind. A Social History of German Political Sentiments, Aspirations and Ideas. The Middle Ages— The Reformation.* London, 1957.

Herz, Hanns-Peter. *Freie Deutsche Jugend. Berichte und Dokumente zur Entwicklung und Tätigkeit der Kommunistischen Jugendorganisation.* Munich, 1957.

Hildebrand, Georg. *Der Religionsunterricht an den öffentlichen Schulen in bisherigen und neuen Recht.* Berlin, 1922.

Hilker, Franz. *Die Schulen in Deutschland (Bundesrepublik und West-Berlin).* Bad Nauheim, 1954.

——— ed. *Pädagogik im Bild.* Freiburg, 1956.

Hiller, Friedrich. *Deutsche Erziehung im neuen Staat.* Langensalza, 1934.

Hinschius, Paul. *Das Kirchenrecht der Katholiken und Protestanten in Deutschland: System des Katholischen Kirchenrechts mit besonderer Rücksicht auf Deutschland.* 6 vols. Berlin, 1869–1897.

Hoche, Werner, ed. *Die Gesetzgebung des Kabinetts Hitler. Die Gesetze in Reich und Preussen seit dem 30. Januar 1933 in systematischer Ordnung mit Sachverzeichnis.* 33 vols. Berlin, 1933–39.

Hofmann, Konrad, ed. *Zeugnis und Kampf des Deutschen Episkopats. Gemeinsame Hirtenbriefe und Denkschriften.* Freiburg im Breisgau, 1946.

Homeyer, Alfred. *Neuordnung des höheren Schulwesens. Sammlung der wichtigsten diesbezüglichen Gesetze, Erlasse, und Verfügungen seit Januar 1933.* 2 ed., Berlin, 1940.

Huber, Ernst, ed. *Quellen zum Staatsrecht der Neuzeit.* Vol. II: *Deutsche Verfassungsdokumente der Gegenwart, 1919–1951.* Tübingen, 1951.

Hunsche, Klara. *Der Kampf um die christliche Schule und Erziehung 1933–1945.* Reprint from *Kirchliches Jahrbuch 1949.* Gütersloh, 1950.

Hylla, Erich J., and Friedrich O. Kegel. *Education in Germany. An Introduction for Foreigners.* Frankfurt am Main, 1954.

——— and W. L. Wrinkle. *Die Schulen in Westeuropa.* Bad Nauheim, 1953.

Institut für Staatslehre und Politik (Mainz). *Der Kampf um den Südweststaat. Verhandlungen und Beschlüsse der gesetzgebenden Körperschaften des Bundes und des Bundesverfassungsgerichtes.* Munich, 1952.

International Bureau of Education. *School Inspection.* Geneva, 1956.

Jahrbuch der Deutschen Demokratischen Republik. Berlin, 1956.

Janssen, Johannes. *History of the German People at the Close of the Middle Ages.* 14 vols. St. Louis, 1909.

Jeremias, N. *Die Jugendweihe in der Sowjetzone.* Bonn, 1956.

The Jewish People, Past and Present. New York: Jewish Encyclopedic Handbooks, 1946– .

Julian, John, ed. *A Dictionary of Hymnology.* Revised ed., London, 1907.

Kabisch, Richard. *Wie lehren wir Religion?* 6 ed., Göttingen, 1923.

Kaeckenbeeckt, Georges. *The International Experiment in Upper Silesia. A Study in the Working of the Upper Silesian Settlement 1922–1937.* London, 1942.

Kaftan, Theodor. *Auslegung des lutherischen Katechismus. Mit einem Anhang: Der Konfirmationsunterricht auf Grund des luth. Katechismus.* Schleswig, 1906.

Kandel, I. L., and T. Alexander, trans. *The Reorganization of Education in Prussia. Based on Official Documents and Publications.* New York, 1927.

Karteibuch des Schulrechts der Deutschen Demokratischen Republik. 2 ed., 10 vols., Berlin, n.d.

Katholische Grundsätze für Schule und Erziehung. Erarbeitet von der Fuldaer Bischofskonferenz 1956. Cologne, 1956.

Katholischer Katechismus der Bistümer Deutschlands. Herausgegeben von den

deutschen Bischöfen. Ausgabe für das Erzbistum Köln. Cologne, 1956.
Katholischer Katechismus vorgeschrieben von den Bischöfen Deutschlands. Ausgabe fur die Diozese Fulda. Fulda, n.d.
Kautz, Heinrich. *Neubau des katholischen Religionsunterrichtes.* 5 ed. 3 vols. Kevelaer, 1924.
Kehr, Dr. C. ed. *Geschichte der Methodik des deutschen Volksschulunterrichts.* 2 ed., 6 vols. Gotha, 1890.
Kern, Dr. Emmanuel. *Der katholische Religionsunterricht an den höheren Schulen Badens seit Beginn des 19. Jahrhunderts.* Freiburg im Breisgau, 1932.
Kirchliches Handbuch. Amtliches statistisches Jahrbuch der katholischen Kirche Deutschlands. Freiburg, 1908– ; Cologne, 1933– .
Kirchliches Jahrbuch für die Evangelische Kirche in Deutschland. Gütersloh, 1874– .
Kittel, Helmuth. *Von Religionsunterricht zur Evangelischen Unterweisung.* Hanover, 1949.
Klärner, K. *Die Simultanschule des ehem. Herzogtums Nassau.* Wiesbaden, 1905.
Kleinert, Heinrich, ed. *Lexikon der Pädagogik.* 3 vols. Berne, 1950–52.
Klinkenberg, Heinrich. *Das Zentrum und die Rechte im Kampf um die christliche Schule seit 1918.* Berlin, 1932.
Kneller, George F. *The Educational Philosophy of National Socialism.* New Haven, 1941.
Köstlin, Julius. *Martin Luther.* 5 ed., 2 vols., Berlin, 1903.
Krebs, Leopold. *Der elementare katholische Religionsunterricht in den Ländern Europas in monographischen Darstellungen.* Vienna, 1938.
Kühn, Walther. *Schulrecht in Preussen. Ein Handbuch für Lehrer, Schulleiter, und Schulverwaltungsbeamte.* Berlin, 1926.
Kultusministerium Württemberg-Baden. *Schule und Lehrerschaft im Dritten Reich.* Stuttgart, 1946.
Künneth, Walter. *Der Grosse Abfall. Eine geschichtstheologische Untersuchung der Begegnung zwischen Nationalsozialismus und Christentum.* Hamburg, 1947.
Landé. Walter. *Aktenstücke zum Reichsvolksschulgesetz.* Leipzig, 1928.
—— *Die Grundschule. Sammlung der Bestimmungen.* 2 ed. Berlin, 1927.
—— *Höhere Schule und Reichsvolksschulgesetz.* Berlin, 1929.
—— *Die Schule in der Reichsverfassung. Ein Kommentar.* Berlin, 1929.
—— *Religionsunterricht. Sammlung der staatlichen Bestimmungen über Religionsunterricht an Volks-, mittleren und höheren Schulen, religiöse Erziehung, Moralunterricht, Konfirmantenunterricht, usw.* Berlin, 1929.
Lange, M. G. *Totalitäre Erziehung. Das Erziehungssystem der Sowjetzone Deutschlands.* Frankfurt am Main, 1954.
Lawin, W. *Methodik des evangelischen Religionsunterrichts in der Volksschule.* Leipzig, 1910.
Learned, William S. *The Oberlehrer. A Study of the Social and Professional Evolution of the German Schoolmaster.* Cambridge, 1914.
Leschnitzer, Adolf. *The Magic Background of Modern Anti-Semitism.* New York, 1956.
Lexikon der Pädagogik. Hrsg. von Ernst M. Roloff. 5 vols. Freiburg im Breisgau: Herder, 1913–1917.
Lexikon der Pädagogik. Verantwortlich für die Schriftleitung, Heinrich Rombach. 4 vols. Freiburg im Breisgau: Herder, 1952–1955.

Lexis, A. *A General View of the History and Organization of Public Education in the German Empire.* Trans. by G. J. Tamsun. Berlin, 1904.

Liddell, Helen, ed. *Education in Occupied Germany.* Paris, 1949.

Lindegren, Alma M. *Education in Germany.* Washington, 1939.

Litchfield, Edward H. et. al. *Governing Postwar Germany.* Ithaca, 1953.

Löffler, L. *Der Religionsunterricht und der konfessionelle Charakter der (Volks-) Schule in den deutschen Ländern.* Düsseldorf, 1937.

Lohmüller, Johannes. *Lebensvoller Religionsunterricht für das erste und zweite Schuljahr (für das dritte und vierte Schuljahr).* 2 vols. Düsseldorf, 1949. Catholic teachers' manual.

McBain, Howard, and Lindsay Rogers. *The New Constitutions of Europe.* New York, 1923.

McClaskey, Beryl R. *The History of U.S. Policy and Program in the Field of Religious Affairs under the Office of the U.S. High Commissioner for Germany.* Office of the U.S. High Commissioner for Germany, 1951.

McGiffert, Arthur C. *Martin Luther, the Man and His Work.* New York, 1911.

Mangoldt, Hermann von. *Das Bonner Grundgesetz.* Berlin and Frankfurt am Main, 1953.

Marquardt, Georg. *Wie lehren wir das Wort Gottes?* Göttingen, 1948.

Martens. *Recueil des Traités.* 1e série to 1847, 2e série to 1907, 3e série since 1908. Göttingen, 1843– .

May, Werner. *Wie lehren wir Christum im Dritten Reich?* Nürnberg, 1935.

Merkt, Hans, ed. *Dokumente zur Schulreform in Bayern.* Munich, 1952.

Meisner, Helmut. *Religiöse Grundlagen der Erwachsenenbildung.* Ratingen bei Düsseldorf, 1957.

Meyer, Jürgen Bona. *Der Kampf um die Schule.* Bonn, 1882.

Micklem, Nathaniel. *National Socialism and the Roman Catholic Church.* London, 1939.

Mission Draussen und Drinnen. Festgabe an Hans Lokies. Berlin, c. 1955.

Möbus, Gerhard. *Kommunistische Jugendarbeit. Zur Psychologie und Pädagogik der kommunistischen Erziehung im sowjetisch besetzten Deutschland.* Munich, 1957.

Morsch, Hans. *Das höhere Lehramt in Deutschland und Österreich.* Berlin, 1910.

Müller, Adolf. *Der Rote Katechismus. Wahrheit oder Lüge.* Dresden, 1910.

Murray, G. "Denominational Education in Germany." British HQ/Educ/82350/ INT: Intelligence and Information Section, October 1948. Mimeographed.

Nazi Conspiracy and Aggression. 8 vols., 2 supp. Washington, 1946–48.

Neisinger, Oskar. *Jungführerbildung.* Altenberg bei Köln, 1955.

Neuhäusler, Johann. *Kreuz und Hakenkreuz. Der Kampf des Nationalsozialismus gegen die katholische Kirche und der kirchliche Widerstand.* Munich, 1946.

Niebergall, Friedrich. *Zur Reform des Religionsunterrichts.* Langensalza, 1921.

Nohl, Hermann, and Ludwig Pallat. *Handbuch der Pädagogik.* 5 vols, 1929–33.

Nohle, C. *Geschichte des deutschen Schulwesens im Umriss.* Reprint from Rein's *Encyklopädisches Handbuch der Pädagogik.* Langensalza, 1896.

Offenstein, W. *Der Kampf um das Reichsschulgetsetz. Die Entwürfe der Jahre 1925 und 1927.* Düsseldorf, 1928.

——— *Die Schulpolitik der Sozialdemokratie.* Düsseldorf, 1926.

Ostermann, W., and L. Wegener. *Lehrbuch der Pädagogik.* 5 vols. Oldenburg, 1908.

Pädagogische Hochschule Berlin. *Vorlesungsverzeichnis Sommersemester, 1957.* Berlin, 1957.

Pädagogische Studienführer. Hrsg. von der Bundesvertretung der Studenten an Pädagogischen Hochschulen. Düsseldorf, 1955.

Papen, Franz von. *Memoirs.* London, 1952.

Pastenaci and Ewers. *Schulrecht für die Volks- mittleren und Privatschulen sowie für die ländlichen Fortbildungsschulen.* 2 ed., Minden in W., 1936.

Paulsen, Friedrich. *Das deutsche Bildungswesen in seiner geschichtlichen Entwickelung.* Leipzig, 1906. Trans. T. Lorenz. London, 1908, as *German Education Past and Present.*

Pernutz, Karl. *Das Verhältnis von Staat und Kirche nach der Weimarer Verfassung.* Strassfurt, 1928.

The Persecution of the Catholic Church in Germany. Facts and Documents translated from the German. London, 1942.

Pfannkuche, August. *Staat und Kirche.* Leipzig, 1915.

Picker, Henry. *Hitlers Tischgespräche im Führerhauptquartier, 1941–42.* Bonn, 1951.

Pinson, Koppel S. *Pietism as a Factor in the Rise of German Nationalism.* New York, 1934.

Pilgert, Henry P. *The West German Educational System.* Office of the U.S. High Commissioner for Germany, 1953.

Plass, Ewald M. *What Luther Says: An Anthology.* 3 vols. St. Louis, 1959.

Poliakov, Leon, and Josef Wulf, eds. *Das Dritte Reich und die Juden. Dokumente und Aufsätze.* Berlin-Grünewald, 1955.

Postwar Changes in German Education U.S. Zone and U.S. Sector Berlin. Office of the United States High Commissioner for Germany, 1951.

Pottag Alfred. *Die Bestimmungen über die Volks- und Mittelschulen und über die Ausbildung und die Prüfungen der Lehrer und Lehrerinnen in Preussen (Gesetze und Ministerial-Erlässe).* Berlin, 1925.

Die Reichsschulkonferenz 1920. Ihre Vorgeschichte und Vorbereitung und ihre Verhandlungen. (Amtlicher Bericht erstattet vom Reichsministerium des Innern). Leipzig, 1921.

Reicke, Emil. *Lehrer und Unterrichtswesen in der deutschen Vergangenheit.* Jena, 1924.

Rein, Dr. W. *Die deutsche Schule im Deutschem Staat mit Beziehung auf die Reichschulgesetzgebung.* Langensalza, 1926.

———— ed. *Encyklopädisches Handbuch der Pädagogik.* 2 ed., 10 vols. and index. Langensalza, 1903–11.

Religious Affairs. Issued by the Office of U.S. Military Government for Germany, August 1946.

Reu, M. *English–German Text. Luther's Small Catechism with Explanation.* 2 ed. Chicago, 1919.

———— *Luther's German Bible. An Historical Presentation together with a Collection of Sources.* Columbus, 1934.

———— *Dr. Martin Luther's Small Catechism. A History of Its Distribution and Its Use.* Chicago, 1929.

Reukauf, A. *Didaktik des evangelischen Religionsunterrichts in der Volksschule.* 2 ed. Leipzig, 1906.

Richter, Karl. *Die Emanzipation der Schule von der Kirche und die Reform des Religionsunterrichts in der Schule.* Leipzig, 1870.

Riede, David C. *The Official Attitude of the Roman Catholic Hierarchy in Germany toward National Socialism, 1933–1945.* University Microfilms, Ann Arbor, Michigan, 1957.

Rietschel, Georg. *Zur Reform des Religionsunterrichts in der Volksschule. Sind die Zwickauer Leitsätze des Sächsischen Lehrervereins geeignet als Grundlage für die Umgestaltung des Religionsunterrichts zu dienen?* Leipzig, 1909.

Robels, Karl. *Das Volksschulunterhaltungsgesetz vom 28. Juli 1906 und seine Ausführung zum 1. April 1908 für Lehrer, Geistliche, Mitglieder von Schuldeputationen, Schulvorständen, Schulkommissionen erläutert.* Breslau, 1908.

Rohrscheidt, Kurt von. *Gesetz betreffend die Unterhaltung der öffentlichen Volksschulen vom 28. Juli 1906. Mit sämtlichen Abänderungsgesetzen und Verordnungen, den Ausführungsanweisungen, zugehörigen Ministerialerlässen sowie weiteren einschlägigen Gesetzbestimmungen. Nach den amtlichen Materialien, der Rechtsprechung, den Erlässen der Zentralbehörden und den Regierungsverfügungen für den praktischen Gebrauch erläutert.* 6 ed. Berlin, 1931.

—— *Gesetz über die Dienstbezüge der Lehrer und Lehrerinnen an den öffentlichen Volksschulen, Volksschullehrer-Besoldungsgesetz vom 1. Mai 1928.* 9 ed. Berlin, 1928.

Rosenberg, Arthur. *A History of the German Republic.* London, 1936.

Rosenberg, (Rabbiner) J. *Methodik des jüdischen Religionsunterrichts.* Berlin, 1924.

Rothaas, Adolf. *Studien zur Lehre von der religiösen Kindererziehung nach dem heutigen Deutschen Rechte.* Fürst, 1933.

Royal Institute of International Affairs. *Survey of International Affairs 1949–50.* London, 1953.

Ruhm von Oppen, Beate. *Documents on Germany Under Occupation 1945–54.* London, 1955.

Russ, Willibald. *Geschichte der Pädagogik im Abriss.* Bad Heilbrunn, 1952.

Russell, James E. *German Higher Schools. The History, Organization and Methods of Secondary Education in Germany.* New York, 1907.

Salomon, Felix. *Die deutschen Parteiprogramme.* 3 vols. Berlin, 1907–1920.

Samuel, R. H., and R. H. Thomas. *Education and Society in Modern Germany.* London, 1949.

Schlemmer, Hans. *Die Schulpolitik der evangelischen Kirche Preussens.* Gölitz, 1928.

Schmid, Eugen. *Geschichte des württembergischen evangelischen Volksschulwesens von 1806 bis 1910.* Stuttgart, 1933.

Schmid, Heinrich. *Apokalyptisches Wetterleuchten. Ein Beitrag der Evangelischen Kirche zum Kampf im " Dritten Reich."* Munich, 1947.

Schmidt, K. A., ed. *Encyklopädie des gesammten Erziehungs- und Unterrichtswesens.* 11 vols. Gotha, 1859–78.

Scholl, Robert. *Biblische Geschichten Kindern erzählt. 80 Beispiele evangelischer Unterweisung für die Sechs- bis Zehnjährigen.* Worms, 1954.

Schöppa, G. *Die Bestimmungen des Königlich Preussischen Ministers der geistlichen, Unterrichts- und medizinal- Angelegenheiten, über die Einrichtung der Volks- , Mittel- und höheren Mädchenschule, sowie über die Prüfungen der Lehrerinnen nebst dem Gesetze über die Beaufsichtigung des Unterrichts- und Erziehungswesens sowie den wichtigsten dazu erlassenen Ministerial-Verfügungen.* 2 ed. Leipzig, 1906.

Schreiber, Georg. *Zwischen Demokratie und Diktatur. Persönliche Erinnerungen an die Politik und Kultur des Reiches 1919–1944.* Regensburg-Münster, 1949.

Schreibmayr, Franz, and Klemens Tilmann. *Handbuch zum katholischen Katechismus.* Vol. I. *Von Gott und unsrer Erlösung,* Part I, *Lehrstücke 1 bis 21;* Part II, *Lehrstücke 22 bis 44.* Freiburg, 1957. One more volume is planned.

Schröteler, Joseph. *Erziehungsverantwortung und Erziehungsrecht. Die Lehre von den Erziehungsträgern im Lichte des päpstlichen Rundschreibens "Divini illius Magistri" vom 31. Dez. 1929.* Munich, 1934.

———— *Katholische Bekenntnisschule und deutsche Volksgemeinschaft.* Limburg a.d.Lahn, 1936.

Schulrecht und Schulverwaltung in der Deutschen Demokratischen Republik. Im Auftrag des Ministeriums für Volksbildung. Berlin, 1956.

Schumann, G., and E. Sperber. *Geschichte des Religionsunterrichts in der evangelischen Volksschule* Vol. VI A of Kehr, C., ed., *Geschichte der Methodik des deutschen Volksschulunterrichts.* Gotha, 1890.

Schuwerack, W. G. *Die Privatschule in der Reichsverfassung vom 11. August 1919.* Vol. 33 of *Schulpolitik und Erziehungs Zeitfragen.* Düsseldorf, n.d.

Schwartz, Hermann, ed. *Pädagogisches Lexikon.* 4 vols. Leipzig, 1928–1931.

Seiler, Freidrich. *Geschichte des deutschen Unterrichtswesens.* 2 vols. Leipzig, 1906. Volumes in the "Sammlung Göschen".

Seipp, Paul, ed., et. al. *Schulrecht. Ergänzbare Sammlung der Vorschriften für Schule und Schulverwaltung: Baden-Württemberg; Bayern; Berlin; Hessen; Nieder-Sachsen; Nordrhein-Westfalen; Rheinland-Pfalz; Schleswig-Holstein.* Karlsruhe, Stuttgart, Berlin, 1954– .

Show, Arley B. *The Movement for Reform in the Teaching of Religion in the Public Schools of Saxony.* United States Bureau of Education Bulletin, 1910, no. 1, Washington, 1910.

Shuster, George N. *Religion Behind the Iron Curtain.* New York, 1954.

Smith, Preserved. *The Life and Letters of Martin Luther.* New York, 1911.

Spieler, Josef, ed. *Lexikon der Pädagogik der Gegenwart.* 2 vols. Freiburg im Breisgau, 1930–32.

Spranger Eduard. *Zur Geschichte der deutschen Volksschule.* Heidelberg, 1949.

Spreng, Rudolf, and Paul Feuchte. *Die Verfassung des Landes Baden-Württemberg.* Stuttgart, 1953.

Statistical Pocket-Book on Expellees. Wiesbaden, 1953.

Statistische Berichte des Niedersächsischen Amts für Landesplanung und Statistik. Die allgemeinbildenden Schulen in Niedersachsen im Schuljahr 1955–1956. Hanover, 1956.

Statistisches Jahrbuch der Deutschen Demokratischen Republik. Herausgegeben von der staatlichen Zentralverwaltung für Statistik, Berlin, 1956. The first volume is for the year 1955.

Statistisches Jahrbuch für die Bundesrepublik Deutschlands. Wiesbaden, 1952– .

Statistisches Jahrbuch für das Deutsche Reich. Berlin, 1880–1942.

Steiner, Rudolf. *Allgemeine Menschenkunde als Grundlage der Pädagogik.* Stuttgart, 1933.

———— *Erziehungskunst, Methodisch-Didaktisches.* Stuttgart, 1948.

Steinhauer, Georg. *Erstes Gesetz zur Ordnung des Schulwesens im Lande Nordrhein-Westfalen vom 8. April 1952 in Frage und Antwort.* Cologne, n.d.

Steward, John S. *Gestapo-Berichte über den Widerstand der Kirchen.* Zurich, 1946.

Stiefelzieher, Max. *Religionsgesellschaften und Weltanschauungsvereinigungen im Volksschulrecht.* Munich, 1931.

Stratemeyer, Clara. *Supervision in German Elementary Education 1918–1933.* New York, 1938.

Strobel, Ferdinand. *Christliche Bewährung. Dokumente des Widerstandes der katholischen Kirche in Deutschland, 1933–1945.* Olten, 1946.

Tews, J. *Ein Jahrhundert preussischer Schulgeschichte. Volksschule und Volksschullehrerstand in Preussen im 19. und 20. Jahrhundert.* Leipzig, 1914.

"Textbooks in Germany, American Zone." Education and Religious Affairs Branch, Office of Military Government (U.S.), mimeographed, August 1946, 1948.

Thieme, Werner. *Deutsches Hochschulrecht.* Berlin, 1956.

Thümmel, Otto. *Evangelisches Kirchenrecht für Preussen.* Berlin, 1930.

Thümmler, Th. *Die Zwickauer Leitsätze und der ministerielle Lehrplan.* Dresden, 1909.

Tieman, Gustav, Franz Dräger and Peter Schumacher. *Die Amtsführung des Lehrers Schulrecht. Ein Ratgeber und Nachschlagebuch für die Fragen des Volksschulwesens.* Düsseldorf, 1941.

Tilmann, Klemens, and Ludwig Wolker. *Christoffer. Vom Diakonat junger Christen in der Gemeinde.* Recklinghausen, 1939.

Tims, Richard W. *Germanizing Prussian Poland. The H-K-T Society and the Struggle for the Eastern Marches in the German Empire 1894–1919.* New York, 1941.

Tobias, Robert. *Communist-Christian Encounter in East Europe.* Indianapolis, 1956.

Tremel, Paul. *Bayerische Volksschulgesetze mit Ausführungs- und Vollzugsvorschriften.* Munich, 1952.

Trial of the Major War Criminals before the International Military Tribunal. 47 vols. Nürnberg, 1947–49.

Uhsadel, Walter. *Evangelische Erziehungs- und Unterrichtslehre.* Heidelberg, 1954.

Ulich, Robert. *Fundamentals of Democratic Education. An Introduction to Educational Philosophy.* New York, 1940.

—— *History of Educational Thought.* New York, 1945.

U.S. State Department. *East Germany under Soviet Control.* Washington, 1952.

—— *Germany 1947–1949. The Story in Documents.* Washington, 1950.

Vischer, Gustav-Adolf. *Aufbau Organisation und Recht der Evang.-Luth. Kirche in Bayern.* 2 vols. Munich, 1953, 1956.

—— *Neuere Rechtsquellen für die Evang.-Luth. Kirche in Bayern.* Munich, 1950.

Volkmer, Dr. *Geschichte der Erziehung und des Unterrichtes.* 5 ed., Habelschwerdt, 1891.

Der Vorstand des Ev.-luth. Schulvereins. *Was aus dem Kleinen Katechismus Dr. Martin Luthers nebst Bibelsprüchen und Kirchenliedern in den evangelischen Schulen des Königreichs Sachsen nach den Beschlüssen der Vertreterversammlung des Sächs. Lehrervereins werden soll. [Roter Katechismus.]* Dresden, 1911. First published in February, 1910.

Wahl, Adalbert. *Deutsche Geschichte. Von der Reichsgründung bis zum Ausbruch des Weltkrieges (1871–1914).* 4 vols. Stuttgart, 1926–1935.

Waite, Robert G. L. *Vanguard of Nazism. The Free Corps Movement in Postwar Germany 1918–1923.* Cambridge, 1952.

Weinryb, Bernard D. *Jewish Emancipation under Attack. Its Legal Recession Until the Present War.* New York, 1942.

Wenke, Hans. *Education in Western Germany.* Washington, 1953.

Werdermann, Hermann. *Geschichte des Religionsunterrichts an preussischen Gymnasien im neunzehnten Jahrhundert.* Gütersloh, 1923.

Werner, Carl Artur. *Das Schulgesetz für Berlin. Handkommentar unter Einbeziehung des Schulrechts der Bundesländer.* Berlin, 1954.

Westhoff, Paul. *Verfassungsrecht der deutschen Schule. Beiträge zur Auslegung der Schulartikel der Reichsverfassung vom 11. August 1919.* Düsseldorf, 1932.

Wohlmuth, Georg. *Zum Streit um die geistliche Schulaufsicht in Bayern.* Augsburg, 1909.

Wurm, Th. *Erinnerungen aus meinem Leben.* Stuttgart, 1953.

Zimmermann, Walter, and Herwig Hafa. *Zur Erneuerung der christlichen Unterweisung.* Berlin, 1957.

NOTES

Complete bibliographical references for all books cited are to be found in the bibliography. For Amtsblätter and periodical literature, see the note on bibliography.

These abbreviations have been used for certain frequently quoted journals, yearbooks, and archives.

ADB   *Allgemeine Deutsche Biographie*
BL   *Berliner Lehrerzeitung*
DJ   *Deutschland Jahrbuch*
EE   *Der evangelische Erzieher*
ELS   *Evangelisch-Lutherisches Schulblatt*
HJ   *Historisches Jahrbuch*
KB   *Katechetische Blätter* (Catholic)
KE   *Der katholische Erzieher*
KH   *Kirchliches Handbuch* (Catholic)
KJ   *Kirchliches Jahrbuch* (Protestant)
KZ   *Kirchliche Zeitschrift* (Protestant)
LJ   *Lutherisches Jahrbuch*
MUND   *Material- und Nachrichten-Dienst der Arbeitsgemeinschaft Deutscher Lehrerverbände*
NKZ   *Neue Kirchliche Zeitschrift* (Protestant)
SA   Schulamt Archives, Frankfurt am Main
SJ   *Statistisches Jahrbuch*

Notes to Chapter I. The Middle Ages and the Reformation

1. Volkmer, *Geschichte der Erziehung und des Unterrichtes*, p. 29.
2. As quoted in *The Church College*, p. 14.
3. Nohle, *Geschichte des deutschen Schulwesens*, p. 15.
4. A large part of this chapter appeared in E. C. Helmreich, "The Reformation and German Education," *Lutheran Education*, LXXXIX (1953), 115–131.
5. Hahn, *Die evangelische Unterweisung in den Schulen des 16. Jahrhunderts*, pp. 17–24.
6. Reu, *Luther's German Bible*, p. 205.
7. *Ibid.*, p. 197.
8. Funck-Brentano, *Luther*, p. 290.
9. *Ibid.*, p. 291. Quoted from *Table Talk* 2758.
10. Goodspeed, *How Came the Bible?*, pp. 91–95.
11. Reu quotes Ranke in *Dr. Martin Luther's Small Catechism*, p. 253. See also M. Reu, "Die Eigenart des Katechismus Luthers und was sich daraus für seine schulmässige Behandlung ergibt," *KZ*, XXX (1906), 208–223; G. Schumann and E. Sperber, "Geschichte des Religionsunterrichts in der evangel-

ischen Volksschule," in Kehr, ed., *Geschichte der Methodik des deutschen Volks-schulunterrichts*, vol. VI, part A, pp. 23–31.

12. McGiffert, *Martin Luther*, p. 317.

13. Julian, ed., *Dictionary of Hymnology*, p. 414.

14. Funck-Brentano, *Luther*, p. 279.

15. Plass, *What Luther Says*, II, 980.

16. Funck-Brentano, *Luther*, p. 304. Quoted from *Table Talk* 968.

17. See Smith, *Life and Letters of Martin Luther*, pp. 85, 186.

18. As quoted in Russell, *German Higher Schools*, p. 32.

19. As quoted in Paulsen, *Das deutsche Bildungswesen*, p. 35.

20. As quoted in McGiffert, *Martin Luther*, pp. 269f.

21. As quoted in Smith, *Life and Letters of Martin Luther*, p. 187.

22. As quoted in Volkmer, *Geschichte der Erziehung und des Unterrichtes*, p. 47. See Ernst Lichtenstein, "Luther und die Schule," in *EE*, VII (1955), 2–13; and Hahn, *Die evangelische Unterweisung in den Schulen des 16. Jahrhunderts*, pp. 25–28, for good brief discussions of Luther's influence on the schools.

23. Hertz, *Development of the German Public Mind*, p. 482.

24. Some of the material in the next pages appeared in E. C. Helmreich, "Joint School and Church Positions in Germany," *Lutheran School Journal*, LXXIX (1943), 157–163.

25. Appens, *Die pädagogischen Bewegungen des Jahres 1848*, pp. 24–26; N. Cant. emer., "Gedanken eines alten Schulmeisters über seinen vierzigjährigen Kirchendienst," reprinted from *Pilger aus Sachsen* in *ELS*, X (July 1875), 213–220; see also Fischer, *Geschichte des deutschen Volksschullehrerstandes*, I, 86–92; 107–111; 115f.; 162–168; II, 48; 91–93; 204; 250–355.

26. "Lord God mercifully grant us peace in our times! There is assuredly no other one who could contend for us than you, our God, alone. Give our country and all in authority peace and good government, that we under them may lead a Christian, honorable, and peaceful life in all godliness and truth, Amen."

27. Fischer, *Geschichte des deutschen Volksschullehrerstandes*, I, 90.

28. *ELS*, X (1875), 213–220; see also the long quotation from Franz Dreising, "Das Amt des Küsters in der evangelischen Kirche" (1854), in Fischer, *Geschichte des deutschen Volksschullehrerstandes*, II, 351–355.

29. *ADB*, XXXVII, 30; Hahn, *Die evangelische Unterweisung*, pp. 51f.

30. Schumann and Sperber, "Geschichte des Religionsunterrichts," in Kehr, ed., *Geschichte der Methodik*, vol. VI, part A, pp. 32ff.; Barth, *Die Geschichte der Erziehung*, pp. 337f.

Notes to Chapter II. The Impact of Pietism and Rationalism

1. As quoted in Volkmer, *Geschichte der Erziehung und des Unterrichtes*, p. 60.

2. As quoted in Reukauf, *Didaktik*, p. 54.

3. M. Reu, "Luther auch der Vater des biblischen Geschichtsunterrichts," *KZ*, XXX (1906), 1–5.

4. F. W. Bürgel, "Geschichte des Religionsunterrichts in den katholischen Volkschulen," in Kehr, ed., *Geschichte der Methodik*, vol. VI, part B, p. 270. The first Bible history for Catholic schools was not published until 1777. See "Biblische Geschichte," in *Lexikon der Pädagogik*, ed. Roloff, I, 498.

5. For a discussion of this aspect of Francke's work see Spranger, *Zur Geschichte der deutschen Volksschule*, pp. 23–27.

6. As quoted in Robert Scholl, "August Hermann Francke als evangelischer Erzieher," *EE*, VII (1955), 45.

7. As quoted in Volkmer, *Geschichte der Erziehung und des Unterrichtes*, p. 74.

8. Schumann and Sperber, "Geschichte des Religionsunterrichts" in Kehr, ed., *Geschichte der Methodik*, vol. VI, part A, pp. 38, 57.

9. Reprinted in G. Giese, *Deutsche Schulgesetzgebung*, pp. 17f.

10. As quoted in Nohle, *Geschichte des deutschen Schulwesens*, p. 33. A contemporary of Frederick William I, the Bishop of Speyer, introduced compulsory education and numerous other reforms in the schools of his state. See Otto B. Roegele, "Ein Schulreformer des 18. Jahrhunderts. Kardinal Damian Hugo von Schönborn und die Reorganisation des Schulwesens in Fürstbistum Speyer," *HJ*, XIV (1955), 351–362.

11. G. Giese, *Deutsche Schulgesetzgebung*, pp. 23–32.

12. *Ibid.*, pp. 32–34.

13. As quoted by G. Giese, "Kirche, Staat und Schule," *BL*, VII (1953), p. 172.

14. Nohle, *Geschichte des deutschen Schulwesens*, p. 37.

15. For the Pietists' emphasis on the practical in religious matters as well as in education, see Pinson, *Pietism as a Factor in the Rise of German Nationalism*, pp. 140–142.

16. See articles on the *Ritterakademien* in Schmid, ed., *Encyklopädie*, VII, 171–203; Schwartz, ed., *Pädagogisches Lexikon*, IV, 186–190; *Lexikon der Pädagogik*, ed. Roloff, IV, 391–394; Rein, ed., *Encyklopädisches Handbuch der Pädagogik*, VII, 545–560.

17. See the extensive article on Basedow in *ADB*, II, 113–124.

18. As quoted in Volkmer, *Geschichte der Erziehung und des Unterrichtes*, p. 126.

19. As quoted in Ostermann and Wegener, eds., *Lehrbuch der Pädagogik*, IV, 24.

20. Paulsen, *Das deutsche Bildungswesen*, pp. 101–104; Nohle, *Geschichte des deutschen Schulwesens*, pp. 30–32.

21. See article on Woellner in *ADB*, XLIV, 148–158; and Fritz Valjavic, "Das Woellnerische Religionsedikt und seine geschichtliche Bedeutung," *HJ*, LXXII (1953), 386–400. The edict of July 9, 1788, itself, is reprinted in G. Giese, *Deutsche Schulgesetzgebung*, pp. 41–46.

22. *Ibid.*, pp. 46f.

23. Fischer, *Geschichte des deutschen Volksschullehrerstandes*, II, 56.

Notes to Chapter III. The Nineteenth Century to 1871

1. Albrecht, *Die Stellung des politischen Katholizismus in Deutschland*, pp. 45f; Ernst G. Gerhard, "Das Ende der kirchlichen Schulhoheit in der Reichstadt Frankfurt im Jahre 1812," *Jahrbuch der Katholiken von Gross-Frankfurt*, 1933, pp. 22–27.

2. See Klärner, *Die Simultanschule des ehem. Herzogtums Nassau;* Karl Broglie, "*Zur Geschichte der Naussauischen Simultanschule*," *Zeitschrift für Geschichte der Erziehung und des Unterrichts*, XXIV (1936), 94–123.

3. As quoted in Ulich, *History of Educational Thought*, p. 286.

4. As quoted in Volkmer, *Geschichte der Erziehung und des Unterrichtes*, p. 124.

5. Paulsen, *Das deutsche Bildungswesen*, p. 155. Translation taken from English edition, *German Education Past and Present*, p. 245.

6. Edgar Loening, "Die Unterhaltung der öffentlichen Volksschulen und die Schulverbände in Preussen," *Jahrbuch des öffentlichen Rechts*, III (1909), 110.

7. As quoted in Tews, *Ein Jahrhundert preussischer Schulgeschichte*, p. 139. One of the main reasons for the failure of the school reform in Württemberg in 1849–50 was the charge that new measures endangered relations between schools and churches. See E. Schmid, *Geschichte des württembergischen evangelischen Volksschulwesens*, pp. 218f., 309f.

8. L. Treitel, "Geschichte des israelitischen Schulwesens in Württemberg," *Mitteilung der Gesellschaft für deutsche Erziehungs- und Schulgeschichte*, IX (1899), 51–65. See also Spatz, "Zur Geschichte der israelitischen Schule zu Affaltrach und Eschenau," *ibid.*, X (1900), 270–285; and the excellent summary of Jewish secular education in Adolf Kober, "Emancipation's Impact on the Education and Vocational Training of German Jewry," *Jewish Social Studies*, XVI (1954), 5–26.

9. Meyer, *Der Kampf um die Schule*, p. 60.

10. For an analysis of the 1847 law and subsequent legislation see Rohrscheidt, *Gesetz betreffend die Unterhaltung der öffentlichen Volksschulen*, pp. 370–379; see also Stiefelzieher, *Religionsgesellschaften und Weltanschauungsvereinigungen*, pp. 42–85; and "Jüdischer Religionsunterricht," in Landé, *Religionsunterricht*, pp. 245–252.

11. Adolf Kober in *Jewish Social Studies*, XVI (1954), 26f.

12. Paulsen, *Das deutsche Bildungswesen*, p. 126; Blättner, *Geschichte der Pädagogik*, pp. 137f.

13. Werdermann, *Geschichte des Religionsunterrichts an preussischen Gymnasien*, p. 19; Seiler, *Geschichte des deutschen Unterrichtswesens*, II, 11–13.

14. Paulsen, *Das deutsche Bildungswesen*, p. 125.

15. As quoted in Nohle, *Geschichte des deutschen Schulwesens*, p. 43.

Notes to Chapter IV. Religion and the Organization of Education and Religion in the Empire

1. Gerhardt Giese, "Die Schule im Reich. Ein Uberblick über 60 Jahre Reichsschulpolitik," *Zeitschrift für Geschichte der Erziehung und des Unterrichts*, XXI (1931), 229–230. After 1912 the debate on the budget of the Reichsschulkommission was extended to a general debate on school affairs, although schools remained under state control.

2. The *Deutscher Lehrerverein* in 1930 was made up of 38 federations and 2762 member organizations. Other teachers' organizations, many on a confessional basis, were founded under the Empire. For a convenient list of the most important organizations as of 1930, see Schwartz, ed., *Pädagogisches Lexikon*, III, 1073–1103.

3. *The Stateman's Yearbook*, 1875, p. 97.

4. Pfannkuche, *Staat und Kirche*, p. 86.

5. Ebers, *Staat und Kirche*, pp. 72f.

6. Martens, *Traités*, 1e Série, III (1808–1818), 106–126.

7. Evangelische Kirche der altpreussischen Union; Evangelisch-Lutherische Landeskirche Hannovers; Evangelische Landeskirche in Hesse-Kassel; Evangelische Landeskirche in Nassau; Evangelische Landeskirche Frankfurt am Main; Evangelisch-Reformierte Landeskirche der Provinz Hannover; Evangelische

Landeskirche von Waldeck und Pyrmont (Rohrscheidt, *Gesetz betreffend die Unterhaltung der öffentlichen Volksschulen*, p. 348).

8. Arndt, *Die Verfassungsurkunde für den Preussischen Staat*, p. 117.

9. Richard Lempp, "Present Religious Conditions in Germany," *Harvard Theological Review*, III (1910), 107, and "Away from the Church in Germany," *The Independent*, LXVIII (1910), 330; Herbert Reich, "Die Aus- und Übertrittsbewegung 1884–1949," *KJ*, LXXVIII (1951), 363–385.

10. Hildebrand, *Religionsunterricht*, pp. 17f.

11. In Germany "the different types of vocational schools are the part-time vocational schools (or *Berufsschulen*), the full-time vocational schools (or *Berufsfachschulen*), or the special vocational schools (*Fachschulen*)." International Bureau of Education, *School Inspection*, p. 177.

12. In 1914 the Catholic schools were private in Brunswick, Bremen, Hamburg, Lippe-Detmold, Lübeck, Mecklenburg-Schwerin, Reuss-j.L., Saxe-Altenburg, Saxe-Coburg-Gotha, Saxe-Meiningen, Schaumburg-Lippe, Schwarzburg-Rudolstadt, Schwarzburg-Sonderhausen, and in part of Anhalt and Saxe-Weimar. There were no Catholic schools in Mecklenburg-Strelitz or Reuss ä.L. See Gerhard Kropotscheck, "Kirche und Schule seit dem Umsturz," *LJ*, 1919, part I, p. 125.

13. Westhoff, *Verfassungsrecht*, p. 1. A law of June 16, 1874, made the Simultanschule a legal school type in Hesse, although some confessional schools continued to exist. See also the section on "Konfessionelle, Simultan- und konfessionslose Schulen," in Hinschius, *Das Kirchenrecht*, IV, 587–594.

14. As quoted in *Neues Zeitblatt für die Angelegenheiten der lutherischen Kirche*, XXV (1880), 60.

15. Edgar Loening in *Jahrbuch des öffentlichen Rechts*, III (1909), 110.

16. The law with good commentary is given in Robels, *Das Volksschulunterhaltungsgesetz;* see also Rohrscheidt, *Gesetz betreffend die Unterhaltung der öffentlichen Volksschulen*.

17. For ordinances (1886–1929) applying to religious education of religious minorities in Prussia see Pastenaci and Ewers, *Schulrecht für die Volks- mittleren und Privatschulen*, pp. 511–513.

18. Frobenius, *Die Entwicklung des Rechts der religiösen Kindererziehung*, p. 101.

19. Stiefelzieher, *Religionsgesellschaften und Weltanschauungsvereinigungen*, p. 47.

20. Robels, *Das Volksschulunterhaltungsgesetz*, p. 69.

21. As quoted in H. Rosin, "Das Verhältnis des Staates zur Kirche und Erziehung in den Programmen der politischen Parteien," *Schulpolitisches Jahrbuch*, 1926, p. 92.

22. "Der höhere Unterricht und die preussischen Juden," *ELS*, VIII (1873), 26–28. In the years 1905–17 in Prussia the relative proportion of Jewish pupils was less than one-half their proportion in the population in elementary schools, but four times their proportion in secondary schools, ten times in girls' higher schools, and about eight times at boys' higher schools. Adolf Kober in *Jewish Social Studies*, XVI (1954), 167.

23. Thümmel, *Evangelisches Kirchenrecht für Preussen*, p. 136.

24. Hammerstein, *Das preussische Schulmonopol*, pp. 149–156. The figure 116 includes the 110 completely Protestant-staffed schools, plus 6 predominantly Protestant-staffed schools where the Catholic teacher was not instructor in religion.

25. Russell, *German Higher Schools*, pp. 124–129.

26. "Der Kampf um den Religionsunterricht in der Volksschule," *KZ*, XXX (1906), 283–286.

27. As quoted in Offenstein, *Schulpolitik der Sozialdemokratie*, p. 10; for the Eisenach, Gotha, and Erfurt programs see Salomon, *Die deutschen Parteiprogramme*, I, 86–88; II, 23–25; 66–71.

28. *Ibid.*, I, 107.

29. Offenstein, *Schulpolitik der Sozialdemokratie*, pp. 61f.

30. As quoted in Russell, *German Higher Schools*, p. 389.

Notes to Chapter V. The Supervision of Schools

1. Richter, *Die Emanzipation der Schule von der Kirche*, p. 21.

2. The following quotation bears this out. "Der Ausdruck 'Schulaufsicht' ein Sammelname für verschiedene staatliche Befügnisse ist, die ihrer Rechtsnatur nach verschieden zu werten sind . . . . Unter 'Leitung' wird auf dem Schulgebiet im einzelnen rechtlich ganz Verschiedenes verstanden derart, dass ein rechtlich relevanter Begriff der Schul-Leitung nicht besteht." Brauchitsch, *Verwaltungsgesetze für Preussen*, vol. VI, part I, p. 23.

3. Prussian constitution articles 23, 24. For various Prussian ordinances from 1850 on, particularly the ordinance of February 18, 1876, see the section "Erteilung, Leitung, Aufsicht über den Religionsunterricht," in Lande, *Religionsunterricht*, pp. 22–59; for provisions regarding "Kirchliche Einsichtnahme in den Religionsunterricht," pp. 59–83.

4. Hildebrand, *Religionsunterricht*, pp. 12–21; see also Henselman, *Schule und evangelische Kirche in Preussen*, pp. 51–65; Hinschius, *Das Kirchenrecht*, IV, 608–616.

5. Schöppa, *Bestimmungen*, p. 5; G. Giese, *Deutsche Schulgesetzgebung*, p. 131.

6. Collmann, "Das Recht und die Beschränkung der kirchlichen Schulaufsicht," *NKZ*, XXII (1911), 335–346.

7. *Neues Zeitblatt für die Angelegenheiten der lutherischen Kirche*, XXIII (1878), 39; see also XXVI (1881), 13.

8. Collman in *NKZ*, XXII (1911), 337.

9. Wohlmuth, *Zum Streit um die geistliche Schulaufsicht in Bayern*, pp. 110, 116. After 1873 the local school inspection for Simultanschulen, of which there were few in Bavaria, could be separated from the clerical office (*ibid.*, p. 79).

10. G. Kropatschek, "Kirche und Schule seit dem Umsturz," *LJ*, 1919, part I, pp. 124f.

11. Kühn, *Schulrecht in Preussen*, p. 179.

12. Robels, *Das Volksschulunterhaltungsgesetz*, Sec. 5.

13. See Chapter I for discussion of the *Küsterschulen*.

14. Janssen, *History of the German People*, XIII, 49–53, 124; Learned, *The Oberlehrer*, pp. 8, 11f., 23; Appens, *Die pädagogischen Bewegungen des Jahres 1848*, pp. 13–16; for a discussion of teachers' salaries during various periods from 1500 to 1892 see Fischer, *Geschichte des Volksschulleherstandes*, I, 36–39, 63–67, 94, 112, 154, 190, 260, 270–280, 344–346; II, 62–64, 73–77, 213–226, 428–437; for salary tables see Lexis, *History and Organization of Public Education in the German Empire*, p. 97.

15. As reported in *Evangelische Kirchenzeitung*, June 8, 1872, and reprinted in *ELS*, VII (1872), 370.

16. Fischer, *Geschichte des deutschen Volksschullehrerstandes*, I, 326; see also

pp. 327, 329; II, 91–93, 203, 274, 349, 355f. Catholic bishops in order to lessen the financial burden of their churches at times advocated the continuance of joint school and church offices (Hinschius, *Das Kirchenrecht*, IV, 618-620).

17. In Prussia a ministerial decree of February 27, 1894, officially designated which were the lower sacristan duties (*niedere Küsterdienste*). Specifically excluded as not belonging to the lower sacristan duties were those belonging to the cantor, organist, or clerical office; those connected with the altar or church service—providing the bread and wine for the Lord's Supper, cleaning the communion service and altar cloths, providing baptismal water, and posting hymn numbers. Rohrscheidt, *Gesetz über die Dientsbezüge der Lehrer und Lehrerinnen*, pp. 170-172; Wahl, *Deutsche Geschichte*, IV, 170; Bertram, "Kurze Einführung in Begriff, Wesen, und Behandlung, Trennung des vereinigten Küsterschulamtes," *Kommunales Archiv* (n.d., ca. 1934), No. 8; Hoche, ed., *Die Gesetzgebung des Kabinetts Hitler*, XXVIII, 654.

18. As quoted in Buch, *Rechtsstellung des Lehrers*, p. 28; see also Schwartz ed., *Pädagogisches Lexikon*, IV, 125; the section on *missio canonica* in Hinschius, *Das Kirchenrecht*, IV, 620-624; Karl Rothenbücher, "Wandlungen in dem Verhältnisse von Staat und Kirche in den neueren Zeit ," *Jahrbuch des öffentlichen Rechts*, III (1909), 360f.

19. *KJ*, 1926, p. 507.

20. Buch, *Rechtsstellung des Lehrers*, p. 46.

21. Rohrscheidt, *Gesetz betreffend die Unterhaltung der öffentlichen Volksschulen*, pp. 347, 363f.

22. Schöppa, *Bestimmungen*, p. 147.

23. Ebers, *Staat und Kirche*, p. 83; Kern, *Der katholische Religionsunterricht*, p. 46. In addition to the Jesuits, the Redemptorists (Liguorians), the Lazarists (Vincentinians), the Priests of the Holy Ghost, and Sisters of the Sacred Heart of Jesus were forbidden to teach in all sections of Germany (Hinschius, *Das Kirchenrecht*, IV, 616-618). For legislation in the period of the Kulturkampf see Franz, *Kulturkampf*, pp. 223–246.

24. Kern, *Der katholische Religionsunterricht*, pp. 134, 215. Kern has a long chapter (pp. 89-143) on "Teachers of Religion," which traces the changes in state requirements in Baden. See also L. Theobald, "Die zukünftige Gestaltung des evangelischen Religionslehramts an den höheren Schulen," *NKZ*, XXXI (1920), 133f.

Notes to Chapter VI. The Content and Method of Religious Instruction

1. Kern, *Der katholische Religionsunterricht*, pp. 79, 87.

2. For the Prussian regulations of 1872 see Schöppa, *Bestimmungen*, pp. 19f.

3. Berndt, *Methodik des Unterrichts in der evangelischen Religion*, pp. 15-19; see also Reukauf, *Didaktik*, pp. 1–8; 119; Kabisch, *Wie lehren wir Religion?* pp. 32–34; Niebergall, *Zur Reform des Religionsunterrichts*, pp. 49ff.

4. *Der evangelische Religionsunterricht im Lehrplan der höheren Schulen*, 2nd ed. (Berlin, 1891), p. 37, as quoted in Kabisch, *Wie lehren wir Religion?* p. 34.

5. As quoted in Burckstümmer, *Der Religionsunterricht in der Volksschule*, p. 96.

6. Reukauf, *Didaktik*, p. 121.

7. Thrändorf, "Religionsunterricht in evangelischen Schulen," in W. Rein, ed., *Encyklopädisches Handbuch der Pädagogik*, VII, 422–423; Thrändorf quotes

Deutschevangelischen Blättern, 1892, p. 271; see also Richter, *Die Emanzipation der Schule von der Kirche*, pp. 84f.

8. Morsch, *Das höhere Lehramt in Deutschland und Österreich*, pp. 227–229.

9. Kern, *Der katholische Religionsunterricht*, p. 49.

10. Reukauf, *Didaktik*, pp. 232–236; see also Hansen, *Über Memoriern*, pp. 46, 61–100. In Württemberg they learned 275 Bible verses, 218 verses of hymns; in Bavaria 345 Bible verses and 26 hymns. A detailed list of memory material for schools in Middle Franconia (Bavaria) and in Berlin is reprinted in *KZ*, XXV (1901), 77–79, 83.

11. Hansen, *Über Memoriern*, p. 101.

12. M. Reu, "Zur Geschichte der Unionskatechismen," *KZ*, XXII (1898), 65–81; and "Der Katechismusangelegenheit in der luth. Landeskirche Bayerns," *KZ*, XXV (1901), 82–83. See also Reukauf, *Didaktik*, p. 187.

13. "Lehrbücher und Lehrpläne," in Kern, *Der katholische Religionsunterricht*, pp. 57–84.

14. As translated in Reu, *English-German Text. Luther's Small Catechism with Explanation*.

15. Schöppa, *Bestimmungen*, pp. 20f.

16. Reukauf, *Didaktik*, p. 215. See also the discussion in Eberhard, *Die wichtigsten Reformbestrebungen*, pp. 6-30. Eberhard advocated having the catechism coordinated with Bible history in the lower and middle grades, but wanted separate instruction in the upper grades.

17. *ADB*, XLV, 229.

18. Volkmer, *Geschichte der Erziehung und des Unterrichtes*, p. 151; Burckstümmer, *Der Religionsunterricht in der Volksschule*, p. 149; Eberhard, *Die wichtigsten Reformbestrebungen*, pp. 25f.; Rein, *Die deutsche Schule*, p. 32. For an orthodox teaching plan see Lawin, *Methodik des evangelischen Religionsunterrichts*, pp. 16–57.

19. As quoted in Rietschel, *Zur Reform des Religionsunterrichts*, pp. 4–6; Thümmler, *Die Zwickauer Leitsätze*, pp. 3–16. Summaries of the conflict in Saxony are given by M. Reu, "Kirchliche Chronik: Deutschland," *KZ*, XXXII (1908), 260f.; XXXIII (1909), 147–150; 304–306; XXXIV (1910), 61f., 234–236, 504–505. See also Show, *Movement for Reform in the Teaching of Religion in the Public Schools of Saxony*.

20. Rietschel, *Zur Reform des Religionsunterrichts*, p. 6.

21. Der Vorstand des Ev.-luth. Schulvereins, *Was aus dem Kleinen Katechismus Dr. Martin Luthers nebst Bibelsprüchen und Kirchenliedern in den evangelischen Schulen des Königreichs Sachsen nach den Beschlüssen der Vertreterversammlung des Sächs.-Lehrervereins werden soll* [*Roter Katechismus*].

22. Müller, *Der Rote Katechismus*, p. 8.

23. Schöppa, *Bestimmungen*, p. 19.

24. "Religionsunterricht," in Schwartz, ed., *Pädagogisches Lexikon*, IV, 111.

25. As quoted in Richter, *Die Emanzipation der Schule von der Kirche*, p. 245.

Notes to Chapter VII. The Revolution and the Weimar Constitution

1. In German the *Unabhängige Sozialdemokratische Partei*. See Bergsträsser, *Geschichte der politischen Parteien in Deutschland*, pp. 186f; Berlau, *The German Social Democratic Party*, pp. 145f.

2. A. Rosenberg, *History of the German Republic*, p. 7.

3. Under Article 21, Paragraph 2, of the Prussian constitution of 1850 every child at school could be compelled to take part in the religious instruction of his confession (Westhoff, *Verfassungsrecht*, pp. 223f.). Actually children could be excused from the regular classes in religion, but then they had to present evidence that they were receiving equivalent instruction. Hoffmann's edict now freed them completely from religious instruction if this was the desire of their parents.

4. Landé, *Religionsunterricht*, pp. 272–275; Hildebrand, *Religionsunterricht*, pp. 23f.; Georg Schreiber, "Deutsche Kirchenpolitik nach dem ersten Welt-kriege. Gestalten und Geschehnisse der Novemberrevolution 1918 und der Weimarer Zeit," *HJ*, LXX (1951), pp. 296f.; G. Kropatschek, "Kirche und Schule seit dem Umsturz," *LJ*, 1919, part I, pp. 3–5.

5. *Ibid.*, pp. 49f.; *KJ*, 1920, pp. 423f.

6. Landé, *Religionsunterricht*, pp. 276ff.; Pottag, *Die Bestimmungen über die Volks- und Mittelschulen*, p. 16.

7. Hildebrand, *Religionsunterricht*, pp. 45, 53; *LJ*, 1919, part I, pp. 29–31; Westhoff, *Verfassungsrecht*, p. 247. The section of the Saxon law abolishing religious instruction from the schools was declared to be contrary to the federal constitution in November 1920.

8. H. Hansen, "Die Rechtlichen Grundlagen der Schulorganisation," *Die Bayerische Schule*, II (1949), 197–199.

9. Offenstein, *Die Schulpolitik der Sozialdemokratie*, p. 99; Hildebrand, *Religionsunterricht*, p. 53; *LJ*, 1919, part I, pp. 44–47. The Hamburg and Bremen laws, like the similar law in Saxony, were later declared to be contrary to the federal constitution.

10. See the different proclamations and party programs as given in Salomon, *Die deutschen Parteiprogramme*, vol. III; also H. Rosin, "Das Verhältnis des Staates zur Kirche und Erziehung in den Programmen der politischen Parteien," *Schulpolitisches Jahrbuch*, 1926, pp. 99–104.

11. As quoted in Rosenberg, *History of the German Republic*, p. 102.

12. Preuss' draft contained in Article 20 only this one sentence: "Der Unter-richt soll allen Deutschen gleichmässig nach Massgabe der Befähigung zugäng-lich sein" (Landé, *Die Schule*, p. 28). Article 31 of the revised draft stated: Für die Bildung der Jugend und des ganzen Volkes soll durch öffentliche Anstalt-en genügend gesorgt werden. Das Schul- und Unterrichtswesen ist in allen Gliedstaaten so einzurichten, dass sich auf die Volksschulbildung der Unterricht in mittleren und höheren Bildungsanstalten aufbaut. Das öffentliche Unter-richtswesen steht unter staatlicher Aufsicht." The government draft presented to the National Assembly contained this article, except that the word "öffentlich" was deleted from the last clause (*ibid.*, p. 29).

13. Westhoff, *Verfassungsrecht*, p. 5. On school questions the Center and German National party united against the left. See Landé, *Die Schule*, p. 33; Klinkenberg, *Das Zentrum und die Rechte im Kampf um die christliche Schule.*

14. Article 149, Sentence 3 as translated in McBain and Rogers, *New Con-stitutions of Europe*, p. 205. The German text reads: "Der Religionsunterricht wird in Übereinstimmung mit den Grundsätzen der betreffenden Religionsgesell-schaft unbeschadet des Aufsichtsrechts des Staates erteilt."

15. Anschütz, *Die Verfassung*, p. 597.

16. "Das öffentliche Schulwesen ist organisch auszugestalten." Anschütz states that this means that the schools were "to be fashioned as a unitary whole

(*einheitlicher Organismus*) in which the single schools and school types were to be considered as members of the whole body. *Ibid.*, p. 586.

17. Good discussions of the school compromises are to be found in Landé, *Die Schule*, pp. 39–48; Westhoff, *Verfassungsrecht*, pp. 33–45.

18. *Ibid.*, p. 36.

19. The constitution does not use the term "Simultanschule" or the term which had begun to replace it "Gemeinschaftsschule."

20. Anschütz, *Die Verfassung*, pp. 495f.; F. Giese, *Verfassung des Deutschen Reichs*, pp. 321f. The Socialists accepted but did not like this clause (Offenstein, *Die Schulpolitik der Sozialdemokratie*, p. 109).

21. Article 146, Paragraph 2. See Anschütz, *Die Verfassung*, p. 584.

22. Westhoff, *Verfassungsrecht*, pp. 24f.; Schuwerack, *Die Privatschule*.

23. Rohrscheidt, *Gesetz betreffend die Unterhaltung der öffentlichen Volksschulen*, p. 336.

24. Anschütz, *Die Verfassung*, p. 597; Pernutz, *Das Verhältnis von Staat und Kirche nach der Weimarer Verfassung*, pp. 50f. There were faculties of Evangelical theology at the Universities of Berlin, Bonn, Breslau, Erlangen, Giessen, Göttingen, Greifswald, Halle, Heidelberg, Jena, Kiel, Königsberg, Leipzig, Marburg, Münster, Rostock, and Tübingen; faculties of Catholic theology at the Universities of Bonn, Breslau, Freiburg, Munich, Münster, Tübingen, and Würzburg. See Lindegren, *Education in Germany*, p. 40.

Notes to Chapter VIII. The National Government and Education under the Weimar Republic

1. Kandel and Alexander, trans., *Education in Prussia*, p. 191; for the text of the law see pp. 187–190.

2. *Reichsgesetzblatt* 1920, no. 222, as quoted in Hildebrand, *Religionsunterricht*, p. 53. The court based its decision on Articles 146, 149, and 174 of the constitution. The court, however, did not restore the schools of Saxony to their former status of confessional schools or repeal other sections of the Saxon law (Westhoff, *Verfassungsrecht*, p. 37).

3. For certain minor exceptions see the discussion below, pp. 134–135, of the so-called *Sammelschulen*.

4. Hildebrand, *Religionsunterricht*, p. 44. The age for majority in religious matters varied in different states. It was the completion of 14 years in Prussia, Nassau, Brunswick, Oldenburg, Hesse-Darmstadt; 16 years in Baden; 21 years in Bavaria and Saxony. For the text of the 1921 law see *Reichsgesetzblatt*, 1921, pp. 939–941; for the law, the supplementary ministerial decree of March 29, 1924, and the official explanation of the law by the government of Breslau of March 13, 1928, see Landé, *Religionsunterricht*, pp. 12–22. Excerpts of the law are given in Kandel and Alexander, *Education in Prussia*, pp. 185f. The law of 1921 is still in force in the Federal Republic of Germany except for changes in the age of religious majority from 14 to 18 in Bavaria, Rhineland-Palatinate, and Saarland.

5. *Die Reichsschulkonferenz 1920. Amtlicher Bericht erstattet vom Reichsministerium des Innern;* the texts of the 1921, 1925, and 1927 drafts of a proposed school law, with excerpts from parliamentary debates, are conveniently reprinted in, Bischöfliche Arbeitstelle für Schule und Erziehung, *Das Ringen um das sogenannte Reichsschulgesetz.*

6. *KJ*, 1936, p. 443; see also pp. 444f.; 1924, pp. 340f.; Gerhardt Giese, "Die Schule im Reich. Ein Uberblick über 60 Jahre Reichsschulpolitik," *Zeitschrift für Geschichte der Erziehung und des Unterrichts*, XXXI (1931), 239.

7. Usually these terms were held to be synonymous, see for example Anschütz, *Die Verfassung*, p. 585; Landé, *Die Schule*, p. 119. See also Rohrscheidt, *Gesetz betreffend die Unterhaltung der öffentlichen Volksschulen*, p. 342; Westhoff, *Verfassungsrecht*, p. 121; Thümmel, *Evangelisches Kirchenrecht für Preussen*, p. 134.

8. For a summary of objections to the measure see *KJ*, 1928, pp. 456–464; the attitude of numerous parties, organizations, and the state governments are discussed in detail in Offenstein, *Der Kampf um das Reichsschulgesetz*, pp. 60–230.

9. Walter Landé, "Die staatrechtlichen Grundlage des deutschen Unter-richtswesens," *Handbuch des Deutschen Staatsrechts*, p. 695, in *Das öffentliche Recht der Gegenwart*, XXIX (1932).

10. Landé, *Die Schule*, p. 219; Westhoff, *Verfassungsrecht*, pp. 26f., 91.

11. Westhoff, *Verfassungsrecht*, pp. 88f. Thuringia later changed this provision slightly. Teachers were to be trained at a pedagogical institute in Jena which was to be separated from the university.

12. Article 106, Paragraph 2; Article 107 of the convention as translated in Kaeckenbeeckt, *The International Experiment in Upper Silesia*, p. 622. In higher schools minority language classes were to be established on application of 25 pupils, minority religion courses on application of 18 pupils (Article 118).

13. Landé, *Religionsunterricht*, pp. 186ff.

14. Tims, *Germanizing Prussian Poland*, p. 275; see also pp. 20, 99.

15. Landé, *Religionsunterricht*, pp. 189-191.

16. Georg Schreiber, *Zwischen Demokratie und Diktatur*, pp. 137f. The Reich Concordat of 1933 concluded by Hitler sought in Article 29 to protect the rights of minorities to religious instruction in their mother tongue (Martens, *Traités*, 3ᵉ série, XXVIII, 40).

17. On the early attempts to conclude a concordat see Schreiber, *Zwischen Demokratie und Diktatur*, pp, 75, 78, 83–86, 116, 133; Georg Schreiber, "Deutsche Kirchenpolitik nach dem ersten Weltkrieg," *HJ*, LXX (1951), 296-333; Albert Fischer, "Schule und Reichskonkordat," in *MUND*, V (1955), no. 68, pp. 7–20; especially valuable is Ernst Deuerlein, *Das Reichskonkordat*, pp. 15–40, 52–70, 87–91.

18. The text of the concordat with Bavaria is to be found in *Gesetz- und Verordnungs-Blatt für den Freistaat Bayern* 1925, No. 3, pp. 53-60; Martens, *Traités*, 3ᵉ série, XX, 310–322; Paul Seipp, ed., with others *Schulrecht: Bayern*, I. (Seipp has edited similar collections for other post-World War II German states.) The Bavarian concordat was ratified on January 24, 1925, on which day it became legally effective (*Gesetz- und Verordnungs-Blatt für den Freistaat Bayern* 1925, no. 4, p. 69). See also Goetz, *Die schulrechtlichen Bestimmungen der europäischen Konkordate*, pp. 112–134.

19. Article 32 of the state treaty with the Evangelical-Lutheran Church in Bavaria Right-of-the-Rhine (*Gesetz- und Verordnungs-Blatt für den Freistaat Bayern* 1925, no. 3, pp. 61–64; Seipp, *Schulrecht: Bayern*, I BI, pp. 7–13); Article 25 of the treaty with the United Protestant Evangelical Christian Church of the Palatinate (*Gesetz- und Verordnungs-Blatt* 1925, no. 3, pp. 65–67; Seipp, *Schulrecht: Rheinland-Pfalz*, I, DI, pp. 109–111). The treaty with the Church

Right-of-the-Rhine went into effect on January 27, 1925, the treaty with the Church of the Palatinate on January 29, 1925, (*Gesetz- und Verordnungs-Blatt für den Freistaat Bayern* 1925, no. 4, p. 76; *Amtsblatt für die evangelisch-lutherische Landeskirche in Bayern rechts des Rheins* 1925, no. 7, p. 31). See also Allgemeiner evang.-luth. Schulverein, *Zum Staatsvertrag*, pp. 3–5.

20. Landé, *Die Schule*, p. 219.

21. Westhoff, *Verfassungsrecht*, p. 93; Landé, *Die Schule*, pp. 55, 62, 197; Anschütz, *Die Verfassung*, pp. 581, 596.

22. Pacelli was appointed nuncio to Bavaria May 1917. Although Prussia had maintained diplomatic relations with the Vatican 1747–1920, 1925–1935, Germany as a united state did not do so until the spring of 1920 when Pacelli, in addition to his Bavarian post, became nuncio at Berlin. He retained his residence in Munich until 1925. In December 1929 he left Berlin when he was appointed to the College of Cardinals. Made secretary of that body on February 29, 1930, he was elected to the Papacy as Pius XII on March 2, 1939, (*Deuerlein, Das Reichskonkordat*, pp. 1f., 11, 75, 87f.).

23. Schreiber, *Zwischen Demokratie und Diktatur*, p. 133; Deuerlein, *Das Reichskonkordat*, pp. 87–91.

24. Martens, *Traités*, 3e série, XXI, 58–70; Deuerlein, *Das Reichskonkordat*, pp. 71–84; Geissler, *Staat und Kirchen in Preussen*, p. 4; Franz von Papen, *Memoirs*, pp. 126, 278. Prussia concluded a treaty with the Evangelical churches on May 11, 1931.

25. Article 11 and the concluding protocol to this article, Martens, *Traités*, 3e série, XXVIII, 21–22, 24f.; Deuerlein, *Das Reichskonkordat*, pp. 85–87. Baden also concluded a treaty with the Vereinigte Evangelisch-Protestantische Landeskirche Badens on November 14, 1932.

Notes to Chapter IX. The Schools under the Weimar Republic

1. To avoid confusion the practice of Landé, Westhoff, and other commentators will be followed and the term "Simultanschule" will be used instead of "Gemeinschaftsschule." although the latter would be more accurate in referring to school reform in Saxony and Thuringia. In Prussia particularly the term "Paritätische Schule" was also used to describe this school type.

2. Landé, *Die Schule*, p. 38. Landé considers it questionable (*streitig*) if these latter territories or Saxony or Thuringia should really be considered Simultanschule territory. See also Löffler, *Der Religionsunterricht und der konfessionelle Charakter der (Volks-) Schule.*

3. Deiters, *Die deutsche Schulreform nach dem Weltkriege*, pp. 85f.

4. C. L. A. Pretsel, "Staat, Kirche und Schule," *Schulpolitisches Jahrbuch*, 1926, p. 19.

5. Landé, *Die Schule*, pp. 131f.; Westhoff, *Verfassungsrecht*, p. 142; Henselmann, *Schule und evangelische Kirche in Preussen*, pp. 34-37; Stiefelzieher, *Religionsgesellschaften und Weltanschauungsvereinigungen*, pp. 98–103.

6. Landé, *Die Schule*, p. 131; *SJ*, 1932, p. 421. In Berlin 3 new Sammelschulen were opened in 1926; 7 in 1927; 3 in 1929; 1 in 1930; and none in 1931 (*KJ*, 1931, p. 258). All Sammelschulen were abolished by Hitler in 1933.

7. *SJ*, 1932, p. 421; Stiefelzieher, *Religionsgesellschaften und Weltanschauungsvereinigungen*, p. 103.

8. *SJ*, 1932, p. 421. These do not include figures on Hamburg; in addition there were 10,785 children who adhered to some other Christian confession,

28,629 Jews, 6,125 who adhered to some other non-Christian religion, and 168,647 without religious affiliation.

9. *KJ*, 1931, p. 232; the figures on private schools are from *SJ*, 1932, p. 424.

10. Out of about 1,200 Prussian public higher schools some 260 were rightly or wrongly classified as confessional schools (Landé, *Höhere Schule und Reichsvolksschulgesetz*, p. 21).

11. *Ibid.*, p. 26.

12. *KJ*, 1931, pp. 262f.

13. Westhoff, *Verfassungsrecht*, p. 174.

14. Stratemeyer, *Supervision in German Elementary Education 1918-1933*, pp. 40–43.

15. Anschütz, *Die Verfassung*, p. 597; Westhoff, *Verfassungsrecht*, pp. 32, 95f.; Landé, *Die Schule*, p. 198; F. Giese, *Die Verfassung des deutschen Reichs*, p. 386; Rothaas, *Studien zur Lehre von der religiösen Kindererziehung*, p. 15; Kühn, *Schulrecht in Preussen*, p. 179; Schlemmer, *Die Schulpolitik der evangelischen Kirche Preussens*, p. 19; Ebers, *Staat und Kirche*, pp. 283f.

16. Buch, *Rechtsstellung des Lehrers*, p. 43; see also p. 109.

17. This summary is taken from Westhoff, *Verfassungsrecht*, p. 131; see also Buch, *Rechtsstellung des Lehrers*, pp. 94–109.

18. Landé, *Die Schule*, p. 207; Westhoff, *Verfassungsrecht*, pp. 203f. There were differences of opinion whether religion had to be given in the Berufsschulen. Anschütz maintains the obligation rested only upon the schools providing a general education and not on specialized and vocational schools (*Die Verfassung*, p. 595). Goetz (*Die schulrechtlichen Bestimmungen der europäischen Konkordate*, p. 183) and Joseph Schröteler ("Das katholische Schulideal und die Bestimmungen des Reichskondordats," *Stimmen der Zeit*, CXXVI (1933), 145–154) hold that under the Concordat of 1933 religious instruction was required at Berufsschulen and that this was a change from existing practice.

19. *KJ*, 1931, p. 272; see also F. Giese, *Religionsunterricht als Pflichtfach der deutschen Berufsschulen*, p. 8.

20. Kandel and Alexander, *Education in Prussia*, pp. 193 ff., 203ff., 231ff., 299ff. By ministerial decrees of June 5, 1920, and July 29, 1921, it was expressly stated that the church authorities must be given a part in drawing up curriculum plans for religious education in Prussia (Henselmann, *Schule und evangelische Kirche in Preussen*, p. 68).

21. The work on this revision was largely done before Hitler took office on January 30, 1933, and the introduction was signed by Bishop Meiser on May 22, 1933. This teaching plan, which covered only the elementary schools, comprises a booklet of 107 pages, which indicates the detail of these regulations (Evang.-Luth. Landeskirchenrat, *Lehrpläne für den evangelisch-lutherischen Religionsunterricht an den Volkshauptschulen in Bayern r.d.Rhs.*).

22. Kautz, *Neubau des katholischen Religionsunterrichtes*, I, 17f. One of the better books on reform of Protestant religious instruction is Niebergall, *Zur Reform des Religionsunterrichts*.

23. *KJ*, 1926, p. 494; 1928, p. 508.

24. Dittmer, *Religionsunterricht*, p. 91.

25. Regulations as printed in Kandel and Alexander, *Education in Prussia*, p. 328.

26. *KJ*, 1924, p. 380.

27. See the Prussian regulation of January 19, 1922 (Landé, *Religionsunter-*

richt, pp. 297f.). In Prussia at the request of parents Jewish children were as hitherto excused from school on Saturday. In 1919 this same privilege was accorded to Adventists (*ibid.*, pp. 310–312).

28. Stiefelzieher, *Religionsgesellschaften und Weltanschauungsvereinigungen*, p. 104; Fleming, *Religionsunterricht? Moralunterricht? Ein Wort für Eltern und Lehrern.*

29. Landé, *Religionsunterricht*, p. 285.

30. SA Frankfurt, T No. 7, vol. I: for material on Jewish education see also Stiefelzieher, *Religionsgesellschaften und Weltanschauungsvereinigungen*, pp. 53–64.

31. Landé, *Religionsunterricht*, p. 253.

32. *Ibid.*, pp. 258–270; J. Rosenberg, *Methodik des jüdischen Religionsunterrichts*, p. vi.

33. Landé, *Die Schule*, pp. 251f.

Notes to Chapter X. The Early Years, 1933–1935

1. Pickers, *Hitlers Tischgespräche*, p. 271.

2. Baynes, *The Speeches of Adolf Hitler*, I, 333; see also the collection of statements by Hitler and other National Socialist leaders in Hermann, *Religionsfreiheit;* Birger Forell, "National Socialism and the Protestant Churches in Germany," in Baumont, et. al., eds., *The Third Reich*, pp. 811–814.

3. Baynes, *The Speeches of Adolf Hitler*, I, 370f. (my italics); Buchheim, *Glaubenskrise im Dritten Reich*, pp. 82, 213. It is interesting to note in view of later developments that the sentence which has been here italicized was omitted in the somewhat abbreviated account of the speech given in the party organ, the *Völkische Beobachter*. Nor did it appear in the official text of the speech published by the Eherverlag in 1934 and in the authorized English translation. Hitler in three major speeches on January 30, August 17, and August 26, 1933, stated that "national socialism affirmed positive Christianity," (Fabricius, *Positive Christianity in the Third Reich*, pp. 7f.).

4. *Zentralblatt für die gesamte Unterrichts-Verwaltung in Preussen*, 1933, p. 65.

5. *Amtsblatt des Bayer. Staatsministeriums für Unterricht und Kultus*, March 28, 1936, p. 36.

6. Von Papen, *Memoirs*, pp. 279ff.; see also von Papen's testimony, *Trial of the Major War Criminals*, XVI, 281–286; Georg Schreiber, "Deutsche Kirchenpolitik nach dem ersten Weltkriege,"*HJ*, LXX (1951), 323, 331f.; Anton Scharnagl, "Das Reichskonkordat und die Länderkonkordate als Konkordatssystem," *HJ*, LXXIV (1955), 601–607; Deuerlein, *Das Reichskonkordat*, pp. 106–135. For earlier attempts to conclude a national concordat see discussion in Chapter Eight.

7. Von Papen, *Memoirs*, pp. 280f.

8. As a consequence of this provision of the concordat Protestant ministers in Baden who had assumed party posts also resigned them. See statement by Alfred Rosenberg in *Völkische Beobachter* (North German edition), August 16, 1953, as quoted in Hermann, *Religionsfreiheit*, p. 31.

9. Joseph Schröteler, "Das katholische Schulideal und die Bestimmungen des Reichskonkordats," *Stimmen der Zeit*, CXXVI (1933), 149, 154.

10. Von Papen, *Memoirs*, p. 282; see also the statement of Pius XII of July 19, 1947, to Prelate Natterer, the secretary of the Bavarian organization of clerics, as quoted in Scharnagl, *HJ*, LXXIV (1955), 607; statements by Papen and

to the ethics of the German race, the following sentences were printed in italics:
"Gewisse Teile des alten Testaments können für den Unterricht nicht in Frage kommen, andere werden stark in den Hintergrund treten müssen . . . . Soweit veraltete Bestimmungen dem entgegenstehen gelten diese als aufgehoben. Mergenthaler."

26. Wurm, *Erinnerungen*, p. 138.

27. *Amtsblatt des Reichsministeriums für Wissenschaft*, 1938, p. 534; *Amtliches Schulblatt für den Regierungsbezirk Kassel*, 1938, p. 2; Tieman, Dräger, and Schumacher, *Die Amtsführung des Lehrers*, p. 389.

28. SA Frankfurt T No. 3, vol. II. The decree was later published; see Homeyer, *Neuordnung des höheren Schulwesens*, p. C 15. For protests of church authorities see Hermelink, *Kirche im Kampf*, pp. 569–575.

29. *Amtsblatt für die Evangelisch-Lutherische Landeskirche in Bayern rechts des Rheins*, January 4, 1939.

30. Hoche, *Gesetzgebung des Kabinetts Hitler*, XXVIII, 654.

31. SA Frankfurt, T No. 1, vol. II; T No. 3, vol. II.

32. *Amtliches Schulblatt für den Regierungsbezirk Kassel*, 1939, p. 85f. *Amtsblatt für die Evangelisch-Lutherische Kirche in Bayern*, September 9, 1946, repealing an ordinance of April 17, 1939, on *Eckstunden*.

33. As quoted in *KH*, 1933–34, p. 80; see also G. Giese, *Staat und Erziehung*, pp. 254, 262f.

34. The campaign for Gemeinschaftsschulen had been carried on intermittently before 1935. As early as December 17, 1933, Bishop Meiser had issued a statement to be read in all Bavarian Lutheran churches affirming that the church still upheld the confessional schools and urging parents to send their children to them ("Kanzelverkündigung am Sonntag, den 17 Dezember nach der Predigt des Hauptgottesdienstes," mimeographed copy obtained at the Pfarramt in Weiltingen, Bavaria). See also Klara Hunsche, "Der Kampf um die christliche Schule und Erziehung 1933-45," in *KJ*, 1949, p. 464.

35. Neuhäusler, *Kreuz und Hakenkreuz*, part I, p. 89.

36. *Ibid.*, p. 88.

37. Schmid, *Apokalyptisches Wetterleuchten*, pp. 325ff. Many individual incidents are cited here as also in Neuhäusler, *Kreuz und Hakenkreuz*, part I, pp. 88–100; Micklem, *National Socialism and the Roman Catholic Church*, pp. 153–156; and *The Persecution of the Catholic Church in Germany*, pp. 143–162; *KH*, 1937–38, pp. 89–96; *KJ*, 1949, pp. 467–477, 485; Merkt, ed., *Dokumente zur Schulreform in Bayern*, p. 17.

38. Schmid, *Apokalyptisches Wetterleuchten*, p. 320.

39. *Amtsblatt des Reichsministeriums für Wissenschaft*, 1938, p. 235; 1939, p. 226; Riede, *Official Attitude of the Roman Catholic Hierarchy*, p. 416.

40. Schröteler, *Katholische Bekenntnisschule und deutsche Volksgemeinschaft*, pp. 24ff. The quotations from canon law and the encyclical of Pius XI are translated from texts given by Schröteler. For statements of the Catholic bishops against the Gemeinschaftsschulen see vol. IV of *Mit Kelle und Schwert*, Bischöfliche Arbeitstelle in Köln, *Stimmen des Episkopates zur Schulfrage in der Zeit des "Dritten Reiches".*

41. As stated in introduction of *Katholische Grundsätze für Schule und Erziehung*. Part I, sec. B, is a concise statement of "the Catholic school ideal." See also vol. III of *Mit Kelle und Schwert*, Bischöfliche Arbeitstelle in Köln, *Die katholische Kirche und ihr Schul- und Erziehungsideal.*

42. *Amtsblatt des Reichsministeriums für Wissenschaft,* 1938, pp. 65f. In the decree of January 22, 1938, an explanation is given of the decree of December 28, 1936. See also *ibid.,* 1939, pp. 258–260.

43. Decision of the Württembergischen Verwaltungsgerichtshof of July 21, 1937, reprinted *ibid.,* 1937, p. 428–432.

44. Neuhäusler, *Kreuz und Hakenkreuz,* part I, pp. 127–143; Micklem, *National Socialism and the Roman Catholic Church,* pp. 118–122, 158–160; *Persecution of the Catholic Church in Germany,* pp. 295–328.

45. Official statistics indicated that of the higher schools on May 25, 1940, there were 63 private boys' schools, 57 private girls' schools, and 23 National Socialist educational institutions. At the same time there were 165 private middle schools. See *SJ,* 1941–42, pp. 368f.

46. See the article by an exchange teacher at one of these schools, J. W. Tate, "The Public Schools of Germany," *Zeitschrift für Erziehung,* VI (1937), 165–170.

47. Samuel and Thomas, *Education and Society in Modern Germany,* pp. 51–53; Hehlmann, *Pädagogisches Wörterbuch,* pp. 1f., 296f.; Alonzo G. Grace, "Education," in Litchfield, *Governing Postwar Germany,* pp. 45f.

48. Benze, *Erziehungsmächte und Erziehungshoheit im Grossdeutschen Reich,* pp. 57–72; for a good brief description of the 1937 decree, see Lindegren, *Education in Germany,* pp. 10–15.

Notes to Chapter XII. The War Years, 1939–1945

1. *KJ,* 1933–1944, pp. 350f. Foreign Minister Ribbentrop informed the Pope in an interview on March 11, 1940, that: "The Führer had quashed no less than seven thousand indictments of Catholic clergymen," *Documents on German Foreign Policy 1918–1945,* Series D, VIII, 697.

2. Hermelink, *Kirche im Kampf,* pp. 494f.

3. *Amtsblatt des Reichsministeriums für Wissenschaft,* 1939, pp. 226-228.

4. SA Frankfurt, T No. 1, vol. IV.

5. Hermelink, *Kirche im Kampf,* pp. 540, 601f.; *Amtsblatt für die Evangelisch-Lutherische Landeskirche in Bayern rechts des Rheins,* 1941, p. 24.

6. *KJ,* 1949, p. 510.

7. SA Frankfurt, T No. 3, vol. II. On May 5, 1950, the writer had an interview with Dr. Herr and among other things questioned him on the quality of religious instruction of lay Catholic teachers during the war years. He replied that it was very satisfactory.

8. *Amtsblatt für die Evangelisch-Lutherische Landeskirche in Bayern rechts des Rheins,* 1944, p. 30.

9. *Amtsblatt des Reichsministeriums für Wissenschaft, usw.,* 1940, p. 212; 1941, p. 138; Homeyer, *Neuordnung des höheren Schulwesens,* pp. A 13a, A 34. Compulsory attendance laws had previously varied in the states, *Internationale Zeitschrift für Erziehung,* VIII (1938), 387.

10. Copy of Minister Rust's decree of October 24, 1942, SA Frankfurt, T No. 3, vol. III; directive of the *Bayerisches Staatsministerium für Unterricht und Kultus* of October 29, 1941, to the *Direktorat der höheren Schulen* (Realgymnasium Archives, Kempten in Allgäu). On difficulties involved in giving instruction to these voluntary groups, see the report of Pfarrer Walter Horkel to the Evang.-Luth. Kreisdekan in Munich: "Jahresbericht über die 'Kirchlichen Arbeitsgemeinschaften' 1941–42 für die Schüler der Oberschule für Jungen in Kempten," (Realgymnasium Archives, Kempten in Allgäu).

11. Neuhäusler, *Kreuz und Hakenkreuz*, part I, p. 107.

12. *Amtsblatt des Reichsministeriums für Wissenschaft, usw.*, 1942, pp. 182, 231; 1943, p. 164; Hehlmann, *Pädagogisches Wörterbuch*, pp. 164-166.

13. Hermelink, *Kirche im Kampf*, p. 589.

14. *Amtsblatt für die Evangelische-Lutherische Landeskirche in Bayern rechts des Rheins*, 1939, p. 40.

15. Homeyer, *Neuordnung des höheren Schulwesens*, pp. B 9a, 8b. This ordinance applied at first only to Volksschulen but it was extended to higher schools on June 26, 1941, and to middle schools on March 3, 1942 (*Amtsblatt des Reichsministeriums für Wissenschaft*, 1942, p. 93).

16. *Amtsblatt für die Evangelisch-Lutherische Landeskirche in Bayern rechts des Rheins*, 1942, p. 31.

17. The Directive of August 23, 1943, was found in the Hamburg Schulamt Archives. See also *KJ*, 1949, pp. 511f.

18. SA Frankfurt, T No. 1, vol. II (Ordinance by Römer).

19. Jewish communities in all Germany were denied the privileges of public law corporations in 1938. On church conditions during the war in annexed sections of Poland see, *KJ*, 1933–1944, pp. 452–457; 1949, p. 511; *Trial of the Major War Criminals*, IV, 510–519; XXXII, pp. 92-105, Doc. 3263PS; Adolph, *Im Schatten des Galgens*, pp. 18–30, 113–115.

Notes to Chapter XIII. Method and Content of Religious Instruction, 1933–1945

1. *Trial of the Major War Criminals*, XXI, 464; XXV, 191–197, Doc. 098–PS; XXXV, 7–13, Dic. 075–D; see also XVII, 264f.; XXI, 464. Borman, who was one of the most anti-Christian and antichurch men among the party leaders, in June 1941 sent a memorandum to all Gauleiter on the "Verhältnis von Nationalsozialismus und Christentum," the opening sentence of which stated: "Nationalsozialistische und christliche Auffassungen sind unvereinbar." The memorandum which elaborated on this thesis got into the hands of some churchmen and caused a furor. Even Rosenberg objected to the memorandum, and Hitler ordered Borman to recall the memorandum and destroy it. Borman's view that Christianity and National Socialism were incompatible was of course echoed by many churchmen. See for example, Feely, *Nazism vs. Religion;* pp. 3–7, Adolf, *Im Schatten des Galgens*, p. 14.

2. Klara Hunsche, "Kirche und Schule im Totalen Staat. Die bekennende Kirche und die Schule im Dritten Reich," *EE*, I (1949), 23f. The Bavarian Protestant curriculum plan of May 15, 1933, must have been largely worked out before the Nazis came to power and was merely a revision of the 1923 plan (*Amtsblatt des Bayer. Staatsministeriums für Unterricht und Kultus*, 1933, p. 67). The new plan introduced a new *Gottbüchlein* which proved very popular and was used throughout the following years. The curriculum plan issued in Thuringia on November 29, 1933, was not very definite or revolutionary (Hiller, *Deutsche Erziehung*, p. 392).

3. *Amtliches Schulblatt für den Regierungsbezirk Wiesbaden*, 1935, p. 58; also *Amtsblatt für die Evangelisch-Lutherische Landeskirche in Bayern rechts des Rheins*, 1938, p. 83; 1941, p. 74.

4. Ellwein, *Der evangelische Religionsunterricht* (Berlin, 1937). In the fourth edition of this volume published in 1939 there is less emphasis laid on the Old Testament. See also Barth, *Die Krisis im evangelischen Religionsunterricht*.

5. Wurm, *Erinnerungen*, p. 138; Hermelink, *Kirche im Kampf*, p. 350. *KJ*, 1949, p. 474; *KH*, 1937–38, p. 80.

6. May, *Wie lehren wir Christum im Dritten Reich?* pp. 14, 16.

7. Otto Eberhard, "Der Geist der Tapferkeit in deutsch-christlichen Unterricht der Volksschule," *Pädagogische Warte*, XL (1933), 1071–1076; Hypocrisy—Matthew 16:23; 17:17; 21:12–13; 23:13–15, 24–28; Pharisees—Luke 18:9–14; 7:36–50; 11:32–52; 12:1; Matthew 5:20; 15:7, 23; following Jesus—Luke 14:15–35; 9:62; 13:23–24; Matthew 7:13–14; 10:22; 20:16; 22:14; 19:25–26; God as father—Matthew 7:23; 10:15, 28, 33; 11:20–24; 12:32, 36, 41–42; 13:30, 40–41, 49.

8. Erwin Wissmann: "Jesus der Führer und Gottesstreiter. Winke für eine neue Sicht und Auswahl der Jesusgeschichten im evangelischen Religionsunterricht der Volksschule," *Pädagogische Warte*, XLII (1935), 204–208; see also Herbert Preisker, "Das Jesusbild der heutigen Theologie und seine Bedeutung für den Religionsunterricht," *ibid.*, 24–30.

9. Shakespeare, *The Merchant of Venice*, Act III, Scene II.

10. Heinrich Schüssler, "Der katholische Religionsunterricht nach der Wende," in Hiller, *Deutsche Erziehung*, p. 247.

11. Cölln, *Lehrplan für deutschen Religionsunterricht*. Cölln was a Mittelschuldirektor and head of the Arbeitsgemeinschaft für deutschen Religionsunterricht. See also the book put out under the auspices of this organization, *Am Urborn deutscher Frömmigkeit;* Neuhäusler, *Kreuz und Hakenkreuz*, part I, pp. 112–115; Friedrich Wieneke, "Die kirchliche Erneuerung und der Religionsunterricht besonders in der Volksschule," *Pädagogische Warte*, L (1933), 1057–1060.

12. A ministerial decree of August 9, 1933, forbade the introduction of any new school books in all subjects before decisions on school reforms had been reached; a decree of February 5, 1937, stated that the same books were to be used in 1937–38. New textbooks began to appear in 1938–39, and these were rather minutely regulated. There were, however, no regulations issued in regard to books for religious instruction (Homeyer, *Neuordnung des höheren Schulwesens*, p. B 21; Neuhäusler, *Kreuz und Hakenkreuz*, part I, pp. 111f).

13. Hermann Werdermann, "Der Katechismus als religionspädagogisches Problem," *Die Deutsche Schule*, XL (1936), 570–576. Werdermann favored retention of the catechism as a book of instruction. See also the article by Erwin Wissmann, "Luthers Kleiner Katechismus in Religionsunterricht der Volksschule," *Die Deutsche Schule*, XXXIX (1935), 33–40.

14. See discussion in Chapter Fifteen.

15. Wurm, *Erinnerungen*, pp. 138f.; Hermelink, *Kirche im Kampf*, pp. 584ff.

16. *Ibid.*, pp. 586 f.; Hermelink, *Geschichte der evangelischen Kirche in Württemberg*, p. 487.

17. Wurm, *Erinnerungen*, p. 139. Local Nazi officials were often concerned at the way the churches maintained their hold on the populace. For examples drawn mostly from South Germany see Steward, *Gestapo-Berichte über den Widerstand der Kirchen*.

18. From a declaration by the Evangelische Oberkirchenrat in Württemberg an die Dekanatsämter (19 Juni 1944) in Hermelink, *Kirche im Kampf*, p. 593.

19. On the basis laid at this time the German Evangelical church after 1945 built its program. The school ideals, as set forth by the chamber for church instruction of the temporary directory of the German Evangelical church at a

meeting in 1943, have been practically realized in West Germany; in East Germany the church program of education today is a continuation and further development of the work begun during the Nazi period by the Confessing church. See Klara Hunsche, "Der Kampf um die christliche Schule und Erziehung 1933–1945," in *KJ*, 1949, pp. 455–519; pp. 514–516 for "Die Forderungen der Kirche für die Gestaltung der christlichen Schule," drawn up in 1943.

Notes to Chapter XIV. Jewish Education in the Third Reich

1. Much of this chapter has appeared in E. C. Helmreich, "Jewish Education in the Third Reich," *Journal of Central European Affairs*, XV (1955), 134–147.

2. *SJ*, 1932, pp. 421–424 indicates there were 97 public Jewish confessional elementary schools, of which 95 were in Prussia and 2 in Württemberg. There were 28,639 students attending these and various other public elementary schools; in addition there were 5,888 attending private elementary schools. Adolf Kober in his excellent article, "Jewish Communities in Germany from the Age of Enlightenment to their Destruction by the Nazis," *Jewish Social Studies*, IX (1947), 214, states: "Before 1933 the Jewish primary schools numbered about 120 in Prussia, 25 in Bavaria, 7 in Württemberg, 1 in Oldenburg (Birkenfeld) making a total of about 155 in the whole German Reich."

3. Hoche, *Gesetzgebung des Kabinetts Hitler*, I, 113–119; II, 66; Blau, *Das Ausnahmerecht für die Juden in Deutschland 1933–1945*, pp. 13–18.

4. Hoche, *Gesetzgebung des Kabinetts Hitler*, II, 365–370.

5. SA Frankfurt, T No. 7, vol. I, May 17, 1933.

6. SA Frankfurt, T No. 7, vol. II, June 2, 1933.

7. SA Frankfurt, T No. 4, vol. II.

8. *Zentralblatt für die gesamte Unterrichts-Verwaltung in Preussen*, 1933, pp. 250f.

9. SA Frankfurt, T No. 7, vol. I, November 1, 1933; January 13, 1934.

10. Hoche, *Gesetzgebung des Kabinetts Hitler*, V, 799f.; Curt L. Heymann, "German Laws against the Jews. A Complete and Factual Survey of the Legal Basis of Anti-Semitism," *Current History*, XLVIII (1938), 42.

11. *Zentralblatt für die gesamte Unterrichts-Verwaltung in Preussen*, 1933, p. 126; 1934, p. 106; *Amtsblatt des Bayer. Staatsministeriums für Unterricht und Kultus*, March 22, 1934.

12. SA Frankfurt, T No. 7, vol. I, September 15, 1933, July 31, 1934, September 12, 1934; *Amtsblatt des Württembergischen Kultusministeriums*, 1935, p. 206; *Amtliches Schulblatt für den Regierungsbezirk Wiesbaden*, August 21, 1934.

13. Hoche, *Gesetzgebung des Kabinetts Hitler*, XV, 49–54.

14. These statistics are taken from Bruno Blau, "The Jewish Population of Germany," *Jewish Social Studies*, XII (1950), 162f.

15. Copy of the directive in SA Frankfurt, T No. 7, vol. I.

16. SA Frankfurt, T No. 7, vol. I, December 13, 1935; July 2, 1937; May 25, 1937.

17. Adolf Kober, "Jewish Communities in Germany from the Age of the Enlightenment to their Destruction by the Nazis," *Jewish Social Studies*, IX (1947), 225f.; Elieser Ehrmann, "Jewish Education in Germany," *Jewish Education*, XI (1939), 95. In 1939 the *Reichsvertretung* was reorganized as the *Reichsvereinigung der Juden in Deutschland* (*American Jewish Yearbook*, 1939–1940, p. 265).

18. SA Frankfurt, E3, No. 1, vol. I, March 24, 1937.

19. Rudolf Stahl, "Vocational Retraining of Jews in Nazi Germany 1933–1938," *Jewish Social Studies*, I (1939), 169–194; Ehrmann in *Jewish Education*, XI (1939), 96.

20. Colodner, *Jewish Education in Nazi Germany*, p. 97.

21. Kober in *Jewish Social Studies*, IX (1947), 229.

22. "Verordnung des Kultusministeriums über die Aufhebung des israelitischen Religionsunterrichts vom 7 Mai 1934," *Amtsblatt des Württembergischen Kultusministeriums*, 1934, p. 88.

23. *Amtsblatt des Bayer. Staatministeriums für Unterricht und Kultus*, 1936, pp. 94, 117.

24. SA Frankfurt, T No. 4, vol. II, summary of measures dated April 5, 1943.

25. SA Frankfurt, T No. 4, vol. II, September 4, 1936; *Amtsblatt des Reichsministeriums für Wissenschaft*, 1936, p. 163.

26. The decree of Kultusminister Boepple of Bavaria of December 1936 is given, *ibid.*, 1937, p. 39; a copy of the decree of August 14, 1941 (Min. Erl. E III a 1657, E III v. E I a) was obtained from the Realgymnasium archives in Kempten in Allgäu. See also the section on Hebrew instruction in Homeyer, *Neuordnung des höheren Schulwesens*.

27. L. Spitzmann, "The Hebrew School Movement," in *The Jewish People Past and Present*, II, 119–127; on the difficulty of providing instruction in Hebrew see Ehrmann in *Jewish Education*, XI (1939), 97f.

28. Oscar Karbach, "The Liquidation of the Jewish Community of Vienna," *Jewish Social Studies*, II (1940), 255–278; Hoche, *Gesetzgebung des Kabinetts Hitler*, XXVI, 523; Weinryb, *Jewish Emancipation under Attack*, p. 48; *American Jewish Yearbook*, 1938–1939, p. 196.

29. SA Frankfurt, T No. 6, vol. III, April 28, 1938.

30. Pertinent sections of the ordinances are conveniently translated in Weinryb, *Jewish Emancipation under Attack*, pp. 47–52.

31. *Documents on German Foreign Policy 1918–1945*, Series D, V, 894.

32. Mark Wischnitzer, "Jewish Emigration from Germany 1933–1938," *Jewish Social Studies*, II (1940), 36.

33. *Nazi Conspiracy and Aggression*, IV, 433f.

34. *Amtsblatt des Reichsministeriums für Wissenschaft*, 1938, p. 520. Jews were also barred from German universities at this time (*Nazi Conspiracy and Aggression*, V, 371f.).

35. SA Frankfurt, 2ha, No. 1, vol. I, summary of February 28, 1941.

36. This school also disappeared in 1943 with the final destruction of the Jewish school system. See Klara Hunsche, "Kirche und Schule im Totalen Staat. Die Bekennende Kirche und die Schule im Dritten Reich," *EE*, I (1949), 26; *KJ*, 1949, pp. 499f.

37. *Amtsblatt des Reichsministeriums für Wissenschaft*, 1938, p. 550.

38. SA Frankfurt, T No. 7, vol. II, December 17, 1938; 2ha No. 1, vol. 1, letter of May 2, 1939 to the Schulrat des Philanthropins.

39. SA Frankfurt, T No. 7, vol. I, August 14, 1939. Section II of the citizenship law of July 4, 1939, dealt with the Jewish schools. See Blau, *Das Ausnahmerecht für die Juden in Deutschland 1933–1945*, pp. 76–78; Colodner, *Jewish Education in Nazi Germany*, pp. 82–85.

40. SA Frankfurt, T No. 7, vol. I, January 13, 1934; May 25, 1937; 2ha, No. 1, vol. I, August 25, 1941; E 3, No. 1, vol. I, February 17, 1942. In April

1950 there were 16 Jewish pupils in the elementary schools of Frankfurt and 9 at the higher schools.

41. Blau, *Das Ausnahmerecht für die Juden in Deutschland 1933–1945*, nos. 109, 313, 364.

42. SA Frankfurt, 2ha, No. 1, vol. I, June 7, 1942.

43. *Amtsblatt des Reichsministeriums für Wissenschaft*, 1942, p. 278; Homeyer, *Neuordnung des höheren Schulwesens*, p. D4; SA Frankfurt, T No. 7, vol. I, September 9, 1942.

44. *Amtsblatt des Reichsministeriums für Wissenschaft*, 1944, p. 78.

Notes to Chapter XV. The Period of Four Power Control

1. Some sentences and paragraphs in this chapter as well as in Chapters XVI and XVII have been taken from E. C. Helmreich, "Religious Education in Germany II: Postwar Measures," *Current History*, XIX (October 1950) 210–216.

2. *DJ*, 1949, p. 351; Pilgert, *The West German Educational System*, pp. 7f.

3. See the section on "Vertriebene und Zugewanderte 1946 bis 1955," *SJ*, 1956, pp. 45–48; *Statistical Pocketbook on Expellees*, p. 5; *The Americana Annual*, 1955, p. 293.

4. For a table showing the religious affiliation of the native populace, expellees, and refugees in each state of the Federal Republic see *DJ*, 1953, p. 464.

5. *SJ*, 1956, p. 43.

6. *KJ*, 1951, pp. 417–420; "Die Heimatvertriebenen; der Stand und die Veränderung der Bevölkerungsverhältnisse in Deutschland nach dem zweiten Weltkriege," *KH*, 1944–51, 219–238; see also the section "The Effect of the East–West Split on the Relative Position of the Two Established Churches in Germany," in McClaskey, *History of U.S. Policy and Program in the Field of Religious Affairs*, pp. 88–91.

7. Pilgert, *The West German Educational System*, p. 10.

8. *DJ*, 1949, p. 352; see also Liddell, ed., *Education in Occupied Germany*, pp. 89, 110, 113, 120, 127.

9. *DJ*, 1949, p. 352.

10. "Textbooks in Germany, American Zone," (mimeographed summary, 1948), p. 5. Through the year 1948, out of 125 books examined 107 were approved 17 conditionally approved, and 1 disapproved. This summary was kindly lent to the author in 1950 by American authorities in Germany.

11. From the summary of the evaluation of books on religion (1945–48) referred to in the above footnote.

12. Quoted by Murray, *Denominational Education in Germany*, paragraph 10.

13. *DJ*, 1949, p. 358.

14. Military Government Regulation 8–112.

15. Article 181. No doubt this article was meant to express validation of both the concordat with the Catholic church and the agreement with the Evangelical Church in Bavaria Right-of-the-Rhine. Actually it confirmed only the concordat, for it alone had validity on January 24, 1925, ratifications of the concordat being exchanged on that day. The agreement with the Bavarian Evangelical Church did not go into effect until January 27, 1925, something the drafters of the constitution no doubt overlooked (see above Chapter VIII, particularly notes 18 and 19). Since the treaties were negotiated in 1924 but

did not become effective until the next year, they are variously referred to as the agreements of 1924 or 1925.

16. As formulated by Murray, *Denominational Education in Germany*, Paragraph 9.

17. Military Government Regulation 8–962; 8–963; reprinted in *Religious Affairs*, (Office of U.S. Military Government in Germany, August 1946), p. 27; U.S. State Department, *Germany 1947–1949. The Story in Documents*, p. 628.

18. *DJ*, 1949, p. 355; Lange, *Totalitäre Erziehung*, pp. 39–41. For a discussion of this law see Chapter XVII.

19. *Constitutions of the German Länder* (Berlin, 1947) is an extremely well-indexed collection of the constitutions, prepared by the Civil Administration Division, Office of U.S. Military Government. For a German collection of the constitutions see Huber, ed., *Quellen zum Staatsrecht der Neuzeit*, vol. II. *Deutsche Verfassungsdokumente der Gegenwart, 1919–1951*. A constitution was adopted in the Saar on December 15, 1947.

20. Point J of American Military Regulation 8–201. The text of Directive 54 is given in U.S. State Department, *Germany 1947–1949. The Story in Documents*. p. 550; *DJ*, 1949, p. 350.

21. Directive 56 in U.S. State Department, *Germany 1947–1949. The Story in Documents*, pp. 550f.

22. As quoted in Giese, *Die Kirche in der Berliner Schule*, p. 9.

23. As quoted by Gerhardt Giese, "Die Schulpolitik der evangelischen Kirche in Berlin," *Mission Draussen und Drinnen*, p. 139.

24. Of the seven districts where religious instruction had not been started, two were in West Berlin and five in East Berlin (Giese, *Die Kirche in der Berliner Schule*, pp. 35–40).

25. Giese in *Mission Draussen und Drinnen*, pp. 147ff.

26. On this campaign and the direct participation of Bishop Dibelius in it see Giese, *Die Kirche in der Berliner Schule*, pp. 61–65.

27. For a history of this important Berlin office see Hermann Kandeler, "Der Rechtliche Aufbau des katechetischen Dienstes in Berlin," in *Mission Draussen und Drinnen*, pp. 112ff.

28. Gerhardt Giese, "Im Auftrage der Kirche," *BL*, IX (1955), 509. Catechists can be divided into three groups in West Berlin: (1) full-time catechists who teach twenty-four hours a week, (2) teachers who give religious instruction, usually two to four hours a week, although the law sets no limit, (3) part-time catechists, usually ministers, choir directors, deaconesses, although others are employed who are not so closely connected with the churches. There are three examinations for catechists: examination C for those who have been trained in short courses; examination B for full-time catechists who have studied two and one-half years in a seminary or have helped at least one year as an assistant catechist, and examination A for specially gifted catechists who have studied four additional semesters at a church seminary and thus become qualified to teach the upper grades at a higher school (Kandeler, in *Mission Draussen und Drinnen*, pp. 125–127).

29. Some 500–600 Protestant teachers took over religion classes in this early postwar period, teaching two to four hours a week. In all they accounted for about ten percent of the religious hours. See Gerhardt Giese, "Im Auftrage der Kirche," *BL*, IX (1955), 509; Klara Hunsche, "Evangelische Lehrerschaft in Berlin," *EE*, II (October 1950), No. 7, pp. 23f.

30. Giese, *Die Kirche in der Berliner Schule*, p. 85.

31. It was not possible to increase the church taxes in Berlin-Brandenburg until 1954 (*ibid.*, p. 49).

32. Seipp, *Schulrecht: Berlin*, I BI, pp. 1–17; *DJ*, 1949, pp. 356f. For a good account of the enactment of the school law which neither the Protestant nor Catholic churches approved, see Giese in *Mission Draussen und Drinnen*, pp. 149–162. See also Spectator, "Das konfessionelle Privatschulwesen in Berlin," *Pädagogische Rundschau*, IV (March 1950), 282–284; Rudolf Diedler, "Vier neue Schulgesetze, Berlin, Bremen, Hamburg, Schleswig-Holstein," *Die Schule*, V (January 1950), 5–10.

33. The Catholics made a strenuous but unsuccessful attempt to have the traditional custom legalized in Berlin. For them the question was not merely an administrative one, but also doctrinal; all baptized children should automatically take part in religion classes (Giese in *Mission Draussen und Drinnen*, p. 154).

34. *DJ*, 1949, p. 357.

35. *Die Evangelischen Grundschulen in Berlin*, p. 8; *Gründungsgeschichte und erster Jahresbericht des Evangelischen Gymnasiums Berlin*, pp. 5–6. For further discussion of these schools see below, Chapter XVII.

Notes to Chapter XVI. Religious Education in the Federal Republic of Germany

1. Murray, *Denominational Education in Germany*.

2. "Gesetz über das öffentliche Schulwesen in Niedersachsen vom 14 September 1954," Paragraph 5, Section 6; "Richtlinien für den Religionskundlichen Unterricht vom 25 April 1955," in Seipp, *Schulrecht: Niedersachsen*, I CI, p. 2; III CI, p. 3.

3. Article 32, author's translation from *Constitutions of the German Länder*, p. 80.

4. In an agreement (1957) between the government of Schleswig-Holstein and the Protestant church, the church delegated its right to inspect religious instruction (*Recht zur Einsichtnahme*) to school inspectors, if they belong to the Evangelical Lutheran church and possess the right to give religious instruction. If this is not the case, the ministry of education will appoint suitable supervisory authorities ("Neue Schulartikel in Schleswig-Holstein," *Die evangelische Elternschaft*, May 1957, pp. 4–7; *Frankfurter Allgemeine Zeitung*, April 24, 1957). In the Weimar Republic and even earlier, the church in Schleswig-Holstein had in practice waived its right to inspect religion classes. See G. Giese, *Staat und Erziehung*, p. 271.

5. This would cover the Bavarian Concordat of January 24, 1925; the Bavarian Agreement with the Evangelical Lutheran Church Right-of-the-Rhine of January 27, 1925; the Bavarian Agreement with the Protestant Christian Church of the Palatinate of January 29, 1925; the Prussian Concordat of August 13, 1929; the Prussian Treaty with the Evangelical Landeskirchen of June 29, 1931; the Baden Concordat of March 11, 1933; the Baden Treaty with the United Evangelical Protestant Landeskirche of March 11, 1933; and the Reich Concordat of September 10, 1933. The dates given are those of ratification when the different agreements became effective.

6. *KJ*, 1945–1948, p. 233.

12*

7. *Bekenntnisfrei* is often translated nonconfessional or nondenominational. The term, however, parallels Articles 149 of the Weimar Constitution where the term is "bekenntnisfreien (weltlichen) Schulen." This has usually been translated "secular schools." It seems clear that the intention was to provide for religious instruction at confessional and Gemeinschaftsschulen, unless the latter were specifically organized on a secular basis. Later in connection with the establishment of private schools the constitution speaks of Gemeinschafts-, Bekenntnis- and Weltanschauungsschulen, but no mention is made of bekenntnisfreien Schulen, which are no doubt covered by the last term used. This interpretation is confirmed by F. Giese, *Grundgesetz für die Bundesrepublik*, p. 24, note 4. Article 12 of the constitution of North Rhine-Westphalia classifies a bekenntnisfreie Schule as a kind of Weltanschauungsschule. See Haugg, *Die Schule in Nordrhein-Westfalen*, vol. I *Der weltanschauliche Charakter der Volksschule*, pp. 16–18.

8. Hermann Lutze, "Um die Bekenntnisschule," *EE*, III (November 1951), no. 8, pp. 2–9; Maria Lövenich, "Zur weltanschaulichen Situation der Volksschulen in Nordrhein-Westfalen," *Pädagogische Rundschau*, IV (1950). 208–212.

9. Seipp, *Schulrecht: Niedersachsen*, I CI; Danehl, *Das Landesrecht in Niedersachsen*, AI.

10. *Hamburgisches Gesetz und Verordnungsblatt*, 1949, pp. 257–263.

11. Spreng and Feuchte, *Die Verfassung des Landes Baden-Württemberg*, pp. 6–21; much of the legal debate leading to the formation of the new state is given in, Institut für Staatslehre und Politik in Mainz, *Der Kampf um den Südweststaat*.

12. Article 18; see also Articles 12, 15, 16.

13. *DJ*, 1953, p. 524. Thirty-two agreements are listed by Fritz Thiele, "Die Einheit der deutschen Schule und die ständige Konferenz der Kultusminister," *BL*, VI (1952), 508. Not all states have as yet adopted the provisions in regard to higher schools. As proposed, all higher schools are henceforth to be known as Gymnasien which are to have a normal "Long Form" starting after four years of Grundschule and continuing nine years, and a "Short Form" starting after seven years of elementary school and continuing for six years. No knowledge of a foreign language is required for entrance to the latter and there are to be two types: a modern language and a mathematics-science line. The "Long Form" is to have three types; a classical language, a modern language, and a mathematics-science line.

14. For a list of the school laws and ordinances enacted in the various states from 1945 to January 1, 1957, see Heckel and Seipp, *Schulrechtskunde*, pp. 347–350. The text of the laws can be found in the volumes of Seipp, *Schulrecht*.

15. Education at elementary and secondary schools is free in Bavaria, Baden-Württemberg, Berlin, Bremen, Hamburg, Hesse, Schleswig-Holstein; is already free for elementary schools and will be for secondary schools after 1959 in Lower Saxony, and after 1960 in North Rhine-Westphalia. Fees for secondary schools are still collected in the Saar. In some states children of nonresident parents have to pay fees, in other states not (Heckel and Seipp, *Schulrechtskunde*, pp. 300f.).

16. For brief descriptions of the West German educational system see: Hylla and Kegel, *Education in Germany;* Wenke, *Education in Western Germany;* Hilker, *Die Schulen in Deutschland;* Pilgert, *The West German Educational System*.

17. Point 7 of "The Objectives of the U.S. Education Program in Germany," in *Postwar Changes in German Education*, p. iv.

18. *Regierungsblatt für das Land Württemberg-Hohenzollern*, 1948, no. 18, p. 90.

19. Becker, *Zur Rechtsproblematik des Reichskonkordat;* Anton Scharnagl, "Das Reichskonkordat und die Länderkonkordate als Konkordatssystem," *HJ*, LXXIV (1955), 602, 606 and the numerous references cited there; Thieme, *Deutsches Hochschulrecht*, p. 121; Albert Discher, "Schule und Reichskonkordat," *MUND*, V (1954), no. 62, pp. 60, 80; Ellwein, *Klerikalismus in der deutschen Politik*, pp. 129–137.

20. For Vatican complaints, the charge of the federal government, and the answer of the government of Lower Saxony see Fischer in *MUND*, VI (1955), no. 68, pp. 49–107; Ellwein, *Klerikalismus in der deutschen Politik*, pp. 183–212. For Lower Saxon law see Seipp, *Schulrecht: Niedersachsen*, I CI.

21. *Frankfurter Allgemeine Zeitung*, March 27, 1957; *Echo der Zeit*, March 31, 1957; *Rheinischer Merkur*, March 29, 1957; for a critical view of the court's decision see W. Böhler, "Zur Karlsruher Entscheidung über das Reichskonkordat," *Echo der Zeit*, April 7, 1957, also reprinted in *Allgemeine Deutsche Lehrerzeitung*, IX (1957), 206f.

22. Based primarily on *SJ*, 1957, pp. 83, 86, 88f. The figures on middle and higher schools do not include Bremen, Hamburg, or the Volksoberschule in Schleswig-Holstein. Statistics on elementary schools in Lower Saxony were obtained from: *Statistische Bericht des Niedersächsischen Amts für Landesplanung und Statistik. Die allgemeinbildenden Schulen in 1955–56*, p. 5.

23. Franz Kelber, "Ein Sonderbericht: K L V Hamburg/Bremen," *KE*, IX (1956), 470f. In 1953 Hamburg paid a subsidy of 186.83 DM for each pupil at Catholic elementary schools, 733.72 DM for each student at Catholic higher schools, and 191.50 DM for each student at the Rudolf Steiner schools (*Hamburger Lehrerzeitung*, VIII (1955), no. 16, p. 12).

24. *DJ*, 1949, p. 533; Edmunds, *Rudolf Steiner Education;* Rudolf Steiner, *Allgemeine Menschenkunde als Grundlage der Pädagogik;* Rudolf Steiner, *Erziehungskunst, Methodisch-Didaktisches.*

25. "Lehrplan für den kirchlichen Unterricht an den Volksschulen. Lehrplan für den kirchlichen Unterricht an den Berufs- und Fachschulen," *Amtsblatt für die Evangelisch-Lutherische Kirche in Bayern*, August 8, 1949, no. 15, pp. 75–77. For a list of curriculum plans for all subjects see W. Schultze and G. Slotta, "Sammlung der zur Zeit gültigen Lehrpläne in den Ländern der Bundesrepublik und in der D.D.R.," (mimeographed, Hochschule für Internationale Pädagogische Forschung, Frankfurt am Main, 1957).

26. *EE*, III (January 1952), no. 1, p. 50.

27. Rudolf Lennert, "Ein Nachwort—Heinrich Marx, Über den Volksschullehrer als Religionslehrer," *Die Sammlung*, IV (1949), 187.

28. Information obtained at the ministry of education and at the Ev. Landeskirchenamt in Munich, May 1957.

29. *Kölnische Rundschau*, April 13, 1950.

30. *Taunus Anzeiger*, December 1, 1955; see also Helmuth Kittel, "Pädagogik und Katechetik in der Vorbildung evangelischer Pfarrer," *EE*, II (June 1950), no. 3, pp. 2–15; (July 1950), no. 4, pp. 6–19.

31. Jules Gerard-Libois, "Où en est l'enseignement religieux dans la République Fedérale allemande," *Lumen Vitae*, X (1956), no. 2, pp. 252f.

32. The minister of education rested his case on Article 34 of the Baden

Education Law of 1910 according to which pupils are to be taught by teachers of the same confession. See *Der Lehrerbote*, February 1950; *Réalités Allemandes*, April 1949, p. 30.

33. Figures compiled from *Pädagogische Studienführer*. In Bavaria the Concordat of 1925 provides for confessional teacher-training institutes. The Institut für Lehrerbildung at Erlangen classes itself as Simultan, but actually is attended only by Protestants. Slightly different totals are presented in *Übersicht über die Regelung der Lehrerbildung in den Ländern der Bundesrepublik Deutschland* compiled by the Bischöfliche Arbeitsstelle für Schule und Erziehung, Köln (1955). See also Hylla and Kegel, *Education in Germany*, p. 50; Ellwein, *Klerikalismus in der deutschen Politik*, pp. 167–182.

34. Pilgert, *The West German Educational System*, pp. 47f.

35. *SJ*, 1957, pp. 90f.

36. Seipp, *Schulrecht: Niedersachsen*, III CI; see also the section on Berufsschulen in *KJ*, 1955, pp. 259–263; Hermann Huber, "Zum Religionsunterricht in der Berufsschule," *KB*, LXXVI (1951), 285–295. In Bavaria the Deutsche Katechetenverein is getting out new material to be used for Catholic instruction in vocational schools, see *KB*, LXXX (1955), 78f.; for Protestant material see the magazine *Der evangelische Religionslehrer an der Berufsschule*.

37. *Katholischer Katechismus der Bistümer Deutschlands*. On the new catechism see Karl Erlinghagen, "Der neue deutsche Katechismus," *KE*, VIII (1955), 347–357; review article in *Rheinischer Merkur*, December 7, 1956; G. Schindler, "Katholische Erziehung," in Hilker, *Pädagogik im Bild*, p. 168. For a brief history of Catholic catechisms see Bopp, *Katechetik*, pp. 53–57.

38. Kittel, *Von Religionsunterricht zur Evangelischen Unterweisung*, p. 10. The constitution of North Rhine-Westphalia in Article 14 speaks of "Religionsunterricht" and also of "religiöse Unterweisung."

39. "Ein Wort zur Schulfrage. Interview Oberkirchenrat Edo Osterloh mit einem Vertreter der 'Ev. Welt'," *EE*, I (April 1950), 27. Osterloh is now (1958) minister of education in Schleswig-Holstein.

40. Giese in *Mission Draussen und Drinnen*, p. 137; Giese, *Erziehung und Bildung in der mündigen Welt*, pp. 82–83; 136–140. See also Oskar Hammelsbeck, "Begegnung zwischen Schule und Kirche in der Evangelischen Unterweisung," *EE*, II (November 1950), no. 8, pp. 2–10.

41. The term "Unterweisung" is also being used more frequently than formerly by Catholics. For an appeal for a renewal of religious vocabulary see Heinz Rennung, "Religionslehrer und Religionsunterricht. Zur Entstehung der Begriffe," *KB*, LXXXVIII (1953), 446–453.

42. "Lehrplan für den kirchlichen Unterricht an den Volksschulen," *Amtsblatt für die Evangelisch-Lutherische Kirche in Bayern*, August 8, 1949, no. 15.

43. For a good discussion on new techniques in religious instruction see Uhsadel, *Evangelische Erziehungs- und Unterrichtslehre*: Marquardt, *Wie lehren wir das Wort Gottes?* See also the following magazines, Protestant: *Der evangelische Erzieher; Schule und Leben, Zeitschrift für christliche Erziehung und Unterrichtspraxis; Evangelische Unterweisung, Mitteilungsblatt für pädagogische Arbeitsgemeinschaften; Die Christenlehre, Zeitschrift für den katechetischen Dienst* (the last is the magazine for the German Democratic Republic); Catholic: *Katechetische Blätter. Der Jugendseelsorger, Zeitschrift für katholische Religionspädagogik und Jugendseelsorger; Der katholische Erzieher*.

44. Adolf Wendel, "Zur Frage der Disziplin in der evangelischen Unter-

weisung," *EE*, IV (1952), 170–174; Konrad Gluckert, "Liebeslied auf die ungezogenen Kinder. Zur Selbstbesinnung des Katechete," *KB*, LXXVIII (1953), 265–267; Bopp, *Katechetik*, pp. 187–192; the excellent article by Klemens Tilmann, "Eine verborgene Grundlage der Schuldisziplin," *KB*, LXXXII (1957), 295–299.

45. Manuscript survey of a study of grades in religion made at the Bischöfliche Arbeitsstelle für Schule und Erziehung, Köln. The headings on the report cards vary, the following terms being used: Religion, Biblische Geschichte, Biblische Geschichte und Katechismus, Religionslehre, Christliche Unterweisung. See also Günter Bezzenberger, "Die Zensur in der Religion," *EE*, I (February 1950), 19; "Die Religionsnote im Urteil der Öffentlichkeit," *EE*, III (May 1951) no. 2, p. 21. For further discussion of the question of grades see Otto Fritz, "Religionsnoten," *EE*, VI (1954), 79f.; A. Niederstenbruch, "Zensuren im Religionsunterricht," *EE*, VII (1955), 26f.; Werner Deems, "Religionsnoten? Zur Fortsetzung einer notwendigen Diskussion," *EE*, VII (1955), 94–96; Hubert Fischer, "Noten im Religionsunterricht," *KB*, LXXIX (1954), 53–55.

46. Hammelsbeck, "Zur Schulgottesdienst, Kritik und Beispiel," in his volume *Glaube Welt Erziehung*, p. 121; *KJ*, 1955, p. 238; Walther Zifreund, "Der Schulgottesdienst in der Spannung zwischen Predigt und Gebet, Passivität und Vollzug," *EE*, IX (1957), 117–125.

Notes to Chapter XVII. Religious Education in the German Democratic Republic

1. For data on party strength see *DJ*, 1949, p. 71; 1953, pp. 105–109.

2. *DJ*, 1949, p. 355; Heinrich Deiters, "Schule und Jugenderziehung in den deutschen Verfassungen der Gegenwart," *pädagogik, beiträge zur erziehungswissenschaft*, IV (1949), no. 8, pp. 21f. Also see discussion in Chapter Fifteen.

3. Hylla and Kegel, *Education in Germany*, p. 65.

4. After some experimentation the "Ten-Year Schools" were given legal status in 1955. *Karteibuch des Schulrechts der DDR*, C 5 1, C 5 1/1; *Schulrecht und Schulverwaltung in der DDR*, p. 55; "Aufgaben und Probleme der deutschen Pädagogik. Referat des Ministers für Volksbildung Fritz Lange auf dem V Pädagogischen Kongress, Leipzig 1956," *Sonderdruck der Deutschen Lehrerzeitung*, p. 25; see also his comments on pp. 4f. on the new centralized school. In 1951 the quota of children of worker or peasant parentage was set at 60 percent for higher schools and 80 percent for "Ten-Year Schools." Bundesministerium für gesamtdeutschen Fragen, *Das Erziehungswesen der Sowjetzone*, pp. 286f. For 1955 regulations see *Karteibuch des Schulrechts der DDR*, B 25.

5. In 1945 out of the 10,500 elementary schools, 4141 (42 percent) were *einklassig*, that is, all eight grades were instructed in one room by one teacher. In 1954–5, only 83 such one-teacher schools remained in the German Democratic Republic. Joseph Müller, "Das ländliche Schulwesen in Ostdeutschland," *Die neue Volksschule in Stadt und Land*, VII (July 1955), no. 4, p. 194.

6. Complaint over conditions in Kreis Güstrow sent to the *Bischöfliche Kommissariat der Diozese Osnabrück für Mecklenburg*, September 18, 1956. Bischöfliche Arbeitsstelle Köln, Archives: *Schulfragen Ostzone*, IX.

7. *DJ*, 1953, p. 525; Lange, *Totalitäre Erziehung*, p. 233. For text of the law see Heilmann and Birnbaum, *Gesetze und Verordnungen*, pp. 80–82. For an official explanation of laws affecting *Elternversammlungen, Elternbeiräte,*

Elternseminare and other parents' organizations see *Schulrecht und Schulverwaltung in der DDR*, pp. 271–276.

8. *Karteibuch des Schulrechts der DDR*, C 5 1; C 5 1/1; Heinrich Deiters, "Schule und Jugenderziehung in den Deutschen Verfassungen der Gegenwart," *pädagogik, beiträge zur erziehungswissenschaft*, IV (1949), no. 8, p. 25. In 1955 when elections to parents' councils were held, the Protestant Bishop of Magdeburg advised parents in his district not to vote "since it is no longer possible for any council member who is not a Marxist to have any say in school matters." "German News Letter," *Christian Century*, LXXIII (1956), 85. On opposition in the parents' councils see Lange, *Totalitäre Erziehung*, pp. 233f.

9. Karl Ellrich, "Die Entwicklung des Grundschulwesens in der Sowjetischen Besatzungszone seit 1945," *pädagogik, beiträge zur erziehungswissenschaft*, IV (1949), no. 6, pp. 24–31. The most important national school laws are the "Gesetz über die Schulpflicht in der Deutschen Demokratischen Republik vom 15 Dezember 1950," and the "Schulordnung für die allgemeinbildenden Schulen der Deutschen Demokratischen Republik vom 24 Mai, 1951," (Heilmann and Birnbaum, *Gesetze und Verordnungen*, pp. 11–17). Laws and ordinances still in effect are to be found in the *Karteibuch des Schulrechts der DDR*.

10. Herman, *Report from Christian Europe*, pp. 27f.; Tobias, *Communist-Christian Encounter in East Europe*, p. 537.

11. *KJ*, 1955, pp. 291ff.; Zimmermann and Hafa, *Unterweisung*, pp. 12, 18. In all East German churches (their jurisdictions do not correspond with present governmental divisions) rules and regulations have been formulated with respect to training and employment of catechists.

12. Shuster, *Religion Behind the Iron Curtain*, p. 43.

13. "German News Letter," *Christian Century*, LXVII (1950), 852; LXIX (1952), 50; LXXIII (1956), 756; Shuster, *Religion Behind the Iron Curtain*, p. 42. Just who are classed as catechists (whether pastors and very limited part-time helpers are included) probably accounts for large discrepancies in figures. Thus *KJ*, 1955, p. 298, refers to 12,000 catechists serving the church in the German Democratic Republic in 1955. President Zimmermann of the Protestant church's Education Chamber assured the writer that the number was about 6,000. This is the figure he gives in his book (Zimmermann and Hafa, *Unterweisung*, p. 7).

14. A sharp reduction in admission of theological students took place in 1956 under a *numerus clausus* policy. (Information from President Zimmermann, July 1957.)

15. Zimmermann and Hafa, *Unterweisung*, pp. 26–29.

16. Information obtained at diocesan headquarters in Berlin, July 1957. Inquiry was made at the Statistical Center of the Catholic Church in Cologne, but no statistics on attendance at Catholic religion classes in the German Democratic Republic as a whole are available.

17. Wulf Thiel, "Der Weg des Kindergottesdienstes seit 1933," in *Mission Draussen und Drinnen*, pp. 89–93.

18. For material on the Youth-Dedication Services (*Jugendweihe*) and statement by leaders see *KJ*, 1954, pp. 141–148; 1955, pp. 113–146; Jeremias, *Die Jugendweihe in der Sowjetzone*, pp. 9f.; Möbus, *Kommunistische Jugendarbeit*, pp. 105–111.

19. *KJ*, 1955, p. 162; Annamarie Doherr, "Die SED macht die Jugendweihe jetzt besonders attractive," *Frankfurter Rundschau*, April 20, 1957.

20. Conversations with men at Catholic and Protestant church offices in Berlin, July 1957; conversation with a church official from Saxony, May 1957. Officially reference was made to an increase of five percent in participation in the Jugendweihe, but the SED paper, *Neues Deutschland*, admitted the failure of the 1957 Jugendweihe campaign and criticized its conduct, see *KE*, X (July 1957), 374. The Jugendweihe apparently made gains, however, in 1958; see *Time* LXXIII (January 5, 1959), 60.

21. "German News Letter," *Christian Century*, LXXIII (1956), 123.

22. *KJ*, 1955, p. 164; "German News Letter," *Christian Century*, LXX (1953), 324, 568.

23. Zimmermann and Hafa, *Unterweisung*, p. 15.

24. Bibelanstalt Altenburg, *Christenlehre*.

25. Church of Scotland, *The Church under Communism*, pp. 22–24; Royal Institute of International Affairs, *Survey of International Affairs 1949–50*, pp. 231f.; U.S. State Department, *East Germany under Soviet Control*, p. 49; Lange, *Totalitäre Erziehung*, pp. 106–109.

26. *KJ*, 1951, pp. 149f.

27. "German News Letter," *Christian Century*, LXIX (1952), 286, 442f., 1044, 1101; see also Amos N. Wilder, "Opening and Closing Doors in Germany," *ibid.*, LXX (1953), 738–740; *New York Times*, December 31, 1952; February 19, 27, 1953; March 26, 1953; April, 13, 23, 24, 27, 28, 1953; Shuster, *Religion Behind the Iron Curtain*, pp. 45–59.

28. *New York Times*, June 8, 1953; "Auflehnung der Oberschüler—Junge Gemeinde", in Lange, *Totalitäre Erziehung*, pp. 408–411; Castellan, *D.D.R. Allemagne de l'est*, pp. 289–294; *KJ*, 1953, pp. 138, 149–155.

29. "Communiqué of the Politburo of the Socialist Unity Party, 1953," in Ruhm von Oppen, *Documents on Germany Under Occupation 1945–54*, p. 587.

30. *New York Times*, June 11, 1953; *Christian Century*, LXX (1953), 731f.; *KJ*, 1953, pp. 178–182.

31. Heilmann and Birnbaum, *Gesetze und Verordnungen*, p. 169; *Karteibuch des Schulrechts der DDR*, B 2 10.

32. *Schulrecht und Schulverwaltung in der DDR*, p. 219.

33. *KJ*, 1954, pp. 285ff.; *Frankfurter Allgemeine Zeitung*, May 21, 1954; Giese in *Mission Draussen und Drinnen*, p. 171.

34. Estimate made by President Zimmermann of the Protestant Church's Education Chamber, July 1957.

35. Zimmermann and Hafa, *Unterweisung*, p. 21.

36. Article in *Neues Deutschland* as reported in *Frankfurter Rundschau*, April 20–21, 1957.

37. *Schulrecht und Schulverwaltung in der DDR*, p. 192. School holidays are announced yearly by the ministry of education. See for example the schedule for 1956–57 in *Karteibuch des Schulrechts der DDR*, C I 10, pp. 4f.

38. Horst Becker, "Wir feiern Weihnachten," *Die Neue Schule*, IV (December 1, 1949), no. 23, pp. 18f.

Notes to Chapter XVIII. Berlin School Developments

1. Seipp, *Schulrecht: Berlin*, I CI, II; see above, Chapter XVII.

2. Seipp, *Schulrecht: Berlin*, III BI, pp. 1f. On the importance of this measure as marking a change in policy see Hans Lokies, "Die Berliner Schulpolitik in kirchlichen Sicht," in Giese, *Die Kirche in der Berliner Schule*, p. 131.

3. Giese, *Die Kirche in der Berliner Schule*, p. 88. So far no regular school prayers or religious services have been inaugurated in the schools of West Berlin. In the district of Steglitz in 1956–57 the district governing officials decided that an opening prayer could be held at the schools, but this is exceptional.

4. "Die evangelischen Lehrer Berlins zur Schulfrage," *EE*, III (July 1951), no. 4, pp. 26f., reprinted from *Die Kirche*, May 20, 1951. This petition was in line with the statement the Protestant church submitted to the Berlin school authorities in November 1949 (Giese in *Mission Draussen und Drinnen*, pp. 177f.). At the meeting of the Catholic teachers of Berlin at Pentecost 1951 somewhat similar views were expressed. See G. Urbanietz, "Zehn Jahre katholischer Lehrerschaft Berlin," *KE*, IX (1956), 536.

5. These are well outlined by Giese in *Mission Draussen und Drinnen*, pp. 172–202.

6. Formerly figured on the basis of forty weeks of instruction, the grant has now been realistically extended to a fifty-two week period, as the churches must pay their catechists on a year-round basis. The subsidy was also increased from 2.50 DM (c. 65 cents) to 3.85 DM (c. 95 cents) for each weekly hour of instruction (Giese, *Die Kirche in der Berliner Schule*, pp. 110–113; Kandeler in *Mission Draussen und Drinnen*, p. 131).

7. *Katholische Nachrichten Agentur*, no. 7 of February 12, 1955; on the school budget of the Protestants in West Berlin see Giese, *Die Kirche in der Berliner Schule*, pp. 112f.

8. Seipp, *Schulrecht: Berlin*, III BI, pp. 2f.; see also ordinance of December 7, 1951, on "Religionsunterricht für katholische Schüler," and the ordinance of March 3, 1952, on "Sicherung des Religionsunterrichts," *ibid.*, III BI, p. 101.

9. Giese in *Mission Draussen und Drinnen*, pp. 197f.; Bischöfliche Arbeitsstelle Köln, Archives, *Schulfragen, Bund-Länder*, IX, letter from Berlin, July 25, 1952.

10. *Dienstblatt des Senat von Berlin*, 1953, III–17; Giese *Die Kirche in der Berliner Schule*, pp. 98, 134. In practice some other than corner hours had been made available for religious instruction on March 31, 1949. Giese in *Mission Draussen und Drinnen*, pp. 176, 201.

11. For the ordinance of November 3, 1952, see Seipp, *Schulrecht: Berlin* I BI, pp. 15f.; the ordinance of July 28, 1954, on "Recht der Lehrer Religionsunterricht zu erteilen," is to be found *ibid.*, III BI, p. 102.

12. The number of regular teachers giving Protestant religious instruction in the schools of West Berlin was 552 in 1953, 530 in 1954, 500 in 1955, and 425 in 1956–57; Catholic, 165 in 1955 and 129 in 1956–57. Gerhardt Giese, "Im Auftrage der Kirche," *BL*, IX (1955), 509f.; "Westberliner Lehrer und neuerer Katechismus," *KE*, IX (1956), 242; information obtained at the Bischöfliches Ordinariat and the Kirchliche Erziehungskammer für Berlin in July, 1957.

13. Law of May 13, 1954; Ordinances of July 7, 1955, October 12, 1955. Seipp, *Schulrecht: Berlin*, X AI, pp. 1–6, 101f.; Heckel, *Deutsches Privatschulrecht*, pp. 160–165.

14. A. Heyder, "Katholische Privatschulen in Westberlin," *KE*, IX (1956), 526f.; "Grundsätzliches zur Schulfrage in Berlin," *EE*, V (1954), 55.

15. Gerhardt Giese, "Werkzeug seines guten Geistes. Unsere kirchliche Schulen im neuen Schuljahr," *Berliner Sonntagsblatt, Die Kirche*, no. 18, May 5, 1957.

16. Information obtained at the Bischöfliches Ordinariat in Berlin, July 1957.

17. Information obtained at the Kirchliche Erziehungskammer für Berlin, July 1957.

18. The Magistrat of Great (East) Berlin on June 2, 1955, (*Dienstblatt*, no. 23/1955, p. 20) ordered that ordinances published in the *Mitteilungsblatt des Ministeriums für Volksbildung der Deutschen Demokratischen Republik* "would also be effective for the Division of Public Education of the Magistrat of Great Berlin, the Division of Public Education of the Councils of the Stadtbezirke and their dependent establishments as well as the directors of the schools, so far as nothing else is expressly ordered." So far (1957) only a directive of October 20, 1954, relative to the school law has not been accepted. The directive thus singled out had to do with attendance of children from families where measles and whooping-cough prevailed, and also contained regulations as to heating of schoolrooms. (*Verfügungen und Mitteilungen des Ministeriums für Volksbildung*, November 2, 1954, no. 30, p. 257). See the note "An alle Berliner Bezieher," p. 4 of "Gesamt-Übersicht über alle im Karteibuch des Schulrechts enthaltenen gesetzlichen Bestimmungen (einschliesslich 90 Nachtrag)," in *Karteibuch des Schulrechts der DDR*. On the other hand educational ordinances of East Berlin do not hold for the German Democratic Republic.

19. *KJ*, 1955, p. 163.

20. Giese, *Die Kirche in der Berliner Schule*, pp. 96, 106.

21. Giese in *Mission Draussen und Drinnen*, p. 171.

22. As quoted in Giese, *Die Kirche in der Berliner Schule*, p. 107.

23. See discussion in Chapter XVII. At this time (November 24, 1953) 16 percent of the East Berlin school classes were without Protestant religious instruction, 50 percent had only one hour a week, and only 34 percent had the regular two-hour-a-week program. Only four regular teachers were still holding religion classes, the rest of the work being carried on by 127 catechists, 55 pastors, and 53 other church personnel (Giese, *Die Kirche in der Berliner Schule*, p. 106).

24. Kirchliche Erziehungskammer für Berlin, report by O. Schikora of January 1, 1956, Anlage zu K IIa 5071/56 vom 18/1/1956; *Katholische Nachrichten Agentur, Schul Katholische Korrespondenz*, February 5, 1956.

25. *Verordnungsblatt für Gross-Berlin*, I, no. 14, 1956, p. 149. The decree is usually referred to as the *Fechner Erlass* because it was signed by Fechner as *Stellvertreter des Oberbürgermeisters*. Reprinted in *KJ*, 1955, p. 300; and in *Die evangelische Elternschaft, Informationsdienst für Schulfragen* (March 1956), no. 3.

26. *KJ*, 1955, p. 302; *Kölnischer Rundschau*, March 5, 1956.

27. Bischöfliche Arbeitsstelle Köln, Archives, *Schulfragen Ostzone*, IX, letter of July 24, 1956, from Berlin.

28. Hans Lokies, "Christian Instruction in Schools in East and West Berlin," *The Bridge*, November 1956, p. 9.

29. Information obtained at the Bischöfliches Ordinariat in Berlin, July 1957.

30. Information obtained at the Kirchliche Erziehungskammer für Berlin, July 1957.

31. Giese, *Die Kirche in der Berliner Schule*, p. 114.

INDEX

Index